THE WEB STANDARD
COLLECTION
REVEALED

ADOBE FLASH CS4,
DREAMWEAVER CS4,
& FIREWORKS CS4

SHERRY BISHOP, JIM SHUMAN & BARBARA M. WAXER

THE WEB
STANDARD
COLLECTION
REVEALED
ADOBE FLASH CS4,
DREAMWEAVER CS4,
& FIREWORKS CS4

SHERRY BISHOP, JIM SHUMAN & BARBARA M. WAXER

DELMAR
CENGAGE Learning™

Australia • Brazil • Japan • Korea • Mexico • Singapore • Spain • United Kingdom • United States

DELMAR
CENGAGE Learning™

The Web Collection Revealed
Standard Edition:
Adobe Dreamweaver CS4, Flash CS4, and
Fireworks CS4

Sherry Bishop, Jim Shuman, and
Barbara M. Waxer

Vice President, Career and Professional Editorial:
Dave Garza

Director of Learning Solutions: Sandy Clark

Senior Acquisitions Editor: Jim Gish

Managing Editor: Larry Main

Product Managers: Jane Hosie-Bounar, Nicole Calisi

Editorial Assistant: Sarah Timm

Vice President Marketing, Career and
Professional: Jennifer McAvey

Executive Marketing Manager:
Deborah S. Yarnell

Marketing Manager: Erin Brennan

Marketing Coordinator: Jonathan Sheehan

Production Director: Wendy Troeger

Senior Content Project Manager:
Kathryn B. Kucharek

Developmental Editors: Barbara Clemens,
Pam Conrad, Barbara Waxer

Technical Editors: John Shanley, Sasha Vodnik,
Susan Whalen

Art Directors: Bruce Bond, Joy Kocsis

Cover Design: Lisa Kuhn, Curio Press, LLC

Cover Photo: Lisa Kuhn, Curio Press, LLC

Text Designer: Ann Small

Proofreader: Wendy Benedetto

Indexer: Alexandra Nickerson

Technology Project Manager:
Christopher Catalina

Production Technology Analyst: Tom Stover

For product information and technology
assistance, contact us at
**Cengage Learning Customer & Sales Support,
1-800-354-9706**

For permission to use material from this text or
product, submit all requests online at
www.cengage.com/permissions.
Further permissions questions can be e-mailed to
permissionrequest@cengage.com

Adobe® Photoshop®, Adobe® InDesign®, Adobe®
Illustrator®, Adobe® Flash®, Adobe® Dreamweaver®,
Adobe® Fireworks®, and Adobe® Creative Suite® are
trademarks or registered trademarks of Adobe Systems,
Inc. in the United States and/or other countries. Third
party products, services, company names, logos, design,
titles, words, or phrases within these materials may be
trademarks of their respective owners.

The Trademark BlackBerry® is owned by Research In
Motion Limited and is registered in the United States and
may be pending or registered in other countries. Delmar
Cengage Learning is not endorsed, sponsored, affiliated
with or otherwise authorized by Research In Motion
Limited.

Coca-Cola® is a registered trademark of The Coca-Cola
Company.

Library of Congress Control Number: 2008910784

Hardcover edition:
ISBN-13: 978-1-4354-8266-1
ISBN-10: 1-4354-8266-2

Soft cover edition:
ISBN-13: 978-1-4354-4198-9
ISBN-10: 1-4354-4198-2

Delmar
5 Maxwell Drive
Clifton Park, NY 12065-2919
USA

Cengage Learning is a leading provider of customized learning solutions with office locations around the globe, including Singapore, the United Kingdom, Australia, Mexico,
Brazil, and Japan. Locate your local office at:
international.cengage.com/region

Cengage Learning products are represented in
Canada by Nelson Education, Ltd.

To learn more about Delmar, visit
www.cengage.com/delmar

Purchase any of our products at your local college
store or at our preferred online store
www.ichapters.com

Notice to the Reader

Printed in the United States of America
2 3 4 5 6 7 13 12 11 10 09

Revealed Series Vision

The Revealed Series is your guide to today's hottest multimedia applications. These comprehensive books teach the skills behind the application, showing you how to apply smart design principles to multimedia products such as dynamic graphics, animation, websites, software authoring tools, and digital video.

A team of design professionals including multimedia instructors, students, authors, and editors worked together to create this series. We recognized the unique learning environment of the multimedia classroom and created a series that:

- Gives you comprehensive step-by-step instructions
- Offers in-depth explanation of the "Why" behind a skill
- Includes creative projects for additional practice
- Explains concepts clearly using full-color visuals

It was our goal to create a book that speaks directly to the multimedia and design community—one of the most rapidly growing computer fields today. We think we've done just that, with a sophisticated and instructive book design.

—The Revealed Series

Authors' Vision

This book will introduce you to three fascinating programs that will hopefully inspire you to create rich and exciting websites. Through the work of many talented and creative individuals, this text was created for you. The Product Manager, Jane Hosie-Bounar, guided and directed the team from start to finish. Working with Barbara Clemens, the Development Editor, is always a joy. It is a bit bittersweet when a project with her is completed. She is such an encourager, both by her words and her example. Although we live thousands of miles apart, I always feel a void when our working time together is over.

The copyright content was generously provided by my dear friend Barbara Waxer. Additional information on locating media on the Internet and determining its legal use is available in her Revealed Series book *Internet Surf and Turf Revealed: The Essential Guide to Copyright, Fair Use, and Finding Media.*

John Shanley and Susan Whalen, the Technical Editors, carefully tested each step to make sure that the end product was error-free. This part of the publishing process is what truly sets Delmar Cengage Learning apart from other publishers.

Tintu Thomas and Kathy Kucharek, our Content Product Managers, kept the schedule on track. We thank them for keeping up with the many details and deadlines.

Janice Jutras patiently contacted the websites we used as examples to obtain permission for their inclusion. Harold Johnson quietly worked behind the scene to ensure that my grammatical and punctuation errors were corrected. Paula Melton authored the test banks.

Special thanks go to Jim Gish, Senior Acquisitions Editor, and Sandy Clark, the Director of Learning Solutions. They have embraced the Revealed books with enthusiasm and grace.

The Beach Club (www.beach-clubal.com) in Gulf Shores, Alabama, generously allowed us to use several photographs of their beautiful property for The Striped Umbrella website. Florence Pruitt, the club director, was extremely helpful and gracious.

Typically, your family is the last to be thanked. My husband, Don, continues to support and encourage me every day, as he has for the last thirty-eight years. Our travels with our children and grandchildren provide happy memories for me and content for the websites. You will see the faces of my precious grandchildren Jacob, Emma, Thomas, and Caroline peeking out from some of the pages.
—Sherry Bishop

I would like to thank Jane Hosie-Bounar for her leadership in guiding us through this project. A very special thanks to Pam Conrad (for her word wizardry and wit) and to my co-authors Barbara and Sherry. I also want to give a heartfelt thanks to my wife, Barbara, for her patience and support.
—Jim Shuman

Huge thanks to my partner, Lindy, and to a house full of animals who deserve the utmost acknowledgement for their spontaneous contributions that never once bordered on combustion. Special thanks to Jane, who led this complex project perfectly.
—Barbara Waxer

SERIES & AUTHORS' VISION

Introduction to The Web Collection Revealed, Standard Edition

Welcome to *The Web Collection Revealed, Standard Edition: Adobe Dreamweaver CS4, Flash CS4, and Fireworks CS4*. This book offers creative projects, concise instructions, and coverage of basic Dreamweaver, Flash, Fireworks, and Creative Suite integration skills, helping you to create polished, professional-looking websites and art work. Use this book both in the classroom and as your own reference guide.

This text is organized into 15 chapters. In these chapters, you will learn many skills, including how to move amongst the Creative Suite applications, which, in this release, provide familiar functionality from one application to the next.

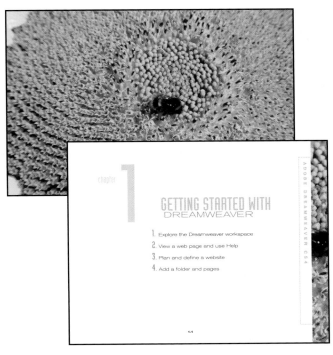

What You'll Do

A What You'll Do figure begins every lesson. This figure gives you an at-a-glance look at what you'll do in the chapter, either by showing you a file from the current project or a tool you'll be using.

Comprehensive Conceptual Lessons

Before jumping into instructions, in-depth conceptual information tells you "why" skills are applied. This book provides the "how" and "why" through the use of professional examples. Also included in the text are tips and sidebars to help you work more efficiently and creatively, or to teach you a bit about the history or design philosophy behind the skill you are using.

Step-by-Step Instructions

This book combines in-depth conceptual information with concise steps to help you learn CS4. Each set of steps guides you through a lesson where you will create, modify, or enhance a CS4 file. Step references to large colorful images and quick step summaries round out the lessons. The Data Files for the steps are provided on the CD at the back of this book.

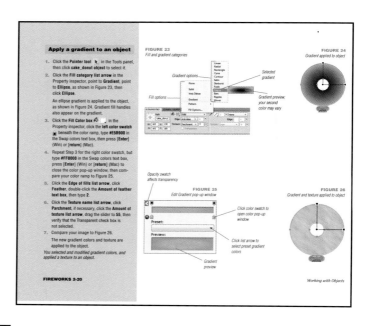

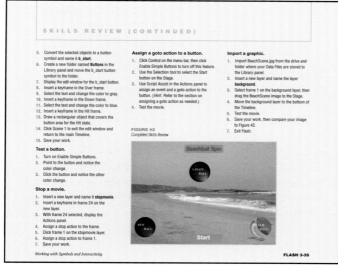

Projects

This book contains a variety of end-of-chapter materials for additional practice and reinforcement. The Skills Review contains hands-on practice exercises that mirror the progressive nature of the lesson material. The chapter concludes with four projects; two Project Builders, one Design Project, and one Portfolio Project. The Project Builders and the Design Project require you to apply the skills you've learned in the chapter. The Portfolio Project encourages students to address and solve challenges based on the content explored in the chapter.

Dreamweaver

Chapter 1 Getting Started with Dreamweaver
Lesson 1 Explore the Dreamweaver Workspace 1-4
2 View a Web Page and Use Help 1-12
3 Plan and Define a Website 1-18
4 Add a Folder and Pages 1-26

Chapter 2 Developing a Web page
Lesson 1 Create Head Content and Set Page Properties 2-4
2 Create, Import, and Format Text 2-10
3 Add Links to Web Pages 2-18
4 Use the History Panel and Edit Code 2-24
5 Modify and Test Web Pages 2-30

Chapter 3 Working with Text and Images
Lesson 1 Create Unordered and Ordered Lists 3-4
2 Create, Apply, and Edit Cascading Style Sheets 3-10
3 Add Rules and Attach Cascading Style Sheets 3-18
4 Insert and Align Graphics 3-22
5 Enhance an Image and Use Alternate Text 3-28
6 Insert a Background Image and Perform Site Maintenance 3-34

Chapter 4 Working with Links
Lesson 1 Create External and Internal Links 4-4
2 Create Internal Links to Named Anchors 4-10
3 Create, Modify, and Copy a Navigation Bar 4-16
4 Create an Image Map 4-24
5 Manage Website Links 4-28

Chapter 5 Positioning Objects with CSS and Tables
Lesson 1 Create a Page using CSS Layouts 5-4
2 Add Content to CSS Layout Blocks 5-8
3 Edit Content in CSS Layout Blocks 5-12
4 Create a Table 5-18
5 Resize, Split, and Merge Cells 5-22
6 Insert and Align Images in Table Cells 5-28
7 Insert Text and Format Cell Content 5-32

Chapter 6 Managing a Web Server and Files
Lesson 1 Perform Website maintenance 6-4
2 Publish a Website and Transfer Files 6-14
3 Check Files Out and In 6-22
4 Cloak Files 6-26
5 Import and Export a Site Definition 6-30
6 Evaluate Web Content for Legal Use 6-34

Flash

Chapter 1 Getting Started with Adobe Flash CS4
Lesson 1 Understand the Adobe Flash CS4 Workspace 1-4
2 Open a Document and Play a Movie 1-12
3 Create and Save a Movie 1-18
4 Work with the Timeline 1-30
5 Distribute an Adobe Flash Movie 1-36
6 Plan an Application or a Website 1-40

Chapter 2 Drawing Objects in Adobe Flash
Lesson 1 Use the Flash Drawing Tools 2-4
2 Select Objects and Apply Colors 2-14
3 Work with Drawn Objects 2-20
4 Work with Text and Text Objects 2-28
5 Work with Layers and Objects 2-34

Chapter 3 Working with Symbols and Interactivity
Lesson 1 Create Symbols and Instances 3-4
2 Work with Libraries 3-10
3 Create Buttons 3-16
4 Assign Actions to Frames and Buttons 3-22
5 Importing Graphics 3-30

Chapter 4 Creating Animations
Lesson 1 Create Motion Tween Animations 4-4
2 Create Classic Tween Animations 4-20
3 Create Frame-by-Frame Animations 4-24
4 Create Shape Tween Animations 4-30
5 Create Movie Clips 4-36
6 Animate Text 4-42

Chapter 5   Creating Special Effects

Lesson 1   Create a Mask Effect 5-4
      2   Add Sound 5-8
      3   Add Video 5-12
      4   Create an Animated
          Navigation Bar 5-18
      5   Create Character Animations Using
          Inverse Kinematics 5-26
      6   Create 3D Effects 5-34

Fireworks

**Chapter 1   Getting Started with Adobe
          Fireworks**

Lesson 1   Understand the Fireworks Work
          Environment 1-4
      2   Work with New and Existing
          Documents 1-8

      3   Work with Layers and Images 1-14
      4   Create Shapes 1-18
      5   Create and Modify Text 1-24

Chapter 2   Working with Objects

Lesson 1   Work with Vector Tools 2-4
      2   Modify Multiple Vector Objects 2-10
      3   Modify Color 2-18
      4   Apply Filters to Objects and
          Text 2-22
      5   Apply a Style to Text 2-26

**Chapter 3   Importing, Selecting, and
          Modifying Graphics**

Lesson 1   Work with Imported Files 3-4
      2   Work with Bitmap Selection
          Tools 3-10
      3   Learn about Selection Areas 3-16
      4   Select Areas Based on Color 3-22

Integration

**Chapter 1   Integrating Adobe CS4
          Web Standard**

Lesson 1   Insert a Fireworks Image into
          a Dreamweaver Document 1-4
      2   Create a Fireworks Image and
          Import It into Flash 1-13
      3   Insert and Edit a Flash Movie in
          Dreamweaver 1-19

Data Files 1

Glossary 11

Index 24

Art Credits 40

Dreamweaver

CHAPTER 1   GETTING STARTED WITH DREAMWEAVER

INTRODUCTION

Getting Started with Dreamweaver 1-2
Introduction 1-2
Using Dreamweaver Tools 1-2

LESSON 1

Explore the Dreamweaver Workspace 1-4
Examining the Dreamweaver Workspace 1-4
Working with Dreamweaver Views 1-7
Tasks   Start Dreamweaver (Windows) 1-8
     Start Dreamweaver (Macintosh) 1-9
     Change views and view panels 1-10

LESSON 2

View a Web Page and Use Help 1-12
Opening a Web Page 1-12
Viewing Basic Web Page Elements 1-12
Getting Help 1-13
Tasks   Open a web page and view basic
     page elements 1-14
     Use Dreamweaver Help 1-16

LESSON 3

Plan and Define a Website 1-18
Understanding the Total Process 1-18
Planning a Website 1-18
Setting Up the Basic Structure 1-19
Creating the Web Pages and Collecting
the Page Content 1-20
Testing the Pages 1-21
Modifying the Pages 1-21
Publishing the Site 1-21
Tasks   Select the location for your website 1-22
     Create a root folder 1-23
     Define a website 1-24
     Set up web server access 1-25

LESSON 4

Add a Folder and Pages 1-26
Adding a Folder to a Website 1-26
Creating the Home Page 1-27
Adding Pages to a Website 1-27
Tasks   Add a folder to a website (Windows) 1-28
     Add a folder to a website (Macintosh) 1-28
     Set the default images folder 1-29
     Create the home page 1-30
     Save an image file in the assets
     folder 1-31
     Add pages to a website (Windows) 1-32
     Add pages to a website (Macintosh) 1-33

CONTENTS

CHAPTER 2   **DEVELOPING A WEB PAGE**

INTRODUCTION
Developing a Web Page 2-2
Introduction 2-2
Understanding Page Layout 2-2

LESSON 1
**Create Head Content and Set Page
Properties** 2-4
Creating the Head Content 2-4
Setting Web Page Properties 2-5
Tasks   Edit a page title 2-6
         Enter keywords 2-7
         Enter a description 2-8
         Set the page background color 2-9

LESSON 2
Create, Import, and Format Text 2-10
Creating and Importing Text 2-10
Formatting Text Using the Property
Inspector 2-11
Using HTML Tags Compared to Using CSS 2-11
Changing Fonts 2-11
Changing Font Sizes 2-11
Formatting Paragraphs 2-11
Tasks   Enter text 2-12
         Format text 2-13
         Save an image file in the assets
         folder 2-14
         Import text 2-15
         Set text properties 2-16
         Check spelling 2-17

LESSON 3
Add Links to Web Pages 2-18
Adding Links to Web Pages 2-18
Using Navigation Bars 2-19
Tasks   Create a navigation bar 2-20
         Insert a horizontal rule 2-20
         Add links to web pages 2-21
         Create an email link 2-22
         View the email link in the Assets panel 2-23

LESSON 4
Use the History Panel and Edit Code 2-24
Using the History Panel 2-24
Viewing HTML Code in the Code
Inspector 2-25
Tasks   Use the History panel 2-26
         Use the Code Inspector 2-27
         Use the Reference panel 2-28
         Insert a date object 2-29

LESSON 5
Modify and Test Web Pages 2-30
Testing and Modifying Web Pages 2-30
Testing a Web Page Using Different
Browsers and Screen Sizes 2-31
Testing a Web Page as Rendered
in a Mobile Device 2-31
Tasks   Modify a web page 2-32
         Test web pages by viewing them
         in a browser 2-33

INTRODUCTION
Working with Text and Images 3-2
Introduction 3-2
Formatting Text as Lists 3-2
Using Cascading Style Sheets 3-2
Using Images to Enhance Web Pages 3-2

LESSON 1
Create Unordered and Ordered Lists 3-4
Creating Unordered Lists 3-4
Formatting Unordered Lists 3-4
Creating Ordered Lists 3-4
Formatting Ordered Lists 3-5
Creating Definition Lists 3-5
Tasks   Create an unordered list 3-6
         Format an unordered list 3-7
         Create an ordered list 3-8
         Format an ordered list 3-9

LESSON 2
Create, Apply, and Edit Cascading Style Sheets 3-10
Understanding Cascading Style Sheets 3-10
Using the CSS Styles Panel 3-10
Comparing the Advantages of Using Style Sheets 3-11
Understanding CSS Style Sheet Code 3-11
Tasks   Create a Cascading Style Sheet
         and a rule 3-12
         Apply a rule in a Cascading
         Style Sheet 3-14
         Edit a rule in a Cascading
         Style Sheet 3-15
         View code with the Code Navigator 3-16
         Use the Code Navigator to edit a rule 3-17

LESSON 3
Add Rules and Attach Cascading Style Sheets 3-18
Understanding External and Embedded Style Sheets 3-18
Tasks   Add rules to a Cascading Style Sheet 3-20
         Attach a style sheet 3-21

LESSON 4
Insert and Align Graphics 3-22
Understanding Graphic File Formats 3-22
Understanding the Assets Panel 3-22
Inserting Files with Adobe Bridge 3-23
Aligning Images 3-23
Tasks   Insert a graphic 3-24
         Use Adobe Bridge 3-25
         Align an image 3-26

LESSON 5
Enhance an Image and Use Alternate Text 3-28
Enhancing an Image 3-28
Using Alternate Text 3-29
Tasks   Add a border 3-30
         Add horizontal and vertical space 3-30
         Edit image settings 3-31
         Edit alternate text 3-32
         Set the alternate text
         accessibility option 3-33

LESSON 6
Insert a Background Image and Perform Site Maintenance 3-34
Inserting a Background Image 3-34
Managing Images 3-34
Removing Colors from a website 3-35
Tasks   Insert a background image 3-36
         Remove a background image from a
         page 3-37
         Delete files from a website 3-38
         Check for Non-web-safe colors 3-39

CHAPTER 4 WORKING WITH LINKS

INTRODUCTION
Working with Links 4-2
Introduction 4-2
Understanding Internal and External Links 4-2

LESSON 1
Create External and Internal Links 4-4
Creating External Links 4-4
Creating Internal Links 4-5
Tasks   Create an external link 4-6
        Create an internal link 4-8
        View links in the Assets panel 4-9

LESSON 2
Create Internal Links to Named Anchors 4-10
Inserting Named Anchors 4-10
Creating Internal Links to Named Anchors 4-11
Tasks   Insert a named anchor 4-12
        Create an internal link to a named anchor 4-14

LESSON 3
Create, Modify, and Copy a Navigation Bar 4-16
Creating a Navigation Bar Using Images 4-16
Copying and Modifying a Navigation Bar 4-17
Tasks   Create a navigation bar using images 4-18
        Add elements to a navigation bar 4-20
        Copy and paste a navigation bar 4-22
        Modify a navigation bar 4-22

LESSON 4
Create an Image Map 4-24
Task   Create an image map 4-26

LESSON 5
Manage Website Links 4-28
Managing Website Links 4-28
Tasks   Manage website links 4-29
        Update a page 4-30

INTRODUCTION
Positioning Objects with CSS and Tables 5-2
Introduction 5-2
Using Div Tags Versus Tables for Page Layout 5-2

LESSON 1
Create a Page Using CSS Layouts 5-4
Understanding Div Tags 5-4
Using CSS Page Layouts 5-4
Viewing CSS Layout Blocks 5-5
Task   Create a page with a CSS layout 5-6

LESSON 2
Add Content to CSS Layout Blocks 5-8
Understanding Div Tag Content 5-8
Understanding CSS Code 5-9
Tasks   Add text to a CSS container 5-10
         Add images to a CSS container 5-11

LESSON 3
Edit Content in CSS Layout Blocks 5-12
Edit Content in CSS Layout Blocks 5-12
Tasks   Format content in CSS layout blocks 5-13
         Edit styles in CSS layout blocks 5-15
         Edit CSS layout block properties 5-15
         Edit page properties 5-17

LESSON 4
Create a Table 5-18
Understanding Table Modes 5-18
Creating a Table 5-18
Using Expanded Tables Mode 5-19
Setting Table Accessibility Preferences 5-19
Tasks   Create a table 5-20
         Set table properties 5-21

LESSON 5
Resize, Split, and Merge Cells 5-22
Resizing Table Elements 5-22
Tasks   Resize columns 5-24
         Resize rows 5-25
         Split cells 5-26
         Merge cells 5-27

LESSON 6
Insert and Align Images in Table Cells 5-28
Inserting Images in Table Cells 5-28
Aligning Images in Table Cells 5-29
Tasks   Insert images in table cells 5-30
         Align graphics in table cells 5-31

LESSON 7
Insert Text and Format Cell Content 5-32
Inserting Text in a Table 5-32
Formatting Cell Content 5-32
Formatting Cells 5-33
Tasks   Insert text 5-34
         Format cells content 5-35
         Format cells 5-36
         Modify cell content 5-37
         Check layout 5-37

CONTENTS

CHAPTER 6   MANAGING A WEB SERVER AND FILES

INTRODUCTION

Managing a Web Server and Files 6-2
Introduction 6-2
Preparing to Publish a Site 6-2

LESSON 1

Perform Website Maintenance 6-4
Maintaining a Website 6-4
Using the Assets Panel 6-4
Checking Links Sitewide 6-4
Using Site Reports 6-4
Validating Markup 6-5
Testing Pages 6-5
Tasks   Check for broken links 6-6
         Check for orphaned files 6-6
         Verify that all colors are web-safe 6-7
         Check for untitled documents 6-8
         Check for missing alternate text 6-9
         Enable Design Notes 6-10
         Associate a Design Note with a file 6-11
         Edit a Design Note 6-12

LESSON 2

Publish a Website and Transfer Files 6-14
Defining a Remote Site 6-14
Viewing a Remote Site 6-14
Transferring Files to and from a Remote Site 6-15
Synchronizing Files 6-16
Tasks   Set up web server access on an FTP site 6-17
         Set up web server access on a local or network folder 6-18
         View a website on a remote server 6-19
         Upload files to a remote server 6-20
         Synchronize files 6-21

LESSON 3

Check Files Out and In 6-22
Managing a Website with a Team 6-22
Checking Out and Checking In Files 6-22
Enabling the Check In/Check Out Feature 6-23
Tasks   Enable the Check In/Check Out feature 6-24
         Check out a file 6-24
         Check in a file 6-25

LESSON 4

Cloak Files 6-26
Understanding Cloaking Files 6-26
Cloaking a Folder 6-26
Cloaking Selected File Types 6-27
Tasks   Cloak and uncloak a folder 6-28
         Cloak selected file types 6-29

LESSON 5

Import and Export a Site Definition 6-30
Exporting a Site Definition 6-30
Importing a Site Definition 6-30
Tasks   Export a site definition 6-31
         Import a site definition 6-32
         View the imported site 6-33

LESSON 6

Evaluate Web Content for Legal Use 6-34
Can I Use Downloaded Media? 6-34
Understanding Intellectual Property 6-34
What Exactly Does the Copyright Owner Own? 6-35
Understanding Fair Use 6-35
How Do I Use Work Properly? 6-35
Understanding Licensing Agreements 6-35
Obtaining Permission or a License 6-36
Posting a Copyright Notice 6-36

Flash

INTRODUCTION
Getting Started with Adobe Flash CS4 1-2
Introduction 1-2

LESSON 1
Understand the Adobe Flash CS4 Workspace 1-4
Organizing the Flash Workspace 1-4
Stage 1-4
Timeline (Frames and Layers) 1-5
Panels 1-5
Tools Panel 1-6
Tasks   Start Adobe Flash and work with
      Panels 1-9
      Change the Stage view and display of the
      Timeline 1-10

LESSON 2
Open a Document and Play a Movie 1-12
Opening a Movie in Flash 1-12
Previewing a Movie 1-12
Control Menu Commands
(and Keyboard Shortcuts) 1-12
Controller 1-13
Testing a Movie 1-13
Documents, Movies, and Applications 1-14
Using the Flash Player 1-14
Tasks   Open and play a movie using the
      Control menu and the Controller 1-15
      Test a movie 1-16
      Change the Document Properties 1-17

LESSON 3
Create and Save a Movie 1-18
Creating a Flash Movie 1-18
Creating an Animation 1-19
The Motion Tween Animation Process 1-20
Motion Presets 1-21
Adding Effects to an Object 1-21
Tasks   Create objects using drawing tools 1-22
      Create a motion tween animation 1-23
      Reshaping the Motion Path 1-24
      Changing the transparency of an object 1-25
      Resize an object 1-26
      Add a filter to an object 1-27
      Add a motion preset 1-28

LESSON 4
Work with the Timeline 1-30
Understanding the Timeline 1-30
Using Layers 1-30
Using Frames 1-30
Using the Playhead 1-31
Understanding Scenes 1-31
Working with the Timeline 1-32
Tasks   Add a layer 1-33
      Create a second animation 1-33
      Work with layers and view
      Timeline features 1-34
      Modify the frame rate 1-35

LESSON 5
Distribute an Adobe Flash Movie 1-36
Distributing Movies 1-36
Tasks   Publish a movie for distribution
      on the web 1-38
      Create a projector file 1-39

LESSON 6
Plan an Application or a Website 1-40
Planning an Application or a Website 1-40
Using Screen Design Guidelines 1-42
Using Interactive Design Guidelines 1-43
The Flash Workflow Process 1-44
Task   Use Flash Help 1-45

INTRODUCTION
Drawing Objects in Adobe Flash 2-2
Introduction 2-2

LESSON 1
Use the Flash Drawing Tools 2-4
Using Flash Drawing and Editing Tools 2-4
Working with Grouped Tools 2-6
Working with Tool Options 2-6
Tools for Creating Vector Graphics 2-6
Positioning Objects on the Stage 2-6
Tasks Show grid lines and check settings 2-8
       Use the Rectangle, Oval, and
       Line tools 2-9
       Use the Pen, Pencil, and Brush tools 2-10
       Modify an object using tool options 2-11
       Use the Spray tool with a symbol 2-12

LESSON 2
Select Objects and Apply Colors 2-14
Selecting Objects 2-14
Using the Selection Tool 2-14
Using the Lasso Tool 2-14
Drawing Model Modes 2-14
Working with Colors 2-15
Working with Gradients 2-15
Tasks Select a drawing using the
       Selection tool 2-16
       Change fill and stroke colors 2-17

Create a gradient and make changes
to the gradient 2-18
Work with the Object Drawing
Model mode 2-19

LESSON 3
Work with Drawn Objects 2-20
Copying and Moving Objects 2-20
Transforming Objects 2-20
Resizing an Object 2-20
Rotating and Skewing an Object 2-21
Distorting an Object 2-21
Reshaping a Segment of an Object 2-21
Flipping an Object 2-21
Tasks Copy and move an object 2-22
       Resize and reshape an object 2-23
       Rotate, skew, and flip an object 2-24
       Use the Zoom, Subselection, and
       Selection tools 2-25
       Use the Primitive Rectangle and
       Oval tools 2-26

LESSON 4
Work with Text and Text Objects 2-28
Learning About Text 2-28
Entering Text and Changing
the Text Block 2-28
Changing Text Attributes 2-28
Working with Paragraphs 2-29

Transforming Text 2-29
Tasks Enter text and change text attributes 2-30
       Add a Filter effect to text 2-31
       Skew text and align objects 2-32
       Reshape and apply a gradient to text 2-33

LESSON 5
Work with Layers and Objects 2-34
Learning About Layers 2-34
Working with Layers 2-35
Using a Guide Layer 2-36
Distributing Text to Layers 2-37
Using Folder Layers 2-37
Tasks Create and reorder layers 2-38
       Rename and delete layers and expand the
       Timeline 2-39
       Hide, lock, and display layer outlines 2-40
       Create a guide for a Guide layer 2-41
       Add objects to a Guide layer 2-42
       Adding text on top of an object 2-43

INTRODUCTION
Working with Symbols and Interactivity 3-2
Introduction 3-2

LESSON 1
Create Symbols and Instances 3-4
Creating a Graphic Symbol 3-4
Working with Instances 3-4
Tasks Create a symbol 3-6
       Create and edit an instance 3-7
       Edit a symbol in the edit window 3-8
       Break apart an instance 3-9

LESSON 2
Work with Libraries 3-10
Understanding the Library 3-10
Tasks Create folders in the Library panel 3-12
       Organize items within Library panel
       folders 3-13
       Display the properties of symbols, rename
       symbols, and delete a symbol 3-14
       Use multiple Library panels 3-15

LESSON 3
Create Buttons 3-16
Understanding Buttons 3-16
Tasks Create a button 3-18
       Edit a button and specify a Hit area 3-19
       Test a button 3-20

LESSON 4
Assign Actions to Frames and Buttons 3-22
Understanding Actions 3-22
Analyzing ActionScript 3-22
ActionScript 2.0 and 3.0 3-22
Tasks Assign a stop action to frames 3-26
       Assign a play action to a button 3-27
       Assign a goto frame action
       to a button 3-28
       Assign a second event to a button 3-29

LESSON 5
Importing Graphics 3-30
Understanding Graphic Types 3-30
Importing and Editing Graphics 3-31
Task   Importing graphics 3-32

CHAPTER 4 CREATING ANIMATIONS

INTRODUCTION

Creating Animations 4-2
Introduction 4-2
How Does Animation Work? 4-2
Flash Animation 4-2

LESSON 1

Create Motion Tween Animations 4-4
Understanding Motion Tween Animations 4-4
Tween Spans 4-5
Motion Path 4-5
Property Keyframes 4-6
Tasks   Create a motion tween animation 4-7
         Edit a motion path 4-8
         Change the ease value of an animation 4-10
         Resize and reshape an object 4-11
         Create a color effect 4-12
         Orient an object to a path 4-13
         Copy a motion path 4-14
         Rotate an object 4-16
         Remove a motion tween 4-17
         Work with multiple motion tweens 4-18

LESSON 2

Create Classic Tween Animations 4-20
Understanding Classic Tweens 4-20
Understanding Motion Guides 4-20
Transformation Point and Registration Point 4-21
Tasks   Create a classic tween animation 4-22
         Add a motion guide and orient the object to the guide 4-22

LESSON 3

Create Frame-by-Frame Animations 4-24
Understanding Frame-by-Frame Animations 4-24
Creating a Frame-by-Frame Animation 4-25
Using the Onion Skin Feature 4-25
Tasks   Create an in-place frame-by-frame animation 4-26
         Copy frames and add a moving background 4-27
         Create a frame-by-frame animation of a moving object 4-28

LESSON 4

Create Shape Tween Animations 4-30
Shape Tweening 4-30
Using Shape Tweening to Create a Morphing Effect 4-30
Properties Panel Options 4-31
Shape Hints 4-31

Tasks   Create a shape tween animation 4-32
         Create a morphing effect 4-33
         Adjust the rate of change in a shape tween animation 4-34
         Use shape hints 4-35

LESSON 5

Create Movie Clips 4-36
Understanding Movie Clip Symbols 4-36
Tasks   Break apart a graphic symbol and select parts of the object to separate from the graphic 4-38
         Create and edit a movie clip 4-39
         Animate a movie clip 4-40

LESSON 6

Animate Text 4-42
Animating Text 4-42

Tasks   Select, copy, and paste frames 4-44
         Create animated text 4-45
         Create rotating text 4-46
         Resize and fade in text 4-47
         Make a text block into a button 4-48
         Add an action to the button 4-49

CHAPTER 5 CREATING SPECIAL EFFECTS

INTRODUCTION
Creating Special Effects 5-2
Introduction 5-2

LESSON 1
Create a Mask Effect 5-4
Understanding Mask Layers 5-4
Tasks   Create a mask layer 5-6
        Create a masked layer 5-7

LESSON 2
Add Sound 5-8
Incorporating Animation and Sound 5-8
Tasks   Add sound to a movie 5-10
        Add sound to a button 5-11

LESSON 3
Add Video 5-12
Incorporating Video 5-12
Using the Adobe Media Encoder 5-13
Using the Import Video Wizard 5-13
Tasks   Import a video 5-14
        Attach actions to video control buttons 5-16
        Synchronize sound to a video clip 5-17

LESSON 4
Create an Animated Navigation Bar 5-18
Understanding Animated Navigation Bars 5-18
Using Frame Labels 5-19
Tasks   Position the drop-down buttons 5-20
        Add a mask layer 5-21
        Assign an action to a drop-down button 5-22
        Add a frame label and assign a rollover
        action 5-23
        Add an invisible button 5-24

LESSON 5
**Create Character Animations Using Inverse
Kinematics** 5-26
Understanding Inverse Kinematics 5-26
Creating the Bone Structure 5-26
Animating the IK Object 5-27
Creating a Movie Clip with an IK Object 5-28
Runtime Feature 5-28
Tasks   Create the bone structure 5-29
        Animate the character 5-30
        Create a movie clip of the IK 5-31
        Apply an ease value 5-32
        Set the play to runtime 5-33

LESSON 6
Create 3D Effects 5-34
The 3D Tools 5-34
Using a Motion Tween with a 3D Effect 5-35
Tasks   Create a 3D animation 5-36

Fireworks

CHAPTER 1 — GETTING STARTED WITH ADOBE FIREWORKS

INTRODUCTION
Getting Started with Adobe Fireworks 1-2
Understanding Fireworks 1-2

LESSON 1
Understand the Fireworks Work Environment 1-4
Viewing the Fireworks Window 1-4
Tasks   Start Fireworks and open a Fireworks
            document 1-6
            Open and adjust panels in the Fireworks
            window 1-7

LESSON 2
Work with New and Existing Documents 1-8
Working with Files 1-8
Working with Pages 1-8
Accessing Help 1-9
Using Filters on Bitmap Images 1-9
Tasks   Create and save a new document 1-10
            Get Help and add a layer 1-11
            Drag and drop an object 1-12
            Apply filters to an image 1-13

LESSON 3
Work with Layers and Images 1-14
Understanding the Layers Panel 1-14
Understanding Bitmap Images and Vector
Objects 1-15
Tasks   Open a document and display the
            Layers panel 1-16
            Edit a bitmap image and
            lock a layer 1-17

LESSON 4
Create Shapes 1-18
Using Rulers, Guides, and
the Grid 1-18
Sizing and Repositioning
Objects 1-18
Using the Tools Panel 1-18
Understanding Auto Shapes 1-19
Applying Fills and Strokes 1-20
Tasks   Display the guides 1-21
            Create a vector object 1-21
            Apply a stroke to an object 1-23

LESSON 5
Create and Modify Text 1-24
Using Text in a Document 1-24
Attaching Text to a Path 1-25
Tasks   Create text using the Text tool 1-26
            Spell check text 1-28
            Create a path, attach text to it, then exit
            Fireworks 1-29

CHAPTER 2 WORKING WITH OBJECTS

INTRODUCTION
Working with Objects 2-2
Understanding Vector Objects 2-2

LESSON 1
Work with Vector Tools 2-4
Understanding Vector Tools and Paths 2-4
Using the Pen Tool and the
Subselection Tool 2-5
Tasks   Create an object using the Pen tool 2-7
        Use the Pen tool and the Line tool to
        modify a path 2-8
        Use the Subselection tool to
        modify an object 2-9

LESSON 2
Modify Multiple Vector Objects 2-10
Aligning and Grouping Objects 2-10
Combining the Paths of Multiple
Objects 2-10
Tasks   Create a vector shape to an
        exact size 2-13
        Copy an object 2-14
        Align objects and combine paths 2-15
        Group objects 2-17

LESSON 3
Modify Color 2-18
Understanding Fills and Gradients 2-18
Tasks   Apply a gradient to an object 2-20
        Transform an object and
        its gradient 2-21

LESSON 4
Apply Filters to Objects and Text 2-22
Understanding Filters 2-22
Using Photoshop Live Effects 2-22
Using the Filters Menu 2-22
Filters and File Size 2-23
Understanding Transparency 2-23
Tasks   Apply filters to objects 2-24
        Apply filters to text 2-25

LESSON 5
Apply a Style to Text 2-26
Using Live Styles and the Styles Panel 2-26
Tasks   Align objects and apply a style to text 2-28
        Create a custom style 2-29

CHAPTER 3 IMPORTING, SELECTING, AND
MODIFYING GRAPHICS

INTRODUCTION

**Importing, Selecting, and Modifying
Graphics** 3-2
Understanding Importing 3-2
Modifying Images 3-2

LESSON 1

Work with Imported Files 3-4
Working with Other Adobe Creative Suite 4
Applications 3-4
Using Files Created in Other Applications 3-4
Importing and Saving Files 3-5
Tasks   Import a .gif file 3-7
        Import a Fireworks .png file 3-7
        Import a vector file as editable paths 3-8
        Edit an imported vector object 3-9

LESSON 2

Work with Bitmap Selection Tools 3-10
Using Selection Tools 3-10
Using the Marquee Tools 3-11
Using the Transformation Tools 3-11
Tasks   Select pixels using the
        Marquee tool 3-12
        Select pixels using the Oval
        Marquee tool 3-13
        Transform a selection 3-14

LESSON 3

Learn About Selection Areas 3-16
Using the Lasso Tools 3-16
Using Select Menu Commands 3-17
Tasks   Select pixels using the Lasso tool 3-18
        Create a selection using the Polygon Lasso
        tool and save it 3-19
        Transform a selection 3-20
        Transform a copied selection 3-21

LESSON 4

Select Areas Based on Color 3-22
Using the Magic Wand Tool 3-22
Merging and Flattening Objects and
Layers 3-22
Tasks   Select and copy pixels using the Magic
        Wand tool 3-24
        Select and alter pixels 3-25
        Merge and flatten objects and
        layers 3-25

Integration

INTRODUCTION
Integrating Adobe CS4 Web Standard 1-2
Introduction 1-2

LESSON 1
**Insert a Fireworks Image into a
Dreamweaver Document** 1-4
Placing a Fireworks Image into
Dreamweaver 1-4
Using Fireworks as the Primary External
Image Editor 1-4
Using Design Notes 1-4
Specifying Launch and Edit Preferences 1-5
Setting up the Dreamweaver Site 1-5
Tasks   Designate the primary external image
           editor 1-6
           Specify launch and edit settings 1-7
           Edit and export an image in Fireworks 1-8
           Insert a Fireworks image into a
           Dreamweaver document 1-9
           Edit a Fireworks image from
           Dreamweaver 1-10
           Copy and paste a Fireworks image in a
           Dreamweaver document 1-11

LESSON 2
**Create a Fireworks Image and Import it into
Flash** 1-13
Import a Fireworks Document into
Flash 1-13
Tasks   Create a Fireworks image with several
           layers 1-14
           Import a Fireworks document into
           Flash 1-15
           Edit a Fireworks image that has been
           imported into Flash 1-16
           Create an animation using a Fireworks text
           object 1-17

LESSON 3
**Insert and Edit a Flash Movie in
Dreamweaver** 1-19
Inserting a Flash Movie into a Dreamweaver
Document 1-19
Using the Property Inspector with the
Movie 1-19

Tasks   Insert a Flash movie into Dreamweaver 1-21
           Play a Flash movie and change settings
           from Dreamweaver 1-22
           Edit a Flash movie from
           Dreamweaver 1-22

Data Files 1

Glossary 11

Index 24

Art Credits 40

What Instructor Resources Are Available with This Book?

The Instructor Resources CD-ROM is Delmar's way of putting the resources and information needed to teach and learn effectively into your hands. All the resources are available for both Macintosh and Windows operating systems.

Instructor's Manual

Available as an electronic file, the Instructor's Manual includes chapter overviews and detailed lecture topics for each chapter, with teaching tips. The Instructor's Manual is available on the Instructor Resources CD-ROM.

PowerPoint Presentations

Each chapter has a corresponding PowerPoint presentation that you can use in lectures, distribute to your students, or customize to suit your course.

Data Files for Students

To complete most of the chapters in this book, your students will need Data Files. The Data Files are available on the CD at the back of this textbook. Instruct students to use the Data Files List at the end of this book. This list gives instructions on organizing files.

Solutions to Exercises

Solution Files are Data Files completed with comprehensive sample answers. Use these files to evaluate your students' work. Or distribute them electronically so students can verify their work. Sample solutions to all lessons and end-of-chapter material are provided.

Test Bank and Test Engine

ExamView is a powerful testing software package that allows instructors to create and administer printed and computer (LAN-based) exams. ExamView includes hundreds of questions that correspond to the topics covered in this text, enabling students to generate detailed study guides that include page references for further review. The computer-based and LAN-based/online testing component allows students to take exams using the EV Player, and also saves the instructor time by grading each exam automatically.

Dreamweaver CS4
System Requirements

For a Windows operating system:

- 2GHz or faster processor
- Microsoft Windows® XP with Service Pack 2 (Service Pack 3 recommended) or Windows Visa Home Premium, Business, Ultimate, or Enterprise with Service Pack 1 (certified for 32-bit Windows XP and Windows Vista)
- 1GB of RAM or more recommended
- 9.3 GB of available hard-disk space for installation; additional free space required during installation (cannot install on flash-based storage devices)
- 1,024×768 display (1,280×800 recommended) with 16-bit video card
- Some GPU-accelerated features require graphics support for Shader Model 3.0 and OpenGL 2.0
- Some features in Adobe® Bridge rely on a DirectX9-capable graphics card with at least 64MB of VRAM
- DVD-ROM drive
- Quicktime 7.4.5 software required for multimedia features
- Broadband Internet connection required for online services

For a Macintosh operating system:

- PowerPC® G5 or multicore Intel® processor
- Mac OS X v10.4.11–10.5.4

- Java™ Runtime Environment 1.5 required for Adobe Version Cue® Server
- 1GB of RAM or more recommended 10.3GB of available hard-disk space for installation; additional hard-disk space required during installation (cannot install on a volume that uses a case-sensitive file system or on flash-based storage devices)
- 1,024×768 display (1,280×800 recommended) with 16-bit video card
- Some GPU-accelerated features require graphics support for Shader Model 3.0 and OpenGL 2.0
- DVD-ROM drive
- QuickTime 7.4.5 software required for multimedia features
- Broadband Internet connection required for online services

Intended Audience

This text is designed for the beginner or intermediate user who wants to learn how to use Dreamweaver CS4. The book is designed to provide basic and in-depth material that not only educates, but also encourages you to explore the nuances of this exciting program.

Approach

The text allows you to work at your own pace through step-by-step tutorials. A concept is presented and the process is explained, followed by the actual steps. To learn the most from the use of the text, you should adopt the following habits:

- Proceed slowly: Accuracy and comprehension are more important than speed.
- Understand what is happening with each step before you continue to the next step.
- After finishing a skill, ask yourself if you could do it on your own, without referring to the steps. If the answer is no, review the steps.

Icons, Buttons, and Pointers

Symbols for icons, buttons, and pointers are shown in the step each time they are used. Icons may look different in the files panel depending on the file association settings on your computer.

Fonts

The Data Files contain a variety of commonly used fonts, but there is no guarantee that these fonts will be available on your computer. In a few cases, fonts other than those common to a PC or a Macintosh are used. If any of the fonts in use is not available on your computer, you can make a substitution, realizing that the results may vary from those in the book.

Windows and Macintosh

Adobe Dreamweaver CS4 works virtually the same on Windows and Macintosh operating systems. In those cases where there is a significant difference, the abbreviations (Win) and (Mac) are used.

Memory Challenges

If, instead of seeing an image on an open page, you see an image placeholder with a large X across it, your RAM is running low. Try closing any other applications that are running to free up memory.

Building a Website

You will create and develop a website called The Striped Umbrella in the lesson material in this book. Because each chapter builds off of the previous chapter, it is recommended that you work through the chapters in consecutive order.

Websites Used in Figures

Each time a website is used for illustration purposes in a lesson, where necessary, a statement acknowledging that we obtained permission to use the website is included, along with the URL of the website. Sites whose content is in the public domain, such

as federal government websites, are acknowledged as a courtesy.

Data Files

To complete the lessons in this book, you need the Data Files on the CD in the back of this book. Your instructor will tell you where to store the files as you work, such as the hard drive, a network server, or a USB storage device. The instructions in the lessons will refer to "where you store your Data Files" when referring to the Data Files for the book.
When you copy the Data Files to your computer, you may see lock icons that indicate that the files are read-only when you view them in the Dreamweaver Files panel. To unlock the files, right-click on the locked file name in the Files panel, and then click Turn off Read Only.

Images vs. Graphics

Many times these terms seem to be used interchangeably. For the purposes of this text, the term images is used when referring to pictures on a Web page. The term graphics is used as a

more encompassing term that refers to non-text items on a web page such as photographs, logos, navigation bars, Flash animations, graphs, background images, and drawings. You may define these terms in a slightly different way, depending on your professional background or business environment.

Preference Settings

The learning process will be much easier if you can see the file extensions for the files you will use in the lessons. To do this in Windows, open Windows Explorer, click Organize, Folder and Search Options, click the View tab, then uncheck the box Hide Extensions for Known File Types. To do this for a Mac, go to the Finder, click the Finder menu, and then click Preferences. Click the Advanced tab, then select the Show all file extensions check box.

To view the Flash content that you will be creating, you must set a preference in your browser to allow active content to run. Otherwise, you will not be able to view objects such as Flash buttons.

To set this preference in Internet Explorer, click Tools, Internet Options, Advanced, then check the box Allow active content to run in files on My Computer. Your browser settings may be slightly different, but look for similar wording. When using Windows Internet Explorer 7, you can also click the information bar when prompted to allow blocked content.

Creating a Portfolio

The Portfolio Project and Project Builders allow students to use their creativity to come up with original Dreamweaver designs. You might suggest that students create a portfolio in which they can store their original work.

Flash CS4
System Requirements
For a Windows operating system:

- 1GHz or faster processor
- Microsoft® Windows® XP with Service Pack 2 (Service Pack 3 recommended) or Windows Vista™ Home Premium, Business, Ultimate, or Enterprise with Service Pack 1 (certified for 32-bit editions)
- 1GB of RAM
- 3.5GB of available hard-disk space (additional free space required during installation)
- 1,024 × 768 monitor resolution with 16-bit video card
- DVD-ROM drive
- QuickTime 7.1.2 software required for multimedia features

For a Macintosh operating system:

- PowerPC® G5 or multicore Intel® processor
- Mac OS X v10.4.11–10.5.4
- 1G of RAM
- 4GB of available hard-disk space (additional free space required during installation)
- 1,024 × 768 display (1,280 × 800 recommended) with 16-bit video card
- DVD-ROM drive
- QuickTime 7.1.2 software required for multimedia features

Projects
Several projects are presented that allow students to apply the skills they have learned in a chapter. Two projects, Ultimate Tours and the Portfolio,

build from chapter to chapter. You will need to contact your instructor if you plan to work on these without having completed the previous chapter's project.

Fireworks System Requirements

For a Windows Operating System

- 1GHz or faster processor
- Microsoft® Windows® XP with Service Pack 2 (Service Pack 3 recommended) or Windows Vista® Home Premium, Business, Ultimate, or Enterprise with Service Pack 1 (certified for 32-bit Windows XP and Windows Vista)
- 512MB of RAM (1GB recommended)
- 1GB of available hard-disk space for installation (additional free space required during installation; cannot install on flash-based storage devices)
- 1,024 × 768 display (1,280 × 800 recommended) with 16-bit video card
- DVD-ROM drive
- Broadband Internet connection required for online services

For a Macintosh Operating System

- PowerPC® G5 or multicore Intel® processor
- Mac OS X v.1-.411–10.5.4
- 512MB of RAM (1GB recommended)
- 1GB of available hard-disk space (additional free space required during installation; cannot install on a volume that uses a case-sensitive file system or on flash-based storage devices)
- 1,024 × 768 display (1,280 × 800 recommended) with 16-bit video card
- DVD-ROM drive
- Broadband Internet connection required for online services

GETTING STARTED WITH
DREAMWEAVER

1. Explore the Dreamweaver workspace

2. View a web page and use Help

3. Plan and define a website

4. Add a folder and pages

GETTING STARTED WITH
DREAMWEAVER

Introduction

Adobe Dreamweaver CS4 is a web development tool that lets you create dynamic, interactive web pages containing text, images, hyperlinks, animation, sounds, video, and other elements. You can use Dreamweaver to create individual web pages or complex websites consisting of many web pages. A **website** is a group of related web pages that are linked together and share a common interface and design. You can use Dreamweaver to create design elements such as text, tables, and interactive buttons, or you can import elements from other software programs. You can save Dreamweaver files in many different file formats, including XHTML, HTML, JavaScript, CSS, or XML, to name a few. **XHTML** is the acronym for eXtensible HyperText Markup Language, the current standard language used to create web pages. You can still use **HTML** (HyperText Markup Language) in Dreamweaver; however, it is no longer considered the standard language. In Dreamweaver, you can easily convert exist-

ing HTML code to XHTML-compliant code. You use a web browser to view your web pages on the Internet. A **web browser** is a program, such as Microsoft Internet Explorer or Mozilla Firefox, that lets you display HTML-developed web pages.

Using Dreamweaver Tools

Creating an excellent website is a complex task. Fortunately, Dreamweaver has an impressive number of tools that can help. Using Dreamweaver's design tools, you can create dynamic and interactive web pages without writing a word of code. However, if you prefer to write code, Dreamweaver makes it easy to type and edit the code directly and see the visual results of the code instantly. Dreamweaver also contains organizational tools that help you work with a team of people to create a website. You can also use Dreamweaver's management tools to help you manage a website. For instance, you can use the **Files panel** to create folders to organize and store the various files for your website, and add pages to your website.

Tools You'll Use

Property inspector

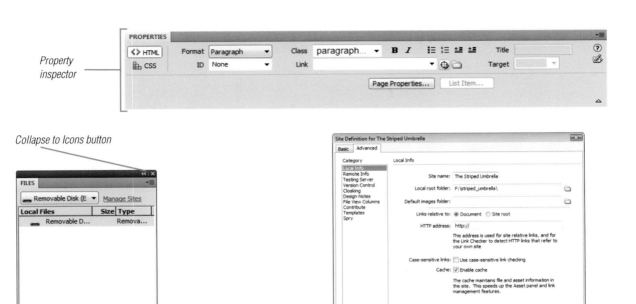

Collapse to Icons button

Show Code and Design views button   Switch Design View to Live View button

Show Code view button   Show Design view button

FIGURE 29
Completed Project Builder 2

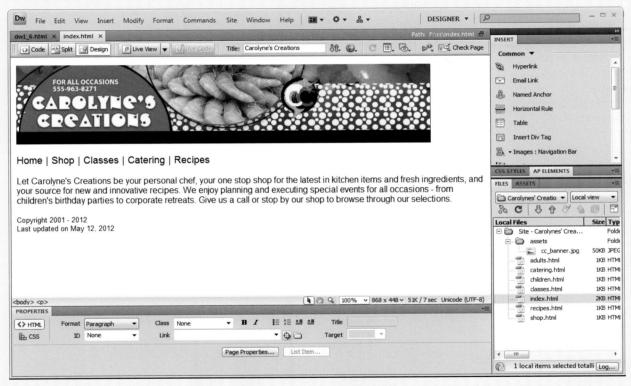

Figure 30 shows the Audi website, a past selection for the Adobe Site of the Day. To visit the current Audi website, connect to the Internet, then go to www.audi.com. The current page might differ from the figure because dynamic websites are updated frequently to reflect current information. Also, your page may default to the Audi of America site. The main navigation structure is accessed through the links along the right side of the page. The page title is Audi Worldwide > Home.

Go to the Adobe website at www.adobe.com, click the Showcase link under the Company menu, then click the current Site of the Day. Explore the site and answer the following questions:

1. Do you see page titles for each page you visit?
2. Do the page titles accurately reflect the page content?
3. View the pages using more than one screen resolution, if possible. For which resolution does the site appear to be designed?

4. Is the navigation structure clear?
5. How is the navigation structure organized?

6. Why do you think this site was chosen as a Site of the Day?

FIGURE 30
Design Project

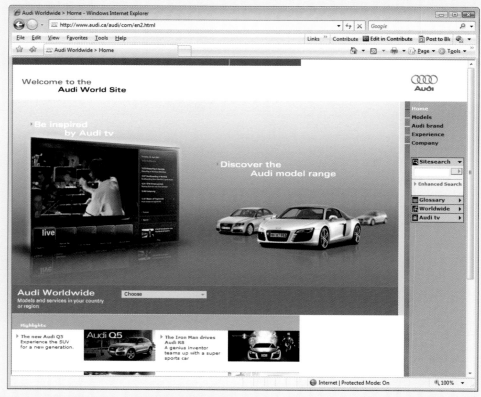

Audi website used with permission from Audi AG – www.audi.com

The Portfolio Project will be an ongoing project throughout the book, in which you will plan and create an original website without any Data Files supplied. The focus of the site can be on any topic, organization, sports team, club, or company that you would like. You will build on this site from chapter to chapter, so you must do each Portfolio Project assignment in each chapter to complete your website. When you finish this book, you should have a completed site that would be an excellent addition to a professional portfolio.

1. Decide what type of site you would like to create. It can be a personal site about you, a business site that promotes a fictitious or real company, or an informational site that provides information about a topic, cause, or organization.
2. Write a list of questions and answers about the site you have decided to create.
3. Create a storyboard for your site to include at least four pages. The storyboard should include the home page with at least three child pages under it.
4. Create a root folder and an assets folder to house the assets, then define your site using the root folder as the website local root folder and the assets folder as the default images folder.
5. Create a blank page named **index.html** as a placeholder for the home page.
6. Begin collecting content, such as pictures or text to use in your website. You can use a digital camera to take photos, use a scanner to scan pictures, or create your own graphics using a program such as Adobe Fireworks or Adobe Illustrator. Gather the content in a central location that will be accessible to you as you develop your site.

chapter

2

DEVELOPING A
WEB PAGE

1. Create head content and set page properties

2. Create, import, and format text

3. Add links to web pages

4. Use the History panel and edit code

5. Modify and test web pages

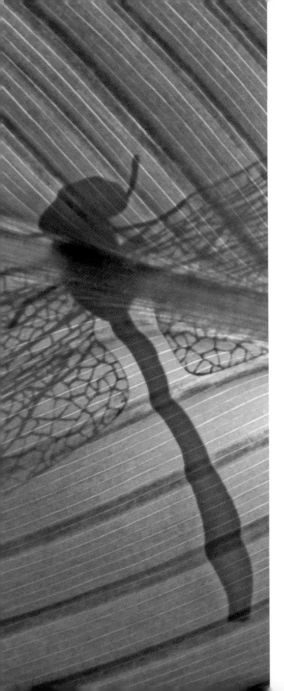

Introduction

The process of developing a web page requires several steps. If the page is a home page, you need to spend some time crafting the head content. The head content contains information used by search engines to help viewers find your website. You also need to choose the colors for the page background and text. You then need to add the page content, format it attractively, and add links to other pages in the site or to other websites. Finally, to ensure that all links work correctly and are current, you need to test them regularly.

Understanding Page Layout

Before you add content to a page, consider the following guidelines for laying out pages:

Use White Space Effectively. A living room crammed with too much furniture makes it difficult to appreciate the individual pieces. The same is true of a web page. Too many text blocks, links, animations, and images can be distracting. Consider leaving some white space on each page.
White space, which is not necessarily white, is the area on a page that contains no text or graphics.

Limit Media Elements. Too many media elements, such as images, video clips, or sounds, may result in a page that takes too much time to load. Viewers may leave your site before the entire page finishes loading. Use media elements only if you have a good reason.

Keep It Simple. Often the simplest websites are the most appealing and are also the easiest to create and maintain. A simple, well-designed site that works well is far superior to a complex one that contains errors.

Use an Intuitive Navigation Structure. Make sure the navigation structure is easy to use. Viewers should always know where they are in the site and be able to easily find their way back to the home page. If viewers get lost, they may leave the site rather than struggle to find their way around.

Apply a Consistent Theme. To help give pages in your website a consistent appearance, consider designing your pages using elements that relate to a common theme. Consistency in the use of color and fonts, the placement of the navigation links, and the overall page design gives a website a unified look and promotes greater ease-of-use and accessibility. Template-based pages and style sheets make this task much easier.

Tools You'll Use

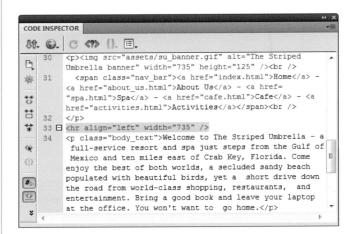

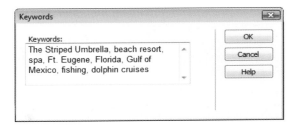

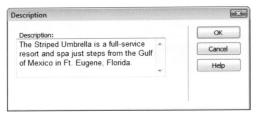

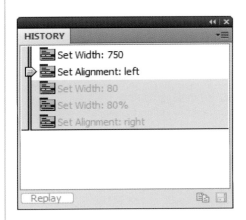

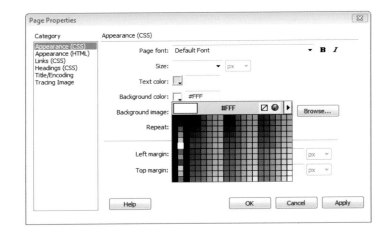

CREATE HEAD CONTENT AND
SET PAGE PROPERTIES

What You'll Do

In this lesson, you will learn how to enter titles, keywords, and descriptions in the head content section of a web page. You will also change the background color for a web page.

Creating the Head Content

A web page is composed of two distinct sections: the head content and the body. The **head content** includes the page title that appears in the title bar of the browser and some important page elements, called meta tags, that are not visible in the browser. **Meta tags** are HTML codes that include information about the page, such as the page title, keywords and descriptions. Meta tags are read by screen readers (for viewers who have visual impairments) and are also used to provide the server information such as the PICS rating for the page. PICS is the acronym for **Platform for Internet Content Selection**. This is a rating system for web pages that is similar to rating systems used for movies. **Keywords** are words that relate to the content of the website.

QUICKTIP

Page titles are not to be confused with filenames, the name used to store each file on the server.

DESIGNTIP   **Using web-safe colors**

Prior to 1994, colors appeared differently on different types of computers. In 1994, Netscape developed the first **web-safe color palette**, a set of colors that appears consistently in all browsers and on Macintosh, Windows, and UNIX platforms. The evolution of video cards has made this less relevant today, although understanding web-safe colors may still prove important given the limitations of other online devices, such as cell phones and PDAs. If you want your web pages to be viewed across a wide variety of computer platforms, choose web-safe colors for all your page elements. Dreamweaver has two web-safe color palettes, Color Cubes and Continuous Tone, each of which contains 216 web-safe colors. Color Cubes is the default color palette. To choose a different color palette, click Modify on the Application bar (Win) or Menu bar (Mac) click Page Properties, click the Appearance (CSS) or Appearance (HTML) category, click the Background, Text, or Links color box to open the color picker, click the color picker list arrow, and then click the color palette you want.

A **description** is a short paragraph that describes the content and features of the website. For instance, the words "beach" and "resort" would be appropriate keywords for The Striped Umbrella website. Search engines find web pages by matching the title, description, and keywords in the head content of web pages with keywords that viewers enter in search engine text boxes. Therefore, it is important to include concise, useful information in the head content. The **body** is the part of the page that appears in a browser window. It contains all the page content that is visible to viewers, such as text, images, and links.

Setting Web Page Properties

When you create a web page, one of the first design decisions that you should make is choosing the **background color**, or the color that fills the entire page. The background color should complement the colors used for text, links, and images that are placed on the page. Many times, images are used for backgrounds for either the entire page or a part of the page, such as a table background or Cascading Style Sheet (CSS) block.

> **QUICK**TIP
>
> A **CSS block** is a section of a web page defined and formatted using a Cascading Style Sheet.
> A **Cascading Style Sheet** is a file used to assign sets of common formatting characteristics to page elements such as text, objects, tags, and tables. We will initially use the Page Properties dialog box to set page properties such as the background color. Later we will learn to do this using Cascading Style Sheets.

A strong contrast between the text color and the background color makes it easier for viewers to read the text on your web page.

You can choose a light background color with a dark text color, or a dark background color with a light text color. A white background with dark text, though not terribly exciting, provides good contrast and is the easiest to read for most viewers. Another design decision you need to make is whether to change the **default font** and **default link colors**, which are the colors used by the browser to display text, links, and visited links. The default color for **unvisited links**, or links that the viewer has not clicked yet, is blue. In Dreamweaver, unvisited links are simply called **links**. The default color for **visited links**, or links that have been previously clicked, is purple. You change the background color, text, and link colors using the color picker in the Page Properties dialog box. You can choose colors from one of the five Dreamweaver color palettes, as shown in Figure 1.

FIGURE 1
Color picker showing color palettes

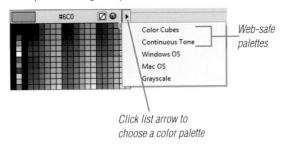

Web-safe palettes

Click list arrow to choose a color palette

Edit a page title

1. Start Dreamweaver, click the **Site list arrow** on the Files panel, then click **The Striped Umbrella** (if necessary).

2. Double-click **index.html** in the Files panel to open The Striped Umbrella home page, click **View** on the Application bar (Win) or Menu bar (Mac), then click **Head Content**.

   The Meta icon 🖳, Title icon ⧉, and CSS icon 🔲 are now visible in the head content section.

3. Click the **Title icon** ⧉ in the head content section.

   The page title The Striped Umbrella appears in the Title text box in the Property inspector, and the selected Title icon in the head content section changes to a blue color, as shown in Figure 2.

4. Click after the end of The Striped Umbrella text in the Title text box in the Property inspector, press **[Spacebar]**, type **beach resort and spa, Ft. Eugene, Florida**, then press **[Enter]** (Win) or **[return]** (Mac).

   Compare your screen with Figure 3. The new title is better, because it incorporates the words "beach resort" and "spa" and the location of the resort—words that potential customers might use as keywords when using a search engine.

   TIP You can also change the page title using the Title text box on the Document toolbar.

You opened The Striped Umbrella website, opened the home page in Design view, viewed the head content section, and changed the page title.

FIGURE 2
Viewing the head content

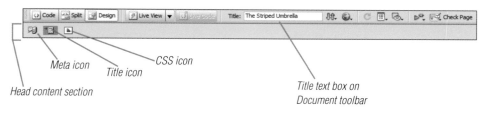

Head content section

Meta icon

Title icon

CSS icon

Title text box on Document toolbar

FIGURE 3
Property inspector displaying new page title

Scroll with arrow key to see the rest of the title

DESIGNTIP   **Using appropriate content for your target audience**

When you begin developing the content for your website, you need to decide what content to include and how to arrange each element on each page. You must design the content with the audience in mind. What is the age group of your audience? What reading level is appropriate? Should you use a formal or informal tone? Should the pages be simple, consisting mostly of text, or rich with images and media files? Your content should fit your target audience. Look at the font sizes used, the number and size of images and animations used, the reading level, and the amount of technical expertise needed to navigate your site, and then evaluate them to see if they fit your audience. If they do not, you will be defeating your purpose. Usually, the first page that your audience will see when they visit your site is the home page. The home page should be designed so that viewers will understand your site's purpose and feel comfortable finding their way around the pages in your site. To ensure that viewers do not get lost in your site, make sure you design all the pages with a consistent look and feel. You can use templates and Cascading Style Sheets to maintain a common look for each page. **Templates** are web pages that contain the basic layout for each page in the site, including the location of a company logo or a menu of buttons. **Cascading Style Sheets** are sets of formatting attributes that are used to format web pages to provide a consistent presentation for content across the site. Cascading Style Sheets make it easy to separate your site content from the site design. The content is stored on web pages, and the formatting styles are stored in a separate style sheet file.

FIGURE 4
*Insert bar displaying the
Common category*

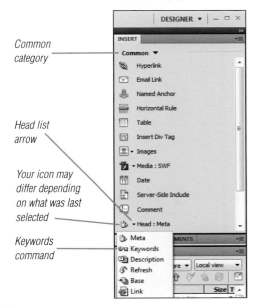

*Common
category*

*Head list
arrow*

*Your icon may
differ depending
on what was last
selected*

*Keywords
command*

Enter keywords

1. Click the **Common category** on the Insert panel (if necessary).

2. Click the **Head list arrow**, as shown in Figure 4, then click **Keywords**.

   TIP   Some buttons on the Insert panel include a list arrow indicating that there is a menu of choices beneath the current button. The button that you select last will appear on the Insert panel until you select another.

FIGURE 5
Keywords dialog box

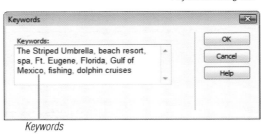

Keywords

3. Type **The Striped Umbrella, beach resort, spa, Ft. Eugene, Florida, Gulf of Mexico, fishing, dolphin cruises** in the Keywords text box, as shown in Figure 5, then click **OK**

   The Keywords icon 🔑 appears in the head content section; click it and the keywords will appear in the Keywords text box in the Property inspector.

You added keywords relating to the beach to the head content of The Striped Umbrella home page.

DESIGNTIP   **Entering keywords and descriptions**

Search engines use keywords, descriptions, and titles to find pages after a user enters search terms. Therefore, it is very important to anticipate the search terms your potential customers would use and include these words in the keywords, description, and title. Many search engines display page titles and descriptions in their search results. Some search engines limit the number of keywords that they will index, so make sure you list the most important keywords first. Keep your keywords and descriptions short and concise to ensure that all search engines will include your site. To choose effective keywords, many designers incorporate the use of focus groups to have a more representative sample of words that potential customers or clients might use. A **focus group** is a marketing tool that asks a group of people for feedback about a product, such as its impact in a television ad or the effectiveness of a website design.

Enter a description

1. Click the **Head list arrow** on the Insert panel, then click **Description**.

2. In the Description text box, type **The Striped Umbrella is a full-service resort and spa just steps from the Gulf of Mexico in Ft. Eugene, Florida**.

   Your screen should resemble Figure 6.

3. Click **OK**, then click the **Description icon** 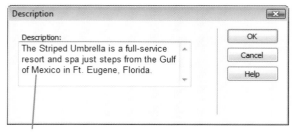 in the Head Content.

   The Description icon appears in the Head Content section and the description appears in the Description text box in the Property inspector.

4. Click the **Show Code view button** Code on the Document toolbar.

   Notice that the title, keywords, and description appear in the HTML code in the document window, as shown in Figure 7.

   | TIP   You can also enter and edit the meta tags directly in the code in Code view.

5. Click the **Show Design view button** Design to return to Design view.

6. Click **View** on the Application bar (Win) or Menu bar (Mac), then click **Head Content** to close the head content section.

You added a description of The Striped Umbrella resort to the head content of the home page. You then viewed the page in Code view and examined the HTML code for the head content.

FIGURE 6
Description dialog box

Description

Description:
The Striped Umbrella is a full-service
resort and spa just steps from the Gulf
of Mexico in Ft. Eugene, Florida.

OK
Cancel
Help

Description

FIGURE 7
Head Content displayed in Code view

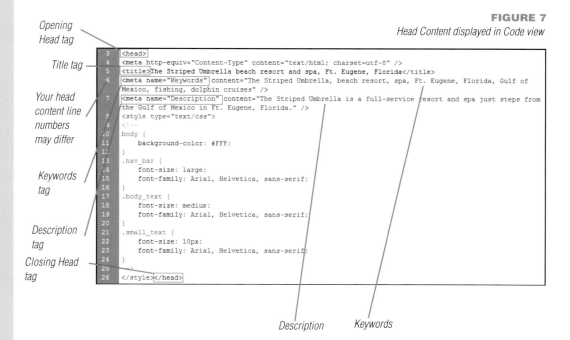

Opening Head tag

Title tag

Your head content line numbers may differ

Keywords tag

Description tag

Closing Head tag

Description   Keywords

FIGURE 8
Page Properties dialog box

Default Color button

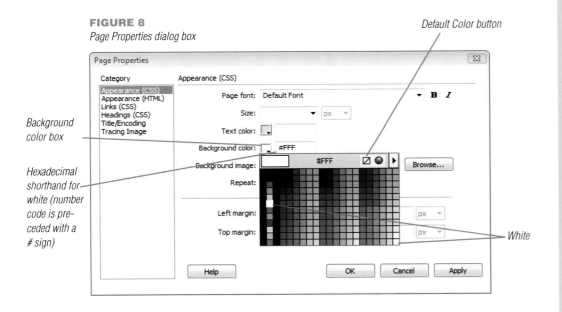

Background color box

Hexadecimal shorthand for white (number code is preceded with a # sign)

White

1. Click **Modify** on the Application bar (Win) or Menu bar (Mac), then click **Page Properties** to open the Page Properties dialog box.

2. Click the **Background color box** to open the color picker, as shown in Figure 8.

3. Click the rightmost color in the bottom row (white).

4. Click **Apply**, then click **OK**.

   Clicking Apply lets you see the changes you made to the web page without closing the Page Properties dialog box.

   TIP If you don't like the color you chose, click the Default Color button in the color picker to switch to the default color.

   The background color of the web page is now white. The black text against the white background provides a nice contrast and makes the text easy to read.

5. Save your work.

You used the Page Properties dialog box to change the background color to white.

Understanding hexadecimal values

Each color is assigned a **hexadecimal RGB value**, a value that represents the amount of red, green, and blue present in the color. For example, white, which is made of equal parts of red, green, and blue, has a hexadecimal value of FFFFFF. This is also referred to as an RGB triplet in hexadecimal format (**hex triplet**). Each pair of characters in the hexadecimal value represents the red, green, and blue values. The hexadecimal number system is based on 16, rather than 10 in the decimal number system. Because the hexadecimal number system includes only numbers up to 9, values after 9 use the letters of the alphabet. "A" represents the number 10 in the hexadecimal number system. "F" represents the number 15. The hexadecimal values are entered in the code using a form of shorthand that shortens the six characters to three characters. For instance: FFFFFF become FFF; 0066CC becomes 06C. The number value for a color is preceded by a pound sign (#) in HTML code.

CREATE, IMPORT, AND
FORMAT TEXT

What You'll Do

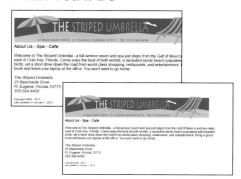

In this lesson, you will apply HTML heading styles and HTML text styles to text on The Striped Umbrella home page. You will also import a file and set text properties for the text on the new page.

Creating and Importing Text

Most information in web pages is presented in the form of text. You can type text directly in Dreamweaver, import, or copy and paste it from another software program. (Macintosh users do not have the option to import text. They must open a text file, copy the text, then paste it into an HTML document.) When using a Windows computer to import text from a Microsoft Word file, you use the Import Word Document command. Not only will the formatting be preserved, but Dreamweaver will generate clean HTML code. Clean HTML code is code that does

what it is supposed to do without using unnecessary instructions, which take up memory. When you format text, it is important to keep in mind that visitors to your site must have the same fonts installed on their computers as the fonts you use. Otherwise, the text may appear incorrectly. Some software programs can convert text into graphics so that the text retains the same appearance no matter which fonts are installed. However, text converted into graphics is no longer editable. If text does not have a font specified, the default font will apply. This means that the default font on

Using keyboard shortcuts

When working with text, the standard Windows keyboard shortcuts for Cut, Copy, and Paste are very useful. These are [Ctrl][X] (Win) or ⌘[X] (Mac) for Cut, [Ctrl][C] (Win) or ⌘[C] (Mac) for Copy, and [Ctrl][V] (Win) or ⌘[V] (Mac) for Paste. You can view all Dreamweaver keyboard shortcuts using the Keyboard Shortcuts dialog box, which lets you view existing shortcuts for menu commands, tools, or miscellaneous functions, such as copying HTML or inserting an image. You can also create your own shortcuts or assign shortcuts that you are familiar with from using them in other software programs. To view or modify keyboard shortcuts, click the Keyboard Shortcuts command on the Edit menu (Win) or Dreamweaver menu (Mac), then select the shortcut key set you want. The Keyboard Shortcuts feature is also available in Adobe Fireworks and Flash. Each chapter in this book includes a list of keyboard shortcuts relevant to that chapter.

the user's computer will be used to display the text. Keep in mind that some fonts may not appear the same on both a Windows and a Macintosh computer. The way fonts are rendered (drawn) on the screen differs because Windows and Macintosh computers use different technologies to render them. It is wise to stick to the standard fonts that work well with both systems. Test your pages using both operating systems.

Formatting Text Using the Property Inspector

Because text is more difficult and tiring to read on a computer screen than on a printed page, you should make the text in your website attractive and easy to read. You can format text in Dreamweaver by changing its font, size, and color, just as you would in other software programs. To apply formatting to text, you first select the text you want to enhance, and then use the Property inspector to apply formatting attributes, such as font type, size, color, alignment, and indents.

Using HTML Tags Compared to Using CSS

The standard practice today is to use Cascading Style Sheets (CSS) to handle the formatting and placement of web page elements. In fact, the default preference in Dreamweaver is to use CSS rather than HTML tags.

QUICKTIP

Tags are the parts of the code that specify formatting for all elements in the document.

However, this is a lot to learn when you are just beginning, so we are going to begin by using HTML tags for formatting until we study CSS in depth in the next chapter. At that point, we will use CSS instead of HTML tags. To change from CSS to HTML and vice versa, you select the CSS or HTML Property inspector. The Property inspector options will change according to which button is selected. Even if you have the HTML Property inspector selected, styles will be created automatically when you apply most formatting attributes.

Changing Fonts

You can format your text with different fonts by choosing a font combination from the Font list in the CSS Property inspector. A **font combination** is a set of three font choices that specify which fonts a browser should use to display the text on your web page. Font combinations are used so that if one font is not available, the browser will use the next one specified in the font combination. For example, if text is formatted with the font combination Arial, Helvetica, sans serif; the browser will first look on the viewer's system for Arial. If Arial is not available, then it will look for Helvetica. If Helvetica is not available, then it will look for a sans-serif font to apply to the text. Using fonts within the default settings is wise, because fonts set outside the default settings may not be available on all viewers' computers.

Changing Font Sizes

There are two ways to change the size of text using the Property inspector. When the CSS option is selected, you can select a numerical value for the size from 9 to 36 pixels or you can use a size expressed in words from xx-small to larger. On the HTML Property inspector, you do not have font sizes available.

Formatting Paragraphs

The HTML Property inspector displays options to format blocks of text as paragraphs or as different sizes of headings. To format a paragraph as a heading, click anywhere in the paragraph, and then select the heading size you want from the Format list in the Property inspector. The Format list contains six different heading formats. Heading 1 is the largest size, and Heading 6 is the smallest size. Browsers display text formatted as headings in bold, setting them off from paragraphs of text. You can also align paragraphs with the alignment buttons on the CSS Property inspector and indent paragraphs using the Text Indent and Text Outdent buttons on the HTML Property inspector.

QUICKTIP

Mixing too many different fonts and formatting attributes on a web page can result in pages that are visually confusing or difficult to read.

Enter text

1. Position the insertion point directly after "want to go home." at the end of the paragraph, press **[Enter]** (Win) or **[return]** (Mac), then type **The Striped Umbrella**.

   Pressing [Enter] (Win) or [return] (Mac) creates a new paragraph. The HTML code for a paragraph break is <p>. The tag is closed with </p>.

   > TIP If the new text does not assume the formatting attributes as the paragraph above it, click the Show Code and Design views button ⬚ Split, position the cursor right after the period after "home", then go back to the page in Design view and insert a new paragraph.

2. Press and hold **[Shift]**, press **[Enter]** (Win) or **[return]** (Mac), then type **25 Beachside Drive**.

   Pressing and holding [Shift] while you press [Enter] (Win) or [return] (Mac) creates a line break. A **line break** places a new line of text on the next line down without creating a new paragraph. Line breaks are useful when you want to add a new line of text directly below the current line of text and keep the same formatting. The HTML code for a line break is <br />.

3. Add the following text below the 25 Beachside Drive text, using line breaks after each line:

   Ft. Eugene, Florida 33775
   555-594-9458

4. Compare your screen with Figure 9.

   You entered text for the address and telephone number on the home page.

FIGURE 9
Entering the address and telephone number on The Striped Umbrella home page

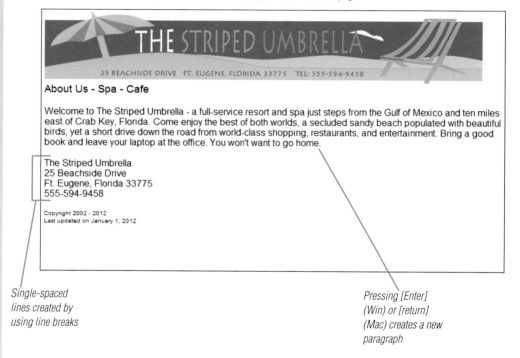

THE STRIPED UMBRELLA

25 BEACHSIDE DRIVE FT. EUGENE, FLORIDA 33775 TEL: 555-594-9458

About Us - Spa - Cafe

Welcome to The Striped Umbrella - a full-service resort and spa just steps from the Gulf of Mexico and ten miles east of Crab Key, Florida. Come enjoy the best of both worlds, a secluded sandy beach populated with beautiful birds, yet a short drive down the road from world-class shopping, restaurants, and entertainment. Bring a good book and leave your laptop at the office. You won't want to go home.

The Striped Umbrella
25 Beachside Drive
Ft. Eugene, Florida 33775
555-594-9458

Copyright 2002 - 2012
Last updated on January 1, 2012

Single-spaced lines created by using line breaks

Pressing [Enter] (Win) or [return] (Mac) creates a new paragraph

Preventing data loss

When you are ready to stop working with a file in Dreamweaver, it is a good idea to save your changes, close the page or pages on which you are working, and exit Dreamweaver. Doing this will prevent the loss of data if power is interrupted. In some cases, loss of power can corrupt an open file and render it unusable.

FIGURE 10

Formatting the address on The Striped Umbrella home page

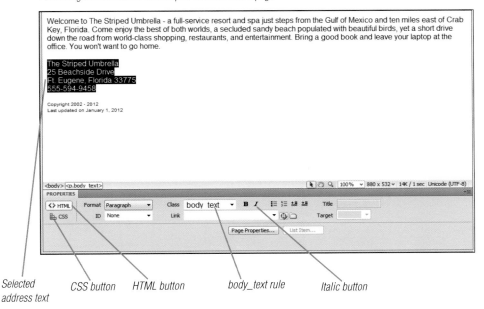

Selected address text — CSS button — HTML button — body_text rule — Italic button

FIGURE 11

Viewing the HTML code for the address and phone number

"body_text" tag defines the CSS style in the original data file

Beginning <em> tag begins italic text

<p> tag begins a new paragraph

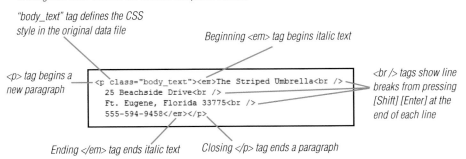

```
<p class="body_text"><em>The Striped Umbrella<br />
   25 Beachside Drive<br />
   Ft. Eugene, Florida 33775<br />
   555-594-9458</em></p>
```


 tags show line breaks from pressing [Shift] [Enter] at the end of each line

Ending </em> tag ends italic text   Closing </p> tag ends a paragraph

Format text

1. Select the entire address and telephone number, as shown in Figure 10, then click the **HTML button** <> HTML in the Property inspector (if it is not already selected) to change to the HTML Property inspector, as shown in Figure 10.

2. Click the **Italic button** I in the Property inspector to italicize the text, then click after the text to deselect it.

   The HTML tag for italic text is <em>.

   > TIP The HTML tag for bold text is <strong></strong>. The HTML tag for underlined text is <u></u>.

3. Click the **Show Code view button** <> Code to view the HTML code, as shown in Figure 11.

   It is always helpful to learn what the HTML code means. As you edit and format your pages, read the code to see how it is written for each element. The more familiar you are with the code, the more comfortable you will feel with Dreamweaver and web design. A strong knowledge of HTML is a necessary skill for professional web designers.

4. Click the **Show Design view button** Design to return to Design view.

5. Save your work, then close the page.

You changed the Property inspector options from CSS to HTML, then formatted the address and phone number for The Striped Umbrella by changing the font style to italic.

Save an image file in the assets folder

1. Open dw2_1.html from where you store your Data Files, save it as **spa.html** in the striped_umbrella folder, overwriting the existing file, then click **No** in the Update Links dialog box.

2. Select **The Striped Umbrella** banner.

   Updating links ties the image or hyperlink to the Data Files folder. Because you already copied su_banner.gif to the website, the banner image is visible. Notice that the Src text box shows the link is to the website assets folder, not to the Data Files folder.

3. Click the **Spa image broken link placeholder** to select it, click the **Browse for File icon** 📁 in the Property inspector next to the Src text box, navigate to the chapter_2 assets folder, click **the_spa.jpg**, then click **OK** (Win) or **Choose** (Mac).

   Because this image was not in the website, it appeared as a broken link. Using the Browse for File icon 📁 selects the source of the original image file. Dreamweaver automatically copies the file to the assets folder of the website and it is visible on the page. You may have to deselect the new image to see it replace the broken link.

4. Click the **Refresh button** 🔄 on the Files panel toolbar if necessary, then click the **plus sign** (Win) or **expander arrow** (Mac) next to the assets folder in the Files panel, (if necessary).

   A copy of the_spa.jpg file appears in the assets folder, as shown in Figure 12.

You opened a new file, saved it as the new spa page, and fixed a broken link by copying the image to the assets folder.

FIGURE 12
Image file added to The Striped Umbrella assets folder

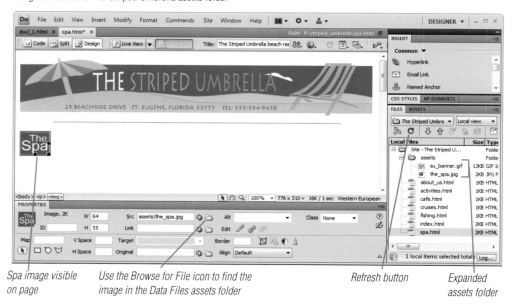

Spa image visible on page

Use the Browse for File icon to find the image in the Data Files assets folder

Refresh button

Expanded assets folder

Choosing filenames for HTML web pages

When you choose a name for a web page, you should use a descriptive name that reflects the contents of the page. For example, if the page is about your company's products, you could name it products.html. You should also follow some general rules for naming web pages, such as naming the home page **index.html**. Most file servers look for the file named index.html to use as the initial page for a website. Do not use spaces, special characters, or punctuation in web page filenames or in the names of any images that will be inserted in your site. Spaces in filenames can cause errors when a browser attempts to read a file, and may cause your images to load incorrectly; use underscores in place of spaces. Forbidden characters include * & ^ % $ # @ ! / and \. You should also never use a number for the first character of a filename. To ensure that everything will load properly on all platforms, including UNIX, assume that filenames are case-sensitive and use lowercase characters. HTML web pages can be saved with the .htm or .html file extension. Although either file extension is appropriate, Dreamweaver uses the default file extension of .html.

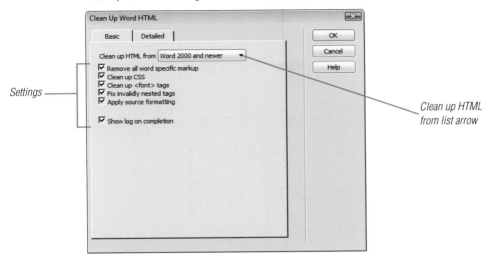

FIGURE 13
Clean Up Word HTML dialog box

Settings ——

Clean up HTML from list arrow

Importing and linking Microsoft Office documents (Windows)

Adobe makes it easy to transfer data between Microsoft Office documents and Dreamweaver web pages. When importing a Word or Excel document, click File on the Application bar, point to Import, then click either Word Document or Excel Document. Select the file want to import, then click the Formatting list arrow to choose between importing Text only; Text with structure (paragraphs, lists, and tables); Text, structure, basic formatting (bold, italic); Text, structure, full formatting (bold, italic, styles) before you click Open. The option you choose depends on the importance of the original structure and formatting. Always use the Clean Up Word HTML command after importing a Word file. You can also create a link to a Word or Excel document on your web page. To do so, drag the Word or Excel document from its current location to the location on the page where you would like the link to appear. (If the document is located outside the site, you can browse for it using the Site list arrow on the Files panel, Windows Explorer, or Mac Finder.) Next, select the Create a link option button in the Insert Document dialog box, then save the file in your root folder so it will be uploaded when you publish your site. If it is not uploaded, the link will be broken.

Import text

1. With the insertion point to the right of the spa graphic on the spa.html page, press **[Enter]** (Win) or **[return]** (Mac).

2. Click **File** on the Application bar, point to **Import**, click **Word Document**, double-click the **chapter_2 folder** from where you store your Data Files, then double-click **spa.doc** (Win); or double-click **spa.doc** from where you store your Data Files, select all, copy, close spa.doc, then paste the copied text on the spa page in Dreamweaver (Mac).

3. Click **Commands** on the Application bar (Win) or Menu bar (Mac), then click **Clean Up Word HTML**.

   TIP   If a dialog box appears stating that Dreamweaver was unable to determine the version of Word used to generate this document, click OK, click the Clean up HTML from list arrow, then choose the Word 2000 and newer version of Word if it isn't already selected.

4. Make sure each check box in the Clean Up Word HTML dialog box is checked, as shown in Figure 13, click **OK**, then click **OK** again to close the results window.

You imported a Word document, then used the Clean Up Word HTML command.

Set text properties

1. Click the Common category on the Insert panel if necessary, then scroll up and place the insertion point anywhere within the words "Spa Services."

2. Click the **Format list arrow** in the HTML Property inspector, click **Heading 4,** click the **Show Code and Design views button** [Split] on the Document toolbar, then compare your screen to Figure 14.

   The Heading 4 format is applied to the paragraph. Even a single word is considered a paragraph if there is a hard return or paragraph break after it. The HTML code for a Heading 4 tag is <h4>. The tag is then closed with </h4>. The level of the heading tag follows the h, so the code for a Heading 1 tag is <h1>.

3. Click **Format** on the Application bar (Win) or Menu bar (Mac), point to **Align,** then click **Center**.

   When the paragraph is centered, the HTML code 'align="center"' is added to the <h4> tag.

You applied a heading format to a heading, viewed the HTML code, then centered the heading.

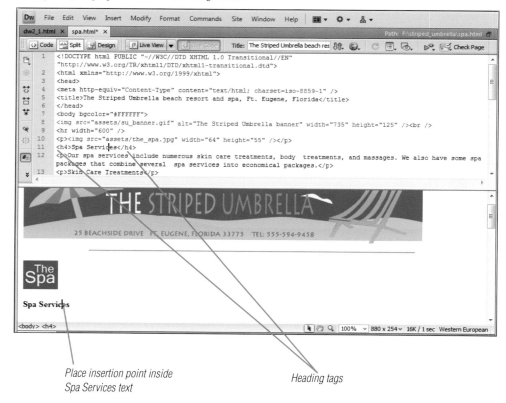

FIGURE 14

Viewing the heading tag in Show Code and Design views

Place insertion point inside Spa Services text

Heading tags

FIGURE 15
Check Spelling dialog box

Our spa services include numerous skin care treatments, body treatments, and massages. We also have some spa
packages that combine several spa se...

Check Spelling

Word not found in dictionary:

masaged   Add to Personal

Skin Care Treatments

Revitalizing Facial   Change to: massaged
A light massage that moisturizes the sk

Suggestions: massaged   Ignore
Gentlemen's Facial   massage
A cleansing facial that includes a neck   messaged   Change
                                        massages
                                        managed   Ignore All
Milk Mask   massager
A mask applied to soften and moisturi   message   Change All
                                        massacred

Body Treatments   Close   Help

Salt Glow
Imported sea salts are **masaged** into the skin, exfoliating and cleansing the pores.

Mud Body Wrap
Relief for your aches and pains.

Misspelled word

*Click "Change" to
correct spelling*

Checking for spelling errors

It is very important to check for spelling and grammatical errors before publishing a
page. A page that is published with errors will cause the viewer to immediately judge
the site as unprofessional and carelessly made, and the accuracy of the data presented
will be in question. If a file you create in a word processor will be imported into
Dreamweaver, run a spell check in the word processor first. Then spell check the
imported text again in Dreamweaver so you can add words such as proper names to
the Dreamweaver dictionary so the program will not flag them again. Click the Add to
Personal button in the Check Spelling dialog box to add a new word to the dictionary.
Even though you may have checked a page using the spell check feature, you still
must proofread the content yourself to catch usage errors such as "to," "too," and
"two." Accuracy in both content and delivery is critical.

Check spelling

1. Click the **Show Design view button** [Design]
   to return to Design view.

2. Place the insertion point in front of the text
   "Spa Services".

   It is a good idea to start a spelling check at
   the top of the document because
   Dreamweaver searches from the insertion
   point down. If your insertion point is in the
   middle of the document, you will receive a
   message asking if you want to check the
   rest of the document. Starting from the
   beginning just saves time.

3. Click **Commands** on the Application bar
   (Win) or Menu bar (Mac), then click
   Check Spelling.

   The word "masaged" is highlighted on the
   page as a misspelled word and suggestions
   are listed to correct it in the Check Spelling
   dialog box, as shown in Figure 15.

4. Click **massaged** in the Suggestions list if
   necessary, then click **Change.**

   The word is corrected on the page.

5. Click **OK** to close the Dreamweaver dialog
   box stating that the Spelling Check is
   completed.

6. Save and close the spa page, then close the
   dw2_1.html page.

You checked the page for spelling errors.

ADD LINKS TO
WEB PAGES

What You'll Do

 In this lesson, you will open the home page and add links to the navigation bar that link to the About Us, Spa, Cafe, and Activities pages. You will then insert an email link at the bottom of the page.

Adding Links to Web Pages

Links provide the real power for web pages. Links make it possible for viewers to navigate all the pages in a website and to connect to other pages anywhere on the web. Viewers are more likely to return to websites that have a user-friendly navigation structure. Viewers also enjoy websites that have interesting links to other web pages or other websites.

To add links to a web page, first select the text or image that you want to serve as a link, and then specify a path to the page to which you want to link in the Link text box in the Property inspector.

When you create links on a web page, it is important to avoid **broken links**, or links that cannot find their intended destinations. You can accidentally cause a broken link by typing the incorrect address for the link in the Link text box. Broken links are often caused by companies merging, going out of business, or simply moving their website addresses.

In addition to adding links to your pages, you should provide a **point of contact**, or a place on a web page that provides viewers with a means of contacting the company. A common point of contact is a **mailto: link**, which is an email address that viewers with questions or problems can use to contact someone at the company's headquarters.

Using Navigation Bars

A **navigation bar** is an area on a web page that contains links to the main pages of a website. Navigation bars are usually located at the top or side of the main pages of a website and can be created with text, images, or a combination of the two. To make navigating a website as easy as possible, you should place navigation bars in the same position on each page. Navigation bars are the backbone of a website's navigation structure, which includes all navigation aids for moving around a website. You can, however, include additional links to the main pages of the website elsewhere on the page. The web page in Figure 16 shows an example of a navigation bar that contains both text and image links that use JavaScript. Notice that when the mouse is placed on an item in the navigation bar, the image expands to include more information.

Navigation bars can also be simple and contain only text-based links to the pages in the site. You can create a simple navigation bar by typing the names of your website's pages at the top of your web page, formatting the text, and then adding links to each page name. It is always a good idea to provide plain text links for accessibility, regardless of the type of navigation structure you choose to use.

FIGURE 16
The CIA website

Additional information appears

Navigation bar with text links using JavaScript

Create a navigation bar

1. Open **index.html**.

2. Position the insertion point to the left of "A" in About Us, then drag to select **About Us - Spa - Cafe**.

3. Type **Home - About Us - Spa - Cafe - Activities,** as shown in Figure 17.

   These five text labels will serve as a navigation bar. You will add the links later.

You created a new navigation bar using text, replacing the original navigation bar.

Insert a horizontal rule

1. Click after the end of the word "Activities" if necessary, then press **[Shift][Enter]** (Win) **or [Shift][return]** (Mac).

2. Click **Horizontal Rule** in the Common category on the Insert panel to insert a horizontal rule under the navigation bar.

   A horizontal rule is a line used to separate page elements or to organize information on a page.

3. Compare your screen to Figure 18, then save your work.

   TIP   An asterisk after the filename in the title bar indicates that you have altered the page since you last saved it. After you save your work, the asterisk does not appear.

You added a horizontal rule to separate the navigation bar from the page content.

FIGURE 17
Viewing the new navigation bar

FIGURE 18
Inserting a horizontal rule

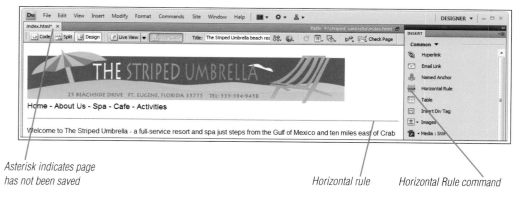

Asterisk indicates page has not been saved

Horizontal rule   *Horizontal Rule command*

FIGURE 19

Selecting text for the Home link

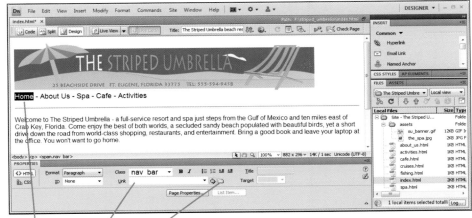

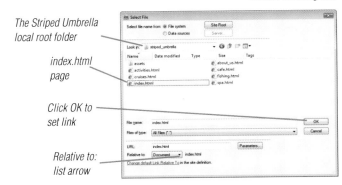

Selected text   *Link text box*   *Browse for File icon*

FIGURE 20

Select File dialog box

The Striped Umbrella
local root folder

index.html
page

Click OK to
set link

Relative to:
list arrow

FIGURE 21

Links added to navigation bar

*Navigation bar
with links added*

Add links to web pages

1. Double-click **Home** to select it, as shown in Figure 19.

2. Click the **Browse for File icon** 🗀 next to the Link text box in the HTML Property inspector, then navigate to the striped_umbrella root folder (if necessary).

3. Verify that the link is set Relative to Document in the Relative to: list.

4. Click **index.html** as shown in Figure 20, click **OK** (Win) or **Choose** (Mac), then click anywhere on the page to deselect Home.

    TIP   Your file listing may differ depending on your view settings.

    Home now appears in blue with an underline, indicating it is a link. However, clicking Home will not open a new page because the link is to the home page. It might seem odd to create a link to the same page on which the link appears, but this will be helpful when you copy the navigation bar to other pages in the site. Always provide viewers a link to the home page.

5. Repeat Steps 1–4 to create links for About Us, Spa, Cafe, and Activities to their corresponding pages in the striped_umbrella root folder.

6. When you finish adding the links to the other four pages, deselect all, then compare your screen to Figure 21.

You created a link for each of the five navigation bar elements to their respective web pages in The Striped Umbrella website.

Create an email link

1. Place the insertion point after the last digit in the telephone number, then insert a line break.

2. Click **Email Link** in the Common category on the Insert panel to insert an email link.

3. Type **Club Manager** in the Text text box, type **manager@stripedumbrella.com** in the E-Mail text box, as shown in Figure 22, then click **OK** to close the Email Link dialog box.

   If the text does not not retain the formatting from the previous line use the Edit, Undo command to undo Steps 1–3. Switch to Code view and place the insertion point immediately to the right of the telephone number, then repeat the steps again in Design view.

4. Save your work.

   The text "mailto:manager@striped_ umbrella.com," appears in the Link text box in the HTML Property inspector. When a viewer clicks this link, a blank email message window opens in the viewer's default email software, where the viewer can type a message. See Figure 23.

   > TIP You must enter the correct email address in the E-Mail text box for the link to work. However, you can enter any descriptive name, such as customer service or Bob Smith in the Text text box. You can also enter the email address as the text if you want to show the actual email address on the web page.

You inserted an email link to serve as a point of contact for The Striped Umbrella.

FIGURE 22
Email Link dialog box

Text for email link on the page (this could also be a person's name or position or the actual email link)

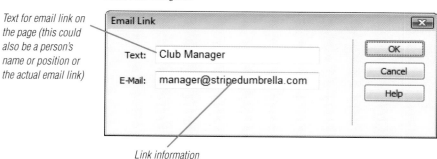

Link information

FIGURE 23
mailto: link on the Property inspector

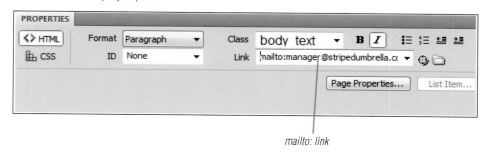

mailto: link

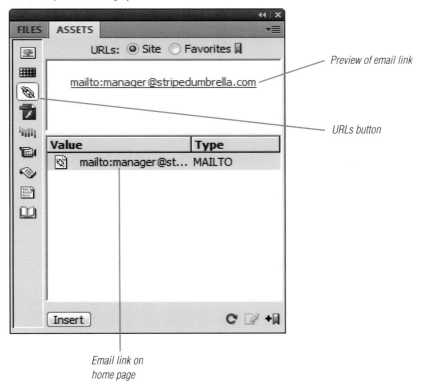

FIGURE 24
The Assets panel URL category

Preview of email link

URLs button

Email link on
home page

1. Click the **Assets panel tab** to view the Assets panel.

2. Click the **URLs button** to display the URLs in the website, as shown in Figure 24.

   URL stands for **Uniform Resource Locator**. The URLs listed in the Assets panel show all of the **external links,** or links pointing outside of the website. An email link is outside the website, so it is an external link. You will learn more about URLs and links in Chapter 4. The links you created to the site pages are internal links (inside the website), and are not listed in the Assets panel.

3. Click the **Files panel tab** to view the Files panel.

You viewed the email link from the home page in the Assets panel.

USE THE HISTORY
PANEL AND EDIT CODE

What You'll Do

In this lesson, you will use the History panel to undo formatting changes you make to a horizontal rule. You will then use the Code Inspector to view the HTML code for the horizontal rule. You will also insert a date object and then view its code in the Code Inspector.

Using the History Panel

Throughout the process of creating a web page, it's likely that you will make mistakes along the way. Fortunately, you have a tool named the History panel to undo your mistakes. The **History panel** records each editing and formatting task performed and displays them in a list in the order in which they were completed. Each task listed in the History panel is called a **step**. You can drag the **slider** on the left side of the History panel to undo

or redo steps, as shown in Figure 25. You can also click in the bar to the left of a step to undo all steps below it. You click the step to select it. By default, the History panel records 50 steps. You can change the number of steps the History panel records in the General category of the Preferences dialog box. However, keep in mind that setting this number too high might require additional memory and could affect Dreamweaver's performance.

Understanding other History panel features

Dragging the slider up and down in the History panel is a quick way to undo or redo steps. However, the History panel offers much more. It has the capability to "memorize" certain tasks and consolidate them into one command. This is a useful feature for steps that you perform repetitively on web pages. Some Dreamweaver features, such as drag and drop, cannot be recorded in the History panel and are noted by a red "x" placed next to them. The History panel does not show steps performed in the Files panel.

Viewing HTML Code in the Code Inspector

If you enjoy writing code, you occasionally might want to make changes to web pages by entering the code rather than using the panels and tools in Design view. You can view the code in Dreamweaver using Code view, Code and Design views, or the Code Inspector. The **Code Inspector**, shown in Figure 26, is a separate window that displays the current page in Code view. The advantage of using the Code Inspector is that you can see a full-screen view of your page in Design view while viewing the underlying code in a floating window that you can resize and position wherever you want.

You can add advanced features, such as JavaScript functions, to web pages by copying and pasting code from one page to another in the Code Inspector. A **JavaScript** function is a block of code that adds dynamic content such as rollovers or interactive forms to a web page. A **rollover** is a special effect that changes the appearance of an object when the mouse moves over it.

FIGURE 25
The History panel

FIGURE 26
The Code Inspector

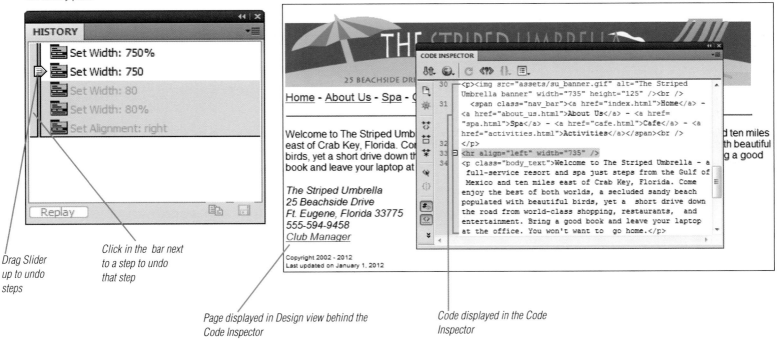

Drag Slider up to undo steps

Click in the bar next to a step to undo that step

Page displayed in Design view behind the Code Inspector

Code displayed in the Code Inspector

Use the History panel

1. Click **Window** on the Application bar (Win) or Menu bar (Mac), then click **History**.

   The History panel opens and displays steps you have recently performed.

2. Click the **History panel options menu button** 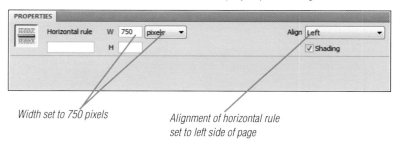, click **Clear History**, as shown in Figure 27, then click **Yes** to close the warning box.

3. Select the **horizontal rule** on the home page.

   The Property inspector shows the properties of the selected horizontal rule.

4. Click the W text box in the Property inspector, type **750**, click the **Align list arrow**, click **Left**, then compare your Property inspector to Figure 28.

   > TIP   Horizontal rule widths can be set in pixels or as a percent of the width of the window. If the width is expressed in pixels, the code will only show the number without the word "pixels". Pixels is understood as the default width setting.

5. Using the Property inspector, change the W text box value to **80**, change the measurement unit to **%**, click the **Align list arrow**, then click **Right**.

6. Drag the **slider** on the History panel up to Set Alignment: Left, as shown in Figure 29.

   The bottom three steps in the History panel appear gray, indicating that these steps have been undone.

7. Right-click (Win) or Control-click (Mac) the **History panel title bar,** then click **Close** to close the History panel.

You formatted the horizontal rule, made changes to it, then used the History panel to undo some of the changes.

FIGURE 27
Clearing the History panel

Options menu button

You will see a additional commands if your panel is displayed in a tab group

Clear History command

FIGURE 28
Property inspector settings for horizontal rule

Width set to 750 pixels

Alignment of horizontal rule set to left side of page

FIGURE 29
Undoing steps using the History panel

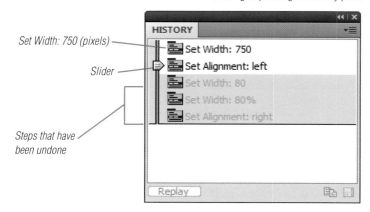

Set Width: 750 (pixels)

Slider

Steps that have been undone

FIGURE 30
Viewing the Options menu in the Code Inspector

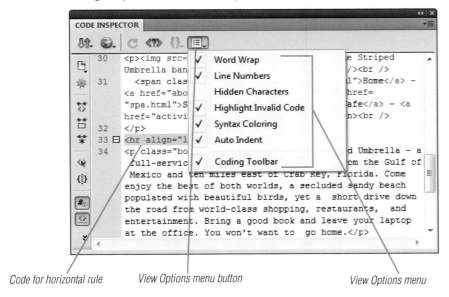

Code for horizontal rule   View Options menu button   View Options menu

Use the Code Inspector

1. Click the **horizontal rule** to select it (if necessary), click **Window** on the Application bar (Win) or Menu bar (Mac), then click **Code Inspector**.

   Because the horizontal rule on the page is selected, the corresponding code is highlighted in the Code Inspector.

   TIP   You can also press [F10](Win) or [option][F10] (Mac) to display the Code Inspector.

2. Click the **View Options menu button** on the Code Inspector toolbar to display the View Options menu, then click **Word Wrap** (if necessary), to activate Word Wrap.

   The Word Wrap feature forces text to stay within the confines of the Code Inspector window, allowing you to read without scrolling sideways.

3. Click the **View Options menu button**, then verify that the Word Wrap, Line Numbers, Highlight Invalid Code, Syntax Coloring, Auto Indent, and the Coding Toolbar menu items are checked, as shown in Figure 30. If they are not checked, check them.

4. Select **750** in the horizontal rule width code, then type **735**.

You changed the width of the horizontal rule by changing the code in the Code Inspector.

POWER USER SHORTCUTS

to do this:	use this shortcut:
Select All	[Ctrl][A] (Win) or ⌘ [A] (Mac)
Copy	[Ctrl][C] (Win) or ⌘ [C] (Mac)
Cut	[Ctrl][X] (Win) or ⌘ [X] (Mac)
Paste	[Ctrl][V] (Win) or ⌘ [V] (Mac)
Line Break	[Shift][Enter] (Win) or [Shift][return] (Mac)
Show or hide the Code Inspector	[F10] (Win) or [option][F10] (Mac)
Preview in browser	[F12] (Win) or [option][F12] (Mac)
Check spelling	[Shift][F7]

Use the Reference panel

1. Click the **Reference button** <?> on the Code Inspector toolbar, as shown in Figure 31, to open the Results Tab Group with the Reference panel visible.

   TIP Verify that the horizontal rule is still selected, or you will not see the horizontal rule description in the Reference panel.

2. Read the information about horizontal rules in the Reference panel, as shown in Figure 32, right-click in an empty area of the **Results Tab Group title bar,** then click **Close Tab Group** (Win) or click the **Panel Options menu button** then click **Close Tab Group** (Mac and Win) to close the Results Tab Group.

3. Close the Code Inspector.

You read information about horizontal rule settings in the Reference panel.

FIGURE 31
Reference button on the Code Inspector toolbar

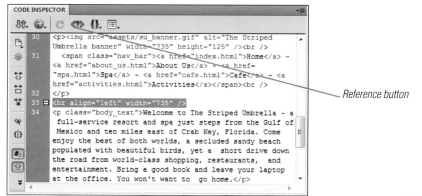

Reference button

FIGURE 32
Viewing the Reference panel

Results tab group

Information on <HR> (horizontal rule tag)

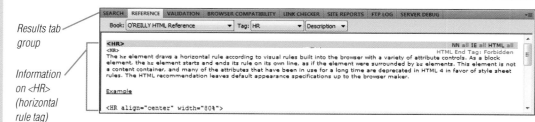

Inserting comments

A handy Dreamweaver feature is the ability to insert comments into HTML code. Comments can provide helpful information describing portions of the code, such as a JavaScript function. You can create comments in any Dreamweaver view, but you must turn on Invisible Elements to see them in Design view. Use the Edit (Win) or Dreamweaver (Mac), Preferences, Invisible Elements, Comments option to enable viewing of comments; then use the View, Visual Aids, Invisible Elements menu option to display them on the page. To create a comment, click the Common category on the Insert panel, click Comment, type a comment in the Comment dialog box, and then click OK. Comments are not visible in browser windows.

Developing a Web Page

FIGURE 33
Insert Date dialog box

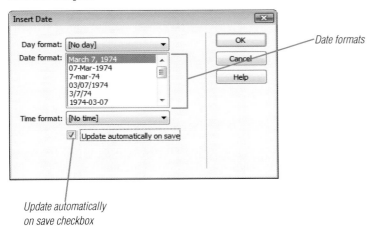

Date formats

Update automatically
on save checkbox

1. Scroll down the page (if necessary) to select **January 1, 2012**, then press **[Delete]** (Win) or **[delete]** (Mac).

2. Click **Date** in the Common category in the Insert panel, then click **March 7, 1974** if necessary in the Date format list box.

3. Click the **Update automatically on save checkbox**, as shown in Figure 33, click **OK**, then deselect the text.

4. Change to Code and Design views.

   The code has changed to reflect the date object, which is set to today's date, as shown in Figure 34. (Your date will be different.) The new code is highlighted with a light yellow background, indicating that it is a date object, automatically coded by Dreamweaver, rather than a date that has been manually typed on the page by the designer.

5. Return to Design view, then save the page.

You inserted a date object that will be updated automatically when you open and save the home page.

FIGURE 34
Viewing the date object code

```
35  <p class="body_text"><em>The Striped Umbrella<br />
36    25 Beachside Drive<br />
37    Ft. Eugene, Florida 33775<br />
38    555-594-9458<br />
39  <a href="mailto:manager@stripedumbrella.com">Club Manager</a></em></p>
40
41  <p class="small_text">Copyright 2002 - 2012 <br />
42  Last updated on
43    <!-- #BeginDate format:Am1 -->July 4, 2008<!-- #EndDate -->
44  </p>
45  </body>
46  </html>
47
```

Code for date object

MODIFY AND TEST
WEB PAGES

What You'll Do

In this lesson, you will preview the home page in the browser to check for typographical errors, grammatical errors, broken links, and overall appearance. After previewing, you will make slight formatting adjustments to the page to improve its appearance.

Testing and Modifying web pages

Testing web pages is a continuous process. You never really finish a website, because there are always additions and corrections to make. As you add and modify pages, you must test each page as part of the development process. The best way to test a web page is to preview it in a browser window to make sure that all text and image elements appear the way you expect them to. You should also test your links to make sure they work properly. You also need to proofread your text to make sure it contains all the necessary information for the page with no typographical or grammatical errors. Designers typically view a page in a browser, return to Dreamweaver to make necessary changes, and then view the page in a browser again. This process may be repeated many times before the page is ready for publishing. In fact, it is sometimes difficult to stop making improvements to a page and move on to another project. You need to strike a balance among quality, creativity, and productivity.

DESIGN TIP Using "Under Construction" or "Come back later" pages

Many people are tempted to insert an unfinished page as a placeholder for a page that will be finished later. Rather than have real content, these pages usually contain text or an image that indicates the page is not finished, or "under construction." You should not publish a web page that has a link to an unfinished page. It is frustrating to click a link for a page you want to open only to find an "under construction" note or image displayed. You want to make the best possible impression on your viewing audience. If you cannot complete a page before publishing it, at least provide enough information on it to make it "worth the trip."

Testing a Web Page Using Different Browsers and Screen Sizes

Because users access the Internet using a wide variety of computer systems, it is important to design your pages so that all browsers and screen sizes can display them well. You should test your pages using different browsers and a wide variety of screen sizes to ensure the best view of your page by the most people possible. Although the most common screen size that designers use today is 1024 × 768, some viewers restore down (reduce) individual program windows to a size comparable to 800 × 600 to be able to have more windows open simultaneously on their screen. In other words, people use their "screen real estate" according to their personal work style. To view your page using different screen sizes, click the Window Size pop-up menu in the status bar, then choose the setting you want to use. Table 1 lists the Dreamweaver default window screen sizes. Remember also to check your pages using Windows and Macintosh platforms. Some page elements such as fonts, colors, table borders, layers, and horizontal rules may not appear consistently in both.

Testing a Web Page as Rendered in a Mobile Device

Dreamweaver has another preview feature that allows you to see what a page would look like if it were viewed on a mobile hand-held device, such as a BlackBerry smartphone. To use this feature, click the Preview/Debug in Browser button on the Document toolbar, then click Preview in Device Central.

TABLE 1: Dreamweaver default window screen sizes

window size (inside dimensions of the browser window without borders)	monitor size
592W	
536 × 196	640 × 480, default
600 × 300	640 × 480, maximized
760 × 420	800 × 600, maximized
795 × 470	832 × 624, maximized
955 × 600	1024 × 768, maximized

Modify a web page

1. Click the **Restore Down button** on the index.html title bar to decrease the size of the home page window (Win) or skip to Step 2 (Mac).

   > TIP   You cannot use the Window Size options if your Document window is maximized (Win).

2. Click the current window size on the status bar, as shown in Figure 35, then click **600 × 300 (640 × 480, Maximized)**, (if necessary).

   A viewer using this setting will be forced to use the horizontal scroll bar to view the entire page.

3. Click the current window size on the status bar, then click **760 × 420 (800 × 600, Maximized)**.

4. Replace the period after the last sentence, "You won't want to go home." with an exclamation point.

5. Click the **Maximize button** on the index.html title bar to maximize the home page window.

6. Save your work.

You viewed the home page using two different window sizes and you made simple formatting changes to the page.

FIGURE 35
Window screen sizes

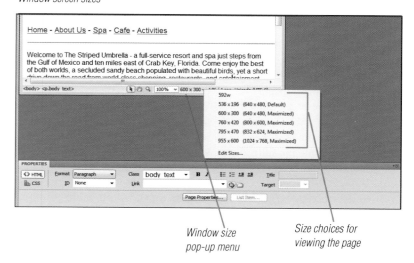

Window size pop-up menu

Size choices for viewing the page

Using smart design principles in web page layout

As you view your pages in the browser, take a critical look at the symmetry of the page. Is it balanced? Are there too many images compared to text, or vice versa? Does everything "heavy" seem to be on the top or bottom of the page, or do the page elements seem to balance with the weight evenly distributed between the top, bottom, and sides? Use design principles to create a site-wide consistency for your pages. Horizontal symmetry means that the elements are balanced across the page. Vertical symmetry means that they are balanced down the page. Diagonal symmetry balances page elements along the invisible diagonal line of the page. Radial symmetry runs from the center of the page outward, like the petals of a flower. These principles all deal with balance; however, too much balance is not good, either. Sometimes it adds interest to place page elements a little off center or to have an asymmetric layout. Color, white space, text, and images should all complement each other and provide a natural flow across and down the page. The rule of thirds—dividing a page into nine squares like a tic-tac-toe grid—states that interest is increased when your focus is on one of the intersections in the grid. The most important information should be at the top of the page where it is visible without scrolling, or "above the fold," as they say in the newspaper business.

FIGURE 36

Viewing The Striped Umbrella home page in the Firefox browser

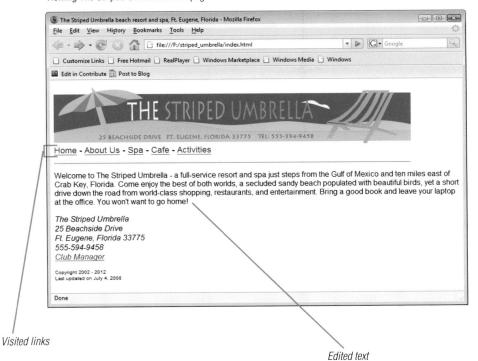

Visited links

Edited text

1. Click the **Preview/Debug in browser button** 🌐 on the Document toolbar, then choose your browser from the menu that opens.

   The Striped Umbrella home page opens in your default browser.

   TIP If previewing the page in Internet Explorer 7, click the Information bar when prompted, click Allow Blocked Content, then click Yes to close the Security Warning dialog box.

2. Click each link on the navigation bar, then after each click, use the Back button on the browser toolbar to return to the home page.

   Pages with no content at this point will appear as blank pages. Compare your screen to Figure 36.

3. Close your browser window, then close all open pages in Dreamweaver.

You viewed The Striped Umbrella home page in your browser and tested each link on the navigation bar.

DESIGNTIP **Choosing a window size**

Today, the majority of viewers are using a screen resolution of 1024×768 or higher. Because of this, more content can be displayed at one time on a computer monitor. Some people may use their whole screen to view pages on the Internet. Others may choose to allocate a smaller area of their screen to the browser window. In other words, people tend to use their "screen real estate" in different ways. The ideal web page will not be so small that it tries to spread out over a larger screen size or so large that the viewer has to use horizontal scroll bars to read the page content. Achieving the best balance is one of the design decisions that must be made during the planning process.

Create head content and set page properties.

1. Open the blooms & bulbs website.
2. Open the index page and view the head content.
3. Add the word "Your" to the page title to read **blooms & bulbs - Your Complete Garden Center**.
4. Insert the following keywords: **garden**, **plants**, **nursery**, **flowers**, **landscape**, **blooms & bulbs**.
5. Insert the following description: **blooms & bulbs is a premier supplier of garden plants for both professional and home gardeners.**
6. Switch to Code view to view the HTML code for the head content, then switch back to Design view.
7. Open the Page Properties dialog box to view the current page properties.
8. Change the background color to a color of your choice.
9. Change the background color to white, then save your work.

Create, import, and format text.

1. Create a new paragraph after the paragraph of text and type the following text, inserting a line break after each line.
   blooms & bulbs
   Highway 43 South
   Alvin, Texas 77511
   (555) 248-0806

2. Verify that the HTML button is selected in the Property inspector, and select it if it is not.
3. Italicize the address and phone number lines.
4. Change to Code view to view the formatting code for the italicized text.
5. Save your work, then close the home page.
6. Open dw2_2.html and save it as **tips.html** in the blooms & bulbs website, overwriting the existing file, but not updating links.
7. Click the broken image link below the blooms & bulbs banner, use the Property inspector to browse to the chapter_2 Data Files folder, select the file garden_tips.jpg in the assets folder, then click OK to save a copy of it in the blooms & bulbs website.
8. Place the insertion point under the Garden Tips graphic.
9. Import gardening_tips.doc from where you store your Data Files, using the Import Word Document command (Win) or copy and paste the text (Mac).
10. Use the Clean Up Word HTML command to correct or remove any unnecessary code.
11. Select the Seasonal Gardening Checklist heading, use the Application bar (Win) or Menu bar (Mac) to center the text, then delete the colon.
12. Use the Property inspector to format the selected text with a Heading 3 format.
13. Check the page for spelling errors by using the Check Spelling command.

14. Save your work and close the tips page and the data file.

Add links to web pages.

1. Open the index page, then select the current navigation bar and replace it with **Home, Featured Plants, Garden Tips,** and **Classes.** Between each item, use a hyphen with a space on either side to separate the items.
2. Add a horizontal rule under the navigation bar, then remove any extra space between the navigation bar and the horizontal rule, so it looks like Figure 37.
3. Use the Property inspector to link Home on the navigation bar to the index.html page in the blooms & bulbs website.
4. Link Featured Plants on the navigation bar to the plants.html page.
5. Link Garden Tips on the navigation bar to the tips.html page.
6. Link Classes on the navigation bar to the classes.html page.
7. Using the Insert panel, create an email link under the telephone number.
8. Type **Customer Service** in the Text text box and **mailbox@blooms.com** in the E-Mail text box.
9. Save your work.
10. View the email link in the Assets panel, then view the Files panel. You may need to click the Refresh button to see the new link.

Use the History panel and edit code.

1. Open the History panel, then clear its contents.
2. Select the horizontal rule under the navigation bar, then change the width to 700 pixels and the alignment to Left.
3. Change the width to 70% and the alignment to Center.
4. Use the History panel to restore the horizontal rule settings to 700 pixels wide, left aligned.
5. Close the History panel.
6. Open the Code inspector and verify that Word Wrap is selected.
7. Edit the code in the Code inspector to change the width of the horizontal rule to 735 pixels.
8. Open the Reference panel and scan the information about horizontal rules.
9. Close the Code inspector and close the Reference panel tab group.
10. Delete the current date in the Last updated on statement on the home page and replace it with a date that will update automatically when the file is saved.
11. Examine the code for the date at the bottom of the page to verify that the code that forces it to update on save is included in the code. (*Hint*: The code should be highlighted with a light yellow background.)
12. Save your work.

Modify and test web pages.

1. Using the Window Size pop-up menu, view the home page at 600 × 300 (640 × 480, Maximized) and 760 × 420 (800 × 600, Maximized), then maximize the Document window.
2. View the page in your browser. (*Hint:* If previewing the page in Internet Explorer 7, click the Information bar when prompted to allow blocked content.)
3. Verify that all links work correctly, then close the browser.
4. On the home page, change the text "Stop by and see us soon!" to **We ship overnight**!
5. Save your work, then view the pages in your browser, comparing your pages to Figure 37 and Figure 38.
6. Close your browser.
7. Adjust the spacing (if necessary), save your work, then preview the home page in the browser again.
8. Close the browser, then save and close all open pages.

FIGURE 37
Completed Skills Review, home page

FIGURE 38
Completed Skills Review, tips page

Home - Featured Plants - Garden Tips - Classes

Welcome to blooms & bulbs. We carry a variety of plants and shrubs along with a large inventory of gardening supplies. Our four greenhouses are full of healthy young plants just waiting to be planted in your yard. Our staff includes a certified landscape architect, three landscape designers, and six master gardeners. We offer detailed landscape plans tailored to your location as well as planting and regular maintenance services. We ship overnight!

blooms & bulbs
Highway 43 South
Alvin, Texas 77511
(555) 248-0806
Customer Service

Copyright 2001 - 2012
Last updated on July 6, 2008

Garden Tips

We have some planting tips we would like to share with you as you prepare your gardens this season. Remember, there is always something to be done for your gardens, no matter what the season. Our experienced staff is here to help you plan your gardens, select your plants, prepare your soil, assist you in the planting, and maintain your beds. Check out our calendar for a list of our scheduled classes. All classes are free of charge and on a first-come, first-served basis!

Seasonal Gardening Checklist

Fall – The time to plant trees and spring blooming bulbs.
Winter – The time to prune fruit trees and finish planting your bulbs.
Spring – The time to prepare your beds, plant annuals, and apply fertilizer to established plants.
Summer – The time to supplement rainfall so that plants get one inch of water per week.

You have been hired to create a website for a TripSmart, a travel outfitter. You have created the basic framework for the website and are now ready to format and edit the home page to improve the content and appearance.

1. Open the TripSmart website, then open the home page.
2. Enter the following keywords: **TripSmart, travel**, **traveling**, **trips**, **vacations**, and **tours**.
3. Enter the following description: **TripSmart is a comprehensive travel store. We can help you plan trips**, **make travel arrangements**, **and supply you with travel gear**.
4. Change the page title to **TripSmart - Serving All Your Travel Needs**.

5. Select the existing navigation bar and replace it with the following text links: **Home**, **Catalog**, **Services**, **Destinations**, and **Newsletter**. Between each item, use a hyphen with a space on either side to separate the items.
6. Replace the date in the last updated statement with a date that will update automatically on save.
7. Type the following address two lines below the paragraph about the company, using line breaks after each line:
TripSmart
1106 Beechwood
Fayetteville, AR 72704
555-848-0807

8. Insert an email link in the line below the telephone number, using **Customer Service** for the Text text box and **mailbox@tripsmart.com** for the E-Mail text box in the Email Link dialog box.
9. Italicize TripSmart, the address, phone number, and email link.
10. Link the navigation bar entries to index.html, catalog.html, services.html, destinations.html, and newsletter.html.
11. View the HTML code for the page.
12. Insert a horizontal rule between the paragraph of text and the address.

13. Change the horizontal rule width to 720 pixels and align to the left side of the page.

14. Save your work.

15. View the page using two different window sizes, then test the links in your browser window.

16. Compare your page to Figure 39, close the browser, then close all open pages.

FIGURE 39
Completed Project Builder 1

Home - Catalog - Services - Destinations - Newsletter

Welcome to TripSmart - the smart choice for the savvy traveler. We're here to help you with all your travel needs. Choose customized trips to any location or our Five-Star Tours, recently rated number one in the country by Traveler magazine. With over 30 years of experience, we can bring you the best the world has to offer.

TripSmart
1106 Beechwood
Fayetteville, AR 72704
555.848.0807
Customer Service

Copyright 2002 - 2012
Last updated on July 6, 2008

Your company has been selected to design a website for a catering business named Carolyne's Creations. You are now ready to add content to the home page and apply formatting options to improve the page's appearance, using Figure 40 as a guide.

1. Open the Carolyne's Creations website, then open the home page.
2. Edit the page title to read **Carolyne's Creations - Premier Gourmet Food Shop.**
3. Add the description **Carolyne's Creations is a full service gourmet food shop. We offer cooking classes, take-out meals, and catering services. We also have a retail shop that stocks gourmet treats and kitchen accessories.**

4. Add the keywords **Carolyne's Creations, gourmet, catering, cooking classes, kitchen accessories, take-out.**
5. Place the insertion point in front of the sentence beginning "Give us a call" and type **Feel like a guest at your own party**.
6. Add the following address below the paragraph using line breaks after each line:
   Carolyne's Creations
   496 Maple Avenue
   Seven Falls, Virginia 52404
   555-963-8271
7. Enter another line break after the telephone number and type **Email**, add a space, then add an email link using Carolyne Kate for the text and carolyne@carolynescreations.com for the email address.

8. Create links from each navigation bar element to its corresponding web page.
9. Replace the date that follows the text "Last updated on" with a date object, then save your work.
10. Insert a horizontal rule below the navigation bar.
11. Set the width of the horizontal rule to 360 pixels.
12. Left-align the horizontal rule.

13. Save your work, view the completed page in your default browser, then test each link. (*Hint*: If previewing the page in Internet Explorer 7, click the Information bar when prompted to allow blocked content.)

14. Close your browser.

15. Close all open pages.

FIGURE 40
Completed Project Builder 2

Home | Shop | Classes | Catering | Recipes

Let Carolyne's Creations be your personal chef, your one stop shop for the latest in kitchen items and fresh ingredients, and your source for new and innovative recipes. We enjoy planning and executing special events for all occasions - from children's birthday parties to corporate retreats. Feel like a guest at your own party. Give us a call or stop by our shop to browse through our selections.

Carolyne's Creations
496 Maple Avenue
Seven Falls, Virginia 52404
555-963-8271
Email Carolyne Kate

Copyright 2001 - 2012
Last updated on July 7, 2008

Angela Lou is a freelance photographer. She is searching the Internet looking for a particular type of paper to use in printing her digital images. She knows that websites use keywords and descriptions in order to receive "hits" with search engines. She is curious about how they work. Follow the steps below and write your answers to the questions.

1. Connect to the Internet, then go to www.snapfish.com to see the Snapfish website's home page, as shown in Figure 41.

2. View the page source by clicking View on the Application bar, then clicking Source (Internet Explorer) or Page Source (Mozilla Firefox).

3. Can you locate a description and keywords? If so, what are they?

4. How many keywords do you find?

5. Is the description appropriate for the website? Why or why not?

6. Look at the numbers of keywords and words in the description. Is there an appropriate number? Or are there too many or not enough?

7. Use a search engine such as Google at www.google.com, then type the words **photo quality paper** in the Search text box.

8. Click the first link in the list of results and view the source code for that page. Do you see keywords and a description? Do any of them match the words you used in the search?

FIGURE 41
Design Project

Snapfish website used with permission from Snapfish - www.snapfish.com

In this assignment, you will continue to work on the website you defined in Chapter 1. In Chapter 1, you created a storyboard for your website with at least four pages. You also created a local root folder for your site and an assets folder to store the site asset files. You set the assets folder as the default storage location for your images. You began to collect information and resources for your site and started working on the home page.

1. Think about the head content for the home page. Add the title, keywords, and a description.
2. Create the main page content for the home page and format it attractively.
3. Add the address and other contact information to the home page, including an email address.
4. Consult your storyboard and design the navigation bar.
5. Link the navigation bar items to the appropriate pages.

6. Add a last updated on statement to the home page with a date that will automatically update when the page is saved.
7. Edit and format the page content until you are satisfied with the results.
8. Verify that all links, including the email link, work correctly.
9. When you are satisfied with the home page, review the checklist questions shown in Figure 42, then make any necessary changes.
10. Save your work.

FIGURE 42
Portfolio Project

Website Checklist

1. Does the home page have a page title?
2. Does the home page have a description and keywords?
3. Does the home page contain contact information, including an email address?
4. Does the home page have a navigation bar that includes a link to itself?
5. Does the home page have a "last updated on" statement that will automatically update when the page is saved?
6. Do all paths for links and images work correctly?
7. Does the home page look good using at least two different browsers and screen resolutions?

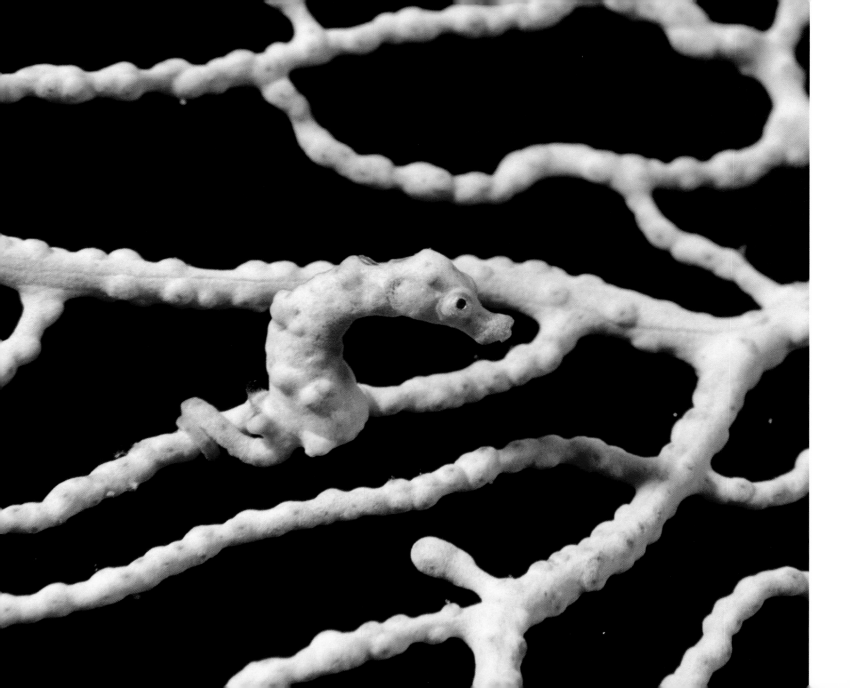

chapter

3

WORKING WITH TEXT
AND IMAGES

1. Create unordered and ordered lists

2. Create, apply, and edit Cascading Style Sheets

3. Add rules and attach Cascading Style Sheets

4. Insert and align graphics

5. Enhance an image and use alternate text

6. Insert a background image and perform site maintenance

3 WORKING WITH TEXT
AND IMAGES

Introduction

Most web pages contain a combination of text and images. Dreamweaver provides many tools for working with text and images that you can use to make your web pages attractive and easy to read. Dreamweaver also has tools that help you format text quickly and ensure a consistent appearance of text elements across all your web pages.

Formatting Text as Lists

If a web page contains a large amount of text, it can be difficult for viewers to digest it all. You can break up the monotony of large blocks of text by dividing them into smaller paragraphs or organizing them as lists. You can create three types of lists in Dreamweaver: unordered lists, ordered lists, and definition lists.

Using Cascading Style Sheets

You can save time and ensure that all your page elements have a consistent appearance by using **Cascading Style Sheets (CSS)**. CSS are sets of formatting instructions, usually stored in a separate file, that control the appearance of content on a web page or throughout a website. You can use CSS to define consistent formatting attributes for page elements such as text and tables throughout your website. You can then apply the formatting attributes you define to any element in a single document or to all of the pages in a website.

Using Images to Enhance Web Pages

Images make web pages visually stimulating and more exciting than pages that contain only text. However, you should use images sparingly. If you think of text as the meat and potatoes of a website, the images would be the seasoning. You should add images to a page just as you would add seasoning to food. A little seasoning enhances the flavor and brings out the quality of the dish. Too much seasoning overwhelms the dish and masks the flavor of the main ingredients. Too little seasoning results in a bland dish. There are many ways to work with images so that they complement the content of pages in a website. There are specific file formats used to save images for websites to ensure maximum quality with minimum file size. You should store images in a separate folder in an organized fashion.

Tools You'll Use

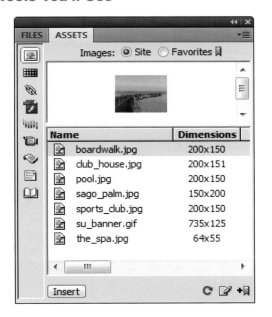

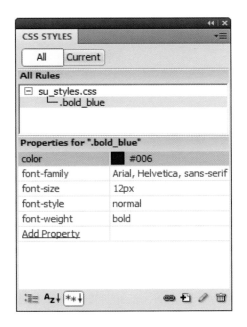

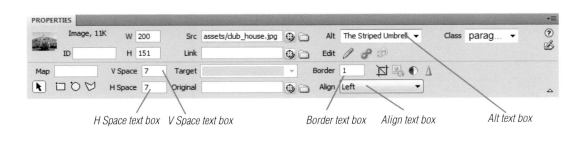

H Space text box   V Space text box   Border text box   Align text box   Alt text box

CREATE UNORDERED AND
ORDERED LISTS

What You'll Do

Spa Packages

- Spa Sampler
  Mix and match any three of our services.
- Girl's Day Out
  One hour massage, a facial, a manicure, and a pedicure.

Call the Spa desk for prices and reservations. Our desk is open from 7:00 a.m. until 5:00 p.m.

Questions you may have

1. How do I schedule Spa services?
   Please make appointments by calling The Club desk at least 24 hours in advance. Please arrive 15 minutes before your appointment to allow enough time to shower or use the sauna.
2. Will I be charged if I cancel my appointment?
   Please cancel 24 hours before your service to avoid a cancellation charge. No-shows and cancellations without adequate notice will be charged for the full service.
3. Are there any health safeguards I should know about?
   Please advise us of medical conditions or allergies you have. Heat treatments like hydrotherapy and body wraps should be avoided if you are pregnant, have high blood pressure, or any type of heart condition or diabetes.
4. What about tipping?
   Gratuities are at your sole discretion, but are certainly appreciated.

In this lesson, you will create an unordered list of spa services on the spa page. You will also import text with questions and format them as an ordered list.

Creating Unordered Lists

Unordered lists are lists of items that do not need to be placed in a specific sequence. A grocery list that lists items in a random order is a good example of an unordered list. Items in unordered lists are usually preceded by a **bullet**, or a small dot or similar icon. Unordered lists that contain bullets are sometimes called **bulleted lists**. Although you can use paragraph indentations to create an unordered list, bullets can often make lists easier to read. To create an unordered list, first select the text you want to format as an unordered list, then use the Unordered List button in the HTML Property inspector to insert bullets at the beginning of each paragraph of the selected text.

Formatting Unordered Lists

In Dreamweaver, the default bullet style is a round dot. To change the bullet style to a square, click inside a bulleted item, expand the Property inspector to its full size, as shown in Figure 1, click the List Item button in the HTML Property inspector to open the List Properties dialog box, and then set the style for bulleted lists to Square. Be aware, however, that not all browsers display square bullets correctly, in which case the bullets will appear differently.

Creating Ordered Lists

Ordered lists, which are sometimes called **numbered lists**, are lists of items that are presented in a specific sequence and that are preceded by sequential numbers or letters. An ordered list is appropriate for a list in which each item must be executed according to its specified order. A list that provides numbered directions for driving from Point A to Point B or a list that provides instructions for assembling a bicycle are both examples of ordered lists.

Formatting Ordered Lists

You can format an ordered list to show different styles of numbers or letters by using the List Properties dialog box, as shown in Figure 2. You can apply numbers, Roman numerals, lowercase letters, or uppercase letters to an ordered list.

Creating Definition Lists

Definition lists are similar to unordered lists but do not have bullets. They are often used with terms and definitions, such as in a dictionary or glossary. To create a definition list, select the text to use for the list, click Format on the Application bar (Win) or Menu bar (Mac), point to List, and then click Definition List.

FIGURE 1

Expanded Property inspector

Property inspector expanded to its full size

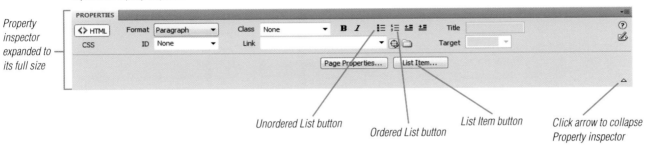

Unordered List button

Ordered List button

List Item button

Click arrow to collapse Property inspector

List type list box

FIGURE 2

Choosing a numbered list style in the List Properties dialog box

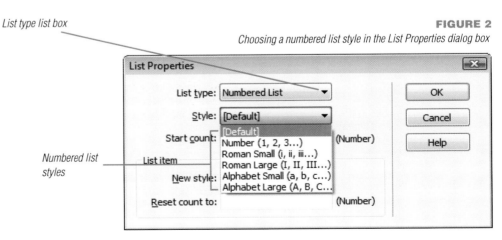

Numbered list styles

Create an unordered list

1. Open the spa page in The Striped Umbrella website.

2. Select the three items under the Skin Care Treatments heading.

3. Click the **HTML button** in the Property inspector to switch to the HTML Property inspector if necessary, click the **Unordered List button** ▤ to format the selected text as an unordered list, click anywhere to deselect the text, then compare your screen to Figure 3.

   Each spa service item and its description is separated by a line break. That is why each description is indented under its corresponding item, rather than formatted as a new list item. You must enter a paragraph break to create a new list item.

4. Repeat Step 3 to create unordered lists of the items under the Body Treatments, Massages, and Spa Packages headings, being careful not to include the contact information in the last sentence on the page as part of your last list.

   TIP Pressing [Enter] (Win) or [return] (Mac) once at the end of an unordered list creates another bulleted item. To end an unordered list, press [Enter] (Win) or [return] (Mac) twice.

You opened the spa page in Design view and formatted four spa services lists as unordered lists.

FIGURE 3
Creating an unordered list

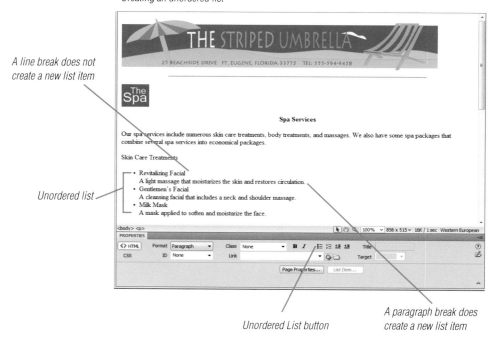

A line break does not create a new list item

Unordered list

Unordered List button

A paragraph break does create a new list item

FIGURE 4

List Properties dialog box

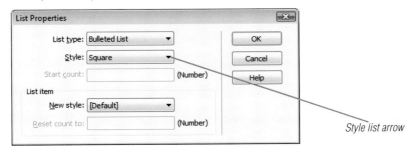

Style list arrow

FIGURE 5

HTML tags in Code view for unordered list

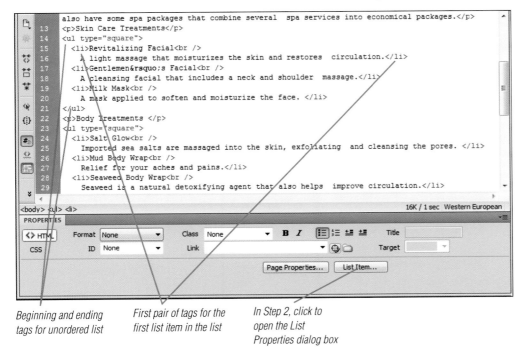

Beginning and ending
tags for unordered list

First pair of tags for the
first list item in the list

In Step 2, click to
open the List
Properties dialog box

1. Click any of the items in the first unordered list to place the insertion point in the list.

2. Expand the Property inspector (if necessary), click **List Item** in the HTML Property inspector to open the List Properties dialog box, click the **Style list arrow**, click **Square**, as shown in Figure 4, then click **OK**.

   The bullets in the unordered list now have a square shape.

3. Repeat Step 2 to format the next three unordered lists.

4. Position the insertion point to the left of the first item in the first unordered list, then click the **Show Code view button** [Code] on the Document toolbar to view the code for the unordered list, as shown in Figure 5.

   Notice that there is a pair of HTML tags surrounding each type of element on the page. The first tag in each pair begins the code for a particular element, and the last tag ends the code for the element. For instance, the tags <ul></ul> surround the unordered list. The tags <li> and </li> surround each item in the list.

5. Click the **Show Design view button** [Design] on the Document toolbar.

6. Save your work.

You used the List Properties dialog box to apply the Square bullet style to the unordered lists. You then viewed the HTML code for the unordered lists in Code view.

Create an ordered list

1. Place the insertion point at the end of the page, after the word "5:00 p.m."

2. Use the Import, Word Document command to import questions.doc from where you store your Data Files (Win) or open questions.doc from where you store your Data Files, select all, copy, then paste the copied text on the page (Mac).

   The inserted text appears on the same line as the existing text.

3. Use the Clean Up Word HTML command, place the insertion point to the left of the text "Questions you may have," then click **Horizontal Rule** in the Common category on the Insert panel.

   A horizontal rule appears and separates the unordered list from the text you just imported.

4. Select the text beginning with "How do I schedule" and ending with the last sentence on the page.

5. Click the **Ordered List button** in the HTML Property inspector to format the selected text as an ordered list.

6. Deselect the text, then compare your screen to Figure 6.

You imported text on the spa page. You also added a horizontal rule to help organize the page. Finally, you formatted selected text as an ordered list.

FIGURE 6
Creating an ordered list

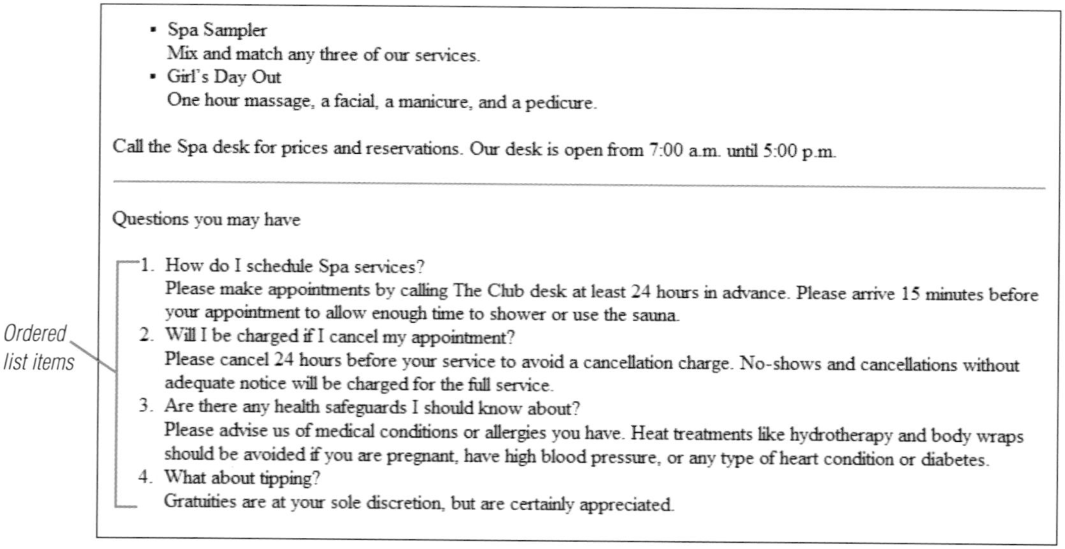

- Spa Sampler
  Mix and match any three of our services.
- Girl's Day Out
  One hour massage, a facial, a manicure, and a pedicure.

Call the Spa desk for prices and reservations. Our desk is open from 7:00 a.m. until 5:00 p.m.

Questions you may have

Ordered list items

1. How do I schedule Spa services?
   Please make appointments by calling The Club desk at least 24 hours in advance. Please arrive 15 minutes before your appointment to allow enough time to shower or use the sauna.
2. Will I be charged if I cancel my appointment?
   Please cancel 24 hours before your service to avoid a cancellation charge. No-shows and cancellations without adequate notice will be charged for the full service.
3. Are there any health safeguards I should know about?
   Please advise us of medical conditions or allergies you have. Heat treatments like hydrotherapy and body wraps should be avoided if you are pregnant, have high blood pressure, or any type of heart condition or diabetes.
4. What about tipping?
   Gratuities are at your sole discretion, but are certainly appreciated.

FIGURE 7

Spa page with ordered list

Formatted heading

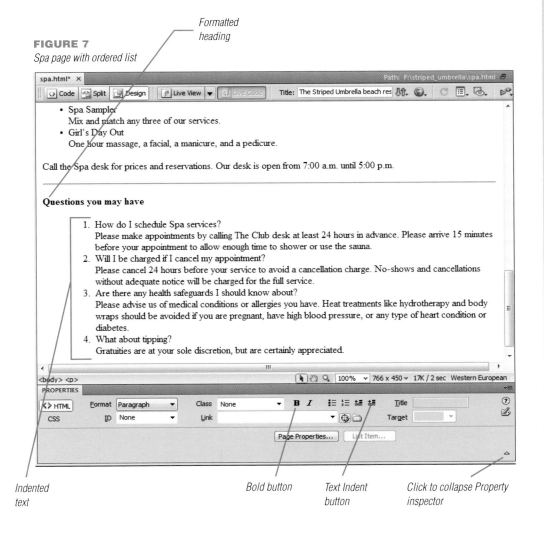

Indented text

Bold button

Text Indent button

Click to collapse Property inspector

1. Select the heading "Questions you may have," then click the **Bold button** **B** in the HTML Property inspector.

2. Select the four questions and answers text, click the **Text Indent button** in the HTML Property inspector, deselect the text, then compare your screen to Figure 7. The Text Indent and Text Outdent buttons are used to indent selected text or remove an indent from selected text.

    TIP If you want to see more of your web page in the Document window, you can collapse the Property inspector.

3. Save your work.

You formatted the "Questions you may have" heading. You also indented the four questions and answers text.

CREATE, APPLY, AND EDIT
CASCADING STYLE SHEETS

What You'll Do

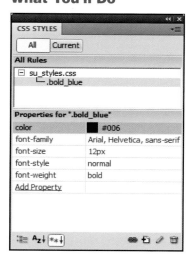

In this lesson, you will create a Cascading Style Sheet file for The Striped Umbrella website. You will also create a rule named bold_blue and apply it to text on the spa page.

Understanding Cascading Style Sheets

CSS are made up of sets of formatting attributes called **rules,** which define the formatting attributes for individual styles, and are classified by where the code is stored. Sometime "style" and "rule" are used interchangeably, but this is not technically accurate. The code can be saved in a separate file (**external style sheet**), as part of the head content of an individual web page (**internal or embedded styles**) or as part of the body of the HTML code (**inline styles**). External CSS style sheets are saved as files with the .css extension and are stored in the directory structure of a website. Figure 8 shows a style sheet named su_styles.css. This style sheet contains a rule called bold_blue. External style sheets are the preferred method for creating and using styles.

CSS are also classified by their type. A **Class type** can be used to format any page element. An **ID type** and a **Tag type** are used to redefine an HTML tag. A **Compound** type is used to format a selection. In this chapter, we will use class type stored in external style sheet files.

Using the CSS Styles Panel

You use the buttons on the CSS Styles panel to create, edit, and apply rules. To add a rule, use the New CSS Rule dialog box to name the rule and specify whether to add it to a new or existing style sheet. You then use the CSS Rule definition dialog box to set the formatting attributes for the rule. Once you add a new rule to a style sheet, it appears in a list in the CSS Styles panel. To apply a rule, you select the text to which you want to apply the rule, and then choose a rule from the Targeted Rule list in the CSS Property inspector. You can apply CSS styles to elements on a single web page or to all of the pages in a website. When you make a change to a rule, all page elements formatted with that rule are automatically updated. Once you create a CSS style sheet, you can attach it to the remaining pages in your website.

The CSS Styles panel is used for managing your styles. The Properties pane displays properties for a selected rule at the bottom of the panel. You can easily change a property's value by clicking an option from a drop-down window.

Comparing the Advantages of Using Style Sheets

You can use CSS styles to save an enormous amount of time. Being able to define a rule and then apply it to page elements on all the pages of your website means that you can make hundreds of formatting changes in a few minutes. In addition, style sheets create a more uniform look from page to page and they generate cleaner code. Using style sheets separates the development of content from the way the content is presented. Pages formatted with CSS styles are much more compliant with current accessibility standards than those with manual formatting.

QUICKTIP

For more information about Cascading Style Sheets, visit www.w3.org or play the audio/video tutorials at www.adobe.com/go/vid0152.

Understanding CSS Style Sheet Code

You can see the code for a CSS rule by opening a style sheet file. A CSS style consists of two parts: the selector and the declaration. The **selector** is the name of the tag to which the style declarations have been assigned. The **declaration** consists of the property and the value. For example, Figure 9 shows the code for the su_styles.css style sheet. In this example, the first property listed for the .bold_blue rule is font-family. The value for this property is Arial, Helvetica, sans-serif. When you create a new CSS, you will see it as an open document in the Document window. Save this file as you make changes to it.

FIGURE 8

Cascading Style Sheet file created in striped_umbrella root folder

New Cascading Style Sheet file

Property   Value   **FIGURE 9**

su_styles.css file

```
1   .bold_blue {
2       font-family: Arial, Helvetica, sans-serif;
3       font-size: 14px;
4       font-style: normal;
5       font-weight: bold;
6       color: #306;
7   }
8   .heading {
9       font-family: Arial, Helvetica, sans-serif;
10      font-size: 16px;
11      font-style: normal;
12      font-weight: bold;
13      color: #036;
14      text-align: center;
15  }
16  .paragraph_text {
17      font-family: Arial, Helvetica, sans-serif;
18      font-size: 14px;
19      font-style: normal;
20  }
21
```

Create a Cascading Style Sheet and a rule

1. Click the **CSS button** [🔳 CSS] in the Property inspector to switch to the CSS Property inspector, as shown in Figure 10.

   From this point forward, we will use CSS rather than HTML tags to format most text.

2. Click **Window** on the Application bar (Win) or Menu bar (Mac), then click **CSS Styles** to open the CSS Styles panel.

3. Click the **Switch to All (Document) Mode button** [All], click the **New CSS Rule button** [🔲] in the CSS Styles panel to open the New CSS Rule dialog box, verify that Class (can apply to any HTML element) is selected under Selector Type, then type **bold_blue** in the Selector Name text box.

   TIP Class names are preceded by a period. If you don't enter a period when you type the name, Dreamweaver will add the period for you.

4. Click the **Rule Definition list arrow**, click **(New Style Sheet File)**, compare your screen with Figure 11, then click **OK**.

5. Type **su_styles** in the File name text box (Win) or the Save As text box (Mac), then click **Save** to open the CSS Rule Definition for .bold_blue in su_styles.css dialog box.

   The .bold_blue rule will be stored within the su_styles.css file.

   (continued)

FIGURE 10
Property inspector after choosing CSS rather than HTML tags option

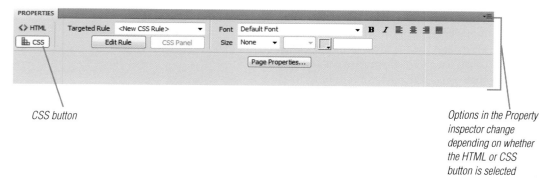

CSS button

Options in the Property inspector change depending on whether the HTML or CSS button is selected

FIGURE 11
New CSS Rule Dialog box

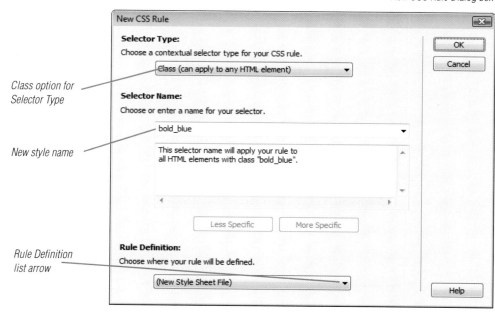

Class option for Selector Type

New style name

Rule Definition list arrow

Working with Text and Images

FIGURE 12
CSS Rule Definition for .bold_blue in the su_styles.css dialog box

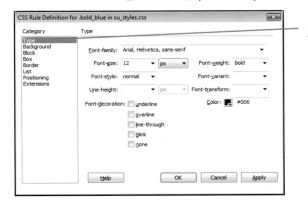

Type category
selected

FIGURE 13
CSS Styles panel with bold_blue rule added

bold_blue
rule

Properties for
bold_blue
rule

6. Verify that Type is selected in the Category list, set the Font-family to **Arial, Helvetica, sans-serif,** set the Font-size to **12 px,** set the Font-weight to **bold**, set the Font-style to **normal,** set the Color to **#006**, compare your screen to Figure 12, then click **OK**.

   TIP You can modify the font combinations in the Font-family list by clicking Format on the Application bar (Win) or Menu bar (Mac), pointing to Font, then clicking Edit Font List.

7. Click the **plus sign** (Win) or the **expander arrow** (Mac) next to su_styles.css in the CSS Styles panel and expand the panel (if necessary) to list the bold_blue style, then select the **bold_blue style**.

   The CSS rule named .bold_blue and the properties appear in the CSS Styles panel, as shown in Figure 13.

   You created a Cascading Style Sheet file named su_styles.css and a rule called .bold_blue.

DESIGNTIP **Choosing fonts**

There are two classifications of fonts: sans-serif and serif. Sans-serif fonts are block-style characters that are often used for headings and subheadings. The headings in this book use a sans-serif font. Examples of sans-serif fonts include Arial, Verdana, and Helvetica. Serif fonts are more ornate and contain small extra strokes at the beginning and end of the characters. Some people consider serif fonts easier to read in printed material, because the extra strokes lead your eye from one character to the next. This paragraph you are reading uses a serif font. Examples of serif fonts include Times New Roman, Times, and Georgia. Many designers feel that a sans-serif font is preferable when the content of a website is primarily intended to be read on the screen, but that a serif font is preferable if the content will be printed. When you choose fonts, you need to keep in mind the amount of text each page will contain and whether most viewers will read the text on-screen or print it. A good rule of thumb is to limit each website to no more than three font variations.

Apply a rule in a Cascading Style Sheet

1. Click **View** on the Application bar (Win) or Menu bar (Mac), point to **Toolbars**, then click **Style Rendering**.

    TIP You can also right-click on an empty area on an open toolbar to see the displayed and hidden toolbars. The displayed toolbars have a check next to them. To display or hide a toolbar, click it.

2. Verify that the **Toggle Displaying of CSS Styles button** 🔳 CSS on the Style Rendering toolbar is active, as shown in Figure 14.

    TIP You can determine if the Toggle Displaying of CSS Styles button is active if it has an outline around the button. As long as this button is active, you do not have to display the toolbar on the screen.

    You use the Toggle Displaying of CSS Styles button to see how styles affect your page. If it is not active, you will not see the effects of your styles.

3. Select the text "Revitalizing Facial," as shown in Figure 15, click the **Targeted Rule text box** in the Property inspector, then click **bold_blue**, as shown in Figure 15.

4. Repeat Step 3 to apply the bold_blue style to each of the spa services bulleted items in the unordered lists, then compare your screen to Figure 16.

    TIP You can use the keyboard shortcut [Ctrl][Y] (Win) or [Command][Y] (Mac) to repeat the previous action.

You applied the bold_blue style to each item in the Spa Services category lists.

FIGURE 14
Style Rendering toolbar

Toggle Displaying of CSS Styles button

FIGURE 15
Applying a CSS rule to selected text — Toggle Displaying of CSS Styles button

Rule applied

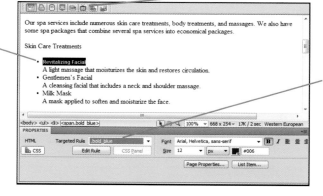

Click to apply bold_blue rule to selected text

FIGURE 16
Unordered list with bold_blue rule applied

bold_blue rule applied to each of the Spa Services items

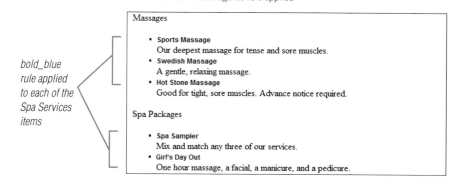

FIGURE 17

Editing a rule

Properties of the bold_blue rule

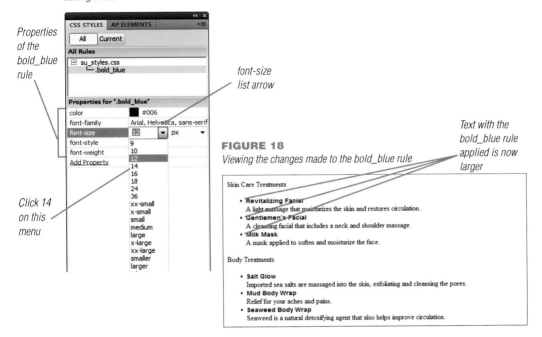

font-size list arrow

Click 14 on this menu

FIGURE 18

Viewing the changes made to the bold_blue rule

Text with the bold_blue rule applied is now larger

Skin Care Treatments

- **Revitalizing Facial**
  A light massage that moisturizes the skin and restores circulation.
- **Gentlemen's Facial**
  A cleansing facial that includes a neck and shoulder massage.
- **Milk Mask**
  A mask applied to soften and moisturize the face.

Body Treatments

- **Salt Glow**
  Imported sea salts are massaged into the skin, exfoliating and cleansing the pores.
- **Mud Body Wrap**
  Relief for your aches and pains.
- **Seaweed Body Wrap**
  Seaweed is a natural detoxifying agent that also helps improve circulation.

Using the Style Rendering toolbar

The Style Rendering toolbar allows you to render your page as different media types, such as print, TV, or handheld. To display it when a page is open, click View on the Application bar (Win); or Menu bar (Mac), point to Toolbars, and then click Style Rendering. The buttons on the Style Rendering toolbar allow you to see how your page will look as you select different media types. The next to the last button on the toolbar is the Toggle Displaying of CSS Styles button, which you can use to view how a page looks with styles applied. It works independently of the other buttons. The last button is the Design-time Style Sheets button, which you can use to show or hide particular combinations of styles while you are working in the Document window.

Edit a rule in a Cascading Style Sheet

1. Click **.bold_blue** in the CSS Styles panel.

   The rule's properties and values appear in the Properties pane, the bottom part of the CSS Styles panel.

   TIP Click the plus sign (Win) or expander arrow (Mac) to the left of su_styles.css in the CSS Styles panel if you do not see .bold_blue. Click the plus sign (Win) or expander arrow (Mac) to the left of <style> if you do not see su_styles.css.

2. Click **12px** in the CSS Styles panel, click the **font-size list arrow**, click **14** as shown in Figure 17, then compare your screen to Figure 18.

   All of the text to which you applied the bold_blue style is larger, reflecting the changes you made to the bold_blue rule. You can also click the **Edit Rule button** in the CSS Styles panel to open the CSS Rule Definition for .bold_blue dialog box.

   TIP If you position the insertion point in text that has a CSS rule applied to it, that rule is displayed in the Targeted Rule text box in the Property inspector.

3. Use the File, Save All command to save the spa page and the style sheet file.

4. Hide the Style Rendering toolbar.

You edited the bold_blue style to change the font size to 14 pixels. You then viewed the results of the edited rule in the unordered list.

View code with the Code Navigator

1. Point to the text "Revitalizing Facial" and hover until the Click indicator to bring up the Code Navigator icon 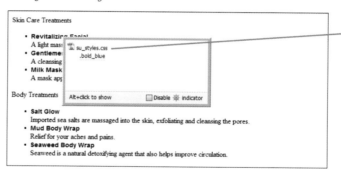 is displayed, as shown in Figure 19.

2. Click the **Click indicator to bring up the Code Navigator icon** 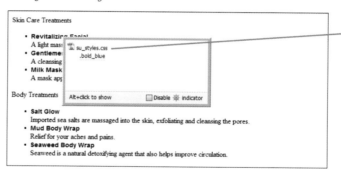.

   A window opens, as shown in Figure 20, with the name of the style sheet that is linked to this page (su_styles.css) and the name of the rule in the style sheet that has been applied to this text (bold_blue).

   | TIP You can also [Alt]-click (Win) or [Command][Option]-click (Mac) the text on the page to display the Code Navigator.

3. Position your cursor over the bold_blue rule name to see the properties of the rule displayed, as shown in Figure 21.

You displayed the Code Navigator to view the properties of the bold_blue rule.

FIGURE 19

Viewing the Click indicator to bring up the Code Navigator icon

Skin Care Treatments

- **Revitalizing Facial**
  A light massage that moisturizes the skin and restores circulation.
- **Gentlemen's Facial**
  A cleansing facial that includes a neck and shoulder massage.
- **Milk Mask**
  A mask applied to soften and moisturize the face.

Body Treatments

- **Salt Glow**
  Imported sea salts are massaged into the skin, exfoliating and cleansing the pores.
- **Mud Body Wrap**
  Relief for your aches and pains.
- **Seaweed Body Wrap**
  Seaweed is a natural detoxifying agent that also helps improve circulation.

Click indicator to bring up the Code Navigator icon

FIGURE 20

Viewing the Code Navigator

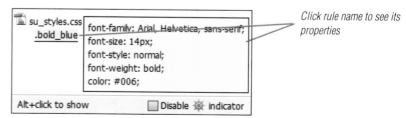

Skin Care Treatments

- **Revitalizing Facial**
  A light mass...
  su_styles.css
- **Gentlemen...**
  .bold_blue
  A cleansing...
- **Milk Mask**
  A mask app...

Body Treatments   Alt+click to show   Disable indicator

- **Salt Glow**
  Imported sea salts are massaged into the skin, exfoliating and cleansing the pores.
- **Mud Body Wrap**
  Relief for your aches and pains.
- **Seaweed Body Wrap**
  Seaweed is a natural detoxifying agent that also helps improve circulation.

Window displays the name of the style sheet file and rule applied from the style sheet

FIGURE 21

Viewing rule properties and values

su_styles.css
.bold_blue
font-family: Arial, Helvetica, sans-serif;
font-size: 14px;
font-style: normal;
font-weight: bold;
color: #006;

Alt+click to show   Disable indicator

Click rule name to see its properties

FIGURE 22

Using Code and Design views to view rule properties

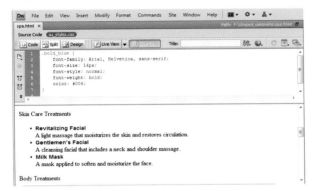

1. Click **.bold_blue** in the Code Navigator.

   The document window is split into two sections. The top section displays the code for the CSS file and the bottom section displays the page in Design view, as shown in Figure 22.

2. Type directly in the code to replace the color "006" with the color "306" as shown in Figure 23.

3. Save all files.

   The font color has changed in Design view to reflect the new shade of blue in the rule.

   | TIP   You can also edit the rule properties in the CSS Styles panel.

4. Click the Show Design view button ![Design].

   You changed the color property in the .bold_blue rule.

FIGURE 23

Using Code and Design views to edit a rule

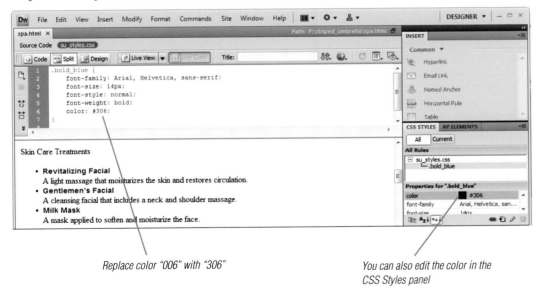

Replace color "006" with "306"

You can also edit the color in the CSS Styles panel

ADD RULES AND ATTACH
CASCADING STYLE SHEETS

What You'll Do

 In this lesson, you will add a style to a Cascading Style Sheet. You will then attach the style sheet file to the index page and apply one of the styles to text on the page.

Understanding External and Embedded Style Sheets

When you are first learning about CSS, the terminology can be very confusing. In the last lesson, you learned that external style sheets are a separate file in a website saved with the .css file extension. You also learned that CSS can be part of an HTML file, rather than a separate file. These are called internal, or embedded, style sheets. External CSS files are created by the web designer. Embedded style sheets are created automatically if the designer does not create them, using default names for the rules. The code for these rules will reside in the head content for that page. These rules will be automatically named style1, style2, and so on. You can rename the rules as they are created to make them more recognizable for you to use, for example, paragraph_text, subheading, or address. Embedded style sheets apply only to a single page, although you can copy them into the code in other pages. Remember that style sheets can be used to format much more than text objects. They can be used to set the page background, link properties, tables, or determine the appearance of almost any object on the page. Figure 24 shows the code for some embedded rules. The code resides in the head content of the web page.

When you have several pages in a website, you will probably want to use the same CSS style sheet for each page to ensure that all your elements have a consistent appearance. To attach a style sheet to another document, click the Attach Style Sheet button on the CSS Styles panel to open the Attach External Style Sheet dialog box, make sure the Add as Link option is selected, browse to locate the file you want to attach, and then click OK. The rules contained in the attached style sheet will appear in the CSS Styles panel, and you can use them to apply rules to text on the page. External style sheets can be attached, or linked, to any page. This is an extremely powerful tool. If you decide to make a change in a rule, it will automatically be made to every object that it formats.

FIGURE 24

Code for embedded rules shown in Code view

Rules are embedded in the head content rather than in an external style sheet file

```
1   <!DOCTYPE html PUBLIC "-//W3C//DTD XHTML 1.0 Transitional//EN"
    "http://www.w3.org/TR/xhtml1/DTD/xhtml1-transitional.dtd">
2   <html xmlns="http://www.w3.org/1999/xhtml">
3   <head>
4   <meta http-equiv="Content-Type" content="text/html; charset=utf-8" />
5   <title>The Striped Umbrella beach resort and spa, Ft. Eugene, Florida</title>
6   <style type="text/css">
7   <!--
8   body {
9       background-color: #FFF;
10  }
11  .nav_bar {
12      font-size: large;
13      font-family: Arial, Helvetica, sans-serif;
14  }
15  .body_text {
16      font-size: medium;
17      font-family: Arial, Helvetica, sans-serif;
18  }
19  .small_text {
20      font-size: 10px;
21      font-family: Arial, Helvetica, sans-serif;
22  }
23  -->
24  </style>
```

Add rules to a Cascading Style Sheet

1. Click the **New CSS Rule button** [icon] in the CSS Styles panel.

2. Type **heading** in the Selector Name text box, as shown in Figure 25, then click **OK**.

3. Set the Font-family to **Arial**, **Helvetica**, **sans-serif**, set the Font-size to **16**, set the Font-style to **normal**, set the Font-weight to **bold**, set the Color to **#036**, compare your screen to Figure 26, then click **OK**.

4. Click the **Edit Rule button** [icon].

5. Click the **Block category** in the CSS Rule Definition for .heading in su_styles.css dialog box, click the **Text align list arrow**, click **center**, as shown in Figure 27, then click **OK**.

6. Select the heading text "Spa Services," click the **HTML button** [icon] in the Property inspector, set the Format to **Paragraph,** then click the **CSS button** [icon] in the Property inspector.

   TIP Before you apply a style to selected text, you need to remove all formatting attributes such as font and color from that text, or the style will not be applied correctly.

7. Click the **Targeted Rule list arrow** in the Property inspector, then click **heading** to apply it to the Spa Services heading.

8. Repeat Steps 1 through 3 to add another rule called **paragraph_text** with the **Arial**, **Helvetica**, **sans-serif** Font-family, size **14**, and **normal** style.

9. Repeat Steps 6 and 7 to apply the paragraph_text style to the all the text on the page except for the blue text that already has the bold_blue style applied to it and the heading text "Questions you may have**.**"

(continued)

FIGURE 25
Adding a rule to a CSS Style sheet

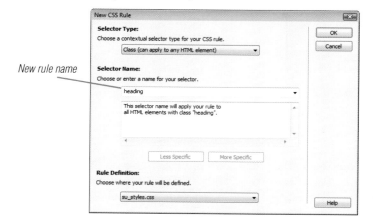

New rule name

FIGURE 26
Formatting options for heading rule

FIGURE 27
Setting text alignment for heading rule

Block category selected

Text align list arrow

Working with Text and Images

FIGURE 28

Spa page with style sheet applied to rest of text on page

heading rule
applied

paragraph_text
rule applied

Spa Services

Our spa services include numerous skin care treatments, body treatments, and massages. We also have some spa packages that combine several spa services into economical packages.

Skin Care Treatments

- **Revitalizing Facial**
  A light massage that moisturizes the skin and restores circulation.
- **Gentlemen's Facial**
  A cleansing facial that includes a neck and shoulder massage.
- **Milk Mask**
  A mask applied to soften and moisturize the face.

su_styles.css style sheet selected

FIGURE 29

Attaching a style sheet to a file

Link option
button

Attach External Style Sheet

File/URL: su_styles.css   Browse...   OK

Add as: ● Link   Preview

○ Import   Cancel

Media:

You may also enter a comma-separated list of media types.

Dreamweaver has sample style sheets to get you started.   Help

FIGURE 30

Viewing the code to link the CSS style sheet file

```
26  <meta name="Description" content="The Striped Umbrella is a full-service resort and spa
    just steps from the Gulf of Mexico in Ft. Eugene, Florida." />
27  <link href="su_styles.css" rel="stylesheet" type="text/css" />
28  </head>
29
30  <body>
31  <p><img src="assets/su_banner.gif" alt="The Striped Umbrella banner" width="735" height=
    "125" /><br />
32  <span class="nav_bar"><a href="index.html">Home</a> - <a href="about_us.html">About Us</a
    > - <a href="spa.html">Spa</a> - <a href="cafe.html">Cafe</a> - <a href="activities.html">
    Activities</a></span><br />
33  </p>
34  <hr align="left" width="735" />
35  <p class="paragraph_text">Welcome to The Striped Umbrella - a full-service resort and spa
    just steps from the Gulf of Mexico and ten miles east of Crab Key, Florida. Come enjoy the
    best of both worlds, a secluded sandy beach populated with beautiful birds, yet a  short
    drive down the road from world-class shopping, restaurants,  and entertainment. Bring a
    good book and leave your laptop at the office. You won't want to  go home!</p>
```

Code linking external style
sheet file to the index page

Code that applies the paragraph_text rule from the
external style sheet to the paragraph

10. Select the heading text **Questions you may have**, click the **HTML button** `<> HTML`, click the **Bold button** `B` to remove the bold setting, click the **CSS button** `css`, click the **Targeted Rule list arrow**, then click **heading** to apply the heading rule.

11. Click **File** on the Application bar (Win) or Menu bar (Mac), then click **Save All**, to save both the spa page and the su_styles.css file.

The styles are saved and applied to the text, as shown in Figure 28.

> TIP You must save the open su_styles.css file after editing it, or you will lose your changes.

You added two new rules called heading and paragraph_text to the su_styles.css file. You then applied the two rules to selected text.

Attach a style sheet

1. Close the spa page and open the index page.

2. Click the **Attach Style Sheet button** on the CSS Styles panel.

3. Browse to select the file su_styles.css (if necessary), click **OK** (Win) or click **Choose** (Mac), verify that the **Link option button** is selected, as shown in Figure 29, then click **OK**.

4. Select the opening paragraph text and the contact information paragraph, click the **HTML button** `<> HTML`, set the Format to **Paragraph**, click the **CSS button** `css`, click the **Targeted Rule text box**, then click **paragraph_text**.

5. Click the **Show Code view button** `Code` and view the code that links the su_styles.css file to the index page, as shown in Figure 30.

6. Click the **Show Design view button** `Design`, save your work, then close the index page.

You attached the su_styles.css file to the index.html page and applied the paragraph_text rule to selected text on the page.

INSERT AND ALIGN
GRAPHICS

What You'll Do

In this lesson, you will insert five images on the about_us page in The Striped Umbrella website. You will then stagger the alignment of the images on the page to make the page more visually appealing.

Understanding Graphic File Formats

When you add graphics to a web page, it's important to choose the appropriate file format. The three primary graphic file formats used in web pages are **GIF** (Graphics Interchange Format), **JPEG** (Joint Photographic Experts Group), and **PNG** (Portable Network Graphics). GIF files download very quickly, making them ideal to use on web pages. Though limited in the number of colors they can represent, GIF files have the ability to show transparent areas. JPEG files can display many colors. Because they often contain many shades of the same color, photographs are often saved in JPEG format. Files saved with the PNG format can display many colors and use various degrees of transparency, called **opacity**. While the GIF format is subject to licensing restrictions, the PNG format is free to use. However, not all older browsers support the PNG format.

QUICKTIP

The status bar displays the download time for the page. Each time you add a new graphic to the page, you can see how much additional time is added to the total download time.

Understanding the Assets Panel

When you add a graphic to a website, it is automatically added to the Assets panel. The **Assets panel**, located in the Files panel group, displays all the assets in a website. The Assets panel contains nine category buttons that you use to view your assets by category. These include Images, Colors, URLs, SWF, Shockwave, Movies, Scripts, Templates, and Library. To view a particular type of asset, click the appropriate category button. The Assets panel is split into two panes. When you click the Images button, as shown in Figure 31, the lower pane displays a list of all the images in your site and is divided into five columns. The top pane displays a thumbnail of the selected image in the list. You can view assets in each category in two ways. You can use the Site option button to view all the assets in a website, or you can use the Favorites option button to view those assets that you have designated as **favorites**, or assets that you expect to use repeatedly while you work on the site. You can use the Assets panel to add an asset to a web page by dragging the asset from the Assets panel to the page or by using the Insert button on the Assets panel.

QUICKTIP

You might need to resize the Assets panel to see all five columns when it is docked. To resize the Assets panel, undock the Files tab group and drag a side or corner of the panel border.

Inserting Files with Adobe Bridge

You can manage project files, including video and Camera Raw files, with a file-management tool called Adobe Bridge. Bridge is an easy way to view files outside the website before bringing them into the website. It is an integrated application, working with other Adobe programs such as Photoshop and Illustrator. You can also use Bridge to add meta tags and search text to your files. To open Bridge, click the Browse in Bridge command on the File menu or click the Browse In Bridge button on the Standard toolbar.

Aligning Images

When you insert an image on a web page, you need to position it in relation to other elements on the page. Positioning an image is referred to as **aligning** an image. By default, when you insert an image in a paragraph, its bottom edge aligns with the baseline of the first line of text or any other element in the same paragraph. When you select an image, the Align text box in the Property inspector displays the

alignment setting for the image. You can change the alignment setting using the options in the Align menu in the Property inspector.

QUICKTIP

The Align menu options function differently from the Align buttons in the Property inspector. You use the Align buttons to center, left-align, or right-align an element without regard to how the element is aligned in relation to other elements. The Align menu options align an image in relation to other elements on the page.

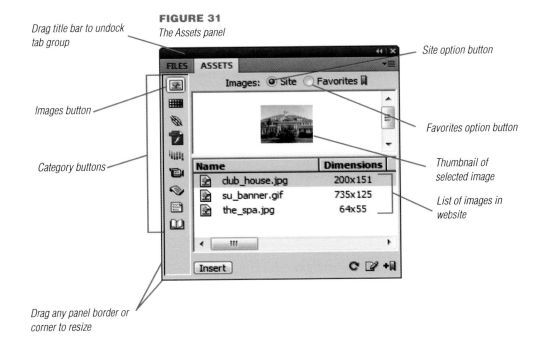

FIGURE 31
The Assets panel

Drag title bar to undock tab group

Images button

Category buttons

Drag any panel border or corner to resize

Site option button

Favorites option button

Thumbnail of selected image

List of images in website

Name	Dimensions
club_house.jpg	200x151
su_banner.gif	735x125
the_spa.jpg	64x55

Insert a graphic

1. Open dw3_1.html from where you store your Data Files, then save it as **about_us.html** in the striped_umbrella root folder.

2. Click **Yes** (Win) or **Replace** (Mac) to overwrite the existing file, click **No** to Update Links, then close dw3_1.html.

3. Click the **Attach Style Sheet button** in the CSS Styles panel, attach the su_styles.css style sheet, select the paragraphs of text on the page, click the **HTML button** ⟨⟩ HTML, verify that the Style is set to **Paragraph**, click the **CSS button** CSS then apply the paragraph_text rule to all of the paragraph text on the page.

4. Place the insertion point before "When" in the first paragraph, click the **Images list arrow** in the Common category in the Insert panel if necessary, then click **Image** to open the Select Image Source dialog box.

5. Navigate to the assets folder where you store your Data Files, double-click **club_house.jpg,** type the alternate text **Club House** if prompted, click **OK,** open the Files panel if necessary, then verify that the file was copied to your assets folder in the striped_umbrella root folder.

    Compare your screen to Figure 32.

6. Click the **Assets panel tab** in the Files tab group, click the **Images button** in the Assets panel (if necessary), then click the **Refresh Site List button** in the Assets panel to update the list of images in The Striped Umbrella website.

    The Assets panel displays a list of all the images in The Striped Umbrella website, as shown in Figure 33.

You inserted one image on the about_us page and copied it to the assets folder of the website.

FIGURE 32

The Striped Umbrella about_us page with inserted image

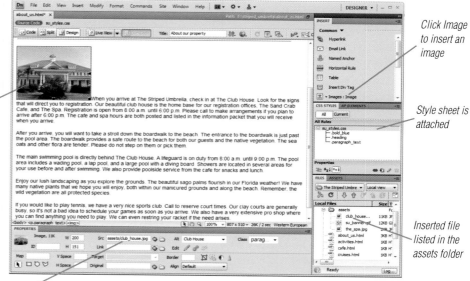

club_house.
jpg file
inserted

Click Image
to insert an
image

Style sheet is
attached

Inserted file
listed in the
assets folder

Path should
begin with the
word "assets"

FIGURE 33

Image files for The Striped Umbrella website listed in Assets panel

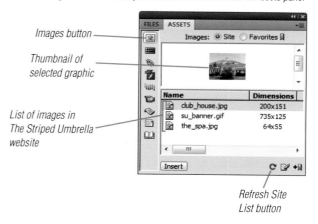

Images button

Thumbnail of
selected graphic

List of images in
The Striped Umbrella
website

Refresh Site
List button

FIGURE 34
Using Adobe Bridge

Your path may
differ

Folders
panel

Folders
tab

boardwalk.jpg
image is selected
in Content panel

Preview panel

Metadata and
Keywords
panels

Use Adobe Bridge

1. Click to place the insertion point before the word "After" at the beginning of the second paragraph.

2. Click **File** on the Application bar (Win) or Menu bar (Mac) click **Browse in Bridge,** close the dialog box asking if you want Bridge to start at login (if necessary), click the **Folders tab**, navigate to where you store your Data Files, then click the thumbnail image **boardwalk.jpg** in the assets folder, as shown in Figure 34. If a dialog box opens asking if you want Bridge to launch at startup, click **Yes** or **No**, depending on your personal preference.

   Bridge is divided into several panels; files and folders are listed in the Folders Panel. The files in the selected folder appear in the Content Panel. A picture of the file appears in the Preview Panel. The Metadata and Keywords Panels list any tags that have been added to the file.

3. Click **File** on the Application bar (Win) or Menu bar (Mac), point to **Place,** then click **In Dreamweaver**.

4. Type the alternate text **Boardwalk to the beach,** if prompted, then click **OK**.

   The image appears on the page.

   > TIP You can also click the Browse in Bridge button [icon] on the Standard toolbar to open Bridge.

(continued)

Using Favorites in the Assets panel

The assets in the Assets panel can be listed two ways: Site and Favorites. The Site option lists all of the assets in the website in the selected category in alphabetical order. As your list of assets grows, you can designate some of the assets that are used more frequently as Favorites for quicker access. To add an asset to the Favorites list, right-click (Win) or [control]-click (Mac) the asset name in the Site list, and then click Add to Favorites. When an asset is placed in the Favorites list, it is still included in the Site list. To delete an asset from the Favorites list, click the Favorites option button in the Assets panel, select the asset you want to delete, and then press [Delete] or the Remove from Favorites button on the Assets panel. If you delete an asset from the Favorites list, it still remains in the Site list. You can further organize your Favorites list by creating folders for similar assets and grouping them inside the folders.

5. Repeat Steps 1–4 to place the **pool.jpg, sago_palm.jpg**, and **sports_club.jpg** files at the beginning of each of the succeeding paragraphs, adding appropriate alternate text if prompted for the pool, sago palm, and sports club images.

After refreshing, your Assets panel should resemble Figure 35.

You inserted four images using Adobe Bridge on the about_us page and copied each image to the assets folder of The Striped Umbrella website.

Align an image

1. Scroll to the top of the page, click the **club house image**, then expand the Property inspector (if necessary).

Because an image is selected, the Property inspector displays tools for setting the properties of an image.

2. Click the **Align list arrow** in the Property inspector, then click **Left**.

The club house photo is now left-aligned with the text and the paragraph text flows around its right edge, as shown in Figure 36.

(continued)

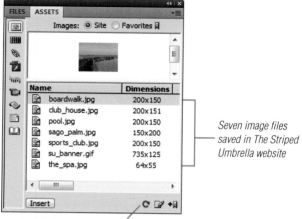

FIGURE 35
Assets panel with seven images

Seven image files saved in The Striped Umbrella website

Click Refresh Site List button to refresh file list

FIGURE 36
Left-aligned club house image

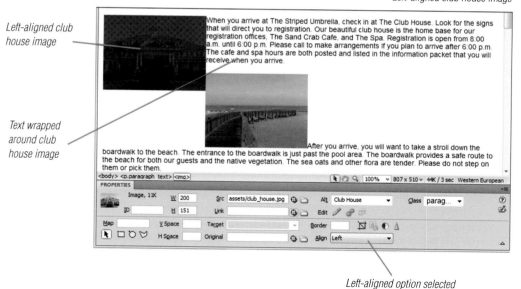

Left-aligned club house image

Text wrapped around club house image

Left-aligned option selected

FIGURE 37
Aligned images on the about_us page

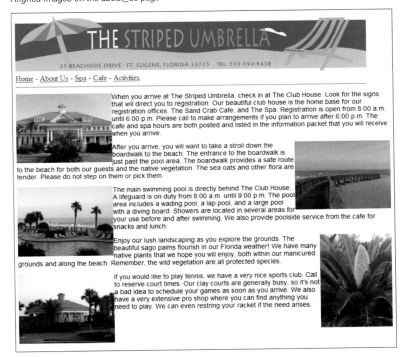

3. Select the boardwalk image, click the **Align list arrow** in the Property inspector, then click **Right**.

4. Align the pool image, using the **Left Align** option.

5. Align the sago palm image, using the **Right Align** option.

6. Align the sports club image, using the **Left Align** option.

7. Save your work.

8. Preview the web page in your browser, compare your screen to Figure 37, then close your browser.

9. Close Adobe Bridge.

You used the Property inspector to set the alignment for the five images. You then previewed the page in your browser.

Graphics versus images

Two terms that sometimes seem to be used interchangeably are graphics and images. For the purposes of discussion in this text, we will use the term **graphics** to refer to the appearance of most non-text items on a web page such as photographs, logos, navigation bars, Flash animations, graphs, background images, and drawings. Files such as these are called graphic files. They are referred to by their file type, or graphic file format, such as JPEG (Joint Photographic Experts Group), GIF (Graphics Interchange Format), or PNG (Portable Network Graphics). We will refer to the actual pictures that you see on the pages as images. Don't worry about which term to use. Many people use one term or the other according to habit or region, or use them interchangeably.

ENHANCE AN IMAGE AND
USE ALTERNATE TEXT

What You'll Do

In this lesson, you will add borders to images, add horizontal and vertical space to set them apart from the text, and then add alternate text to each image on the page.

Enhancing an Image

After you place an image on a web page, you have several options for **enhancing** it, or improving its appearance. To make changes to the image itself, such as removing scratches from it, or erasing parts of it, you need to use an image editor such as Adobe Fireworks or Adobe Photoshop. To edit an image directly in Fireworks from Dreamweaver, first select the image, and then click Edit in the Property inspector. This will open the Fireworks program if it is installed on your computer.

Complete your editing, and then click Done to return to Dreamweaver.

QUICKTIP

You can copy a Photoshop PSD file directly into Dreamweaver. After inserting the image, Dreamweaver will prompt you to optimize the image for the web.

You can use Dreamweaver to enhance certain aspects of how images appear on a page. For example, you can add borders around an image or add horizontal and

---

DESIGNTIP **Resizing graphics using an external editor**

Each image on a web page takes a specific number of seconds to download, depending on the size of the file. Larger files (in kilobytes, not width and height) take longer to download than smaller files. It's important to determine the smallest acceptable size for an image on your web page. Then, if you need to resize an image to reduce the file size, use an external image editor to do so, *instead* of resizing it in Dreamweaver. Although you can adjust the width and height settings of an image in the Property inspector to change the size of the image as it appears on your screen, these settings do not affect the file size. Decreasing the size of an image using the H (height) and W (width) settings in the Property inspector does *not* reduce the time it will take the file to download. Ideally you should use images that have the smallest file size and the highest quality possible, so that each page downloads as quickly as possible.

vertical space. **Borders** are frames that surround an image. Horizontal and vertical space is blank space above, below, and on the sides of an image that separates the image from text or other elements on the page. Adding horizontal or vertical space is the same as adding white space, and helps images stand out on a page. In the web page shown in Figure 38, the horizontal and vertical space around the images helps make these images more prominent. Adding horizontal or vertical space does not affect the width or height of the image. Spacing around web page objects can also be created by using "spacer" images, or clear images that act as placeholders.

Using Alternate Text

One of the easiest ways to make your web page viewer-friendly and accessible to people of all abilities is to use alternate text. **Alternate text** is descriptive text that appears in place of an image while the image is downloading or when the mouse pointer is placed over it. You can program some browsers to display only alternate text and to download images manually. Alternate text can be "read" by a **screen reader**, a device used by persons with visual impairments to convert written text on a computer monitor to spoken words. Screen readers and alternate text make it possible for viewers who have visual impairments to have an image described to them in detail. One of the default preferences in Dreamweaver is to

prompt you to enter alternate text whenever you insert an image on a page.

The use of alternate text is the first checkpoint listed in the World Wide Web Consortium (W3C) list of Priority 1 accessibility checkpoints. The Priority 1 checkpoints dictate the most basic level of

accessibility standards to be used by web developers today. The complete list of these and the other priority-level checkpoints are listed on the W3C website, www.w3.org (use the search "text accessibility level checkpoints"). You should always strive to meet these criteria for all web pages.

FIGURE 38
National Park Service website

National Park Service website – www.nps.gov

Add a border

1. Select the club house image, then expand the Property inspector (if necessary).

2. Type **1** in the Border text box, press **[Tab]** to apply the border to the club house image, then select the image, as shown in Figure 39.

   The border setting is not visible until you preview the page in a browser.

3. Repeat Step 2 to add borders to the other four images.

You added a 1-pixel border to each image on the about_us page.

Add horizontal and vertical space

1. Select the club house image, type **7** in the V Space text box in the Property inspector, press **[Tab]**, type **7** in the H Space text box, press **[Tab]**, then compare your screen to Figure 40.

   The text is more evenly wrapped around the image and is easier to read, because it is not so close to the edge of the image.

2. Repeat Step 1 to set the V Space and H Space to 7 for the other four images.

   The spacing under each picture differs because of the difference in the lengths of the paragraphs.

You added horizontal spacing and vertical spacing around each image on the about_us page.

FIGURE 39
Using the Property inspector to add a border

Selected image
with 1-pixel border

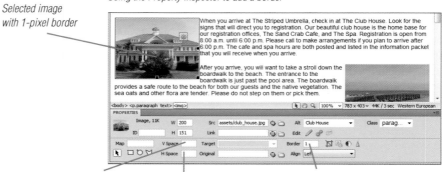

V Space text box   H Space text box   Border text box

FIGURE 40
Comparing images with and without horizontal and vertical space

Image with horizontal
and vertical space

Image without
horizontal and
vertical space

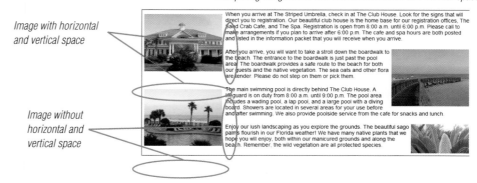

5. Create another rule called **heading** using appropriate formatting options and apply it to the text "Cranberry Ice" and "Directions."

6. Create another rule called **nav_bar** using appropriate formatting options and apply it to the navigation bar.

7. Insert the file cranberry_ice.jpg from where you store your Data Files, then place it on the page, using alignment, horizontal space, and vertical space settings. (*Hint*: In Figure 55 the align setting is set to left, H space is set to 30, and V space is set to 10.

8. Add appropriate alternate text to the banner, then save and close the page and the style sheet file.

9. Open dw3_6.html from where you store your Data Files and save it as **shop.html**, overwriting the existing file and not updating the links.

10. Attach the cc_styles.css style sheet and create a new rule named **sub_head** to use in formatting the text "January Specials - Multifunctional Pot and Cutlery Set." Use any formatting options that you like. Apply the nav_bar rule to the navigation bar. Apply the **paragraph_text** rule to the rest of the text on the page.

11. Insert the pot_knives.jpg image from the assets folder where you store your Data Files next to the paragraph beginning

"We try," choosing your own alignment and spacing settings and adding appropriate alternate text.

12. Save the shop page and the style sheet file, then preview both new pages in the browser, (*Hint:* If previewing the page in Internet Explorer 7, click the Information bar when prompted to allow blocked content.)

13. Close your browser, then close all open pages.

Don Chappell is a new sixth-grade history teacher. He is reviewing educational websites for information he can use in his classroom.

1. Connect to the Internet, then navigate to the Library of Congress website at www.loc.gov. The Library of Congress website is shown in Figure 57.
2. Which fonts are used for the main content on the home—serif or sans-serif? Are the same fonts used consistently on the other pages in the site?
3. Do you see ordered or unordered lists on any pages in the site? If so, how are they used?
4. Use the Source command on the View menu to view the source code to see if a style sheet was used.
5. Do you see the use of Cascading Style Sheets noted in the source code?

FIGURE 57
Design Project

The Library of Congress website - www.loc.gov

In this assignment, you will continue to work on the website that you started in Chapter 1, and continued to build in Chapter 2. No Data Files are supplied. You are building this site from chapter to chapter, so you must do each Portfolio Project assignment in each chapter to complete your website.

You continue building your website by designing and completing a page that contains a list, headings, paragraph_text, images, and a background. During this process, you will develop a style sheet and add several rules to it. You will insert appropriate images on your page and enhance them for maximum effect. You will also check for non-web-safe colors and remove any that you find.

1. Consult your storyboard and decide which page to create and develop for this chapter.
2. Plan the page content for the page and make a sketch of the layout. Your sketch should include at least one ordered or unordered list, appropriate headings, paragraph text, several images, and a background color or image. Your sketch should also show where the paragraph text and headings should be placed on the page and what rules should be used for each type of text. You should plan on creating at least two rules.

3. Create the page using your sketch for guidance.
4. Create a Cascading Style Sheet for the site and add to it the rules you decided to use. Apply the rules to the appropriate content.
5. Access the images you gathered in Chapter 2, and place them on the page so that the page matches the sketch you created in Step 2. Add a background image if you want, and appropriate alternate text for each image.
6. Remove any non-web-safe colors.
7. Identify any files in the Assets panel that are currently not used in the site. Decide which of these assets should be removed, then delete these files.

8. Preview the new page in a browser, then check for page layout problems and broken links. Make any necessary corrections in Dreamweaver, then preview the page again in the browser. Repeat this process until you are satisfied with the way the page looks in the browser. (*Hint:* If previewing the page in Internet Explorer 7, click the Information bar when prompted to allow blocked content.)
9. Use the checklist in Figure 58 to check all the pages in your site.
10. Close the browser, then close the open pages.

FIGURE 58
Portfolio Project checklist

Website Checklist

1. Does each page have a page title?
2. Does the home page have a description and keywords?
3. Does the home page contain contact information?
4. Does every page in the site have consistent navigation links?
5. Does the home page have a last updated statement that will automatically update when the page is saved?
6. Do all paths for links and images work correctly?
7. Do all images have alternate text?
8. Are all colors web-safe?
9. Are there any unnecessary files you can delete from the assets folder?
10. Is there a style sheet with at least two rules?
11. Did you apply the rules to all text blocks?
12. Do all pages look good using at least two different browsers?

4 WORKING WITH
LINKS

1. Create external and internal links

2. Create internal links to named anchors

3. Create, modify, and copy a navigation bar

4. Create an image map

5. Manage website links

4 WORKING WITH
LINKS

Introduction

What makes websites so powerful are the links that connect one page to another within a website or to any page on the web. Although you can add graphics, animations, movies, and other enhancements to a website to make it visually attractive, the links you include are often a site's most essential components. Links that connect the pages within a site are always very important because they help viewers navigate between the pages of the site. However, if one of your goals is to keep viewers from leaving your website, you might want to avoid including links to other websites. For example, most e-commerce sites include only links to other pages in the site to discourage shoppers from leaving the site. In this chapter, you will create links to other pages in The Striped Umbrella website and to other sites on the web. You will also insert a navigation bar that contains images instead of text, and check the links in The Striped

Umbrella website to make sure they all work correctly.

Understanding Internal and External Links

Web pages contain two types of links: internal links and external links. **Internal links** are links to web pages in the same website, and **external links** are links to web pages in other websites or to email addresses. Both internal and external links have two important parts that work together. The first part of a link is the element that viewers see and click on a web page, for example, text, an image, or a button. The second part of a link is the **path**, or the name and location of the web page or file that will open when the element is clicked. Setting and maintaining the correct paths for all your links is essential to avoid having broken links in your site, which can easily cause a visitor to click away immediately.

Tools You'll Use

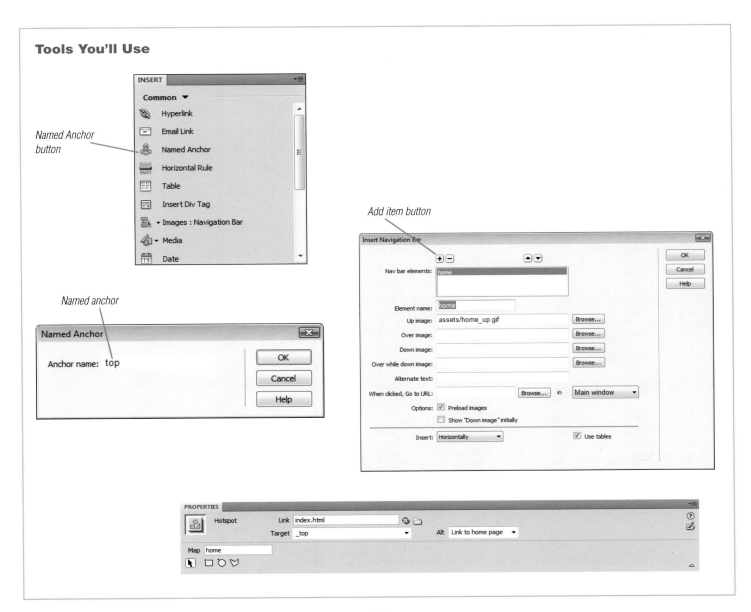

Named Anchor button

Named anchor

Add item button

CREATE EXTERNAL AND INTERNAL LINKS

What You'll Do

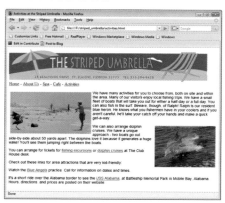

 In this lesson, you will create external links on The Striped Umbrella activities page that link to websites related to area attractions. You will also create internal links to other pages within The Striped Umbrella website.

Creating External Links

A good website often includes a variety of external links to other related websites so that viewers can get more information on a particular topic. To create an external link, you first select the text or object that you want to serve as a link, then you type the absolute path to the destination web page in the Link text box in the Property inspector. An **absolute path** is a path used for external links that includes the complete address for the destination page, including the protocol (such as http://) and the complete **URL** (Uniform Resource Locator), or address, of the destination page. When necessary, the web page filename and folder hierarchy are also part of an absolute path. Figure 1 shows an example of an absolute path showing the protocol, URL, and filename. An example for the code for an external link would be <a href="http://www.adobe.com"> Adobe website</a>.

FIGURE 1
An example of an absolute path

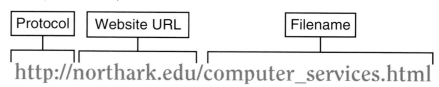

Creating Internal Links

Each page in a website usually focuses on an individual category or topic. You should make sure that the home page provides links to each major page in the site, and that all pages in the site contain numerous internal links so that viewers can move easily from page to page. To create an internal link, you first select the text element or image that you want to use to make a link, and then use the Browse for File icon next to the Link text box in the HTML Property inspector to specify the relative path to the destination page. A **relative path** is a type of path used to reference web pages and image files within the same website. Relative paths include the filename and folder location of a file. Figure 2 shows an example of a relative path. Table 1 describes absolute paths and relative paths. Relative paths can either be site-root relative or document-relative. You can also use the Point to File icon in the HTML Property inspector to point to the file you want to use for the link, or drag the file you want to use for the link from the Files panel into the Link text box in the Property inspector.

You should take great care in managing your internal links to make sure they work correctly and are timely and relevant to the page content. You should design the navigation structure of your website so that viewers are never more than three or four clicks away from the page they are seeking. An example for the code for a relative internal link would be <a href="activities.html"> Activities</a>.

FIGURE 2
An example of a relative path

TABLE 1: Description of absolute and relative paths

type of path	description	examples
Absolute path	Used for external links and specifies protocol, URL, and filename of destination page	http://www.yahoo.com/recreation
Relative path	Used for internal links and specifies location of file relative to the current page	spa.html or assets/heron.gif
Root-relative path	Used for internal links when publishing to a server that contains many websites or where the website is so large it requires more than one server	/striped_umbrella/activities.html
Document-relative path	Used in most cases for internal links and specifies the location of file relative to current page	cafe.html or assets/heron.gif

Create an external link

1. Open The Striped Umbrella website, open dw4_1.html from where you store your Chapter 4 Data Files, then save it as **activities** in the striped_umbrella root folder, overwriting the existing activities page, but not updating links.

2. Attach the su_styles.css file, then apply the **paragraph_text rule** to the paragraphs of text on the page (not to the navigation bar).

3. Select the first broken image link, click the **Browse for File icon** □ next to the Src text box, then select the **heron_waiting_small.jpg** in the Data Files assets folder to save the image in your assets folder.

4. Click on the page next to the broken image link to see the heron_waiting_small image, as shown in Figure 3.

(continued)

FIGURE 3
Saving an image file in the assets folder

Broken image is replaced when file is saved in the assets folder

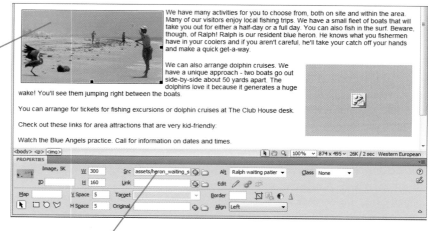

Image is saved in assets folder

Typing URLs

Typing URLs in the Link text box in the Property inspector can be very tedious. When you need to type a long and complex URL, it is easy to make mistakes and create a broken link. You can avoid such mistakes by copying and pasting the URL from the Address text box (Internet Explorer) or Location bar (Mozilla Firefox) to the Link text box in the Property inspector. Copying and pasting a URL ensures that the URL is entered correctly.

FIGURE 4

Assets panel with two new images added

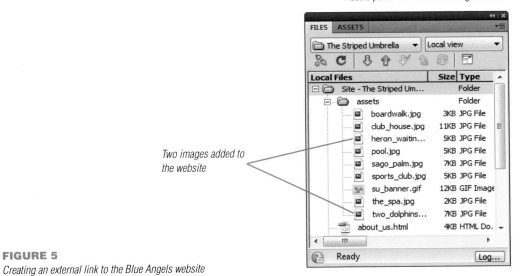

Two images added to
the website

5. Repeat Step 3 for the second image, **two_dolphins_small.jpg.** The two new files are copied into the assets folder, as shown in Figure 4.

6. Scroll down, then select the text "Blue Angels."

7. Click the **HTML button** <> HTML in the Property inspector to switch to the HTML Property inspector, click in the Link text box, type **http://www.blueangels.navy.mil**, press **[Enter]** (Win) or **[return]** (Mac), deselect the link, then compare your screen to Figure 5.

8. Repeat Steps 6 and 7 to create a link for the USS Alabama site in the next paragraph: **http://www.ussalabama.com**.

9. Save your work, preview the page in your browser, test all the links to make sure they work, then close your browser.

> TIP You must have an active Internet connection to test the links. If clicking a link does not open a page, make sure you typed the URL correctly in the Link text box.

You opened The Striped Umbrella website, replaced the existing activities page, attached the su_styles.css.file, applied the paragraph_text style to the text, then imported the new images into the site. You added two external links to other sites on the page, then tested each link in your browser.

FIGURE 5

Creating an external link to the Blue Angels website

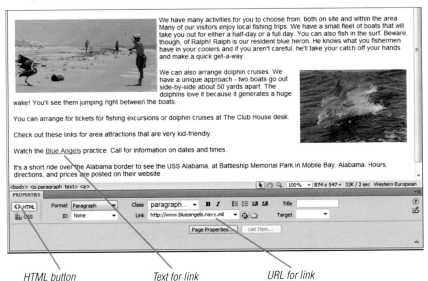

HTML button   Text for link   URL for link

Create an internal link

1. Select the text "fishing excursions" in the third paragraph.

2. Click the **Browse for File icon** 🗀 next to the Link text box in the HTML Property inspector, then double-click **fishing.html** in the Select File dialog box to set the relative path to the fishing page.

   Notice that fishing.html appears in the Link text box in the Property inspector, as shown in Figure 6.

   > TIP Pressing [F4] will hide or redisplay all panels, including the ones on the right side of the screen.

3. Select the text "dolphin cruises" in the same sentence.

4. Click the **Browse for File icon** 🗀 next to the Link text box in the HTML Property inspector, then double-click **cruises.html** in the Select File dialog box to specify the relative path to the cruises page.

   The words "dolphin cruises" are now a link to the cruises page.

5. Save your work, preview the page in your browser to verify that the internal links work correctly, then close your browser.

   The fishing and cruises pages do not have page content yet, but serve as placeholders until they do.

You created two internal links on the activities page, and then tested the links in your browser.

FIGURE 6

Creating an internal link on the activities page

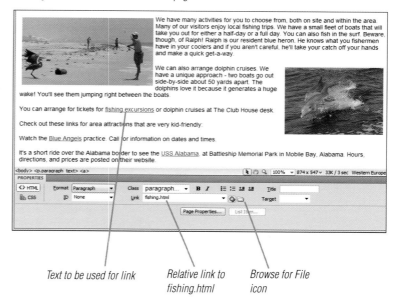

Text to be used for link

Relative link to fishing.html

Browse for File icon

Using case-sensitive links

When text is said to be "case sensitive," it means that the text will be treated differently when it is typed using uppercase letters rather than lowercase letters, or vice-versa. With some operating systems, such as Windows, it doesn't matter which case you use when you enter URLs. However, with other systems, such as UNIX, it does matter. To be sure that your links will work with all systems, use lowercase letters for all links. This is another good reason to select and copy a URL from the browser address bar, and then paste it in the link text box or code in Dreamweaver when creating an external link. You won't have to worry about missing a case change.

FIGURE 7
Assets panel with three external links

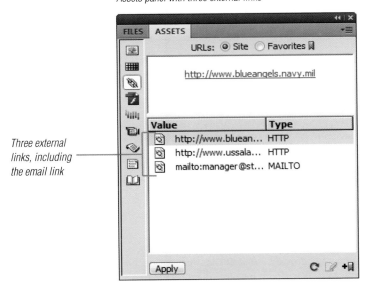

Three external links, including the email link

1. Click the **Assets panel tab** to view the Assets panel.

2. Click the **URLs button** in the Assets panel.

3. Click the **Refresh Site List button** .

    Three links are listed in the Assets panel: one external link for the email link and two external links to the Blue Angels and USS Alabama websites, as shown in Figure 7. Notice that the internal links are not displayed in the Assets panel.

4. Click the **Files panel tab** to view the Files panel.

5. Close the activities page and the dw4_1.html page.

You viewed the external links on the activities page in the Assets panel.

CREATE INTERNAL LINKS
TO NAMED ANCHORS

What You'll Do

In this lesson, you will insert five named anchors on the spa page: one for the top of the page and four for each of the spa services lists. You will then create internal links to each named anchor.

Inserting Named Anchors

Some web pages have so much content that viewers must scroll repeatedly to get to the bottom of the page and then back up to the top of the page. To make it easier for viewers to navigate to specific areas of a page without scrolling, you can use a combination of internal links and named anchors. A **named anchor** is a specific location on a web page that has a descriptive name. Named anchors act as targets for internal links and make it easy for viewers to jump to a particular place on the same page quickly. A **target** is the location on a web page that a browser displays when an internal link is clicked. For example, you can insert a named anchor called "top" at the top of a web page, and then create a link to it from the bottom of the page.

You can also insert named anchors in strategic places on a web page, such as at the beginning of paragraph headings.

You insert a named anchor using the Named Anchor button in the Common category on the Insert panel, as shown in Figure 8. You then enter the name of the anchor in the Named Anchor dialog box. You should choose short names that describe the named anchor location on the page. Named anchors are represented by yellow anchor icons on a web page when viewed in Design view. Selected anchors are represented by blue icons. You can show or hide named anchor icons by clicking View on the Application bar (Win) or Menu bar (Mac), bar, pointing to Visual Aids, and then clicking Invisible Elements.

Creating Internal Links to Named Anchors

Once you create a named anchor, you can create an internal link to it using one of two methods. You can select the text or image on the page that you want to use to make a link, and then drag the Point to File icon from the Property inspector to the named anchor icon on the page. Or, you can select the text or image to which you want to use to make a link, then type # followed by the named anchor name (such as "#top") in the Link text box in the Property inspector.

QUICKTIP

To avoid possible errors, you should create a named anchor before you create a link to it.

FIGURE 8

Using the Point to File icon

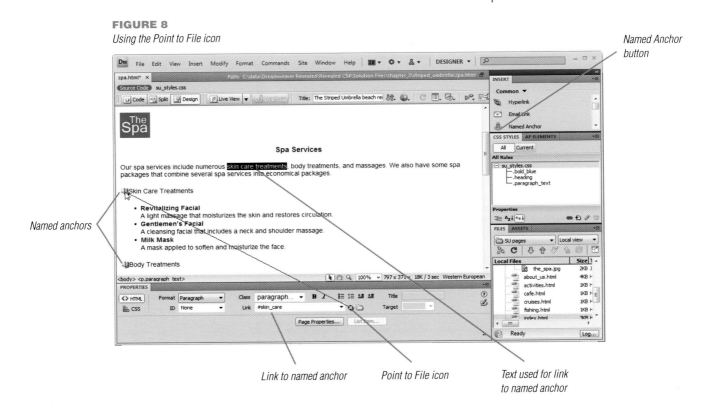

Named Anchor button

Named anchors

Link to named anchor   Point to File icon   Text used for link to named anchor

Insert a named anchor

1. Open the spa page, click the **banner image** to select it, then press [←] to place the insertion point to the left of the banner.

2. Click **View** on the Application bar (Win) or Menu bar (Mac), point to **Visual Aids**, then verify that Invisible Elements is checked.

   | TIP If there is no check mark next to Invisible Elements, this feature is turned off. Click Invisible Elements to turn this feature on.

3. Click the **Common** category on the Insert panel (if necessary).

4. Click **Named Anchor** on the Insert panel to open the Named Anchor dialog box, type **top** in the Anchor name text box, compare your screen with Figure 9, then click **OK**.

   An anchor icon now appears before The Striped Umbrella banner.

   | TIP Use lowercase letters, no spaces, and no special characters in named anchor names. You should also avoid using a number as the first character in a named anchor name.

   (continued)

FIGURE 9
Named Anchor dialog box

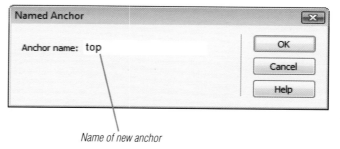

Name of new anchor

FIGURE 10
Named anchors on the activities page

Named anchor icons

Selected named anchor icon

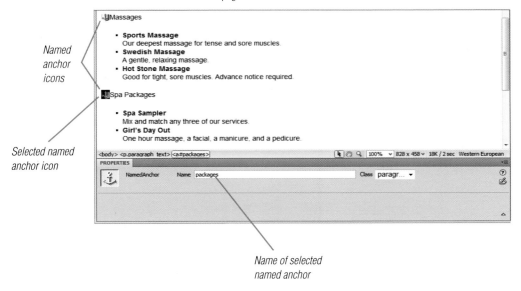

Name of selected named anchor

5. Click to the left of the Skin Care Treatments heading, then insert a named anchor named **skin_care**.

6. Insert named anchors to the left of the Body Treatments, Massages, and Spa Packages headings using the following names: **body_treatments**, **massages**, and **packages**.

Your screen should resemble Figure 10.

You created five named anchors on the activities page; one at top of the page, and four that will help viewers quickly access the Spa Services headings on the page.

Create an internal link to a named anchor

1. Select the words "skin care treatments" in the first paragraph, then drag the **Point to File icon** 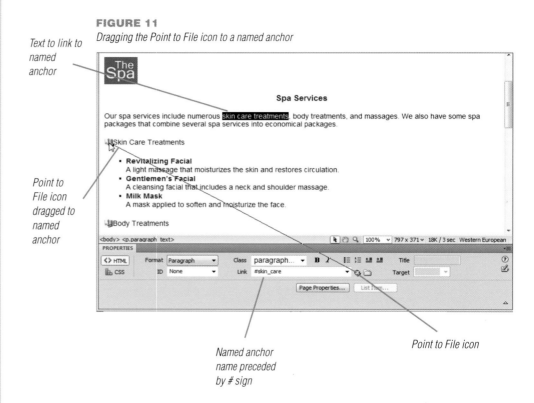 from the Property inspector to the anchor named skin_care, as shown in Figure 11.

   The words "skin care treatments" are now linked to the skin_care named anchor. When viewers click the words "skin care treatments" the browser will display the Skin Care Treatments heading at the top of the browser window.

   | TIP The name of a named anchor is always preceded by a pound (#) sign in the Link text box in the Property inspector.

2. Create internal links for body treatments, massages, and spa packages in the first paragraph by first selecting each of these words or phrases, then dragging the **Point to File icon** to the appropriate named anchor icon.

   The words "body treatments," "massages," and "spa packages" are now links that connect to the Body Treatments, Massages, and Spa Packages headings.

   | TIP Once you select the text on the page you want to link, you might need to scroll down to view the named anchor on the screen. Once you see the named anchor on your screen, you can drag the Point to File icon on top of it. You can also move the pointer to the edge of the page window (still in the white area of the page) to scroll the page.

   (continued)

FIGURE 11

Dragging the Point to File icon to a named anchor

Text to link to named anchor

Point to File icon dragged to named anchor

Named anchor name preceded by # sign

Point to File icon

FIGURE 12

Spa page in Mozilla Firefox with internal links to named anchors

Internal links to named anchors

3. Scroll down to the bottom of the page, then place the insertion point at the end of the last sentence on the page.

4. Press [**Enter**] (Win) or [**return**] (Mac) twice to insert two paragraph breaks, then type **Top of page**.

5. Click the **CSS button** [🔣 CSS] to switch to the CSS Property inspector, then apply the paragraph_text rule to "Top of Page."

6. Click the **HTML button** [<> HTML] to switch to the HTML Property inspector, then use the Point to File icon to link the text to the top named anchor.

7. Save your work, preview the page in your browser, as shown in Figure 12, then test the links to each named anchor.

   Notice that when you click the spa packages link in the browser, the associated named anchor appears in the middle of the page instead of at the top. This happens because the spa page is not long enough to position this named anchor at the top of the page.

8. Close your browser.

You created internal links to the named anchors next to the Spa Services headings and to the top of the spa page. You then previewed the page in your browser and tested each link.

CREATE, MODIFY, AND COPY
A NAVIGATION BAR

What You'll Do

 In this lesson, you will create a navigation bar on the spa page that can be used to link to each major page in the website. The navigation bar will have five elements: home, about _us, cafe, spa, and activities. You will also copy the new navigation bar to other pages in the website. On each page you will modify the appropriate element state to reflect the current page.

Creating a Navigation Bar Using Images

To make your website more visually appealing, you can create a navigation bar with images rather than text. Any images you use in a navigation bar must be created in a graphics software program, such as Adobe Fireworks or Adobe Illustrator. For a browser to display a navigation bar correctly, all image links in the navigation bar must be exactly the same size. You insert a navigation bar by clicking Insert on the Application bar (Win) or Menu bar (Mac), pointing to Image Objects, then clicking Navigation Bar. The Insert Navigation Bar dialog box appears. You use this dialog box to specify the appearance of each link, called an **element**, in each of four possible states. A **state** is the condition of the element relative to the mouse pointer. The four states are as follows: **Up image** (the state when the mouse pointer is not on top of the element), **Over image** (the state when the mouse pointer is positioned on top of the element), **Down image** (the state when you click the element), and **Over while down image** (the state when the mouse pointer is positioned over an element that has been clicked). You can create a rollover effect by using different colors or images to represent each element state. You can add many special effects to navigation bars or to links on a web page. For instance, the website shown in Figure 13 contains a navigation bar that uses rollovers and also contains images that link to featured items in the website.

When a navigation bar is inserted on a web page using the Insert Navigation Bar command, JavaScript code is added to the page to make the interaction work with the navigation bar elements. Dreamweaver also creates a Scripts folder and adds it to the root folder to store the newly created AC-RunActiveContent.js file. When a viewer views a web page with one of these navigation bars, the JavaScript that runs is stored on the user's, or client's, computer.

QUICKTIP

You can insert only one navigation bar using the Insert, Image Objects, Navigation Bar command or by clicking the Common category in the Insert panel and then selecting Navigation Bar from the Images menu.

Copying and Modifying a Navigation Bar

After you create a navigation bar, you can reuse it and save time by copying and pasting it to the other main pages in your site. Make sure you place the navigation bar in the same position on each page. This practice ensures that the navigation bar will look the same on each page, making it much easier for viewers to navigate to all the pages in your website. If you are even one line or one pixel off, the navigation bar will appear to "jump" as it changes position from page to page.

You use the Modify Navigation Bar dialog box to customize the appearance of the copied navigation bar on each page. For example, you can change the appearance of the spa navigation bar element on the spa page so that it appears in a different color. Highlighting the navigation element for the current page provides a visual reminder so that viewers can quickly tell which page they are viewing. This process ensures that the navigation bar will not only look consistent across all pages, but will be customized for each page.

FIGURE 13
NASA website

Navigation bar
with rollovers

Navigation links
with rollovers

Rollover images
serving as links

Create a navigation bar using images

1. Select the banner on the spa page, press the **right arrow key,** then press **[Shift][Enter]** (Win) or **[Shift][return]** (Mac) to enter a line break after the banner.

   The insertion point is now positioned between the banner and the horizontal rule.

2. Click the **Common** category on the Insert panel (if necessary), click the **Images list arrow,** then click **Navigation Bar.**

3. Type **home** in the Element name text box, in the Insert Navigation Bar dialog box, click the **Insert list arrow** as shown in Figure 14, click **Horizontally** (if necessary), to specify that the navigation bar be placed horizontally on the page.

   Be sure to choose Horizontally for the navigation bar orientation. The two options below the horizontal rule will not be available in the Modify Navigation Bar dialog box. If you miss these settings now, you will either have to make your corrections directly in the code or start over.

4. Click **Browse** next to the Up image text box, navigate to the assets folder where you store your Data Files, then double-click **home_up.gif.**

   The path to the file home_up.gif appears in the Up image text box, as shown in Figure 14.

5. Click **Browse** next to the Over image text box to specify a path to the file home_down.gif located in the chapter_4 Data Files assets folder.

6. Click **Browse** next to the Down image text box to specify a path to the file home_down.gif

   (continued)

FIGURE 14
Insert Navigation Bar dialog box

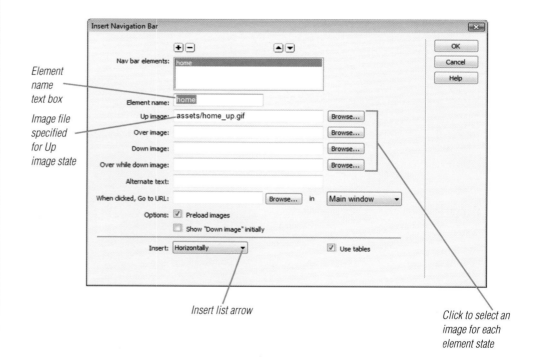

Element name text box

Image file specified for Up image state

Insert list arrow

Click to select an image for each element state

FIGURE 15
Insert Navigation Bar dialog box

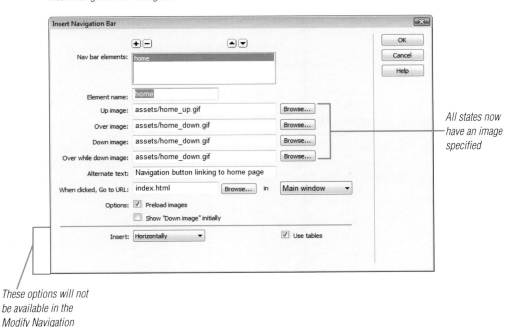

All states now have an image specified

These options will not be available in the Modify Navigation Bar dialog box

located in the chapter_4 Data Files assets folder, overwriting the existing file.

Because this is a simple navigation bar, you use the home_down.gif image for the Over, Down, and Over while down image states.

> TIP Instead of clicking Browse in Steps 6 and 7, you could copy the path of the home_down.gif file in the Over image text box and paste it to the Down image and Over while down image text boxes. You could also reference the home_down.gif file in The Striped Umbrella assets folder once it is copied there in Step 5.

7. Click **Browse** next to the Over while down image text box to specify a path to the file home_down.gif located in the chapter_4 Data Files assets folder, overwriting the existing file.

   By specifying one graphic for the Up image state, and another graphic for the Over image, Down image, and Over while down image states, you will create a rollover effect.

8. Type **Navigation button linking to home page** in the Alternate text text box, click **Browse** next to the When clicked, Go to URL text box, double-click **index.html** in the striped_umbrella root folder, then compare your screen to Figure 15.

You used the Insert Navigation Bar dialog box to create a navigation bar for the spa page and added the home element to it. You used one image for the Up state and one for the other three states.

Add elements to a navigation bar

1. Click the **Add item button** ⊞ in the Insert Navigation Bar dialog box, then type **about_us** in the Element name text box.

   TIP You use the Add item button ⊞ to add a new navigation element to the navigation bar, and the Delete item button ⊟ to delete a selected navigation bar element from the navigation bar.

2. Click **Browse** next to the Up image text box, navigate to the chapter_4 assets folder, click **about_us_up.gif**, then click **OK** (Win) or **Choose** (Mac).

3. Click **Browse** next to the Over image text box to specify a path to the file **about_us_down.gif** located in the chapter_4 assets folder.

4. Click **Browse** next to the Down image text box to specify a path to the file **about_us_down.gif** located in the chapter_4 assets folder, over-writing the existing file.

5. Repeat Step 4 for the Over while down image.

6. Type **Navigation button linking to about_us page** in the Alternate text text box, click **Browse** next to the When clicked, Go to URL text box, double-click **about_us.html**, then compare your screen to Figure 16.

(continued)

FIGURE 16
Add elements to a navigation bar

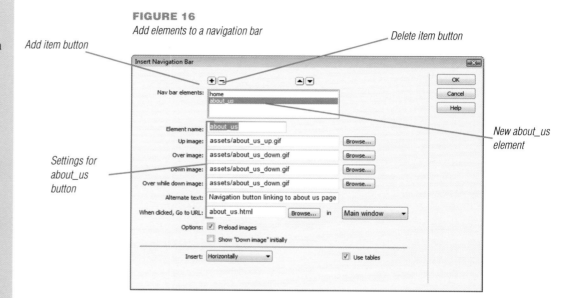

Add item button

Delete item button

New about_us element

Settings for about_us button

FIGURE 17

Navigation bar with all elements added

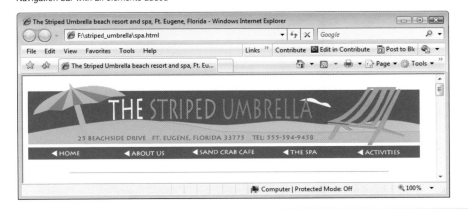

TABLE 2: Settings to use in the Insert Navigation Bar dialog box for each new element

dialog box item	cafe element	spa element	activities element
Up image file	cafe_up.gif	spa_up.gif	activities_up.gif
Over image file	cafe_down.gif	spa_down.gif	activities_down.gif
Down image file	cafe_down.gif	spa_down.gif	activities_down.gif
Over while down image file	cafe_down.gif	spa_down.gif	activities_down.gif
Alternate text	Navigation button linking to cafe page	Navigation button linking to spa page	Navigation button linking to activities page
When clicked, Go to URL	cafe.html	spa.html	activities.html

7. Using the information provided in Table 2, add three more navigation bar elements in the Insert Navigation Bar dialog box called **cafe**, **spa**, and **activities.**

   TIP All files listed in the table are located in the assets folder of the chapter_4 folder where you store your Data Files.

8. Click **OK** to close the Insert Navigation Bar dialog box.

9. Save your work, preview the page in your browser, compare your screen to Figure 17, check each link to verify that each element works correctly, then close your browser.

You completed The Striped Umbrella navigation bar by adding four more elements to it, each of which contain links to four pages in the site. All images added to the navigation bar are now stored in the assets folder of The Striped Umbrella website.

Copy and paste a navigation bar

1. Place the insertion point to the left of the navigation bar, press and hold **[Shift]**, then click to the right of the navigation bar. Since this navigation bar was created using the tables option in the Insert Navigation Bar dialog box, table tags are used to place the navigation bar. To make sure you have selected the entire table that formats the navigation bar, verify in the Tag selector that the <table> tag is selected, as shown in Figure 18.

2. Click **Edit** on the Application bar (Win) or Menu bar (Mac) then click **Copy**.

3. Double-click **activities.html** on the Files panel to open the activities page.

4. Select the original navigation bar on the page, click **Edit** on the Application bar (Win) or Menu bar (Mac) click **Paste**, then compare your screen to Figure 19.

You copied the navigation bar from the spa page and pasted it on the activities page.

Modify a navigation bar

1. Click **Modify** on the Application bar (Win) or Menu bar (Mac), then click **Navigation Bar** to open the Modify Navigation Bar dialog box.

2. Scroll down and click **activities** in the Nav bar elements list box, then click the **Show "Down image" initially check box**, as shown in Figure 20.

   An asterisk appears next to activities in the Nav bar elements list box, indicating that this element will be displayed in the Down image state initially. The sand-colored activities navigation

(continued)

FIGURE 18
Table tag selected in Tag selector

Table tag
is selected

FIGURE 19
Navigation bar copied to the activities page

FIGURE 20
Changing settings for the activities element

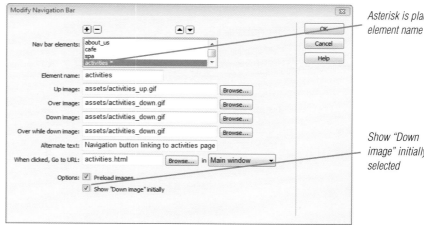

Asterisk is placed next to the element name

Show "Down image" initially is selected

FIGURE 21

About Us page with the modified navigation bar

element normally used for the Down image state of the activities navigation bar element will remind viewers that they are on the activities page.

3. Click **OK** to save the new settings and close the Modify Navigation Bar dialog box, then save and close the activities page.

4. Repeat Steps 1 through 3 to modify the navigation bar on the spa page to show the Down image initially for the spa element, then save and close the spa page.

   TIP The Show "Down image" initially check box should be checked only for the element that links to the current page.

5. Open the home page, paste the navigation bar on top of the original navigation bar, then modify the navigation bar to show the Down image initially for the home element.

6. Save and close the home page.

7. Open the about_us page, paste the navigation bar on top of the original navigation bar, then use the Modify Navigation Bar dialog box to specify that the Down image be displayed initially for the about_us element, then compare your screen to Figure 21.

8. Save your work, preview the current page in your browser, test the navigation bar on the home, about_us, spa, and activities pages, then close your browser.

   The cafe page is blank at this point, so use the Back button when you test the cafe link to return to the page you were viewing previously.

You modified the navigation bar on the activities page to show the activities element in the Down state initially. You then copied the navigation bar to two additional pages in The Striped Umbrella website, modifying the navigation bar elements each time to show the Down image state initially.

CREATE AN
IMAGE MAP

What You'll Do

In this lesson, you will create an image map by placing a hotspot on The Striped Umbrella banner that will link to the home page.

Another way to create links for web pages is to combine them with images by creating an image map. An **image map** is an image that has one or more hotspots placed on top of it. A **hotspot** is a clickable area on an image that, when clicked, links to a different location on the page or to another web page. For example, a map of the United States could have a hotspot placed on each individual state so that viewers could click a state to link to information about that state. The National Park Service website is shown in Figure 22. As you place your mouse over a state, the state name, a photo, and introductory sentences from that state's page are displayed. When you click a state, you will be linked to information about national parks in that state. You

can create hotspots by first selecting the image on which you want to place a hotspot, and then using one of the hotspot tools in the Property inspector to define its shape.

There are several ways to create image maps to make them user-friendly and accessible. One way is to be sure to include alternate text for each hotspot. Another is to draw the hotspot boundaries a little larger than they need to be to cover the area you want to set as a link. This allows viewers a little leeway when they place their mouse over the hotspot by creating a larger target area for them.

The hotspot tools in Dreamweaver make creating image maps a snap. In addition to the Rectangle Hotspot Tool, there is a

Circle Hotspot Tool and a Polygon Hotspot Tool for creating different shapes. These tools can be used to create any shape hotspot that you need. For instance, on a map of the United States, you can draw an outline around each state with the Polygon Hotspot Tool.

You can then make each state "clickable." Hotspots can be easily changed and rearranged on the image. Use the Pointer Hotspot Tool to select the hotspot you would like to edit. You can drag one of the hotspot selector handles to change the size or shape of a hotspot. You can also

move the hotspot by dragging it to a new position on the image. It is a good idea to limit the number of complex hotspots in an image because the code can become too lengthy for the page to download in a reasonable length of time.

FIGURE 22

Viewing an image map on the National Park Service website

The pointer is over Hawaii, which causes a window with a photo and introductory text about Hawaii to display

Clicking on an individual state will link to information about parks in that state

National Park Service website - www.nps.gov

Create an image map

1. Open the activities page, if necessary, select the banner, then click the **Rectangle Hotspot Tool** □ in the Property inspector.

2. Drag the **pointer** to create a rectangle over the umbrella in the banner, as shown in Figure 23, then click **OK** to close the dialog box that reminds you to supply alternate text for the hotspot.

   TIP To adjust the shape of a hotspot, click the Pointer Hotspot Tool ▶ in the Property inspector, then drag a sizing handle on the hotspot.

3. Drag the **Point to File icon** ⊕ in the Property inspector to the index.html file on the Files panel to link the index page to the hotspot.

4. Replace the default text "Map" with **home** in the Map text box in the Property inspector to give the image map a unique name.

5. Click the **Target list arrow** in the Property inspector, then click **_top**.

   When the hotspot is clicked, the _top option causes the home page to open in the same window. See Table 3 for an explanation of the four target options.

   (continued)

FIGURE 23
Properties of the rectangular hotspot on the banner

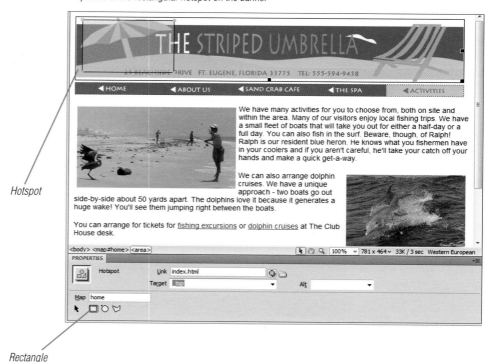

Hotspot

Rectangle Hotspot Tool

TABLE 3: Options in the Target list

target	result
_blank	Displays the destination page in a separate browser window
_parent	Displays the destination page in the parent frameset (replaces the frameset)
_self	Displays the destination page in the same frame or window
_top	Displays the destination page in the whole browser window

FIGURE 24
Hotspot properties

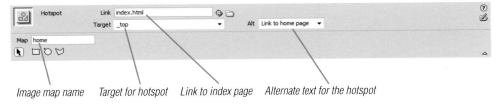

Image map name   Target for hotspot   Link to index page   Alternate text for the hotspot

FIGURE 25
Image map preview on the activities page in the browser

Alternate text
for hotspot

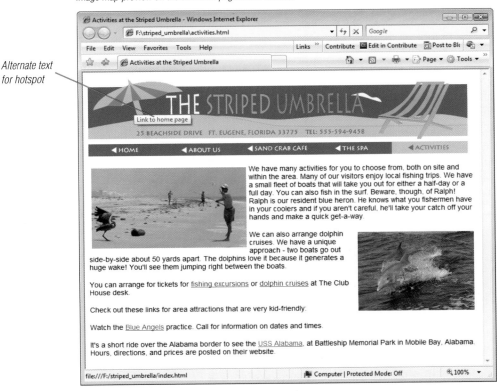

6. Type **Link to home page** in the Alt text box in the Property inspector, as shown in Figure 24. then press **[Enter]** (Win) or **[return]** (Mac).

7. Save your work, preview the page in your browser, then place the pointer over the image map.

   As you place the pointer over the hotspot, you see the alternate text displayed and the pointer indicates the link (Win), as shown in Figure 25.

8. Click the link to test it, close the browser, then close all open pages.

You created an image map on the banner of the activities page using the Rectangle Hotspot Tool. You then linked the hotspot to the home page.

MANAGE WEBSITE
LINKS

What You'll Do

In this lesson, you will use some of Dreamweaver's reporting features to check The Striped Umbrella website for broken links and orphaned files.

Managing Website Links

Because the World Wide Web changes constantly, websites may be up one day and down the next. If a website changes server locations or goes down due to technical difficulties or a power failure, the links to it become broken. Broken links, like misspelled words on a web page, indicate that a website is not being maintained diligently.

Checking links to make sure they work is an ongoing and crucial task you need to perform on a regular basis. You must check external links manually by reviewing your website in a browser and clicking each link to make sure it works correctly. The Check Links Sitewide feature is a helpful tool for managing internal links. You can use it to check your entire website for the total number of links and the number of links that are okay, external, or broken, and then view the results in the Link Checker panel. The Link Checker panel also provides a list of all of the files used in a website, including those that are **orphaned files**, or files that are not linked to any pages in the website.

DESIGN TIP   Considering navigation design issues

As you work on the navigation structure for a website, you should try to limit the number of links on each page to no more than is necessary. Too many links may confuse visitors to your website. You should also design links so that viewers can reach the information they want within a few clicks. If finding information takes more than three or four clicks, the viewer may become discouraged or lost in the site. It's a good idea to provide visual clues on each page to let viewers know where they are, much like a "You are here" marker on a store directory at the mall, or a bread crumbs trail. A **bread crumbs trail** is a list of links that provides a path from the initial page you opened in a website to the page that you are currently viewing.

FIGURE 26

Link Checker panel displaying external links

List of external links   Show list arrow

FIGURE 27

Link Checker panel displaying no orphaned files

No orphaned
files shown

Show list arrow

FIGURE 28

Assets panel displaying links

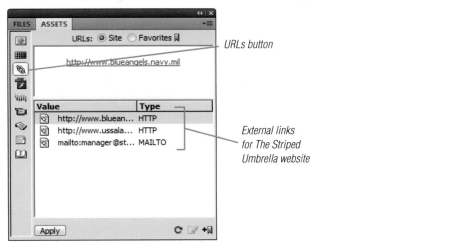

URLs button

External links
for The Striped
Umbrella website

Manage website links

1. Click **Site** on the Application bar (Win) or Menu bar (Mac), point to **Advanced**, then click **Recreate Site Cache**.

2. Click **Site** on the Application bar (Win) or Menu bar (Mac), then click **Check Links Sitewide**.

   The Results tab group opens with the Link Checker panel displayed. By default, the Link Checker panel initially displays any broken internal links found in the website. The Striped Umbrella website has no broken links.

3. Click the **Show list arrow** in the Link Checker panel, click **External Links**, then compare your screen to Figure 26.

4. Click the **Show list arrow**, then click **Orphaned Files** to view the orphaned files in the Link Checker panel, as shown in Figure 27.

   The Striped Umbrella website has no orphaned files.

5. Right-click in an empty area of the Results tab group title bar, then click **Close tab group**.

6. Display the Assets panel (if necessary), then click the **URLs button** in the Assets panel if necessary to display the list of links in the website.

   The Assets panel displays the external links used in the website, as shown in Figure 28.

You used the Link Checker panel to check for broken links, external links, and orphaned files in The Striped Umbrella website. You also viewed the external links in the Assets panel.

Update a page

1. Open dw4_2.html from where you store your Data Files, then save it as **fishing.html** in the striped_umbrella root folder, overwriting the existing fishing page, but not updating the links.

2. Click the broken link image placeholder, click the **Browse for File icon** 📁 next to the Src text box in the Property inspector, then browse to the chapter_4 Data Files folder and select the file **heron_small.jpg** to copy the file to the striped_umbrella assets folder.

3. Deselect the image placeholder and the image will appear as shown in Figure 29.

   Notice that the text is automatically updated with the paragraph_text style. The code was already in place on the page linking the su_styles.css to the file.

4. Save and close the fishing page, then close the dw4_2.html page.

(continued)

(continued)

FIGURE 29
Fishing page updated

POWER USER SHORTCUTS

to do this:	use this shortcut:
Close a file	[Ctrl][W] (Win) or ⌘[W] (Mac)
Close all files	[Ctrl][Shift][W] (Win) or ⌘[Shift][W] (Mac)
Print Code	[Ctrl][P] (Win) or ⌘[P] (Mac)
Check page links	[Shift][F8]
Undo	[Ctrl][Z], [Alt][BkSp] (Win) or ⌘[Z], [option][delete] (Mac)
Redo	[Ctrl][Y], [Ctrl][Shift][Z] (Win) or ⌘[Y], ⌘[Shift][Z] (Mac)
Refresh Design View	[F5]
Hide all Visual Aids	[Ctrl][Shift][I] (Win) or ⌘[Shift][I] (Mac)
Insert a Named Anchor	[Ctrl][Alt][A] (Win) or ⌘[option][A] (Mac)
Make a Link	[Ctrl][L] (Win) or ⌘[L] (Mac)
Remove a Link	[Ctrl][Shift][L] (Win) or ⌘[Shift][L] (Mac)
Check Links Sitewide	[Ctrl][F8] (Win) or ⌘[F8] (Mac)
Show Files tab group	[F8] (Win) or ⌘[Shift][F] (Mac)

Working with Links

FIGURE 30
Cruises page updated

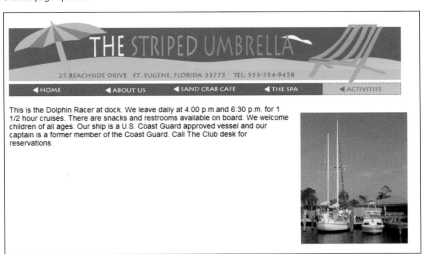

5. Open dw4_3.html from where you store your Data Files, then save it as **cruises.html** in the striped_umbrella root folder, overwriting the existing cruises page, but not updating the links.

6. Click the broken link graphic placeholder, click the **Browse for File icon** 🗁 next to the Src text box in the Property inspector, then browse to the chapter_4 Data Files folder and select the file **boats.jpg** to copy the file to the striped_umbrella assets folder.

7. Deselect the image placeholder and the image will appear as shown in Figure 30.

   Notice that the text is automatically updated with the paragraph_text style. The code was already in place on the page linking the su_styles.css to the file.

8. Save and close the page.

9. Open each page that has a horizontal rule under the navigation bar, delete the horizontal rule, then save each page.

   Each page did not have a horizontal rule. By deleting each existing horizontal rule after the navigation bars were added, all pages now have a consistent look.

10. Preview each page in the browser, close the browser, then close all open pages.

You added content to two previously blank pages in the website, then deleted horizontal rules under navigation bars to provide a consistent look for each page in the site.

Create external and internal links.

1. Open the blooms & bulbs website.
2. Open dw4_4.html from where you store your Data Files, then save it as **newsletter.html** in the blooms & bulbs website, overwriting the existing file without updating the links. Close dw4_4.html.
3. Verify that the banner path is set correctly to the assets folder in the website and correct it, if it is not.
4. Scroll to the bottom of the page, then link the National Gardening Association text to http://www.garden.org.
5. Link the Organic Gardening text to http://www.organicgardening.com.
6. Link the Southern Living text to http://www.southernliving.com/southern.
7. Save the file, then preview the page in your browser, verifying that each link works correctly.
8. Close your browser, then return to the newsletter page in Dreamweaver.
9. Scroll to the paragraph about gardening issues, select the gardening tips text in the last sentence, then link the selected text to the tips.html file in the blooms root folder.
10. Apply the paragraph_text rule from the blooms_styles.css file to all of the text on the page except the subheadings and heading.
11. Apply the headings rule to the text "Gardening Matters," and the bold_blue rule to the subheadings on the page.
12. Change the page title to **Gardening Matters**, then save your work.
13. Open the plants page and add the following sentence to the end of the last paragraph: **We have many annuals, perennials, and water plants that have just arrived**.
14. Link the "annuals" text to the annuals.html file, link the "perennials" text to the perennials.html file, and the "water plants" text to the water_plants.html file.
15. Save your work, test the links in your browser, then close your browser. (*Hint*: These pages do not have content yet, but are serving as placeholders.)

Create internal links to named anchors.

1. Show Invisible Elements (if necessary).
2. Click the Common category in the Insert panel.
3. Switch to the newsletter page, then insert a named anchor in front of the Grass heading named **grass**.
4. Insert a named anchor in front of the Plants heading named **plants**.
5. Insert a named anchor in front of the Trees heading named **trees**.
6. Use the Point to File icon in the Property inspector to create a link from the word "grass" in the Gardening Issues paragraph to the anchor named "grass."
7. Create a link from the word "trees" in the Gardening Issues paragraph to the anchor named "trees."
8. Create a link from the word "plants" in the Gardening Issues paragraph to the anchor named "plants."
9. Save your work, view the page in your browser, test all the links to make sure they work, then close your browser.

Create, modify, and copy a navigation bar.

1. Select the banner, press the right arrow key, click the Images list arrow on the Insert panel, then click Navigation Bar to insert a horizontal navigation bar at the top of the newsletter page below the banner. Verify that the option to use tables is selected.

2. Type **home** as the first element name, then use the **b_home_up.jpg** file for the Up image state. This file is in the assets folder where you store your Data Files.

3. Specify the file **b_home_down.jpg** for the three remaining states. This file (and all files for the remainder of this exercise) are in the assets folder where you store your Data Files.

4. Enter **Link to home page** as the alternate text, then set the index.html file as the link for the home element.

5. Create a new element named **plants** and use the **b_plants_up.jpg** file for the Up image state and the **b_plants_down.jpg** file for the remaining three states.

6. Enter **Link to plants page** as the alternate text, then set the **plants.html** file as the link for the plants element.

7. Create a new element named **tips** and use the **b_tips_up.jpg** file for the Up image state and the **b_tips_down.jpg** file for the remaining three states.

8. Enter **Link to tips page** as the alternate text, then set the **tips.html** file as the link for the tips element.

9. Create a new element named **classes** and use the **b_classes_up.jpg** file for the Up image state and the **b_classes_down.jpg** file for the remaining three states.

10. Enter **Link to classes page** as the alternate text, then set the **classes.html** file as the link for the classes element.

11. Create a new element named **newsletter**, then use the **b_newsletter_up.jpg** file for the Up image state and the **b_newsletter_down.jpg** file for the remaining three states.

12. Enter the alternate text **Link to newsletter page**, then set the **newsletter.html** file as the link for the newsletter element.

13. Save the page and test the links in your browser, then close the browser.

14. Select and copy the navigation bar, then open the home page.

15. Delete the current navigation bar on the home page, paste the new navigation bar under the banner, then delete the horizontal rule under the navigation bar. Remove any space between the banner and navigation bar if necessary. (*Hint*: The easiest way to remove any extra space is to go to Code view and delete any space between the end of the banner code and the beginning table tag for the navigation bar.

16. Modify the home element on the navigation bar to show the Down image state initially.

17. Save the page, test the links in your browser, then close the browser and the page.

18. Modify the navigation bar on the newsletter page so the Down image is shown initially for the newsletter element.

19. Paste the navigation bar on the plants page and the tips page, making the necessary modifications so that the Down image is shown initially for each element.

20. Save your work, preview all the pages in your browser, compare your newsletter page to Figure 31, test all the links, then close your browser.

Create an image map.

1. Use the Rectangle Hotspot Tool to draw an image map across the left side of the banner on the newsletter page that will link to the home page.

2. Name the image map **home** and set the target to **_top**.

3. Add the alternate text **Link to home page**, save the page, then preview it in the browser to test the link. (*Hint*: In the Internet Explorer browser, you may see a space between the banner and the navigation bar that is caused by the image map on the banner. Mozilla Firefox will display the page correctly without the space.)

4. Close the page.

Manage website links.

1. Use the Link Checker panel to view and fix broken links and orphaned files in the blooms & bulbs website.

2. Open dw4_5.html from where you store your Data Files, then save it as **annuals.html**, replacing the original file. Do not update links, but save the file **fuschia.jpg** in the assets folder of the website. Close dw4_5.html.

3. Repeat Step 2 using **dw4_6.html** to replace **perennials.html**, saving the **iris.jpg** file in

the assets folder and using **dw4_7.html** to replace **water_plants.html**, saving the **water_hyacinth.jpg** file in the assets folder.

FIGURE 31
Completed Skills Review

4. Save your work, then close all open pages.

Use Figure 32 as a guide to continue your work on the TripSmart website that you began in Project Builder 1 in Chapter 1 and developed in the previous chapters. You have been asked to create a new page for the website that lists helpful links for customers. You will also add content to the destinations, kenya, and amazon pages.

1. Open the TripSmart website.
2. Open dw4_8.html from where you store your Data Files, then save it as **services.html** in the TripSmart website root folder, replacing the existing file and not updating links. Close dw4_8.html.
3. Verify that the TripSmart banner is in the assets folder of the root folder.
4. Apply the paragraph_text rule to the paragraphs of text and the heading rule to the four main paragraph headings.
5. Create named anchors named **reservations**, **outfitters**, **tours**, and **links** in front of the respective headings on the page, then link each named anchor to "Reservations," "Travel Outfitters," "Escorted Tours," and "Helpful Links in Travel Planning" in the first paragraph.

6. Link the text "on-line catalog" in the Travel Outfitters paragraph to the catalog.html page.
7. Link the text "CNN Travel Channel" under the heading Travel Information Sites to http://www.cnn.com/TRAVEL.
8. Repeat Step 7 to create links for the rest of the websites listed:
   US Department of State:
   http://travel.state.gov
   Yahoo!:
   http://yahoo.com/Recreation/Travel
   MapQuest:
   http://www.mapquest.com
   Rand McNally:
   http://www.randmcnally.com
   AccuWeather:
   http://www.accuweather.com
   The Weather Channel:
   http://www.weather.com
9. Save the services page, then open the index page.
10. Reformat the navigation bar on the home page with a style of your choice. If you decide to use graphics for the navigation bar, you will have to create your own graphic files using a graphics program. There are no Data Files for you to use.

(*Hint*: If you create your own graphic files, be sure to create two graphic files for each element: one for the Up image state and one for the Down image state.) To design a navigation bar using text, you simply type the text for each navigation bar element, format the text appropriately using styles, and insert links to each text element as you did in Chapter 2. The navigation bar should contain the following elements: Home, Catalog, Services, Destinations, and Newsletter. In Figure 32, the navigation bar style was edited to incorporate letter spacing to spread the text slightly. Indents were then used to center the navigation bar under the banner. (Letter spacing and indents are in the Block category in the CSS Rule definition dialog box. You can also use the Text Indent button on the HTML Property inspector.)
11. Copy the navigation bar, then place it on each completed page of the website.

12. Save each page, then check for broken links and orphaned files. (*Hint*: The two orphaned files will be removed after completing the next steps.)

13. Open the destinations.html file in your root folder and save it as **kenya.html**, overwriting the existing file, then close the file.

14. Open dw4_9.html from where you store your Data Files, then save it as **amazon.html**, overwriting the existing file. Do not update links, but save the **water_lily.jpg** and **sloth.jpg** files in the assets folder of the website, then save and close the file. Close dw4_9.html.

15. Open dw4_10.html from where you store your Data Files, then save the file as **destinations.html**, overwriting the existing file. Do not update links, but save the **parrot.jpg** and **giraffe.jpg** files in the assets folder of the website. Close dw4_10.html.

16. Link the text "Amazon" in the second sentence of the first paragraph to the **amazon.html** file.

17. Link the text "Kenya" in the first sentence in the second paragraph to the **kenya.html** file.

18. Copy your customized navigation bar to the two new pages so they will match the other pages.

19. Check all text on all pages to make sure each text block uses a style for formatting. Correct those that don't.

20. Save all files.

21. Test all links in your browser, close your browser, then close all open pages.

FIGURE 32
Sample Project Builder 1

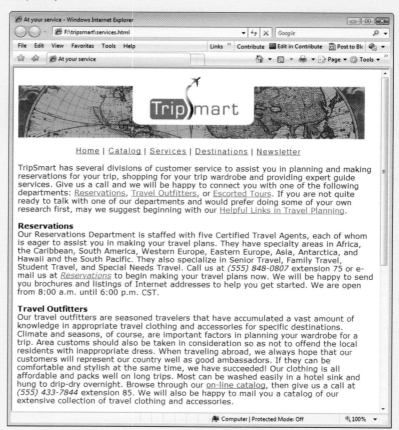

You are continuing your work on the Carolyne's Creations website, that you started in Project Builder 2 in Chapter 1 and developed in the previous chapters. Chef Carolyne has asked you to create a page describing her cooking classes offered every month. You will create the content for that page and individual pages describing the children's classes and the adult classes. Refer to Figures 33-36 for possible solutions.

1. Open the Carolyne's Creations website.
2. Open dw4_11.html from where you store your Data Files, save it as **classes.html** in the root folder of the Carolyne's Creations website, overwriting the existing file and not updating the links. Close dw4_11.html.
3. Check the path of the banner to make sure it is linking to the banner in the assets folder of the website. Notice that styles have already been applied to the text, because the CSS code was already in the Data File.
4. Select the text "adults' class" in the last paragraph, then link it to the adults.html page. (*Hint*: This page has not been developed yet.)
5. Select the text "children's class" in the last paragraph and link it to the children.html page. (*Hint*: This page has not been developed yet.)

6. Create an email link from the text "Sign me up!" that links to **carolyne@carolynescreations.com**
7. Insert the file **fish.jpg** from the assets folder where you store your Data Files at the beginning of the second paragraph, add

appropriate alternate text, then choose your own alignment and formatting settings.
8. Add the file **children_cooking.jpg** from the assets folder where you store your Data Files at the beginning of the third paragraph.

FIGURE 33
Completed Project Builder 2

Cooking Classes are fun!

Chef Carolyne loves to offer a fun and relaxing cooking school each month in her newly refurbished kitchen. She teaches an **adult class** on the fourth Saturday of each month from 6:00 to 8:00 pm. Each class will learn to cook a complete dinner and then enjoy the meal at the end of the class with a wonderful wine pairing. This is a great chance to get together with friends for a fun evening.

Chef Caroline also teaches a **children's class** on the second Tuesday of each month from 4:00 to 5:30 pm. Our young chefs will learn to cook two dishes that will accompany a full meal served at 5:30 pm. Kids aged 5–8 years accompanied by an adult are welcome. We also host small birthday parties where we put the guests to work baking and decorating the cake! Call for times and prices.

We offer several special adult classes throughout the year. The **Valentine Chocolate Extravaganza** is a particular favorite. You will learn to dip strawberries, make truffles, and bake a sinful Triple Chocolate Dare You Torte. We also host the **Not So Traditional Thanksgiving** class and the **Super Bowl Snacks** class each year with rave reviews. Watch the Web site for details!

Prices are $40.00 for each adults' class and $15.00 for each children's class. Sign up for classes by calling 555-963-8271 or by emailing us: Sign me up!

See what's cooking this month for the adults' class and children's class.

9. Compare your work to Figure 33 for a possible solution, then save and close the file.

10. Open dw4_12.html from where you store your Data Files, then save it as **children.html,** overwriting the existing file and not updating links. Save the image **cookies_oven.jpg** from the assets folder where you store your Data Files to the website assets folder. Close dw4_12.html.

11. Use your own alignment and formatting settings, compare your work to Figure 34 for a possible solution, then save and close the file.

FIGURE 35
Completed Project Builder 2

FIGURE 34
Completed Project Builder 2

12. Repeat Steps 10 and 11 to open the dw4_13.html file and save it as **adults.html**, overwriting the existing file and saving the files **dumplings1.jpg, dumplings2.jpg,** and **dumplings3.jpg** in the assets folder, then use alignment settings of your choice. Compare your work to Figure 35 for a possible solution, then save and close the file.

13. Open the index page and delete the banner, navigation bar, and horizontal rule.

14. Insert the file **cc_banner_with_text.jpg** from where you store your Data Files in place, of what you just deleted adding appropriate alternate text.

15. Create an image map for each word at the bottom of the navigation bar to be used as a link to that page, as shown in Figure 36. Use **_top** as the target, the names of the "buttons" as the image map names, and appropriate alternate text. Link each image map to its corresponding page.

16. Copy the new banner with the navigation bar to each completed page, deleting existing navigation bars and banners.

17. Save all the pages, then check for broken links and orphaned files. You will see one orphaned file, the original version of the banner.

18. Apply a rule from the style sheet to any text that is not formatted with a style.

19. Preview all the pages in your browser, check to make sure the links work correctly, close your browser, then close all open pages.

FIGURE 36
Completed Project Builder 2

Let Carolyne's Creations be your personal chef, your one stop shop for the latest in kitchen items and fresh ingredients, and your source for new and innovative recipes. We enjoy planning and executing special events for all occasions - from children's birthday parties to corporate retreats. Feel like a guest at your own party. Give us a call or stop by our shop to browse through our selections.

Carolyne's Creations
496 Maple Avenue
Seven Falls, Virginia 52404
555-963-8271
E-mail <u>Carolyne Kate</u>

Copyright 2001 - 2012
Last updated on July 29, 2008

Grace Keiko is a talented young water-color artist who specializes in botanical works. She wants to develop a website to advertise her work, but isn't sure what she would like to include in a website or how to tie the pages together. She decides to spend several hours looking at other artists' websites to help her get started.

1. Connect to the Internet, then navigate to the Kate Nessler website pictured in Figure 37, www.katenessler.com.

2. Spend some time looking at several of the pages in the site to get some ideas.

3. What categories of page content would you include on your website if you were Grace?

4. What external links would you consider including?

5. Describe how you would place external links on the pages and list examples of ones you would use.

6. Would you use text or images for your navigation bar?

7. Would you include rollover effects on the navigation bar elements? If so, describe how they might look.

8. How could you incorporate named anchors on any of the pages?

9. Would you include an image map on a page?

10. Sketch a website plan for Grace, including the pages that you would use as links from the home page.

11. Refer to your website sketch, then create a home page for Grace that includes a navigation bar, a short introductory paragraph about her art, and a few external links.

FIGURE 37
Design Project

Kate Nessler website used with permission from Kate Nessler - www.katenessler.com

In this assignment, you will continue to work on the website that you started in Chapter 1 and developed in the previous chapters.

You will continue building your website by designing and completing a page with a navigation bar. After creating the navigation bar, you will copy it to each completed page in the website. In addition to the navigation bar, you will add several external links and several internal links to other pages as well as to named anchors. You will also link text to a named anchor. After you complete this work, you will check for broken links and orphaned files.

1. Consult your storyboard to decide which page or pages you would like to develop in this chapter. Decide how to design and where to place the navigation bar, named anchors, and any additional page elements you decide to use. Decide which reports should be run on the website to check for accuracy.

2. Research websites that could be included on one or more of your pages as external links of interest to your viewers. Create a list of the external links you want to use. Using your storyboard as a guide, decide where each external link should be placed in the site.

3. Add the external links to existing pages or create any additional pages that contain external links.

4. Create named anchors for key locations on the page, such as the top of the page, then link appropriate text on the page to them.

5. Decide on a design for a navigation bar that will be used on all pages of the website.

6. Create the navigation bar and copy it to all finished pages on the website. If you decided to use graphics for the navigation bar, create the graphics that will be used.

7. Think of a good place to incorporate an image map, then add it to a page.

8. Use the Link Checker panel to check for broken links and orphaned files.

9. Use the checklist in Figure 38 to make sure your website is complete, save your work, then close all open pages.

FIGURE 38
Portfolio Project checklist

> **Website Checklist**
> 1. Do all pages have a page title?
> 2. Does the home page have a description and keywords?
> 3. Does the home page contain contact information?
> 4. Does every page in the website have consistent navigation links?
> 5. Does the home page have a last updated statement that will automatically update when the page is saved?
> 6. Do all paths for links and images work correctly?
> 7. Do all images have alternate text?
> 8. Are all colors web-safe?
> 9. Are there any unnecessary files that you can delete from the assets folder?
> 10. Is there a style sheet with at least two styles?
> 11. Did you apply the style sheet to page content?
> 12. Does at least one page contain links to one or more named anchors?
> 13. Does at least one page contain an internal link?
> 14. Do all pages look good using at least two different browsers?

chapter

5 POSITIONING OBJECTS
WITH CSS AND TABLES

1. Create a page using CSS layouts

2. Add content to CSS layout blocks

3. Edit content in CSS layout blocks

4. Create a table

5. Resize, split, and merge cells

6. Insert and align images in table cells

7. Insert text and format cell content

9. Type **Lunch Boxes**, **Brunch Boxes**, and **Gift Baskets** in the three cells in the third row.

10. Type **Soups**, **Entrees**, and **Desserts** in the three cells in the seventh row.

11. Apply the nav_bar rule to the text you typed in Steps 9 and 10.

12. Use a color of your choice for the background for each cell in the third and seventh rows.

13. Type the text **Call/fax by 9:00 a.m. for lunch orders, Call/fax by 1:00 p.m. for dinner orders, Fax number: 555-963-5938** in the first cell in the last row using a line break to separate each line.

14. Apply the paragraph_text rule to the text you typed in Step 13.

15. Use your word processor to open the file menu items.doc from your Data Files folder. Copy and paste each text block into the cells in the fourth and eighth rows, apply the paragraph_text rule to each text block, then center align each text block in the cells, using Figure 44 as a guide.

16. Merge the last two cells in the last row, then insert the image muffins.jpg with alternate text and any additional formatting of your choice.

17. Delete the footer placeholder text and change the background color of the footer to white.

18. Save your work, preview the page in your browser, make any adjustments that you feel would improve the page appearance, then close all open files.

FIGURE 44
Completed Project Builder 2

Jon Bishop is opening a new restaurant and wants to have the restaurant website launched two weeks before his opening. He has hired you to create the site and has asked for several design proposals. You begin by looking at some restaurant sites with pleasing designs.

1. Connect to the Internet, then go to www.jamesatthemill.com, as shown in Figure 45.

2. How are CSS used in this site?
3. How are CSS used to prevent an overload of information in one area of the screen?
4. View the source code for the page and locate the html tags that control the CSS on the page.
5. Use the Reference panel in Dreamweaver to look up the code used in this site to place the content on the page. (To do this, make note of a tag that you don't understand, then open the Reference panel and find that tag the Tag list box in the Reference panel. Select it from the list and read the description in the Reference panel.)
6. Do you see any tables on the page? If so, how are they used?

FIGURE 45
Design Project

James at the Mill website used with permission from Miles James – www.jamesatthemill.com

For this assignment, you will continue to work on the portfolio project that you have been developing since Chapter 1. There will be no Data Files supplied. You are building this website from chapter to chapter, so you must do each Portfolio Project assignment in each chapter to complete your website.

You will continue building your website by designing and completing a page that uses layers rather than tables to control the layout of information.

1. Consult your storyboard to decide which page to create and develop for this chapter. Draw a sketch of the page to show how you will use CSS to lay out the content.

2. Create the new page for the site and set the default preferences for div tags. Add the appropriate number of div tags to the new page and configure them appropriately, making sure to name them and set the properties for each.

3. Add text, background images, and background colors to each container.

4. Create the navigation links that will allow you to add this page to your site.

5. Update the other pages of your site so that each page includes a link to this new page.

6. Add images in the containers (where appropriate), making sure to align them with text so they look good.

7. Review the checklist in Figure 46 and make any necessary modifications.

8. Save your work, preview the page in your browser, make any necessary modifications to improve the page appearance, close your browser, then close all open pages.

FIGURE 46
Portfolio Project checklist

```
                        Website Checklist
1.      Do all pages have titles?
2.      Do all navigation links work correctly?
3.      Are all colors in your layers web-safe?
4.      Does the use of CSS in your website improve the site navigation?
5.      Do your pages look acceptable in at least the two major browsers?
6.      Do all images in your CSS containers appear correctly?
```

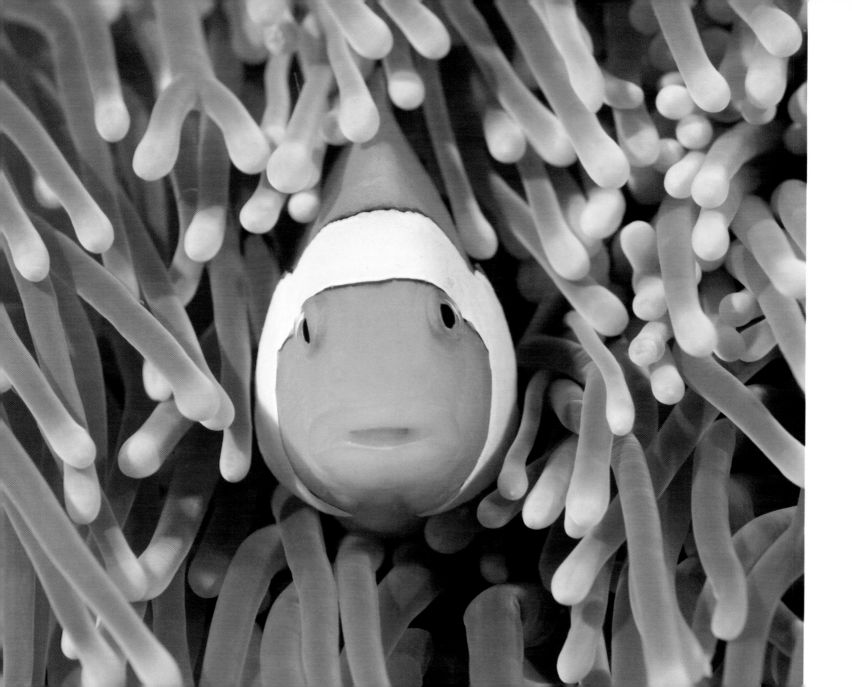

6

MANAGING A WEB
SERVER AND FILES

1. Perform website maintenance

2. Publish a website and transfer files

3. Check files out and in

4. Cloak files

5. Import and export a site definition

6. Evaluate web content for legal use

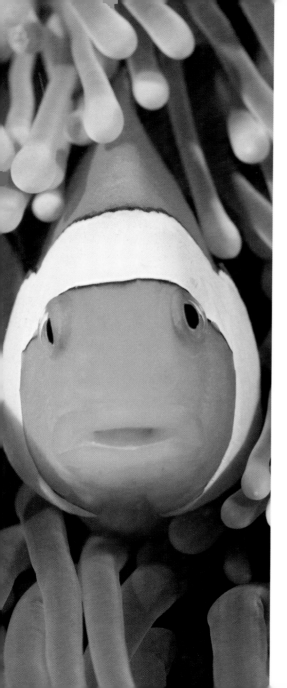

6 MANAGING A WEB
SERVER AND FILES

Introduction

Once you have created all the pages of your website, finalized all the content, and performed site maintenance, you are ready to publish your site to a remote server so the rest of the world can access it. In this chapter, you will start by running some reports to make sure the links in your site work properly, that the colors are web-safe, and that orphaned files are removed. Next, you will set up a connection to the remote site for The Striped Umbrella website. You will then transfer files to the remote site and learn how to keep them up to date. You will also check out a file so that it is not available to other team members while you are editing it and you will learn how to cloak files. When a file is **cloaked**, it is excluded from certain processes, such as being transferred to the remote site. Next, you will export the site definition file from The Striped Umbrella website so that other designers can import the site. Finally, you will research important copyright issues that affect all websites.

Preparing to Publish a Site

Before you publish a site, it is extremely important that you test it regularly to make sure the content is accurate and up to date and that everything is functioning properly. When viewing pages over the Internet, it is very frustrating to click a link that doesn't work or have to wait for pages that load slowly because of large graphics and animations. Remember that the typical viewer has a short attention span and limited patience. Before you publish your site, make sure to use the Link Checker panel to check for broken links and orphaned files. Make sure that all image paths are correct and that all images load quickly and have alternate text. Verify that all pages have titles, and remove all non-web-safe colors. View the pages in at least two different browsers and different versions of the same browser to ensure that everything works correctly. The more frequently you test, the better the chance that your viewers will have a positive experience at your site and want to return. *Before you publish your pages, verify that all content is original to the website, has been obtained legally, and is used properly without violating the copyright of someone else's work.*

Tools You'll Use

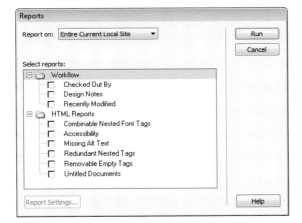

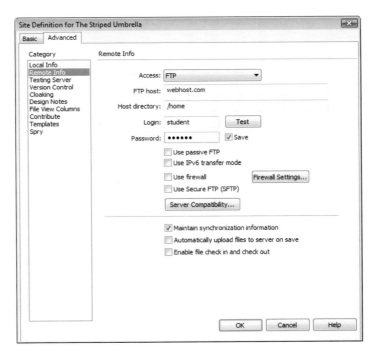

PERFORM WEBSITE
MAINTENANCE

What You'll Do

 In this lesson, you will use some Dreamweaver site management tools to check for broken links, orphaned files, and missing alternate text. You will also verify that all colors are web-safe. You will then correct any problems that you find.

Maintaining a Website

As you add pages, links, and content to a website, it can quickly become difficult to manage. It's easier to find and correct errors as you go, rather than waiting until the end of the design phase. It's important to perform maintenance tasks frequently to make sure your website operates smoothly and remains "clean." You have already learned about some of the tools described in the following paragraphs. Although it is important to use them as you create and modify your pages, it is also important to run them at periodic intervals after publishing your website to make sure it is always error-free.

Using the Assets Panel

You should use the Assets panel to check the list of images and colors used in your website. If you see images listed that are not being used, you should move them to a storage folder outside the website until you need them. You should also check to see if all of the colors used in the site are web-safe. If there are non-web-safe colors in the list, locate the elements to which

these colors are applied and apply web-safe colors to them.

Checking Links Sitewide

Before and after you publish your website, you should use the Link Checker panel to make sure all internal links are working. If the Link Checker panel displays any broken links, you should repair them. If the Link Checker panel displays any orphaned files, you should evaluate whether to delete them or link them with existing pages.

Using Site Reports

You can use the Reports command in the Site menu to generate six different HTML reports that can help you maintain your website. You choose the type of report you want to run in the Reports dialog box, shown in Figure 1. You can specify whether to generate the report for the current document, the entire current local site, selected files in the site, or a selected folder. You can also generate workflow reports to see files that have been checked out by others or recently modified or you can view the Design Notes attached to files.

Design Notes are separate files in a website that contain additional information about a page file or a graphic file. In a collaborative situation, designers can record notes to exchange information with other designers. Design Notes can also be used to record sensitive information that would not be included in files that could be viewed on the website. Information about the source files for graphic files, such as Flash files or Fireworks files, are also stored in Design Notes.

Validating Markup

One of the report features in Dreamweaver is the ability to validate markup. This means that Dreamweaver will go through the code to look for errors that could occur with different language versions, such as XHTML or XML. To validate code for a page, click File on the Application bar (Win) or Menu bar (Mac) point to Validate, and then click Markup. The Results tab group displaying the Validation panel opens and lists any pages with errors, the line numbers where the errors occur, and an explanation of the errors. The Validate button on the Validation panel offers the choice of validating a single document, an entire local website, or selected files in a local website.

Testing Pages

Finally, you should test your website using many different types and versions of browsers, platforms, and screen resolutions. You can use the Check Page button on the Document toolbar to check browser

compatibility. This feature lists issues with the pages in your site that may cause problems when the pages are viewed using certain browsers, such as the rendering of square bullets in Mozilla Firefox. If you find such issues, you then have the choice to make changes to your page to eliminate the problems. The Results Tab group's Browser Compatibility window includes a URL that you can visit to find the solutions to problems. You should test every link to make sure it connects to a valid, active website.

Pages that download slowly should be reduced in size to improve performance. You should analyze all user feedback on the website objectively, saving both positive and negative comments for future reference to help you make improvements to the site.

FIGURE 1
Reports dialog box

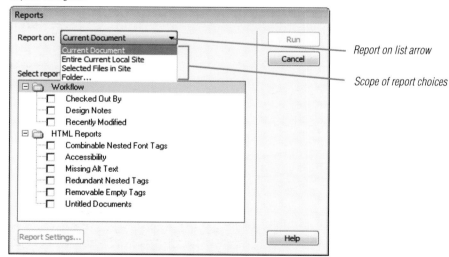

Report on list arrow

Scope of report choices

Check for broken links

1. Open The Striped Umbrella website.

2. Show the Files panel (if necessary).

3. Click **Site** on the Application bar (Win) or Menu bar (Mac), point to **Advanced**, then click **Recreate Site Cache**.

4. Click **Site** on the Application bar (Win) or Menu bar (Mac), then click **Check Links Sitewide**.

   No broken links are listed in the Link Checker panel of the Results tab group, as shown in Figure 2.

You verified that there are no broken links in the website.

Check for orphaned files

1. On the Link Checker panel, click the **Show list arrow**, then click **Orphaned Files**.

   There are no orphaned files, as shown in Figure 3.

2. Close the Results tab group.

You verified that there are no orphaned files in the website.

FIGURE 2

Link Checker panel displaying no broken links

No broken links listed

FIGURE 3

Link Checker panel displaying no orphaned files

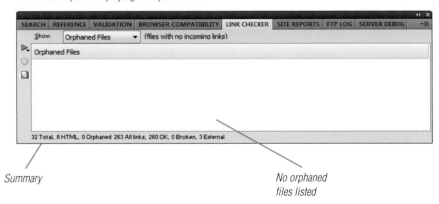

Summary

No orphaned files listed

FIGURE 4

Assets panel displaying web-safe colors

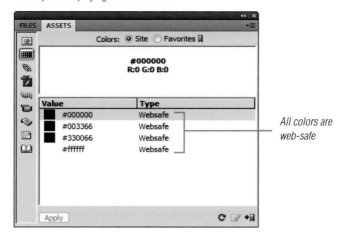

All colors are
web-safe

Verify that all colors are web-safe

1. Click the **Assets panel tab**, then click the **Colors button** ▦ to view the website colors, as shown in Figure 4.

   The Assets panel shows that all colors used in the website are web-safe.

You verified that the website contains all web-safe colors.

Using Find and Replace to locate non-web-safe colors

As with many software applications, Dreamweaver has a Find and Replace feature that can be used both in Design view and in Code view on the Edit menu. This command can be used to search the current document, selected files, or the entire current local site. If you are looking for a particular non-web-safe color, you will probably save time by using the Find and Replace feature to locate the hexadecimal color code in Code view. If a site has many pages, this will be the fastest way to locate it. The Find and Replace feature can also be used to locate other character combinations, such as a phrase that begins or ends with a particular word or tag. These patterns of character combinations are referred to as **regular expressions**. To find out more, search for "regular expressions" in Dreamweaver Help.

Check for untitled documents

1. Click **Site** on the Application bar (Win) or Menu bar (Mac), then click **Reports** to open the Reports dialog box.

2. Click the **Report on list arrow**, click **Entire Current Local Site**, click the **Untitled Documents check box**, as shown in Figure 5, then click **Run**.

   The Site Reports panel opens in the Results tab group, and shows that the cafe page does not have a page title, as shown in Figure 6.

3. Open the cafe page, replace the current page title "Untitled Document" with the title **The Sand Crab Cafe**, then save the file.

4. Close the cafe page.

5. Run the report again to check the entire site for untitled documents.

   No files should appear in the Site Reports panel.

You ran a report for untitled documents, then added a page title to the cafe page.

FIGURE 5

Reports dialog box with Untitled Documents option selected

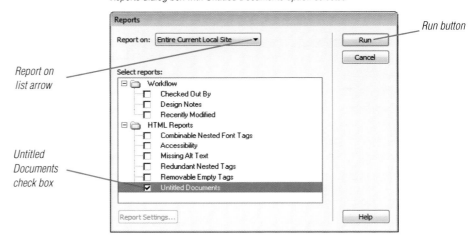

Run button

Report on list arrow

Untitled Documents check box

FIGURE 6

Site Reports panel showing one page without a page title

Cafe page does not have a page title

FIGURE 7

FIGURE 7

Reports dialog box with Missing Alt text option selected

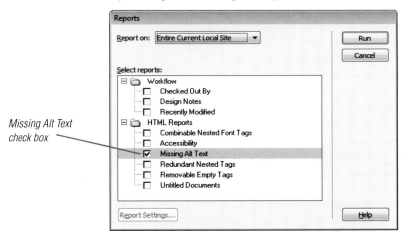

Missing Alt Text
check box

FIGURE 8

Site Reports panel displaying missing "alt" tag

Line number in code
with missing "alt" tag

One missing "alt" tag
found on one page

Check for missing alternate text

1. Using Figure 7 as a guide, run another report that checks the entire current local site for missing alternate text.

    The results show that the spa page contains an image that is missing alternate text, as shown in Figure 8.

2. Open the spa page, then find the image that is missing alternate text.

    TIP   The Site Reports panel documents the code line number where the missing alt tag occurs. Sometimes it is faster to locate the errors in Code view, rather than in Design view.

3. Add appropriate alternate text to the image.

4. Save your work, then run the report again to check the entire site for missing alternate text.

    No files should appear in the Site Reports panel.

5. Close the Results tab group, then close all open pages.

You ran a report to check for missing alternate text in the entire site. You then added alternate text for one image and ran the report again.

Validating Accessibility Standards

There are many accessibility issues to consider to ensure that your website conforms to current accessibility standards. HTML Reports provide an easy way to check for missing alternate text, missing page titles, and other accessibility concerns such as improper markup, deprecated features, or improper use of color or images. HTML Reports can be run on the current document, selected files, or the entire local site. You can also use the Check Page, Accessibility command under the File menu to check for accessibility issues on an open page. After the report is run, a list of issues will open in the Site Reports panel with the line number and description of each problem. If you right-click a description, you will see the option "More Info. . ." Click on this option to read a more detailed description and solutions to correct the issue.

Enable Design Notes

1. Click **Site** on the Application bar (Win) or Menu bar (Mac), click **Manage Sites**, verify that The Striped Umbrella site is selected, click **Edit**, click the **Advanced tab** (if necessary), then click the **Design Notes category**.

2. Click the **Maintain Design Notes check box**, to select it (if necessary), as shown in Figure 9.

   Selecting this option enables the designer to record notes about a page in a separate file linked to the page. For instance, a Design Note for the index.html file would be saved in a file named index.html.mno. This file would be automatically saved in a folder that is created by Dreamweaver named _notes. This folder does not appear in the Files panel, but can be seen using Windows Explorer (Win) or Finder (Mac).

3. Click the **File View Columns category**, then click **Notes** in the File View Columns list.

4. Click the **Options**: **Show check box**, to select it (if necessary).

   The Notes column now displays the word "Show" in the Show column, as shown in Figure 10, indicating that the Notes column will be visible in the Files panel.

5. Click **OK**, then click **Done** in the Manage Sites dialog box.

You set the preference to use Design Notes in the website. You also set the option to display the Notes column in the Files panel.

FIGURE 9

Design Notes category in the Site Definition for The Striped Umbrella

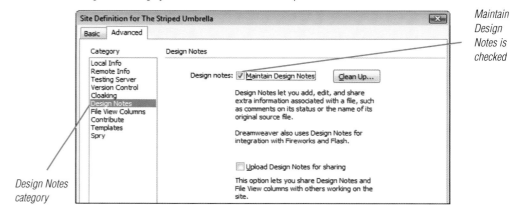

Maintain Design Notes is checked

Design Notes category

FIGURE 10

File View Columns category in the Site Definition for The Striped Umbrella

File View Columns category

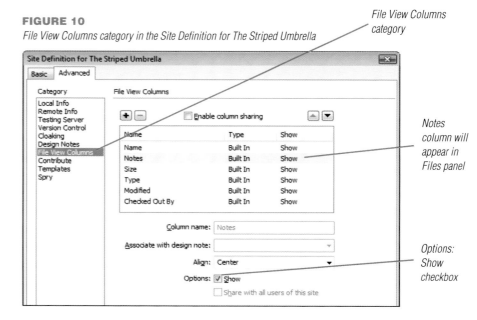

Notes column will appear in Files panel

Options: Show checkbox

FIGURE 11
Design Notes dialog box

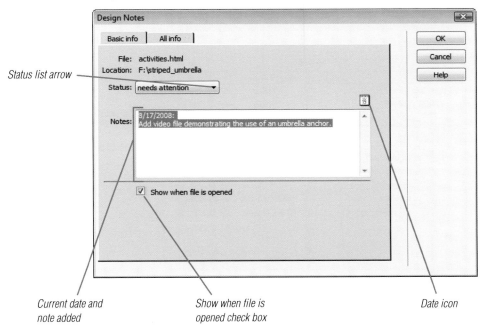

Status list arrow

Current date and
note added

Show when file is
opened check box

Date icon

Associate a Design Note with a file

1. Open the activities page, click **File** on the Application bar (Win) or Menu bar (Mac), click **Design Notes**, then click the **Basic info tab** (if necessary).

   The Design Notes dialog box opens with a text box to record a note related to the open file, the option to display the note each time the file is opened, an option to include the current date, and a status indicator.

2. Click the **Date icon** above the Notes text box on the right.

   The current date is added to the Notes text box.

3. Type **Add video file demonstrating the use of an umbrella anchor.** in the Notes text box beneath the date.

4. Click the **Status list arrow**, then click **needs attention**.

5. Click the **Show when file is opened** check box to select it, as shown in Figure 11, then click **OK**.

You added a design note to the activities page with the current date and a status indicator. The note will open each time the file is opened.

Using Version Cue to manage assets

Another way to collaborate with team members is through Adobe Version Cue, a workgroup collaboration system that is included in Adobe Creative Suite 4. You can perform such functions such as managing security, backing up data, and using metadata to search files. **Metadata** includes information about a file such as keywords, descriptions, and copyright information. Adobe Bridge also organizes files with metadata.

Edit a Design Note

1. Click **File** on the Application bar (Win) or Menu bar (Mac), then click **Design Notes** to open the Design Note associated with the activities page.

   You can also right-click (Windows) or control-click (Mac) the filename in the Files panel, then click Design Notes, or double-click the yellow Design Notes icon in the Files panel next to the filename to open a Design Note, as shown in Figure 12.

   | TIP   You may have to click the Refresh button 🔄 to display the Notes icon.

2. Edit the note by adding the sentence **Ask Jane Pinson to send the file.** after the existing text in the Notes section, then click **OK** to close it.

   A file named activities.html.mno has been created in a new folder called _notes. This folder and file will not display in the Files panel unless you have the option to show hidden files and folders selected. However, you can switch to Windows Explorer to see them without selecting this option.

   (continued)

FIGURE 12
Files panel with Notes icon displayed

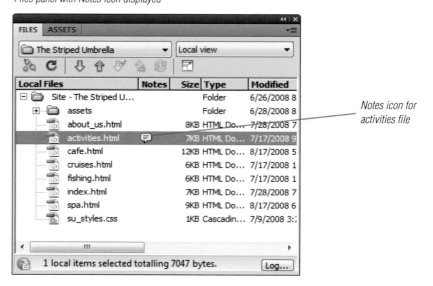

Notes icon for activities file

Deleting a Design Note

There are two steps to deleting a Design Note that you don't need anymore. The first step is to delete the Design Note file. To delete a Design Note, right-click the filename in the Files panel that is associated with the Design Note you want to delete, and then click Explore (Win) or Reveal in Finder (Mac) to open your file management system. Open the _notes folder, then delete the .mno file in the files list, and then close Explorer (Win) or Finder (Mac). The second step is done in Dreamweaver. Click Site on the Application bar (Win) or Menu bar (Mac), click Manage Sites, click Edit, and then select the Design Notes category. Click the Clean Up button. (*Note*: Don't do this if you deselect Maintain Design Notes first or it will delete all of your design notes!) The Design Notes icon will be removed from the Notes column in the Files panel.

FIGURE 13
Windows Explorer displaying the _notes file and folder

Notes file
in _notes folder

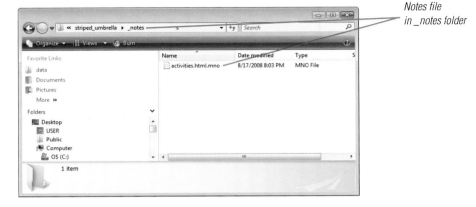

FIGURE 14
Code for the activities.html.mno file

```
1  <?xml version="1.0" encoding="utf-8" ?>
2  <info>
3     <infoitem key="notes" value="8/17/2008: &#xD;Add video file demonstrating the use of an
   umbrella anchor. Ask Jane Pinson to send the file." />
4     <infoitem key="status" value="needs attention" />
5     <infoitem key="showOnOpen" value="true" />
6  </info>
7
```

3. Right-click (Win) or control-click (Mac) **activities.html** in the Files panel, then click **Explore** (Win) or **Reveal in Finder** (Mac).

4. Double-click the folder **_notes** to open it, then double-click the file **activities.html.mno**, shown in Figure 13, to open the file in Dreamweaver.

   The notes file opens in Code view in Dreamweaver, as shown in Figure 14.

5. Read the file, close it, close Explorer (Win) or Finder (Mac), then close the activities page.

You opened the Design Notes dialog box and edited the note in the Notes text box. Next, you viewed the .mno file that Dreamweaver created when you added the Design Note.

PUBLISH A WEBSITE
AND TRANSFER FILES

What You'll Do

 In this lesson, you will set up remote access to either an FTP folder or a local/network folder for The Striped Umbrella website. You will also view a website on a remote server, upload files to it, and synchronize the files.

Defining a Remote Site

As you learned in Chapter 1, publishing a site means transferring all the site's files to a web server. A **web server** is a computer that is connected to the Internet with an IP (Internet Protocol) address so that it is available on the Internet. Before you can publish a site to a web server, you must first define the remote site by specifying the Remote Info settings on the Advanced tab of the Site Definition dialog box. You can specify remote settings when you first create a new site and define the root folder (as you did in Chapter 1 when you defined the remote access settings for The Striped Umbrella website), or you can do it after you have completed all of your pages and are confident that your site is ready for public viewing. To specify the remote settings for a site, you must first choose an Access setting, which specifies the type of server you will use. The most common Access setting is FTP (File Transfer Protocol). If you specify FTP, you will need to specify an address for the server and the name of the folder on the FTP site in which your root folder will be stored. You can also use **Secure FTP (SFTP)**, an FTP option that enables you to encrypt file transfers. This option will pro-

tect your files, user names, and passwords. To use SFTP, check the Use Secure FTP (SFTP) check box in the Site Definition dialog box. You will also need to enter login and password information. Figure 15 shows an example of FTP settings in the Remote Info category of the Site Definition dialog box.

QUICKTIP

If you do not have access to an FTP site, you can publish a site to a local/network folder. This is referred to as a **LAN**, or a Local Area Network. Use the alternate steps provided in this lesson to publish your site to a local/network folder.

Viewing a Remote Site

Once you have defined a site to a remote location, you can then view the remote folder in the Files panel by choosing Remote view from the View list. If your remote site is located on an FTP server, Dreamweaver will connect to it. You will see the File Activity dialog box showing the progress of the connection. You can also use the Connects to remote host button on the Files panel toolbar to connect to the remote site. If you defined your site on a local/network folder, then you don't need to use the Connects to remote host button; the root folder and any files and folders it contains will appear in the Files panel when you switch to Remote view.

Transferring Files to and from a Remote Site

After you define a remote site, you will need to transfer or **upload** your files from the local version of your site to the remote host. To do this, view the site in Local view, select the files you want to upload, and then click the Put File(s) button on the Files panel toolbar. Once you click this button, the files will be transferred to the remote site. To view the uploaded files, switch to Remote view, as shown in Figure 16. Or, you can

expand the Files panel to view both the Remote Site and the Local Files panes by clicking the Expand to show local and remote sites button in the Files panel.

If a file you select for uploading requires additional files, such as graphics, a dialog box will open after you click the Put File(s) button and ask if you want those files (known as **dependent files**) to be uploaded. By clicking Yes, all dependent files in the selected page will be uploaded to the appropriate folder in the remote site. If a file that you want to upload is located in a folder in the local site, the folder will be automatically transferred to the remote site.

QUICKTIP

To upload an entire site to a remote host, select the root folder, then click the Put File(s) button.

If you are developing or maintaining a website in a group environment, there might be times when you want to transfer or **download** files that other team members have created from the remote site to your local site. To do this, switch to Remote view, select the files you want to download, then click the Get File(s) button on the Files panel toolbar.

FIGURE 15
FTP settings in the Site Definition for The Striped Umbrella dialog box

FIGURE 16
Files panel with Remote view selected

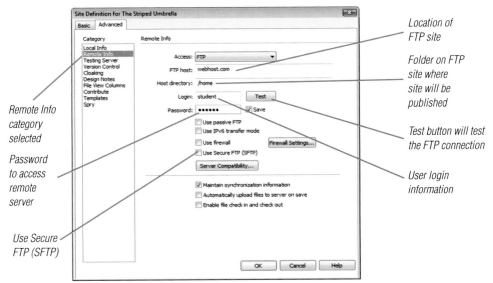

Remote Info category selected

Password to access remote server

Use Secure FTP (SFTP)

Location of FTP site

Folder on FTP site where site will be published

Test button will test the FTP connection

User login information

Expand to show local and remote sites button

Remote view

Synchronizing Files

To keep a website up to date—especially one that contains several pages and involves several team members—you will need to update and replace files. Team members might make changes to pages on the local version of the site or make additions to the remote site. If many people are involved in maintaining a site, or if you are constantly making changes to the pages, ensuring that both the local and remote sites have the most up-to-date files could get confusing. Thankfully, you can use the Synchronize command to keep things straight. The Synchronize command instructs Dreamweaver to compare the dates of the saved files in both versions of the site, then transfers only the files that have changed. To synchronize files, use the Synchronize Files dialog box, as shown in Figure 17. You can synchronize an entire site or selected files. You can also specify whether to upload newer files to the remote site, download newer files from the remote site, or both.

FIGURE 17
Synchronize Files dialog box

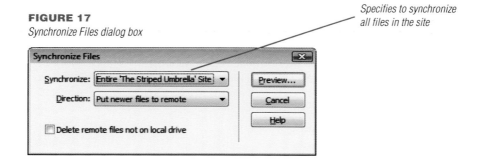

Specifies to synchronize
all files in the site

Understanding Dreamweaver connection options for transferring files

The connection types with which you are probably the most familiar are FTP and Local/Network. Other connection types that you can use with Dreamweaver are Microsoft Visual SafeSource **(VSS)**, WebDav, and RDS. VSS is used only with the Windows operating system with Microsoft Visual SafeSource Client version 6. **WebDav** stands for Web-based Distributed Authoring and Versioning. This type of connection is used with the WebDav protocol. An example would be a website residing on an Apache web server. The **Apache web server** is a public domain, open source web server that is available using several different operating systems including UNIX and Windows. **RDS** stands for Remote Development Services, and is used with web servers using Cold Fusion.

FIGURE 18

FTP settings specified in the Site Definition for The Striped Umbrella dialog box

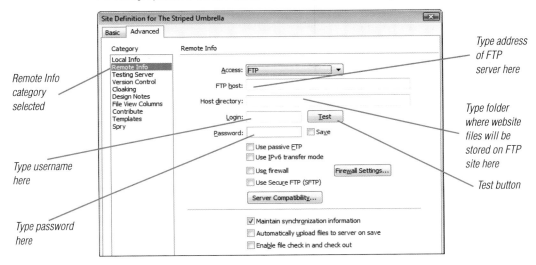

Remote Info category selected

Type username here

Type password here

Type address of FTP server here

Type folder where website files will be stored on FTP site here

Test button

Comparing two files for differences in content

There are situations where it would be helpful to be able to compare the contents of two files, such as a local file and the remote version of the same file; or an original file and the same file that has been saved with a different name. Once the two files are compared and differences are detected, you can merge the information in the files. A good time to compare files is before you upload them to a remote server to prevent accidentally writing over a file with more recent information. To compare files, you must first locate and install a third-party file comparison utility, or "dif" tool, such as Araxis Merge or Beyond Compare. (Dreamweaver does not have a file comparison tool included as part of the software. You will have to download one. If you are not familiar with these tools, find one using your favorite search engine.)

After installing the files comparison utility, use the Preferences command on the Edit menu, and then select the File Compare category. Next, browse to select the application to compare files. After you have set your Preferences, click the Compare with Remote command on the File menu to compare an open file with the remote version.

Set up web server access on an FTP site

NOTE: Complete these steps only if you know you can store The Striped Umbrella files on an FTP site and you know the login and password information. If you do not have access to an FTP site, complete the exercise called Set up web server access on a local or network folder on Page 6-18.

1. Click **Site** on the Application bar (Win) or Menu bar (Mac), then click **Manage Sites**.

2. Click **The Striped Umbrella** in the Manage Sites dialog box (if necessary), then click **Edit**.

3. Click the **Advanced tab**, click **Remote Info** in the Category list, click the **Access list arrow**, click **FTP**, then compare your screen to Figure 18.

4. Enter the FTP host, Host directory, Login, and Password information in the dialog box.

   TIP   You must have file and folder permissions to use FTP. The server administrator will also tell you the folder name and location to use to publish your files.

5. Click the **Test button** to test the connection to the remote site.

6. If the connection is successful, click **Done** to close the dialog box; if it is not successful, verify that you have the correct settings, then repeat Step 4.

7. Click **OK**, click **OK** to restore the cache, then click **Done** to close the Manage Sites dialog box.

You set up remote access information for The Striped Umbrella website using FTP settings.

Set up web server access on a local or network folder

NOTE: Complete these steps if you do not have the ability to post files to an FTP site and could not complete the previous lesson.

1. Using Windows Explorer (Win) or Finder (Mac), create a new folder on your hard drive or on a shared drive named **su_yourlastname** (e.g., if your last name is Jones, name the folder **su_jones**.)

2. Switch back to Dreamweaver, open The Striped Umbrella website, then open the Manage Sites dialog box.

   TIP You can also double-click the site name in the Site Name list box in the Files panel to open the Advanced tab in the Site Definition dialog box.

3. Click **The Striped Umbrella**, click **Edit** to open the Site Definition for The Striped Umbrella dialog box, click the **Advanced tab**, then click **Remote Info** in the Category list.

4. Click the **Access list arrow**, then click **Local/Network**.

5. Click the **Browse for File icon** ☐ next to the Remote folder text box to open the Choose remote root folder for site The Striped Umbrella dialog box, navigate to the folder you created in Step 1, select the folder, click **Open**, then click **Select** (Win) or **Choose** (Mac).

6. Compare your screen to Figure 19, click **OK**, click **OK** in the message window about the site cache, then click **Done**.

You created a new folder and specified it as the remote location for The Striped Umbrella website, then set up remote access to a local or network folder.

FIGURE 19

Local/Network settings specified in the Site Definition for The Striped Umbrella dialog box

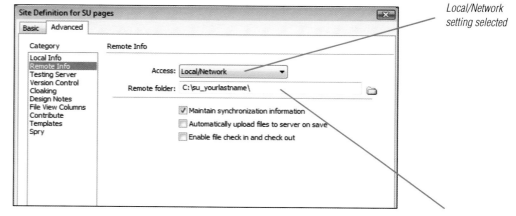

Local/Network setting selected

Local or network drive and folder where remote site will be published (your folder name should end with your last name)

FIGURE 20

Connecting to the remote site

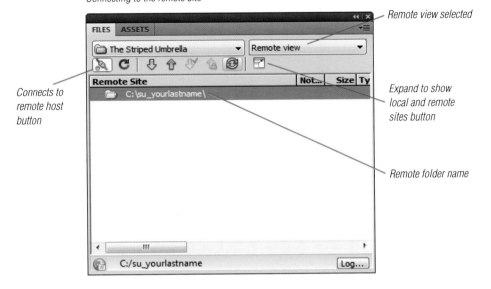

Remote view selected

Connects to remote host button

Expand to show local and remote sites button

Remote folder name

View a website on a remote server

1. Click the **View list arrow** in the Files panel, then click **Remote view**, as shown in Figure 20.

   If you specified your remote access to a local or network folder, then the su_yourlastname folder will now appear in the Files panel. If your remote access is set to an FTP site, Dreamweaver will connect to the host server to see the remote access folder.

2. Click the **Expand to show local and remote sites button** to view both the Remote Site and Local Files panes. The su_yourlast-name folder appears in the Remote Site portion of the expanded Files panel.

   TIP If you don't see your remote site files, click the Connects to remote host button or the Refresh button If you don't see two panes, one with the remote site files and one with the local files, drag the panel border to enlarge the panel.

You used the Files panel to set the view for The Striped Umbrella site to Remote view. You then connected to the remote server to view the contents of the remote folder you specified.

Using a site usability test to test your site

Once you have at least a prototype of the website ready to evaluate, it is a good idea to conduct a site usability test. This is a process that involves asking unbiased people, who are not connected to the design process, to use and evaluate the site. A comprehensive usability test will include pre-test questions, participant tasks, a post-test interview, and a post-test survey. This will provide much-needed information as to how usable the site is to those unfamiliar with it. Typical questions include: "What are your overall impressions?"; "What do you like the best and the least about the site?"; and "How easy is it to navigate inside the site?" For more information, go to www.w3.org and search for "site usability test."

Upload files to a remote server

1. Click the **about_us.html file**, then click the **Put File(s) button** ⬆ on the Files panel toolbar.

   The Dependent Files dialog box opens, asking if you want to include dependent files.

2. Click **Yes**.

   The about_us file, the style sheet file, and the image files used in the about_us page are copied to the remote server. The Background File Activity dialog box appears and flashes the names of each file as they are uploaded.

3. Expand the assets folder in the remote site (if necessary), then compare your screen to Figure 21.

   The remote site now contains the about_us page as well as the images on that page, and the striped_umbrella external style sheet file, all of which are needed by the about_us page.

   TIP   You might need to expand the su_yourlastname folder in order to view the assets folder.

You used the Put File(s) button to upload the about_us file and all files that are dependent files of the about_us page.

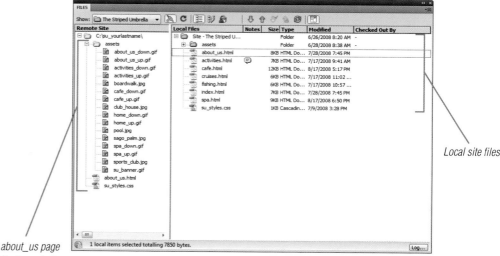

FIGURE 21
Remote view of the site after uploading the about_us page

Local site files

The about_us page and its dependent files in remote site

Continuing to work while transferring files to a remote server

During the process of uploading files to a remote server, there are many Dreamweaver functions that you can continue to use while you wait. For example, you can create a new site, create a new page, edit a page, add files and folders, and run reports. However, there are some functions that you cannot use while transferring files, many of which involve accessing files on the remote server or using Check In/Check Out.

FIGURE 22
Synchronize Files dialog box

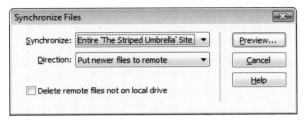

FIGURE 23
Files that need to be uploaded to the remote site

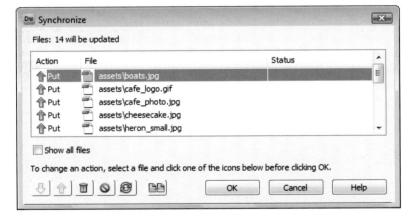

Synchronize files

1. Click the **Synchronize button** 🖲 on the Files panel toolbar to open the Synchronize Files dialog box.

2. Click the **Synchronize list arrow**, then click **Entire 'The Striped Umbrella' Site**.

3. Click the **Direction list arrow**, click **Put newer files to remote** (if necessary), then compare your screen to Figure 22.

4. Click **Preview**.

   The Background File Activity dialog box might appear and flash the names of all the files from the local version of the site that need to be uploaded to the remote site. The Synchronize dialog box shown in Figure 23 then opens and lists all the files that need to be uploaded to the remote site.

5. Click **OK**.

   All the files from the local The Striped Umbrella site are now contained in the remote version of the site. Notice that the remote folders are yellow and the local folders are green.

You synchronized The Striped Umbrella website files to copy all remaining files from the local root folder to the remote root folder.

CHECK FILES
OUT AND IN

What You'll Do

In this lesson, you will use the Site Definition dialog box to enable the Check In/Check Out feature. You will then check out the cafe page, make a change to it, and then check it back in.

Managing a Website with a Team

When you work on a large website, chances are that many people will be involved in keeping the site up to date. Different individuals will need to make changes or additions to different pages of the site by adding or deleting content, changing graphics, updating information, and so on. If everyone had access to the pages at the same time, problems could arise. For instance, what if you and another team member both made edits to the same page at the same time? If you post your edited version of the file to the site after the other team member posts his edited version of the same file, the file that you upload will overwrite his version and none of his changes will be incorporated.

Not good! Fortunately, you can avoid this scenario by using Dreamweaver's collaboration tools.

Checking Out and Checking In Files

Checking files in and out is similar to checking library books in and out or video/DVD rentals. No one else can read the same copy that you have checked out. Using Dreamweaver's Check In/Check Out feature ensures that team members cannot overwrite each other's pages. When this feature is enabled, only one person can work on a file at a time. To check out a file, click the file you want to work on in the Files panel, and then click the Check Out File(s) button on the Files panel toolbar. Files that you have checked out are marked with green check marks in the Files panel. Files that have been checked in are marked with padlock icons.

After you finish editing a checked-out file, you need to save and close the file, and then click the Check In button to check the file back in and make it available to other users. When a file is checked in, you cannot make edits to it unless you check it out again. Figure 24 shows the Check Out File(s) and Check In buttons on the Files panel toolbar.

Enabling the Check In/Check Out Feature

To use the Check In/Check Out feature with a team of people, you must first enable it. To turn on this feature, check the Enable file check in and check out check box in the Remote Info settings of the Site Definition dialog box.

Check Out
File(s) button   Check In button

FIGURE 24

Check Out File(s) and Check In buttons on the Files Panel toolbar

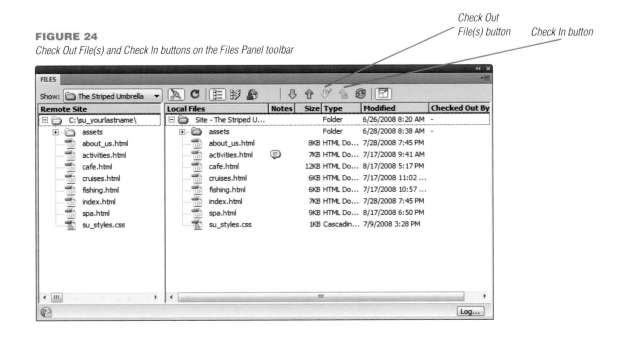

Enable the Check In/Check Out feature

1. Verify that the Site panel is in expanded view, click **Site** on the menu bar, click **Manage Sites** to open the Manage Sites dialog box, click **The Striped Umbrella** in the list, then click **Edit** to open the Site Definition for The Striped Umbrella dialog box.

2. Click **Remote Info** in the Category list, then click the **Enable file check in and check out check box** to select it.

3. Check the **Check out files when opening check box** to select it (if necessary).

4. Type your name using all lowercase letters and no spaces in the Check out name text box.

5. Type your email address in the Email address text box.

6. Compare your screen to Figure 25, click **OK** to close the Site Definition for The Striped Umbrella dialog box, then click **Done** to close the Manage Sites dialog box. Your dialog box will look different if you are using FTP access.

You used the Site Definition for The Striped Umbrella dialog box to enable the Check In/Check Out feature to let team members know when you are working with a file in the site.

Check out a file

1. Click the **cafe page** in the Local Files list in the Files panel to select it.

(continued)

FIGURE 25
Enabling the Check In/Check Out feature

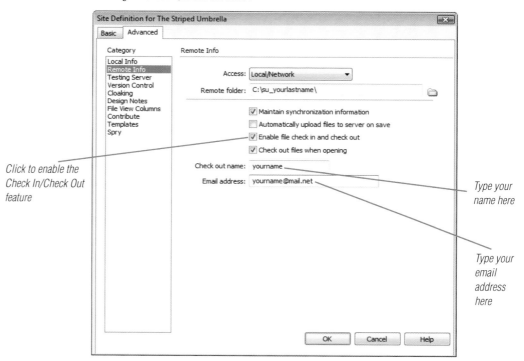

Click to enable the Check In/Check Out feature

Type your name here

Type your email address here

FIGURE 26

Files panel in Local view after checking out cafe page

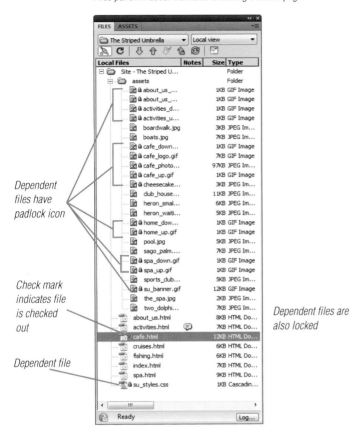

Dependent files have padlock icon

Check mark indicates file is checked out

Dependent file

FIGURE 27

Files panel after checking in cafe page

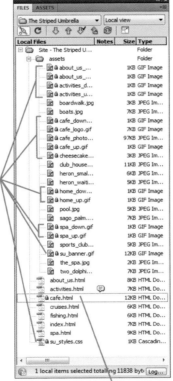

Dependent files are also locked

Padlock icon indicates file is read-only and cannot be edited unless it is checked out

2. Click the **Check Out File(s) button** on the Files panel toolbar.

   The Dependent Files dialog box appears, asking if you want to include all files that are needed for the cafe page.

3. Click **Yes**, expand the assets folder if necessary, collapse the Files panel, click the **View list arrow**, click **Local view**, then compare your screen to Figure 26.

   The cafe file has a check mark next to it indicating you have checked it out. The dependent files have a padlock icon.

   TIP If a dialog box appears asking "Do you wish to overwrite your local copy of cafe.html?", click Yes.

You checked out the cafe page so that no one else can use it while you work on it.

Check in a file

1. Open the cafe page, change the closing hour for the The Cabana in the table to **7:00 p.m.**, then save your changes.

2. Close the cafe page, then click the **cafe page** in the Files panel to select it.

3. Click the **Check In button** on the Files panel toolbar.

   The Dependent Files dialog box opens, asking if you want to include dependent files.

4. Click **Yes**, click another file in the Files panel to deselect the cafe page, then compare your screen to Figure 27.

   A padlock icon appears instead of a green check mark next to the cafe page on the Files panel.

You made a content change on the cafe page, then checked in the cafe page, making it available for others to check it out.

CLOAK
FILES

What You'll Do

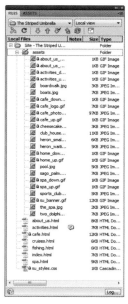

 In this lesson, you will cloak the assets folder so that it is excluded from various operations, such as the Put, Get, Check In, and Check Out commands. You will also use the Site Definition dialog box to cloak all .gif files in the site.

Understanding Cloaking Files

There may be times when you want to exclude a particular file or files from being uploaded to a server. For instance, suppose you have a page that is not quite finished and needs more work before it is ready to be viewed by others. You can exclude such files by **cloaking** them, which marks them for exclusion from several commands, including Put, Get, Synchronize, Check In, and Check Out. Cloaked files are also excluded from site-wide operations, such as checking for links or updating a template or library item. You can cloak a folder or specify a type of file to cloak throughout the site.

QUICKTIP

By default, the cloaking feature is enabled. However, if for some reason it is not turned on, open the Site Definition dialog box, click the Advanced tab, click the Cloaking category, then click the Enable cloaking check box.

Cloaking a Folder

There may be times when you want to cloak an entire folder. For instance, if you are not concerned with replacing outdated image files, you might want to cloak the assets folder of a website to save time when synchronizing files. To cloak a folder, select the folder, click the Options menu button in the Files panel, point to Site, point to Cloaking, and then click Cloak. The folder you cloaked and all the files it contains appear with red slashes across them, as shown in Figure 28. To uncloak a folder, click the Options menu button on the Files panel, point to Site, point to Cloaking, and then click Uncloak.

QUICKTIP

To uncloak all files in a site, click the Files panel Options menu button, point to Site, point to Cloaking, then click Uncloak All.

Cloaking Selected File Types

There may be times when you want to cloak a particular type of file, such as a .jpg file. To cloak a particular file type, open the Site Definition dialog box, click the Cloaking category, click the Cloak files ending with check box, and then type a file extension in the text box below the check box. All files throughout the site that have the specified file extension will be cloaked.

FIGURE 28
Cloaked assets folder in the Files panel

Options menu button

Red slash indicates folder is cloaked

Cloaked files

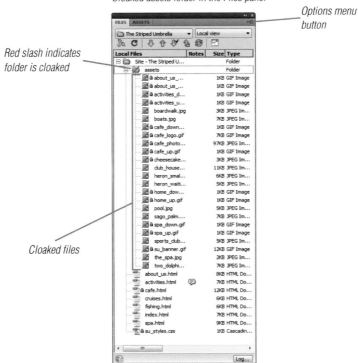

Cloak and uncloak a folder

1. Verify that Local view is displayed in the Files panel, then open the Manage Sites dialog box.

2. Click **The Striped Umbrella** (if necessary), click **Edit** to open the Site Definition for The Striped Umbrella dialog box, click **Cloaking** in the Category list, verify that the Enable cloaking check box is checked, click **OK**, then click **Done**.

3. Click the **assets folder** in the Files panel, click the **Options menu button**, point to **Site**, point to **Cloaking**, click **Cloak**, then compare your screen to Figure 29.

   A red slash now appears on top of the assets folder in the Files panel, indicating that all files in the assets folder are cloaked and will be excluded from putting, getting, checking in, checking out, and many other operations.

   | TIP   You can also cloak a folder by right-clicking (Win) or [control]-clicking (Mac) the folder, pointing to Cloaking, then clicking Cloak.

4. Right-click (Win) or [control]-click (Mac) the **assets folder**, point to **Cloaking**, then click **Uncloak**.

   The assets folder and all the files it contains no longer appear with red slashes across them, indicating they are no longer cloaked.

You cloaked the assets folder so that this folder and all the files it contains would be excluded from many operations, including uploading and downloading files. You then uncloaked the assets folder.

FIGURE 29
Assets folder after cloaking

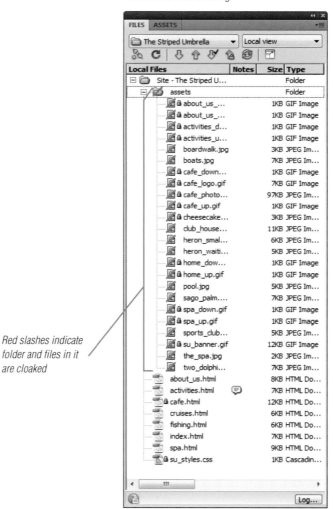

Red slashes indicate folder and files in it are cloaked

FIGURE 30
Specifying a file type to cloak

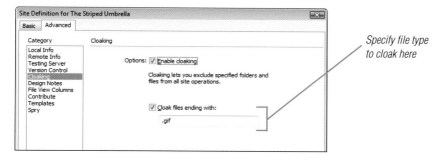

Specify file type
to cloak here

FIGURE 31
Assets folder in Files panel after cloaking .gif files

Assets folder
is not cloaked

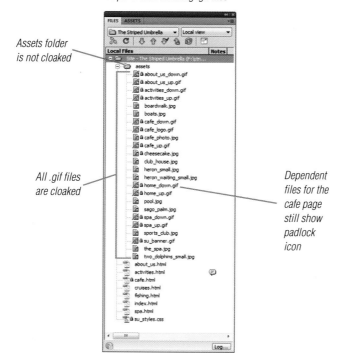

All .gif files
are cloaked

Dependent
files for the
cafe page
still show
padlock
icon

Cloak selected file types

1. Right-click (Win) or [control]-click (Mac) the **assets folder** in the Files panel, point to **Cloaking**, then click **Settings** to open the Site Definition for The Striped Umbrella dialog box with the Cloaking category selected.

2. Click the **Cloak files ending with check box**, select the text in the text box that appears, type **.gif** in the text box, then compare your screen to Figure 30.

3. Click **OK**.

   A dialog box opens, indicating that the site cache will be re-created.

4. Click **OK**, expand the assets folder (if necessary), then compare your screen to Figure 31.

   All of the .gif files in the assets folder appear with red slashes across them, indicating that they are cloaked. Notice that the assets folder is not cloaked.

You cloaked all the .gif files in The Striped Umbrella website.

IMPORT AND EXPORT
A SITE DEFINITION

What You'll Do

In this lesson, you will export the site definition file for The Striped Umbrella website. You will then import The Striped Umbrella website.

Exporting a Site Definition

When you work on a website for a long time, it's likely that at some point you will want to move it to another machine or share it with other collaborators who will help you maintain it. The site definition for a website contains important information about the site, including its URL, preferences that you've specified, and other secure information, such as login and password information. You can use the Export command to export the site definition file to another location. To do this, open the Manage Sites dialog box, click the site you want to export, and then click Export. Because the site definition file contains password information that you will want to keep secret from other site users, you should never save the site definition file in the website. Instead, save it in an external folder.

Importing a Site Definition

If you want to set up another user with a copy of your website, you can import the site definition file. To do this, click Import in the Manage Sites dialog box to open the Import Site dialog box, navigate to the .ste file you want to import, then click Open.

FIGURE 32

Saving The Striped Umbrella.ste file in the su_site_definition folder

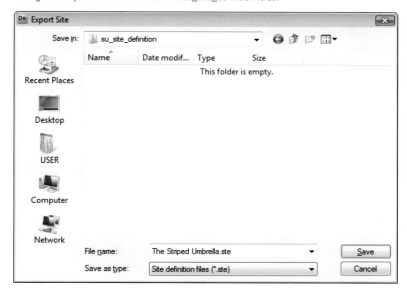

1. Use Windows Explorer (Win) or Finder (Mac) to create a new folder on your hard drive or external drive named **su_site_definition**.

2. Switch back to Dreamweaver, open the Manage Sites dialog box, click **The Striped Umbrella**, then click **Export** to open the Export Site dialog box. If you see a message asking if you are exporting the site to back up your settings or to share your settings with other users, choose the Back up my settings option, then click **OK**.

3. Navigate to and double-click to open the **su_site_definition folder** that you created in Step 1, as shown in Figure 32, click **Save**, then click **Done**.

You used the Export command to create the site definition file and saved it in the su_site_definition folder.

Import a site definition

1. Open the Manage Sites dialog box, click **The Striped Umbrella**, then click **Import** to open the Import Site dialog box.

2. Navigate to the su_site_definition folder, compare your screen to Figure 33, select **The Striped Umbrella.ste**, then click **Open**.

   A dialog box opens and says that a site named The Striped Umbrella already exists. It will name the imported site The Striped Umbrella 2 so that it has a different name.

3. Click **OK**.

4. Click **The Striped Umbrella 2** (if necessary), click **Edit**, then compare your screen to Figure 34.

   The settings show that the The Striped Umbrella 2 site has the same root folder and default images folder as the The Striped Umbrella site. Both of these settings are specified in the The Striped Umbrella.ste file that you imported. Importing a site in this way makes it possible for multiple users with different computers to work on the same site.

   TIP   Make sure you know who is responsible for which files to keep from overwriting the wrong files when they are published. The Synchronize Files and Check In/Check Out features are good procedures to use with multiple designers.

5. Click **OK**, click **OK** to close the warning message, then click **Done**.

   TIP   If a dialog box opens warning that the root folder chosen is the same as the folder for the site "The Striped Umbrella," click OK.

You imported The Striped Umbrella.ste file and created a new site, The Striped Umbrella 2.

FIGURE 33
Import Site dialog box

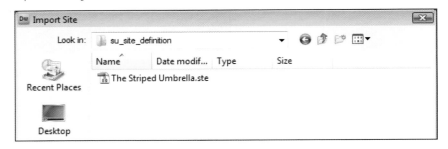

FIGURE 34
Site Definition for the The Striped Umbrella 2 dialog box

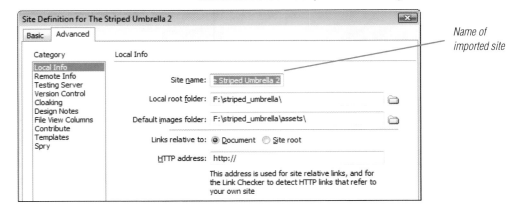

Name of imported site

FIGURE 35

Viewing The Striped Umbrella 2 website files

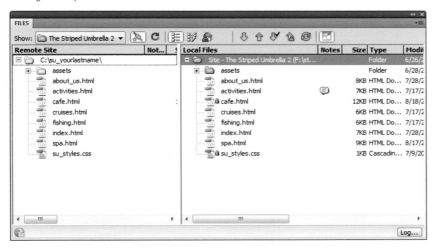

1. Click the **Expand to show local and remote sites button** 🔲 on the Files panel toolbar to expand the Files panel.

2. Expand the Site root folder to view the contents (if necessary).

3. Click the **Refresh button** 🔃 to view the files in the Remote Site pane.

   As shown in Figure 35, the site looks identical to the original The Striped Umbrella site, except the name has been changed to The Striped Umbrella 2.

   > TIP If you don't see your remote site files, click the Connects to remote host button.

4. Click the **Collapse to show only local or remote site button** 🔲 to collapse the Files panel.

5. Open the Manage Sites dialog box, verify that The Striped Umbrella 2 site is selected, click **Remove**, click **Yes** to clear the warning dialog box, then click **Done** to delete The Striped Umbrella 2 website.

6. Close all open pages, then close Dreamweaver.

You viewed the expanded Files panel for The Striped Umbrella 2 website and then deleted The Striped Umbrella 2 website.

POWER USER SHORTCUTS

to do this:	use this shortcut:
Validate Markup	[Shift][F6]
Get	[Ctrl][Shift][D] (Win) or ⌘ [Shift][D] (Mac)
Check Out	[Ctrl][Alt][Shift][D] (Win) or ⌘ [option][Shift][D] (Mac)
Put	[Ctrl][Shift][U] (Win) or ⌘ [Shift][U] (Mac)
Check In	[Ctrl][Alt][Shift][U] (Win) or ⌘ [option][Shift][U] (Mac)
Check Links	[Shift][F8]
Check Links Sitewide	[Ctrl][F8] (Win) or ⌘ [F8] (Mac)

EVALUATE WEB CONTENT FOR
LEGAL USE

What You'll Do

In this lesson, you will examine copyright issues in the context of using content gathered from sources such as the Internet.

Can I Use Downloaded Media?

The Internet has made it possible to locate compelling and media-rich content to use in websites. A person who has learned to craft searches can locate a multitude of interesting material, such as graphics, animations, sounds, and text. But just because you can find it easily does not mean that you can use it however you want or under any circumstance. Learning about copyright law can help you decide whether or how to use content created and published by someone other than yourself.

Understanding Intellectual Property

Intellectual property is a product resulting from human creativity. It can include inventions, movies, songs, designs, clothing, and so on.

The purpose of copyright law is to promote progress in society, not expressly to protect the rights of copyright owners. However, the vast majority of work you might want to download and use in a

project is protected by either copyright or trademark law.

Copyright protects the particular and tangible *expression* of an idea, not the idea itself. If you wrote a story using the idea of aliens crashing in Roswell, New Mexico, no one could copy or use your story without permission. However, anyone could write a story using a similar plot or characters— the *idea* of aliens crashing in Roswell is not copyright-protected. Generally, copyright lasts for the life of the author plus 70 years.

Trademark protects an image, word, slogan, symbol, or design used to identify goods or services. For example, the Nike swoosh, Disney characters, or the shape of a classic Coca-Cola bottle are works protected by trademark. Trademark protection lasts for 10 years with 10-year renewal terms, lasting indefinitely provided the trademark is in active use.

What Exactly Does the Copyright Owner Own?

Copyright attaches to a work as soon as you create it; you do not have to register it with the U.S. Copyright Office. A copyright owner has a "bundle" of six rights, consisting of:

1) reproduction (including downloading)
2) creation of **derivative works** (for example, a movie version of a book)
3) distribution to the public
4) public performance
5) public display
6) public performance by digital audio transmission of sound recordings

By default, only a copyright holder can create a derivative work of his or her original by transforming or adapting it.

Understanding Fair Use

The law builds in limitations to copyright protection. One limitation to copyright is **fair use**. Fair use allows limited use of copyright-protected work. For example, you could excerpt short passages of a film or song for a class project or parody a television show. Determining if fair use applies to a work depends on the *purpose* of its use, the *nature* of the copyrighted work, *how much* you want to copy, and the *effect* on the market or value of the work. However, there is no clear formula on what constitutes fair use. It is always decided on a case-by-case basis.

How Do I Use Work Properly?

Being a student doesn't mean you can use any amount of any work for class.

On the other hand, the very nature of education means you need to be able to use or reference different work in your studies. There are many situations that allow you to use protected work.

In addition to applying a fair use argument, you can obtain permission, pay a fee, use work that does not have copyright protection, or use work that has a flexible copyright license, where the owner has given the public permission to use the work in certain ways. For more information about open-access licensing, visit www.creativecommons.org. Work that is no longer protected by copyright is in the **public domain**; anyone can use it however

they wish for any purpose. In general, the photos and other media on federal government websites are in the public domain.

Understanding Licensing Agreements

Before you decide whether to use media you find on a website, you must decide whether you can comply with its licensing agreement. A **licensing agreement** is the permission given by a copyright holder that conveys the right to use the copyright holder's work under certain conditions.

Websites have rules that govern how a user may use its text and media, known as **terms of use**. Figures 36, 37, and 38 are great

FIGURE 36
The Library of Congress home page

Link to legal information regarding the use of content on the website

Library of Congress website – www.loc.gov

examples of clear terms of use for the Library of Congress website.

A site's terms of use do not override your right to apply fair use. Also, someone cannot compile public domain images in a website and then claim they own them or dictate how the images can be used. Conversely, someone can erroneously state in their terms of use that you can use work on the site freely, but they may not know the work's copyright status. The burden is on you to research the veracity of anyone claiming you can use work.

Obtaining Permission or a License

The **permissions process** is specific to what you want to use (text, photographs, music, trademarks, merchandise, and so on) and how you want to use it (school term paper, personal website, fabric pattern). How you want to use the work will determine the level and scope of permissions you need to secure. The fundamentals, however, are the same. Your request should contain the following:

- Your full name, address, and complete contact information.
- A specific description of your

intended use. Sometimes including a sketch, storyboard, or link to a website is helpful.

- A signature line for the copyright holder.
- A target date when you would like the copyright holder to respond. This can be important if you're working under deadline.

Posting a Copyright Notice

The familiar © symbol or "Copyright" is no longer required to indicate copyright, nor does it automatically register your work,

FIGURE 37
Library of Congress website legal page

Library of Congress website – www.loc.gov

FIGURE 38
Library of Congress website copyright page

About Copyright and the Collections

Whenever possible, the Library of Congress provides factual information about copyright owners and related matters in the catalog records, finding aids and other texts that accompany collections. As a publicly supported institution, the Library generally does not own rights in its collections. Therefore, it does not charge permission fees for use of such material and generally does not grant or deny permission to publish or otherwise distribute material in its collections. Permission and possible fees may be required from the copyright owner independently of the Library. It is the researcher's obligation to determine and satisfy copyright or other use restrictions when publishing or otherwise distributing materials found in the Library's collections. Transmission or reproduction of protected items beyond that allowed by fair use requires the written permission of the copyright owners. Researchers must make their own assessments of rights in light of their intended use.

If you have any more information about an item you've seen on our website or if you are the copyright owner and believe our website has not properly attributed your work to you or has used it without permission, we want to hear from you. Please contact OGC@loc.gov with your contact information and a link to the relevant content.

but it does serve a useful purpose. When you post or publish it, you are stating clearly to those who may not know anything about copyright law that this work is claimed by you and is not in the public domain. Your case is made even stronger if someone violates your copyright and your notice is clearly visible. That way, violator can never claim ignorance of the law as an excuse for infringing. Common notification styles include:

Copyright 2013
Delmar, Cengage Learning
or
© 2013 Delmar, Cengage Learning

Giving proper attribution for text excerpts is a must; giving attribution for media is excellent practice, but is never a substitute for applying a fair use argument, buying a license, or simply getting permission.

You must provide proper citation for materials you incorporate into your own work, such as the following:

References
Waxer, Barbara M., and Baum, Marsha L. 2006. *Internet Surf and Turf – The Essential Guide to Copyright, Fair Use, and Finding Media.* Boston: Thomson Course Technology.

This expectation applies even to unsigned material and material that does not display the copyright symbol (©). Moreover, the expectation applies just as certainly to ideas you summarize or paraphrase as to words you quote verbatim.

Guidelines have been written by the American Psychological Association (APA) to establish an editorial style to be used to present written material. These guidelines include the way citations are referenced.

Here's a list of the elements that make up an APA-style citation of web-based resources:
- Author's name (if known)
- Date of publication or last revision (if known), in parentheses
- Title of document
- Title of complete work or website (if applicable), underlined
- URL, in angled brackets
- Date of access, in parentheses

Following is an example of how you'd reference the APA Home page on the Reference page of your paper:

APA Style.org. Retrieved August 22, 2012, from APA Online website: http://www.apastyle.org/electext.html

Another set of guidelines used by many schools and university and commercial presses is the Modern Language Association (MLA) style. For more information, go to http://www.mla.org.

Perform website maintenance.

1. Open the blooms & bulbs website, then re-create the site cache.
2. Use the Link Checker panel to check for broken links, then fix any broken links that appear.
3. Use the Link Checker to check for orphaned files. If any orphaned files appear in the report, take steps to link them to appropriate pages or remove them.
4. Use the Assets panel to check for non-web-safe colors. (*Hint*: If you do see any non-web-safe colors, recreate the site cache again, then refresh the Assets panel.)
5. Run an Untitled Documents report for the entire local site. If the report lists any pages that have no titles, add page titles to the untitled pages. Run the report again to verify that all pages have page titles.
6. Run a report to look for missing alternate text. Add alternate text to any graphics that need it, then run the report again to verify that all images contain alternate text.
7. Enable the Design Notes preference and add a Design Note to the classes page as follows: **Shoot a video of the hanging baskets class to add to the page**. Add the status **needs attention** and check the Show when file is opened option.

Publish a website and transfer files.

1. Set up web server access for the blooms & bulbs website on an FTP server or a local/network server (whichever is available to you) using blooms_yourlastname as the remote folder name.
2. View the blooms & bulbs remote site in the Files panel.
3. Upload the iris.jpg file to the remote site, then view the remote site.
4. Synchronize all files in the blooms & bulbs website, so that all files from the local site are uploaded to the remote site.

Check files out and in.

1. Enable the Check In/Check Out feature.
2. Check out the plants page and all dependent pages.
3. Open the plants page, then change the heading style of "Drop by to see our Featured Spring Plants" to bold_blue, then save the file.
4. Check in the plants page and all dependent files.

Cloak files.

1. Verify that cloaking is enabled in the blooms & bulbs website.
2. Cloak the assets folder, then uncloak it.
3. Cloak all the .jpg files in the blooms & bulbs website.

Import and export a site definition.

1. Create a new folder named **blooms_site_ definition** on your hard drive or external drive.

2. Export the blooms & bulbs site definition to the blooms_site_definition folder.

3. Import the blooms & bulbs site definition to create a new site called **blooms & bulbs 2**.

4. Make sure that all files from the blooms & bulbs website appear in the Files panel for the imported site, then compare your screen to Figure 39.

5. Remove the blooms & bulbs 2 site.

6. Close all open files.

FIGURE 39
Completed Skills Review

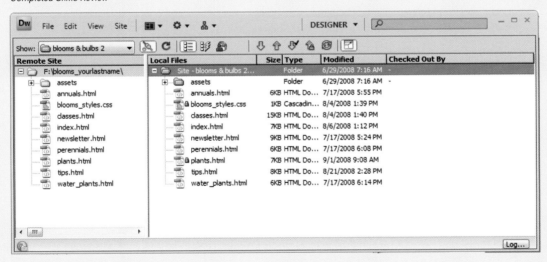

In this Project Builder, you will publish the TripSmart website that you have developed throughout this book to a local/network folder. Mike Andrew, the owner, has asked that you publish the site to a local folder as a backup location. You will first run several reports on the site, specify the remote settings for the site, upload files to the remote site, check files out and in, and cloak files. Finally, you will export and import the site definition.

1. Use the TripSmart website that you began in Project Builder 1 in Chapter 1 and developed in previous chapters.

2. Use the Link Checker panel to check for broken links, then fix any broken links that appear.

3. Use the Link Checker to check for orphaned files. If any orphaned files appear in the report, take steps to link them to appropriate pages or remove them.

4. Use the Assets panel to check for non-web-safe colors.

5. Run an Untitled Documents report for the entire local site. If the report lists any pages that lack titles, add page titles to the untitled pages. Run the report again to verify that all pages have page titles.

6. Run a report to look for missing alternate text. Add alternate text to any graphics that need it, then run the report again to verify that all images contain alternate text.

7. Enable the Design Notes preference, if necessary, and add a design note to the newsletter page as follows: **Add a Flash video showing the river route**. Add the status **needs attention** and check the Show when file is opened option.

8. If you did not do so in Project Builder 1 in Chapter 1, use the Site Definition dialog box to set up web server access for a remote site using a local or network folder.

9. Upload the index page and all dependent files to the remote site.

10. View the remote site to make sure that all files uploaded correctly.

11. Synchronize the files so that all other files on the local TripSmart site are uploaded to the remote site.

12. Enable the Check In/Check Out feature.

13. Check out the index page in the local site and all dependent files.

14. Open the index page, close the index page, then check in the index page and all dependent pages.

15. Cloak all .jpg files in the website.

16. Export the site definition to a new folder named **tripsmart_site_definition**.

17. Import the TripSmart.ste file to create a new site named TripSmart 2.

18. Expand the assets folder in the Files panel (if necessary), then compare your screen to Figure 40.

19. Remove the TripSmart 2 site.

20. Close any open files.

FIGURE 40
Sample Project Builder 1

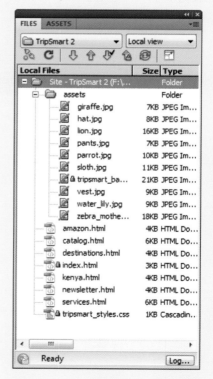

In this Project Builder, you will finish your work on the Carolyne's Creations website. You are ready to publish the website to a remote server and transfer all the files from the local site to the remote site. First, you will run several reports to make sure the website is in good shape. Next, you will enable the Check In/Check Out feature so that other staff members may collaborate on the site. Finally, you will export and import the site definition file.

1. Use the Carolyne's Creations website that you began in Project Builder 1 in Chapter 1 and developed in previous chapters.

2. If you did not do so in Project Builder 2 in Chapter 1, use the Site Definition dialog box to set up web server access for a remote site using either an FTP site or a local or network folder.

3. Run reports for broken links and orphaned files, correcting any errors that you find. The cc_banner.jpg file is no longer needed, so delete the file.

4. Run reports for untitled documents and missing alt text, correcting any errors that you find.

5. Check for non-web-safe colors.

6. Upload the classes.html page and all dependent files to the remote site.

7. View the remote site to make sure that all files uploaded correctly.

8. Synchronize the files so that all other files on the local Carolyne's Creations site are uploaded to the remote site.

9. Enable the Check In/Check Out feature.

10. Check out the classes page and all its dependent files.

11. Open the classes page, then change the price of the adult class to **$45.00**.

12. Save your changes, close the page, then check in the classes page and all dependent pages.

13. Export the site definition to a new folder named **cc_site_definition**.

14. Import the Carolyne's Creations.ste file to create a new site named Carolyne's Creations 2.

15. Expand the root folder in the Files panel (if necessary), compare your screen to Figure 41, then remove the Carolyne's Creations2 site.

FIGURE 41
Completed Project Builder 2

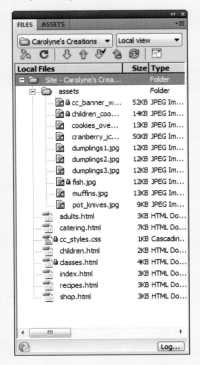

Throughout this book you have used Dreamweaver to create and develop several websites that contain different elements, many of which are found in popular commercial websites. For instance, Figure 42 shows the National Park Service website, which contains photos and information on all the national parks in the United States. This website contains many types of interactive elements, such as image maps and tables—all of which you learned to create in this book.

1. Connect to the Internet, then go to the National Park Service website at www.nps.gov.
2. Spend some time exploring the pages of this site to familiarize yourself with its elements.
3. Type a list of all the elements in this site that you have learned how to create in this book. After each item, write a short description of where and how the element is used in the site.
4. Print the home page and one or two other pages that contain some of the elements you described and attach it to your list.

FIGURE 42
Design Project

National Park Service website – www.nps.gov

In this project, you will finish your work on the website that you created and developed throughout this book.

You will publish your site to a remote server or local or network folder.

1. Before you begin the process of publishing your website to a remote server, make sure that it is ready for public viewing. Use Figure 43 to assist you in making sure your website is complete. If you find problems, make the necessary changes to finalize the site.

2. Decide where to publish your site. The folder where you will publish your site can be either an FTP site or a local/network folder. If you are publishing to an FTP site, be sure to write down all the information you will need to publish to the site, including the URL of the FTP host, the directory on the FTP server where you will publish your site's root folder, and the login and password information.

3. Use the Site Definition dialog box to specify the remote settings for the site using the information that was decided upon in Step 2.

4. Transfer one of the pages and its dependent files to the remote site, then view the remote site to make sure the appropriate files were transferred.

5. Synchronize the files so that all the remaining local pages and dependent files are uploaded to the remote site.

6. Enable the Check In/Check Out feature.

7. Check out one of the pages. Open the checked-out page, make a change to it, save the change, close the page, then check the page back in.

8. Cloak a particular file type.

9. Export the site definition for the site to a new folder on your hard drive or on an external drive.

10. Import the site to create a new version of the site.

11. Close the imported site, save and close all open pages (if necessary), then exit Dreamweaver.

FIGURE 43
Portfolio Project checklist

Website Checklist

1. Are you satisfied with the content and appearance of every page?
2. Are all paths for all links and images correct?
3. Does each page have a title?
4. Do all images appear?
5. Are all colors web-safe?
6. Do all images have appropriate alternate text?
7. Have you eliminated any orphaned files?
8. Have you deleted any unnecessary files?
9. Have you viewed all pages using at least two different browsers?
10. Does the home page have keywords and a description?

GETTING STARTED WITH
ADOBE FLASH CS4

1. Understand the Adobe Flash CS4 workspace

2. Open a document and play a movie

3. Create and save a movie

4. Work with the Timeline

5. Distribute an Adobe Flash movie

6. Plan an application or a website

Introduction

Adobe Flash CS4 Professional is a development tool that allows you to create compelling interactive experiences, often by using animation. You can use Flash to create entire websites, including e-commerce, entertainment, education, and personal use sites. In addition, Flash is an excellent program for developing animations that are used in websites, such as product demonstrations, banner ads, online tutorials, and electronic greeting cards. Also, Flash can be used to create applications, such as games and simulations, that can be delivered over the web and on DVDs. These applications can even be scaled to be displayed on mobile devices, such as cell phones. While it is known as a tool for creating complex animations for the web, Flash also has excellent drawing tools and tools for creating interactive controls, such as navigation buttons and menus. Furthermore, Flash provides the ability to incorporate sounds and video easily into an application.

Flash has become the standard for both professional and casual applications as well as for web developers. Flash is popular because the program is optimized for the web. Web developers need to provide high-impact experiences for the user, which means making sites come alive and turning them from static

text and pictures to dynamic, interactive experiences. The problem has been that incorporating high-quality graphics and motion into a website can dramatically increase the download time and frustrate viewers as they wait for an image to appear or for an animation to play. Flash directly addresses this problem by allowing developers to use vector images, which reduce the size of graphic files. Vector images appeal to designers because they are scalable, which means they can be resized and reshaped without distortion. For example, using a vector graphic, you can easily have an object, such as an airplane, become smaller as it moves across the screen without having to create the plane in different sizes.

In addition, Flash provides for streaming content over the Internet. Instead of waiting for the entire contents of a web page to load, the viewer sees a continuous display of images. Another reason Flash has become a standard is that it is made by Adobe. Adobe makes other programs, such as Dreamweaver, Fireworks, Photoshop, and Illustrator. Together these products can be used to create compelling interactive websites and applications. This chapter provides an overview of Flash and presents concepts that are covered in more detail in later chapters.

Tools You'll Use

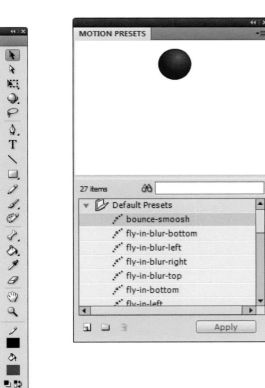

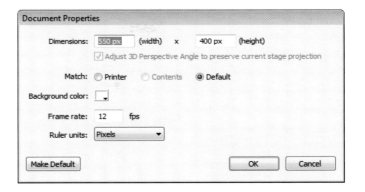

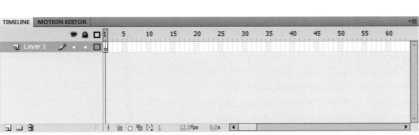

UNDERSTAND THE
ADOBE FLASH CS4
WORKSPACE

What You'll Do

 In this lesson, you will learn about the development workspace in Adobe Flash and how to change Flash settings to customize your workspace.

Organizing the Flash Workspace

As a designer, one of the most important things for you to do is to organize your workspace—that is, to decide what to have displayed on the screen and how to arrange the various tools and panels. Because **Flash** is a powerful program with many tools, your workspace may become cluttered. Fortunately, it is easy to customize the workspace to display only the tools needed at any particular time.

The development process in Flash operates according to a movie metaphor: objects placed on the Stage also appear in frames on a Timeline. As you work in Flash, you create a movie by arranging objects (such as graphics and text) on the Stage, and then animating the objects using the Timeline. You can play the movie on the Stage as you are working on it by using the movie controls (start, stop, rewind, and so on). When done the movie can be incorporated into a website or as part of an application, such as a game.

When you start Flash, three basic parts of the workspace are displayed: a menu bar that organizes commands within menus, a Stage where objects are placed, and a Timeline used to organize and control the objects on the Stage. In addition, one or more panels may be displayed. Panels, such as the Tools panel, are used when working with objects and features of the movie. Figure 1 shows a typical Flash workspace.

Stage

The **Stage** contains all of the objects (such as drawings, photos, clip art, and text) that are part of the movie that will be seen by your viewers. It shows how the objects behave within the movie and how they interact with each other. You can resize the Stage and change the background color applied to it. You can draw objects directly on the Stage or drag them from the Library panel to the Stage. You can also import objects developed in another program directly to the Stage. You can specify the size of the Stage (in pixels), which will be the size of the area within your browser window that displays the movie. The gray area surrounding the Stage is the Pasteboard. You can place objects on the Pasteboard as you are creating a movie. However, neither the Pasteboard nor the objects on it will appear when the movie is played in a browser or the Flash Player.

Timeline (Frames and Layers)

The **Timeline** is used to organize and control the movie's contents by specifying when each object appears on the Stage. The Timeline is critical to the creation of movies because a movie is merely a series of still images that appear over time. The images are contained within **frames**, which are segments of the Timeline. Frames in a Flash movie are similar to frames in a motion picture. When a Flash movie is played, a playhead moves from frame to frame on the Timeline, causing the contents of each frame to appear on the Stage in a linear sequence.

The Timeline indicates where you are at any time within the movie and allows you to insert, delete, select, copy, and move frames. It shows the animation in your movie and the layers that contain objects. **Layers** help to organize the objects on the Stage. You can draw and edit objects on one layer without affecting objects on other layers. Layers are a way to stack objects so they can overlap and give a 3D appearance on the Stage.

Panels

Panels are used to view, organize, and modify objects and features in a movie. The most commonly used panels are the Tools panel, the Properties panel (also called the Property inspector), and the Library panel.

FIGURE 1
A typical Flash workspace

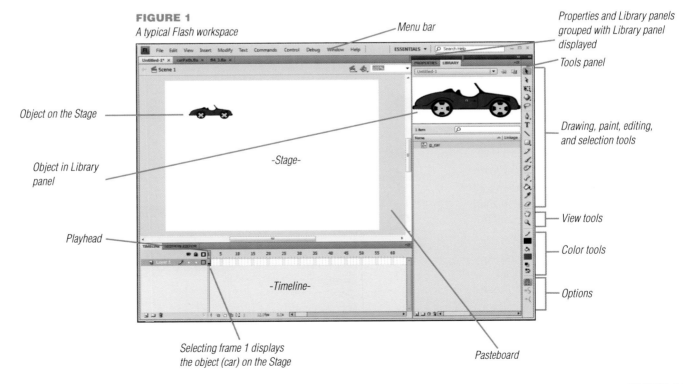

Menu bar

Properties and Library panels grouped with Library panel displayed

Tools panel

Object on the Stage

Object in Library panel

-Stage-

Drawing, paint, editing, and selection tools

Playhead

-Timeline-

View tools

Color tools

Options

Selecting frame 1 displays the object (car) on the Stage

Pasteboard

For example, the Properties panel is used to change the properties of an object, such as the fill color of a circle. The Properties panel is context sensitive, so that if you are working with text it displays the appropriate options, such as font and font size.

You can control which panels are displayed individually or you can choose to display panel sets. Panel sets are groups of the most commonly used panels. For example, the Properties and the Library panels are often grouped together to make a panel set. You use the Window menu on the menu bar to display and hide panels.

Tools Panel

The **Tools panel** contains a set of tools used to draw and edit graphics and text. It is divided into four sections.

The **Tools** section includes draw, paint, text, and selection tools, which are used to create lines, shapes, illustrations, and text. The selection tools are used to select objects so that they can be modified in several ways.

The **Views** section includes the Zoom tool and the Hand tool, which are used to zoom in on and out of parts of the Stage and to pan the Stage window, respectively.

The **Colors** section includes tools and icons used to change the stroke (border of an object) and fill (area inside an object) colors.

The **Options** section includes options for selected tools, such as allowing you to choose the size of the brush when using the Brush tool.

Although several panels open automatically when you start Flash, you may choose to display them only when they are needed. This keeps your workspace from becoming too cluttered. Panels are floating windows, meaning that you can move them around the workspace. This allows you to group (dock) panels together as a way to organize them in the workspace. In addition, you can control how a panel is displayed. That is, you can expand a panel to show all of its features or collapse it to show only the title bar. Collapsing panels reduces the clutter on your workspace, provides a larger area for the Stage, and still provides easy access to often used panels.

If you choose to rearrange panels, first decide if you want a panel to be grouped (docked) with another panel, stacked above or below another panel, a floating panel, or simply a stand-alone panel. An example of each of these is shown in Figure 2.

Arranging panels can be a bit tricky. It's easy to start moving panels around and find that the workspace is cluttered with panels arranged in unintended ways. While you cannot use the Flash Undo feature on the Edit menu to undo a panel move, you can always close a panel or choose the Reset Essentials option from the Workspace command on the Windows

FIGURE 2
Arranging panels

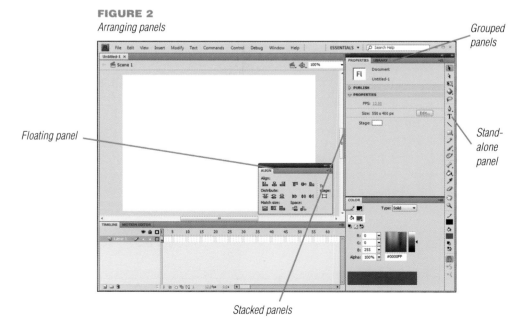

Floating panel

Stacked panels

Grouped panels

Stand-alone panel

Getting Started with Adobe Flash CS4

menu. This command displays the default panel arrangement, which is a good starting position when working with Flash.

The key to rearranging panels is the blue drop zone that appears when a panel is being moved. Refer to Figure 3. The drop zone is the area to which the panel can move and is indicated by either a blue line or a rectangle with a blue border. A single blue line indicates the position for stacking a panel above or below another panel. A rectangle with a blue border indicates the position for grouping panels. If you move a panel without using a drop zone, the panel becomes a floating panel and is neither grouped nor stacked with other panels. To move a panel, you drag the panel by its tab until the desired blue drop zone appears, then you release the mouse button. (*Note*: Dragging a panel by its tab moves only that panel. To move a panel set you must drag the group by its title bar.)

Figure 3 shows the Library panel being grouped with the Properties panel. The process is to drag the Library panel tab adjacent to the Properties panel tab. Notice the rectangle with the blue border that surrounds the Properties panel. This indicates the drop zone for the Library panel which groups them together. Figure 4 shows the Library panel after being ungrouped and placed as a floating panel.

FIGURE 3
Grouping the Library panel

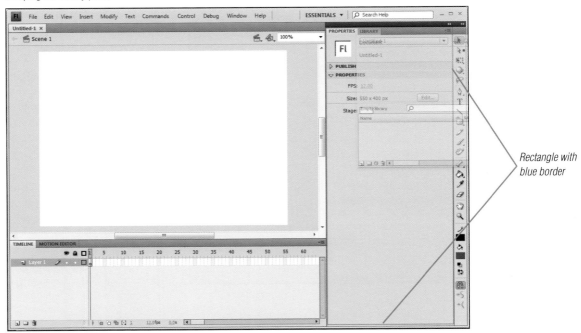

Rectangle with blue border

In addition to moving panels, you can collapse them so that only the title bar appears, and then you can expand them to display the entire panel. The Collapse to Icons button is located in the upper-right corner of each panel, as shown in Figure 4. The Collapse to Icons button is a toggle button, which means it changes or toggles between two states. When

clicked, the Collapse to Icons button changes to the Expand Panels button. Finally, if you want to close a panel, you can use the Close option from the drop down menu on the panel title bar, as shown in Figure 4 or you can deselect a panel option on the Windows menu.

Regardless of how you decide to customize your development workspace,

the Stage and the menu bar are always displayed. Usually, you display the Timeline, Tools panel, Library panel, Properties panel, and one or more other panels.

Other changes that you can make to the workspace are to change the size of the Stage, move the Stage around the Pasteboard, and change the size of the Timeline panel. To increase the size of the Stage so that the objects on the Stage can be more easily edited, you can change the magnification setting using commands on the View menu or by using the View tools on the Tools panel. The Hand tool on the Tools panel and the scroll bars at the bottom and right of the Stage can be used to reposition the Stage. The Timeline can be resized by dragging the top border. The more complex your Flash movie, the more layers that are used in the Timeline. Increasing the size of the Timeline allows you to view several layers at one time.

FIGURE 4
Ungrouping the Library panel

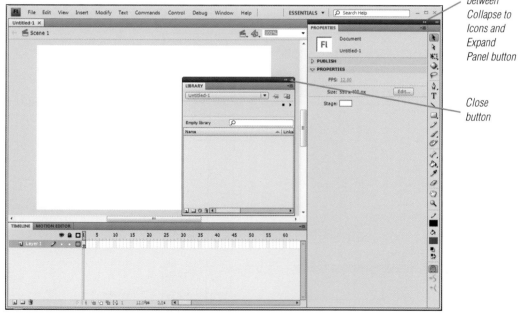

Toggle
between
Collapse to
Icons and
Expand
Panel button

Close
button

QUICKTIP

When working with panels, you can collapse, move, and close them as suits your working style. Settings for an object are not lost if you close or collapse a panel. If, at any time the panels have become confusing, simply return to the Essentials workspace and open panels as needed.

FIGURE 5

The Flash Welcome screen

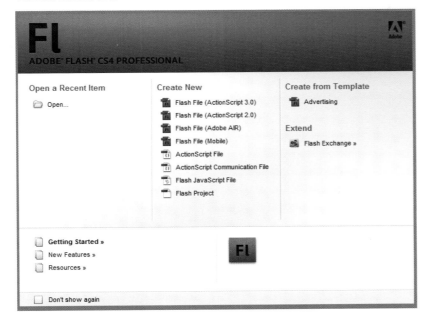

Start Adobe Flash and work with panels

1. Start the Adobe Flash CS4 program **Fl** .

   The Adobe Flash CS4 Welcome screen appears, as shown in Figure 5. This screen allows you to open a recent document or create a new Flash file.

2. Click **Flash File (ActionScript 3.0)** under Create New.

3. Click **Window** on the menu bar, point to **Workspace**, then click **Reset 'Essentials'**.

   TIP As you are rearranging your workspace, you can always select the Reset 'Essentials' option on the Window Workspace submenu to display the default workspace.

4. Click **Window** on the menu bar, then note the panels with check marks. The check marks identify which panels are open.

   TIP The Properties and Library panels may be grouped depending upon the configuration of your Essentials workspace. If so, only the panel that is active (the tab that is selected) will have a check mark.

5. With the Windows menu still open, click **Hide Panels**.

6. Click **Window** on the menu bar, then click **Timeline**.

7. Click **Window** on the menu bar, then click **Tools**.

8. Click **Window** on the menu bar, then click **Library**.

9. Click **Window** on the menu bar, then click **Properties**.

   At this point the Library and Properties panels should be grouped.

10. Click the **Library panel tab** to display the panel.

11. Click the **Properties panel tab** to display the panel.

(continued)

12. Click the **Library panel tab**, then drag the **panel** to the Stage as a floating panel.

13. Click the **Collapse to Icons button** on the Library panel title bar.

14. Click the **Expand Panels button** on the Library panel title bar.

15. Click the **Library panel tab**, drag the **panel** to the right of the Properties panel tab, then when a rectangle with a blue border appears, release the mouse button to group the panels, as shown in Figure 6.

    Note: If the panels do not appear as shown in Figure 6, repeat the step making sure there is a rectangle with a blue border before releasing the mouse button.

16. Click the **Collapse to Icons button** in the upper-right corner of the grouped panels, as shown in Figure 6.

17. Click the **Expand Panels button** delete icon to display the grouped panels.

18. Click **Window** on the menu bar, point to **Workspace**, then click **Reset 'Essentials'**.

    The Essentials workspace appears.

You started Flash and configured the workspace by hiding, moving, and displaying selected panels.

Change the Stage view and display of the Timeline

1. Click **View** on the menu bar, point to **Magnification**, then click **50%**.

2. Click the **Hand tool** ✋ on the Tools panel, click the middle of the Stage, then drag the **Stage** around the Pasteboard.

(continued)

FIGURE 6
Library panel grouped with the Properties panel

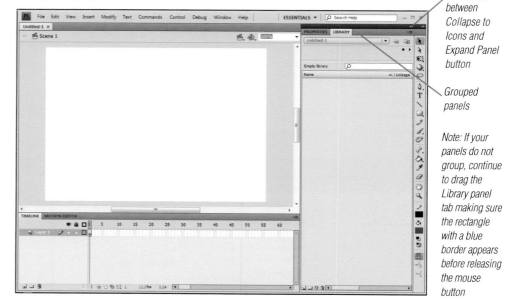

Use to toggle between Collapse to Icons and Expand Panel button

Grouped panels

Note: If your panels do not group, continue to drag the Library panel tab making sure the rectangle with a blue border appears before releasing the mouse button

Understanding your workspace

Organizing the Flash workspace is like organizing your desktop. You may work more efficiently if you have many of the most commonly used items in view and ready to use. Alternately, you may work better if your workspace is relatively uncluttered, giving you more free "desk space." Fortunately, Flash makes it easy for you to decide which items to display and how they are arranged while you work. For example, to toggle the Main toolbar, click Window on the menu bar, point to Toolbars, then click Main. You should become familiar with quickly opening, collapsing, expanding, and closing the various windows, toolbars, and panels in Flash, and experimenting with different layouts and screen resolutions to find the workspace that works best for you.

FIGURE 7
Changing the size of the Timeline panel

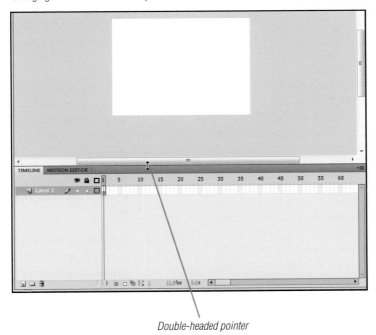

Double-headed pointer

3. Move the pointer to the top of the Timeline title bar, when the pointer changes to a double-headed pointer ↕ , click and drag up to increase the size of the Timeline, as shown in Figure 7.

   Increasing the size of the Timeline panel allows you to view more layers as you add them to the Timeline.

4. Point to the top of the Timeline title bar, when the pointer changes to a double-headed pointer ↕ , click and drag the **title bar** down to decrease the size of the Timeline.

5. Double-click the word **TIMELINE** to collapse the Timeline.

6. Double-click the word **TIMELINE** again to expand the Timeline.

7. Click **View** on the menu bar, point to **Magnification**, then click **100%**.

8. Click **ESSENTIALS** on the menu bar, then click **Reset 'Essentials'**.

   This resets the workspace to the Essentials template.

9. Click the **Selection tool** ▸ on the Tools panel.

10. Click **File** on the menu bar, then click **Save**.

11. Navigate to the drive and folder where your Data Files are stored, type **workspace** for the filename, then click **Save**.

12. Click **File** on the menu bar, then click **Close**.

You used a View command to change the magnification of the Stage; you used the Hand tool to move the Stage around the workspace; you resized, collapsed, and expanded the Timeline panel; then you saved the document.

OPEN A DOCUMENT
AND PLAY A MOVIE

What You'll Do

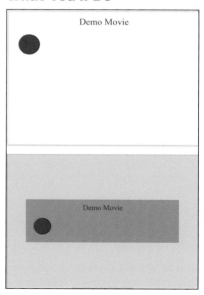

In this lesson, you will open a Flash document (movie); preview, test, and save the movie; then change the movie's document settings.

Opening a Movie in Flash

Flash files are called documents (or movies, interchangeably) and have an .fla file extension. If you have created a movie in Flash and saved it with the name mymovie, the filename will be mymovie.fla. Files with the .fla file extension can only be opened and edited using Flash. After they are opened, you can edit and resave them.

In order for Flash movies to be viewed on computers that do not have the Flash program installed, the movies must be changed to the Flash Player (.swf) file format. Files using the .swf file format are created from Flash movies using the Publish command. Flash .swf movies can be played in a browser without the Flash program, but the Flash Player must be installed on the computer. Flash Players are pre-installed on almost all computers. For those that do not have the player, it can be downloaded free from the Adobe website, *www.adobe.com*. Because .swf files cannot be edited in the Flash program, you should preview the Flash .fla files on the Stage and test them before you publish them as .swf files. Be sure to keep the original .fla

file so that you can make changes if needed at a later date.

Previewing a Movie

After creating a new Flash movie or opening a previously saved movie, you can preview it within the workspace in several ways. When you preview a movie, you play the frames by directing the playhead to move through the Timeline, and you watch the movement on the Stage.

Control Menu Commands (and Keyboard Shortcuts)

Figure 8 shows the Control menu commands, which resemble common DVD-type options:

- Play ([Enter] (Win) or [return] (Mac)) begins playing the movie frame by frame, from the location of the playhead to the end of the movie. For example, if the playhead is on frame 5 and the last frame is frame 40, choosing the Play command will play frames 5–40 of the movie.

- Rewind ([Shift][,] (Win)) or [option] $\mathcal{H}$ [R] (Mac) moves the playhead to frame 1.
- Step Forward One Frame (.) moves the playhead forward one frame at a time.
- Step Backward One Frame (,) moves the playhead backward one frame at a time.

You can turn on the Loop Playback setting to allow the movie to continue playing repeatedly. A check mark next to the Loop Playback command on the Control menu indicates that the feature is active. To turn off this feature, click the Loop Playback command.

Controller

You can also preview a movie using the Controller. To display the Controller, click the Controller option on the Toolbars command of the Window menu.

Testing a Movie

When you play a movie within the Flash workspace, some interactive functions (such as buttons that are used to jump from one part of the movie to another) do not work. To preview the full functionality of a movie you need to play it using a Flash Player. You can use the Test Movie command on the Control menu to test the movie using a Flash Player.

FIGURE 8
Control menu commands

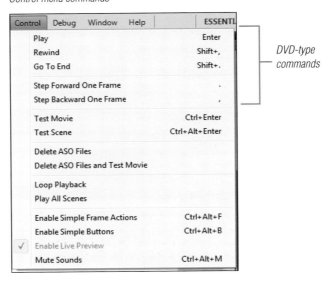

DVD-type commands

Documents, Movies, and Applications

As you work in Flash, you are creating a document. When you save your work as an .fla file, you are saving the document. This is consistent with other Adobe products such as Photoshop that use the word *document* to refer to work created in that progam. In addition, because Flash uses a movie metaphor with a Stage, timeline, frames, animations, and so on, the work done in Flash is often referred to as a movie. So, the phrase *Flash document* and the phrase *Flash movie* are synonymous. Movies can be as small and simple as a ball bouncing across the screen or as complex as a full-length interactive adventure game. Products such as games and educational software, as well as online advertisements and product demonstrations, are referred to as applications (see Figure 9). Applications usually contain multiple Flash documents or movies that are linked.

Using the Flash Player

To view a Flash movie on the web, your computer needs to have the Flash Player installed. An important feature of multimedia players, such as Flash Player, is the ability to decompress a file that has been compressed to give it a small file size that can be delivered more quickly over the Internet. In addition to Adobe, companies such as Apple (QuickTime), Microsoft (Windows Media Player), and RealNetworks (RealPlayer) create players that allow applications, developed with their and other companies' products, to be viewed on the web. The multimedia players are distributed free and can be downloaded from the company's website. The Flash Player is created by Adobe and the latest version is available at *www.adobe.com*.

FIGURE 9
Example of an application

FIGURE 10

Playhead moving across Timeline

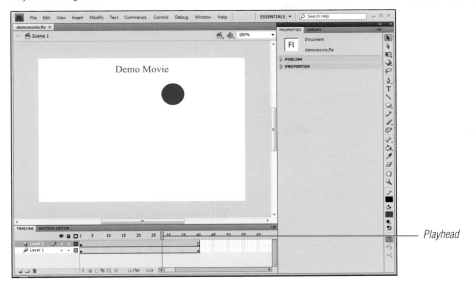

Playhead

Using options and shortcuts

There is often more than one way to complete a particular function when using Flash. For example, if you want to rewind a movie you can use the controls on the controller panel; press [Shift] + [.]; or drag the playhead to frame 1. In addition, Flash provides context menus that are relevant to the current selection. For example, if you point to a graphic and right-click (Win) or [control] click (Mac), a menu opens with graphic-related commands, such as cut and copy. Shortcut keys are also available for many of the most common commands, such as [Ctrl][Z] (Win) or ⌘ [Z] (Mac) for Undo.

Open and play a movie using the Control menu and the Controller

1. Open fl1_1.fla from the drive and folder where your Data Files are stored, then save it as **demomovie.fla**.

2. Click **View** on the menu bar, point to **Magnification**, then click **Fit in Window**.

3. Click **Control** on the menu bar, then click **Play**.

   Notice how the playhead moves across the Timeline as the blue circle moves from the left to the right, as shown in Figure 10.

4. Click **Control** on the menu bar, then click **Rewind**.

5. Press [**Enter**] (Win) or [**return**] (Mac) to play the movie, then press [**Enter**] (Win) or [**return**] (Mac) again to stop the movie before it ends.

6. Click **Window** on the menu bar, point to **Toolbars**, then click **Controller**.

7. Use all the buttons on the Controller to preview the movie, then close the Controller.

8. Point to the **playhead** on the Timeline, then click and drag the **playhead** back and forth to view the contents of the frames and view the movie.

9. Click **frame 1** on the Timeline.

10. Press the **period key** several times, then press the **comma key** several times to move the playhead one frame at a time forward and backward.

You opened a Flash movie and previewed it, using various controls.

Lesson 2   Open a Document and Play a Movie

FLASH 1-15

Test a movie

1. Click **Control** on the menu bar, then click **Test Movie**.

   The Flash Player window opens, as shown in Figure 11 and the movie starts playing automatically.

2. Click **Control** on the menu bar of the Flash Player window (Win) or application menu bar (Mac), then review the available commands.

3. Click **File** on the menu bar of the Flash Player window (Win) or application menu bar (Mac), then click **Close** to close the Flash Player window.

4. Use your file management program to navigate to the drive and folder where you saved the demomovie.fla file and notice the demomovie.swf file that was created when you tested the movie in the Flash Player window.

   TIP   When you test a movie, Flash automatically creates a file that has an .swf extension in the folder where your movie is stored and then plays the movie in the Flash Player.

5. Return to the Flash program.

You tested a movie in the Flash Player window and viewed the .swf file created as a result of testing the movie.

FIGURE 11
Flash Player window

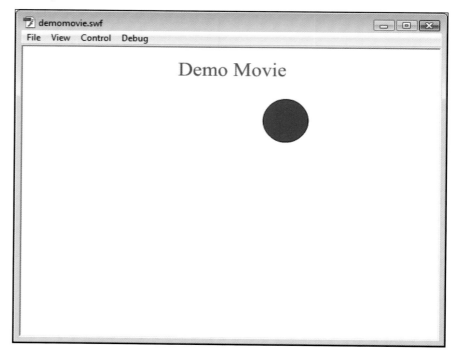

FIGURE 12

Document Properties dialog box

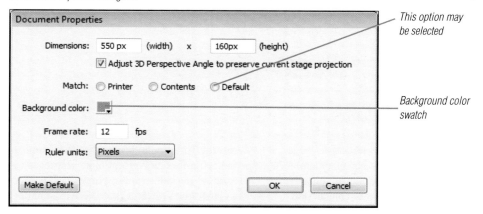

This option may be selected

Background color swatch

1. Click **Modify** on the menu bar, then click **Document** to display the Document Properties dialog box.

2. Double-click the number in the **height text box**, then type **160**.

3. Click the **Background color swatch**, then click the **middle gray (#999999) color swatch** in the far-left column of the color palette.

   Note: The Color Swatch palette allows you to click a color to choose it or to enter a number that represents the color.

4. Review the remaining default values shown in Figure 12, then click **OK**.

5. Click **View** on the menu bar, point to **Magnification**, then click **Fit in Window** if it is not already selected. Your screen should resemble Figure 13.

6. Click **File** on the menu bar, then click **Save As**.

7. Navigate to the drive and folder where your Data Files are stored, type **demomovie banner** for the filename, then click **Save** (Win) or **Save As** (Mac).

8. Click **File** on the menu bar, then click **Close**.

You set the document properties including the size of the Stage and background color, then set the magnification and saved the document.

FIGURE 13

Completed changes to document properties

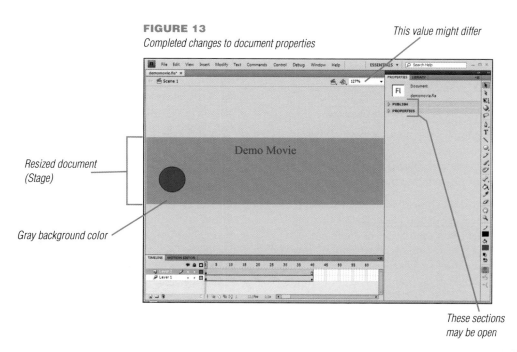

This value might differ

Resized document (Stage)

Gray background color

These sections may be open

CREATE AND SAVE
A MOVIE

What You'll Do

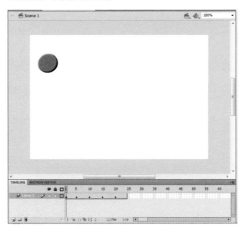

In this lesson, you will create a Flash movie that will include a simple animation, you will add animation effects, and then save the movie.

Creating a Flash Movie

Flash movies are created by placing objects (graphics, text, sounds, photos, and so on) on the Stage, editing these objects (for example, changing their brightness), animating the objects, and adding interactivity with buttons and menus. You can create graphic objects in Flash using the drawing tools, or you can create them in another program, such as Adobe Fireworks, Illustrator, or Photoshop, and then import them into a Flash movie. In addition, you can acquire clip art and stock photographs and import them into a movie. When objects are placed on the Stage, they are automatically placed on a layer and in the currently selected frame of the Timeline.

Figure 14 shows a movie that has an oval object created in Flash. Notice that the playhead is on frame 1 of the movie. The object placed on the Stage appears in frame 1 and appears on the Stage when the playhead is on frame 1. The dot in frame 1

on the Timeline indicates that this frame is a keyframe. The concept of keyframes is critical to understanding how Flash works. A **keyframe** indicates that there is a change in the movie, such as the start or end of an animation, or the playing of a sound. A keyframe is automatically designated in frame 1 of every layer. In addition, you can designate any frame to be a keyframe.

The circle object in Figure 14 was created using the Oval tool. To create an oval or a rectangle, you select the desired tool and then drag the pointer over an area on the Stage. *Note:* Flash groups the Oval and Rectangle tools, along with three other drawing tools, using one button on the Tools panel. To display a menu of these tools, click and hold the rectangle (or oval) button on the Tools panel to display the menu and then click the tool you want to use. If you want to draw a perfect circle or square, press and hold [Shift] after the tool is selected, and then drag the pointer.

If you make a mistake, you can click Edit on the menu bar, and then click Undo. To make changes to an object, such as resizing or changing its color, or to animate an object, you must first select it. You can use the Selection tool to select an entire object or group of objects. You drag the Selection tool pointer around the entire object to make a **marquee**. An object that has been selected displays a dot pattern or a blue border.

Creating an Animation

Figure 15 shows another movie that has 12 frames, as specified in the Timeline. The blue background color on the Timeline indicates a motion animation that starts in frame 1 and ends in frame 12. The dotted line indicates the path the object will follow during the animation. In this case, the object will move from left to right across the Stage. The movement of the object is caused by having the object in different

places on the Stage in different frames of the movie. In this case, frame 6 will display the object midway through the animation. A basic motion animation requires two keyframes. The first keyframe sets the starting position of the object, and the second keyframe sets the ending position of the object. The number of frames between the two keyframes determines the length of the animation. For example, if the starting keyframe is frame 1 and the ending

FIGURE 14
Circle object in frame 1

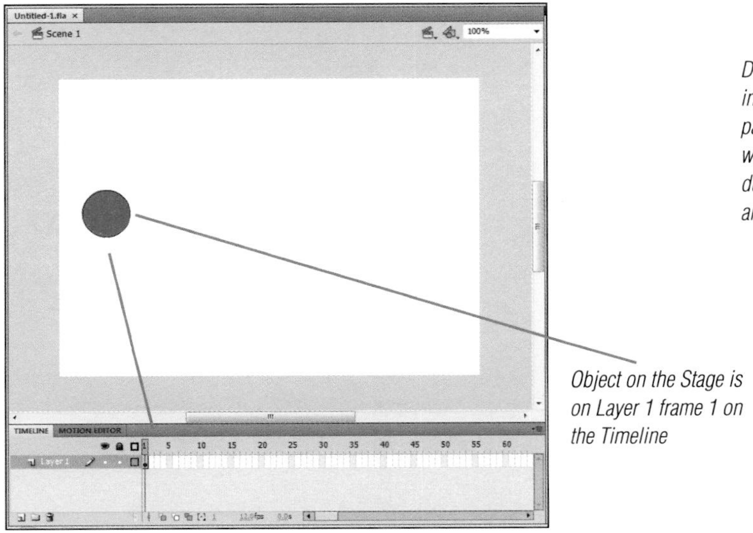

Object on the Stage is on Layer 1 frame 1 on the Timeline

FIGURE 15
Motion animation

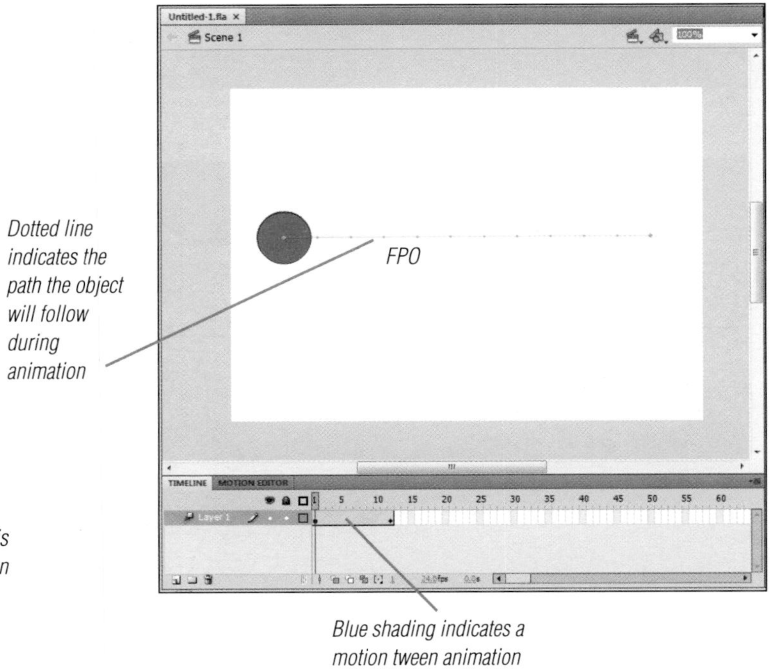

Dotted line indicates the path the object will follow during animation

FPO

Blue shading indicates a motion tween animation

keyframe is frame 12, the object will be animated for 12 frames. As an object is being animated, Flash automatically fills in the frames between them, with a process called **motion tweening**.

The Motion Tween Animation Process

Having an object move around the screen is one of the most common types of animations. Flash provides a process called motion tween that makes it relatively simple to move objects. The process is to select an object on the Stage, then select the Motion Tween command from the Insert menu. If the object is not a symbol, a dialog box opens asking if you want to change the object into a symbol. Creating a symbol allows you to reuse the object for this and other movies, as well as to apply a motion tween. Only symbols can be motion tweened. The final step in the animation process is to select the ending frame for the animation and drag the object to another location on the Stage.

Two important things happen during the animation process. First, the Timeline shows the **tween span** (also called motion span), that is the number of frames in the motion tween. The tween span can be identified on the Timeline by a blue color, which in this case extends for 12 frames. A tween span is equal to one second in duration. The number of frames in a tween span varies and is determined by the number of frames per second setting. In this example, we set the number of frames per second to 12, so the number of frames in a tween for this movie is 12 frames. You can increase or decrease the length of the animation by pointing to either end of the span and dragging it to a new frame. Second, a dotted line, as shown in Figure 16, called the **motion path**, represents the path

FIGURE 16
Line showing the motion path

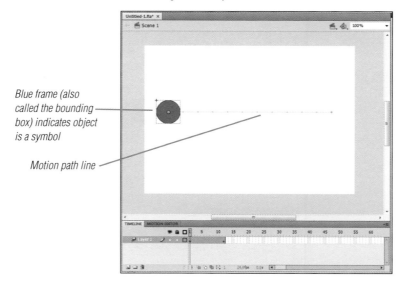

Blue frame (also called the bounding box) indicates object is a symbol

Motion path line

the object takes from the beginning frame to the ending frame. This path can be reshaped to cause the object to travel in a non-linear way. Reshaping a path can be done by using the Selection tool on the Tools panel.

Motion Presets

Flash provides several preconfigured motion tweens that you can apply to an object on the Stage. These allow you to bounce an object across the Stage, fly-in an object from off the Stage, cause an object to pulsate and to spiral in place, as well as many other types of object animations. Figure 17 shows the Motion Presets panel where you choose a preset and apply it to an object. You can preview each preset before applying it and you can easily change to a different preset, if desired.

Adding Effects to an Object

In addition to animating the location of an object (or objects), you can also animate an object's appearance. Objects have proper-ties such as color, brightness, and size. You can alter an object's properties as it is being animated using the motion tween process. For example, you could give the appearance of the object fading in by changing its transparency (alpha setting) or having it grow larger by altering its size over the course of the animation. Another useful effect is applying filters, such as drop shadows or bevels. All of these changes can be made using the Properties panel after selecting the object.

FIGURE 17
Motion Presets panel

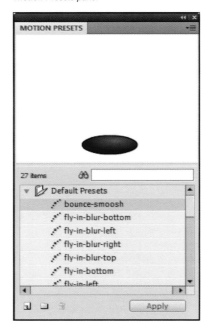

Create objects using drawing tools

1. Click **File** on the menu bar, then click **New**.

2. Click **OK** in the New Document window to choose Flash File (ActionScript 3.0) as the new document to create, then save the movie as **tween**.

3. Click **View** on the menu bar, point to **Magnification**, then click **100%**.

4. Click and hold the **Rectangle tool** ▭ (or the Oval tool if it is displayed) on the Tools panel to display the list of tools, as shown in Figure 18, then click the **Oval tool** ◯.

5. Verify that the Object Drawing option ◯ in the Options area of the Tools panel is deselected, as shown in Figure 18.

6. Click the **Fill Color tool color swatch** 🎨 on the Tools panel, then, if necessary, click the **red color swatch** in the left column of the color palette.

7. Click the **Stroke Color tool color swatch** 🎨 on the Tools panel, then, if necessary, click the **black color swatch** in the left column of the color palette.

8. Press and hold **[Shift]**, drag the **pointer** on the left side of the Stage to draw the circle, as shown in Figure 19, then release the mouse button.

   Pressing and holding [Shift] creates a circle.

9. Click the **Selection tool** ➤ on the Tools panel, then drag a **marquee** around the object to select it, as shown in Figure 20, then release the mouse button

   The object appears covered with a dot pattern.

You created an object using the Oval tool and then selected the object using the Selection tool.

FIGURE 18
Drawing tools menu

FIGURE 19
Drawing a circle

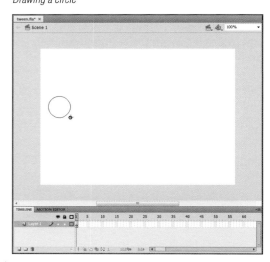

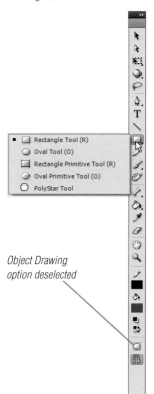

- ▪ ▭ Rectangle Tool (R)
- ◯ Oval Tool (O)
- ▭ Rectangle Primitive Tool (R)
- ◯ Oval Primitive Tool (O)
- ◯ PolyStar Tool

Object Drawing option deselected

FIGURE 20
Creating a marquee selection

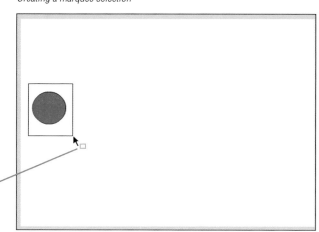

Use the Selection tool to draw a marquee, which selects the entire object

FIGURE 21
The circle on the right side of the Stage

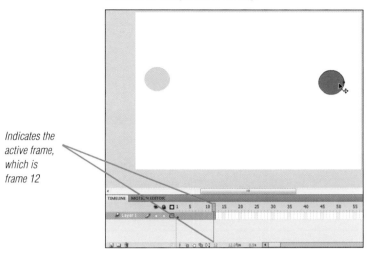

Indicates the active frame, which is frame 12

FIGURE 22
Pointing to the end of the tween span

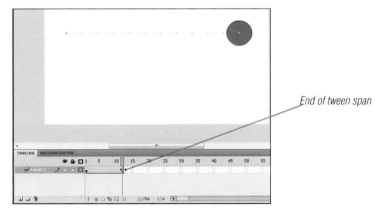

End of tween span

Create a motion tween animation

1. Click **Insert** on the menu bar, then click **Motion Tween**, which opens the Convert selection to symbol for tween dialog box.

2. Click **OK**.

   A blue border surrounds the object indicating that the object is selected. Notice in this case that the playhead automatically moved to frame 12, the last frame in the tween span.

3. Click and then drag the **circle** to the right side of the Stage, as shown in Figure 21.

4. Press **[Enter]**(Win) or **[return]**(Mac) to play the movie.

   The playhead moves through frames 1–12 on the Timeline, and the circle moves across the Stage.

5. Click **frame 6** on Layer 1 on the Timeline.

   Notice that the object is halfway across the screen. This is the result of the tweening process in which the frames between 1 and 12 are filled in with the object in the correct location for each frame.

6. Verify the Selection tool ♦ is selected, point to the end of the tween span until the pointer changes to a double-headed arrow ↔, as shown in Figure 22.

7. Click and drag the **tween span** to frame 48.

8. Press **[Enter]**(Win) or **[return]**(Mac) to play the movie.

   Notice it now takes longer (4 seconds, not 1 second) to complete the animation. Also notice that a diamond symbol appears in

   (continued)

frame 48 indicating that a keyframe has been placed in that frame. The diamond symbol indicates a change in the animation. In this case it indicates the end of the animation.

9. Click **frame 24** and notice that the object is still halfway across the screen.

10. Click **File** on the menu bar, then click **Save**.

You created a motion tween animation and changed the length of the tween span.

Reshaping the Motion Path

1. Click **File** on the menu bar, click **Save As**, then save the document with the filename **tween-effects.fla**.

2. Verify the Selection tool ↖ is selected.

3. Click **frame 1** to select it.

   Note: When you see the direction to click a frame, click the frame on the layer not the number on the Timeline.

4. Point to just below the middle of the path until the pointer changes to a pointer with an arc ↳ , as shown in Figure 23.

5. Click and drag the **path** to reshape the path, as shown in Figure 24.

6. Play the movie.

   Note: When you see the direction to play the movie, press [Enter] (Win) or [return] (Mac).

7. Test the movie.

   Note: When you see the direction to test the movie, click Control on the menu bar, then click Test Movie.

8. View the movie, then close the Flash Player window.

(continued)

FIGURE 23
Using the Selection tool to reshape a motion path

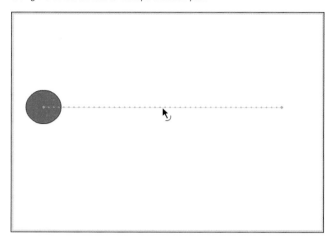

FIGURE 24
Reshaping the motion path

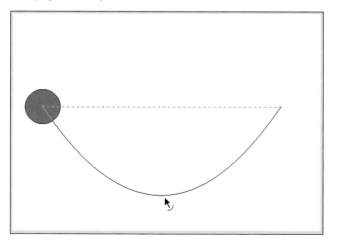

9. Click **Edit** on the menu bar, then click **Undo Reshape**.

You used the Selection tool to reshape a motion path and the Undo command to undo the reshape.

Changing the transparency of an object

1. Click the **Properties panel tab** to display the Properties panel, as shown in Figure 25.

Note: If the Properties panel is not open, click Window on the menu bar, then click Properties.

2. Verify frame 1 is selected, then click the **object** on the Stage to select it.

Note: To verify the object is selected, review the available settings in the Properties panel. Make sure POSITION AND SIZE is one of the options.

3. Click **COLOR EFFECT** on the Properties panel, click the **Style list arrow**, then click **Alpha**.

4. Drag the **Alpha slider** to **0**.

This causes the object to become transparent.

5. Click **frame 48** on the layer to select it.

6. Click **the middle of the bounding box** on the Stage to select the object and check that the object's properties are displayed in the Properties panel.

Note: To verify the object is selected, review the available settings in the Properties panel. Make sure POSITION AND SIZE is one of the options.

(continued)

FIGURE 25
The Properties panel displayed

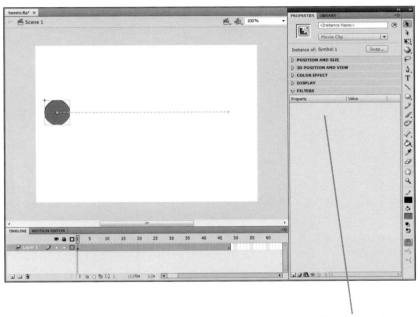

Properties panel

7. Drag the **Alpha slider** ⌂ to **100**.

8. Play the movie.

9. Test the movie.

10. View the movie, then close the Flash Player window.

You used the Color Effect option on the Properties panel to change the transparency of an object.

Resize an object

1. Click **frame 1** select it.

2. Click the **object** to select it.

3. Click **POSITION AND SIZE** on the Properties panel if this section is not already open.

4. Review the width (W) and height (H) of the object.

   The width and height are the dimensions of the bounding box around the circle.

5. Click **frame 48** to select it, then click the **object** to select it.

6. Point to the number for the width and when the pointer changes into a double-headed arrow ⇹ , drag the ⇹ **pointer** right to increase the width so that the circle grows in size to 80, as shown in Figure 26.

   Hint: You can also double-click a value in the Properties panel and type the new value.

7. Play the movie.

8. Test the movie.

9. View the movie, then close the Flash Player window.

(continued)

FIGURE 26
Resizing the circle

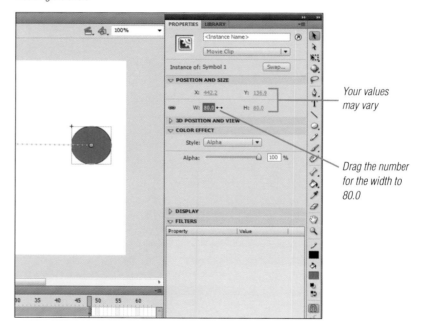

Your values may vary

Drag the number for the width to 80.0

10. Click **frame 1** to select it, then click the **object** to select it.

11. Drag the **Alpha slider** ⬡ to **100**.

You used the Position and Size option on the Properties panel to change the size of an object.

Add a filter to an object

1. Verify the object is selected by viewing the Properties panel and verifying the object's properties are displayed.

2. Click **FILTERS** on the Properties panel to display the Filters section if it is not already displayed.

3. Click the **Add filter icon** 🔳 at the bottom of the Filters section, as shown in Figure 27.

4. Click **Drop Shadow**, point to the number for the angle, when the pointer changes to a double-headed arrow 🖑 , drag the 🖑 **pointer** right to change the number of degrees to **100**.

5. Play the movie.

6. Click **frame 1** to select it, then click the **object** to select it.

7. Click the **Delete Filter icon** 🔳 at the bottom of the Filters section to remove the drop shadow filter.

8. Click the **Add filter icon** 🔳 at the bottom of the panel.

(continued)

FIGURE 27
The Add filter icon

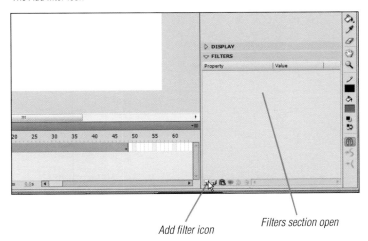

Add filter icon   Filters section open

9. Click **Bevel**, test the movie, then close the Flash Player window.

10. Point to the number for the Filter distance and when the pointer changes into a double-headed arrow , drag the **pointer** right to increase the setting to **35**.

You used the Filters option in the Properties panel to add and delete filters.

Add a motion preset

1. Verify the playhead is on frame 1 and the object is selected.

2. Click **Window** on the menu bar, then click **Motion Presets**.

3. Drag the **Motion Presets panel** so that it does not obscure the Stage.

4. Click the **list arrow** for the Default Presets, then click **bounce-smoosh** and watch the animation in the preview widow, as shown in Figure 28.

5. Click **Apply**.

    A dialog box opens asking if you want to replace the current motion object with the new selection. You can only apply one motion tween or motion preset to an object at any one time.

6. Click **Yes**.

    The bevel filter is deleted and a new path is displayed.

7. Play the movie, then test the movie.

    Notice the object disappears from the Stage.

    (continued)

FIGURE 28
The Motion Presets panel

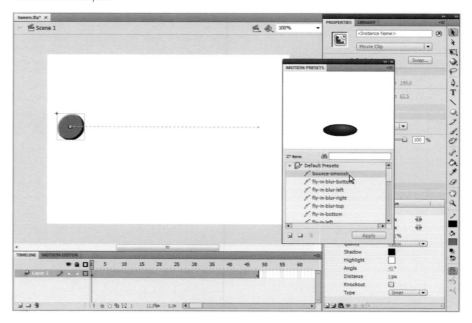

FIGURE 29

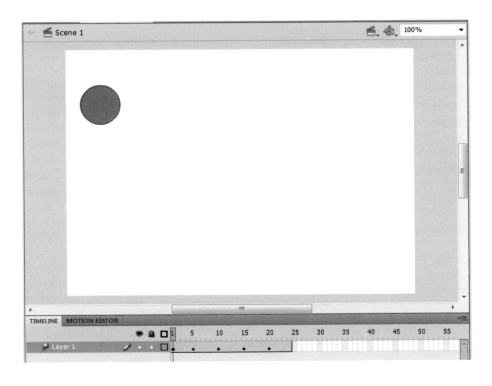

8. Close the Flash Player window.

9. Scroll as needed to see the object, click the **object**, hold **[Shift]**, then click the **path** to select both of them.

10. Press the **up arrow key [↑]** to move the object and the path toward the top of the Stage.

11. Play the movie.

12. Scroll the list of presets, click **pulse**, click **Apply**, then click **Yes**.

13. Play the movie.

Notice the Timeline has four diamond symbols, as shown in Figure 29. Each one is a keyframe and indicates that there is a change in the motion tween. In this case the change comes each time the ball is resized.

14. Click **frame 1** to select it, then drag the **playhead** from frame 1 to the last frame and notice the change that occurs at each keyframe.

15. Close the Motion Presets panel.

16. Save and close the movie.

You applied motion presets to an object and viewed how keyframes identify changes in the motion tween.

WORK WITH
THE TIMELINE

What You'll Do

 In this lesson, you will add another layer, allowing you to create an additional animation, and you will use the Timeline to help organize your movie.

Understanding the Timeline

The Timeline organizes and controls a movie's contents over time. By learning how to read the information provided on the Timeline, you can determine and change what will be happening in a movie, frame by frame. You can determine which objects are animated, what types of animations are being used, when the various objects will appear in a movie, which objects will appear on top of others, and how fast the movie will play. Features of the Timeline are shown in Figure 30 and explained in this lesson.

Using Layers

Each new Flash movie contains one layer, named Layer 1. **Layers** are like transparent sheets of acetate that are stacked on top of each other. This is shown in Figure 31, which also shows how the stacked objects appear on the Stage. Each layer can contain one or more objects. You can add layers using the Layer command on the Insert menu or by clicking the Insert Layer icon on the Timeline. Placing objects on different layers and locking the layers helps avoid accidentally making changes to one object while editing another.

When you add a new layer, Flash stacks it on top of the other layer(s) in the Timeline. The stacking order of the layers in the Timeline is important because objects on the Stage appear in the same stacking order. For example, if you have two overlapping objects, and the top layer has a drawing of a tree and the bottom layer has a drawing of a house, the tree appears as though it is in front of the house. You can change the stacking order of layers simply by dragging them up or down in the list of layers. You can name layers, hide them so their contents do not appear on the Stage, and lock them so that they cannot be edited.

Using frames

The Timeline is made up of individual segments called **frames**. The content of each layer appears as the playhead moves over the frames while the movie plays so any object in frame 1, no matter which layer it is on, appears on the Stage whenever frame 1 is played. Frames are numbered in increments of five for easy reference, while symbols and colors are used to indicate the type of frame (for example, keyframe (symbol) or motion animation (color)). The upper-right corner of the Timeline contains a Frame View icon. Clicking this icon displays a menu that provides different views of the Timeline, showing more frames or showing a preview (thumbnails) of the objects on a layer, for example. The status bar at the bottom of the Timeline indicates the current frame (the frame that the playhead is currently on), the frame rate (frames per second, also called fps), and the elapsed time from frame 1 to the current frame. Frames per second is the unit of measure for movies.

Using the Playhead

The **playhead** indicates which frame is playing. You can manually move the playhead by dragging it left or right. This makes it easier to locate a frame that you may want to edit. Dragging the playhead also allows you to do a quick check of the movie without having to play it.

Understanding Scenes

When you create a movie, the phrase Scene 1 appears above the Stage. You can add scenes to a movie at any time. Scenes are a way to organize long movies. For example, a movie created for a website could be divided into several scenes: an introduction, a home page,

and content pages. Each scene has its own Timeline. You can insert new scenes by using the Insert menu. Scenes can be given descriptive names, which will help you find them easily if you need to edit a particular scene. The number of scenes is limited only by the computer's memory. There are some drawbacks to using scenes, including potentially larger file sizes and longer download times for the viewer.

FIGURE 30
Elements of the Timeline

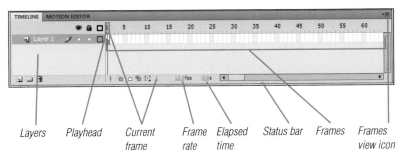

Layers   Playhead   Current frame   Frame rate   Elapsed time   Status bar   Frames   Frames view icon

FIGURE 31
The concept of layers

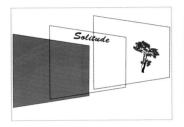 

Working with the Timeline

Figure 32 shows the Timeline of a movie created in Lesson 3 with a second object, a square at the top of the Stage. By studying the Timeline, you can learn several things about the square object and this movie. First, the second object (in this example, the square) is placed on its own layer, Layer 2. Second, the layer has a motion animation (indicated by the blue background in the frames and the motion path on the Stage).

Third, the animation runs from frame 1 to frame 48. Fourth, if the objects intersect during the animation, the square will be on top of the circle, because the layer it is placed on (Layer 2) is above the layer that the circle is placed on (Layer 1). Fifth, the frame rate is set to 12, which means that the movie will play 12 frames per second. Sixth, the play-head is at frame 1, which causes the contents of frame 1 for both layers to appear on the Stage.

QUICKTIP

You can adjust the height of the Timeline by positioning the pointer over the top edge of the Timeline title bar until a double-headed pointer appears, and, then dragging the border up or down.

FIGURE 32

The Timeline of a movie with a second object

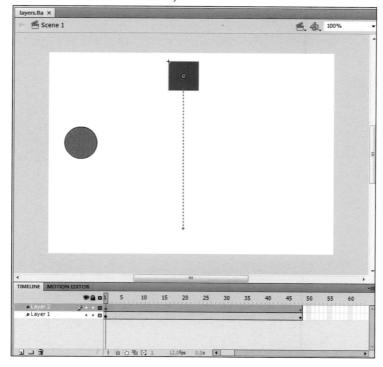

FIGURE 33
Drawing a square

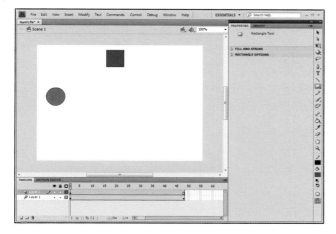

FIGURE 34
Positioning the square at the bottom of the Stage

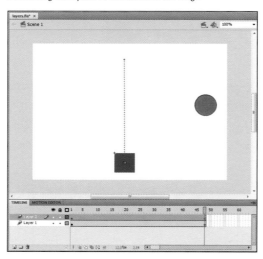

Add a layer

1. Open tween.fla and save it as **layers.fla**.
2. Click **frame 1** on Layer 1.
3. Click **Insert** on the menu bar, point to **Timeline**, then click **Layer**.

   A new layer—Layer 2—appears at the top of the Timeline.

You added a layer to the Timeline.

Create a second animation

1. Click **frame 1** on Layer 2.
2. Select the **Rectangle tool** ☐ on the Tools panel.
3. Click the **Fill Color tool color swatch** 🎨 on the Tools panel, then click the **blue color swatch** in the left column of the color palette.
4. Press and hold [**Shift**], then draw a square resembling the dimensions and position of the square, as shown in Figure 33.
5. Click the **Selection tool** ▶ on the Tools panel, then drag a **marquee** around the square to select the object.
6. Click **Insert** on the menu bar, click **Motion Tween**, then click **OK** in the Convert selection to symbol for tween dialog box.
7. Click **frame 48** on Layer 2, then drag the **square** to the bottom of the Stage, as shown in Figure 34.
8. Play the movie.

   The square appears on top if the two objects intersect.

You drew an object and used it to create a second animation.

Work with layers and view Timeline features

1. Click **Layer 2** on the Timeline, then drag it below Layer 1, as shown in Figure 35.

   Layer 2 is now the bottom layer.

2. Play the movie and notice how the square appears beneath the circle if the objects intersect.

3. Click **Layer 2** on the Timeline, then drag it above Layer 1.

4. Play the movie and notice how the square appears above the circle if they intersect.

5. Click the **Frame View icon** ![frame view icon] on the right corner of the Timeline title bar, as shown in Figure 36, to display the menu.

6. Click **Tiny** to display more frames.

   Notice how more frames appear on the Timeline, but each frame is smaller.

7. Click the **Frame View icon** ![icon], then click **Short**.

8. Click the **Frame View icon** ![icon], click **Preview**, then note the object thumbnails that appear on the Timeline.

9. Click the **Frame View icon** ![icon], then click **Normal**.

You changed the order of the layers, the display of frames, and the way the Timeline is viewed.

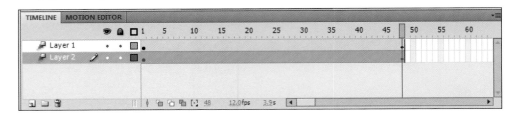

FIGURE 35

Changing the stacking order of layers

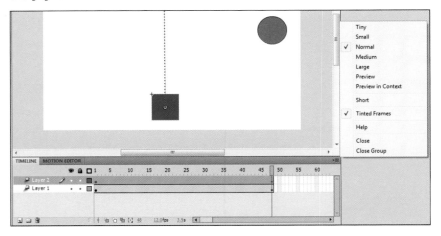

FIGURE 36

Changing the view of the Timeline

FIGURE 37
Changing the frame rate

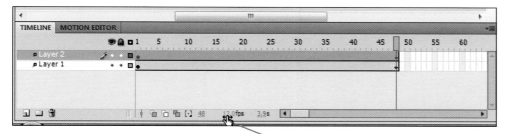

Pointer changes to double-
headed arrow

FIGURE 38
Displaying the Properties option

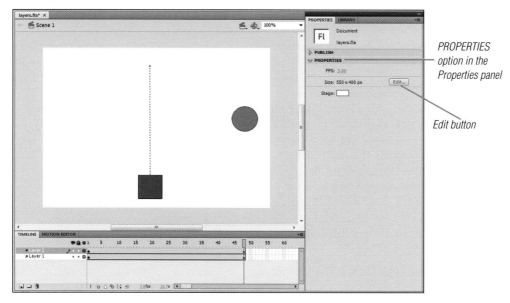

PROPERTIES
option in the
Properties panel

Edit button

1. Point to the **Frame Rate (fps)** on the bottom of the Timeline so the pointer changes to a double-headed arrow ⇳ in Figure 37.

2. Drag the ⇳ **pointer** to change the frame rate to 3.

   TIP Alternately, you can double-click the frame rate number, then type a new number.

3. Play the movie and notice that the speed of the movie changes.

4. Click a blank area of the Stage, then verify the Properties panel is the active panel. If not, click **Window, Properties**.

5. If the PROPERTIES options are not displayed, click **PROPERTIES** on the Properties panel to display the options, as shown in Figure 38.

   The Properties panel provides information about the Stage, including size and background color.

6. Click the **Edit button** in the PROPERTIES section of the Properties panel to display the Document Properties dialog box.

   TIP Another way to open the Document Properties dialog box is using the Modify menu.

7. Change the frame rate to **18**, click **OK**, then play the movie.

8. Change the frame rate to **12** using the Properties panel.

9. Click **frame 20** on the Timeline and notice the position of the objects on the Stage.

10. Drag the **playhead** left and right to display specific frames.

11. Save your work.

You changed the frame rate of the movie and used the playhead to display the contents of frames.

DISTRIBUTE AN ADOBE
FLASH MOVIE

What You'll Do

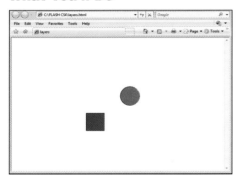

In this lesson, you will prepare a movie for distribution in various formats.

Distributing Movies

When you develop Flash movies, the program saves them in a file format (.fla) that only users who have the Flash program installed on their computers can view. Usually, Flash movies are viewed on the web as part of a website or directly from a viewer's computer using the Flash Player. Flash files (.fla) cannot be viewed on the web using a web browser. They must be converted into a Flash Player file (.swf) so that the web browser knows the type of file to play (.swf) and the program needed to play the file (Flash Player). In addition, the HTML code needs to be created that instructs the web browser to play the swf file. Fortunately, Flash generates both the swf and HTML files when you use the publish feature of Flash.

The process for publishing a Flash movie is to create and save a movie and then click the Publish command on the File menu. You can specify various settings, such as dimensions for the window in which the movie plays in the browser, before publishing the movie. Publishing a movie creates two files: an HTML file and a Flash Player (.swf) file. Both the HTML and swf files retain the same name as the Flash movie file, but with different file extensions:

- .html—the HTML document
- .swf—the Flash Player file

For example, publishing a movie named layers.fla generates two files–layers.html and layers.swf. The HTML document contains the code that the browser interprets to display the movie on the web. The code also specifies which Flash Player movie the browser should play. Sample HTML code referencing a Flash Player movie is shown in Figure 39. If you are familiar with HTML code, you will recognize this as a complete HTML document. Even if you are not familiar with HTML code, you might recognize the code, as seen in Figure 39, that the browser uses to display the Flash movie. For example, the movie source is set to layers.swf; the background color is set to white (#ffffff is the code for white), and the display dimensions (determined by the size of the Stage) are set to 550 × 400.

Flash provides several other ways to distribute your movies that may or may not involve delivery on the web. You can create a stand-alone movie called a **projector**. Projector files, such as Windows .exe files, maintain the movie's interactivity. Alternately, you can create self-running movies, such as QuickTime .mov files, that are not interactive.

You can play projector and non-interactive files directly from a computer, or you can incorporate them into an application, such as a game, that is downloaded or delivered on a CD or DVD. In addition, Flash provides features for creating movies specifically for mobile devices, such as cell phones.

FIGURE 39
Sample HTML code

```
</head>
<body bgcolor="#ffffff">
<!--url's used in the movie-->
<!--text used in the movie-->
<!-- saved from url=(0013)about:internet -->
<script language="JavaScript" type="text/javascript">
          AC_FL_RunContent (
                  'codebase',
'http://download.macromedia.com/pub/shockwave/cabs/flash/swflash.cab#version=10,0,0,0',
                  'width', '550',
                  'height', '400',
                  'src', 'layers',
                  'quality', 'high',
                  'pluginspage', 'http://www.adobe.com/go/getflashplayer',
                  'align', 'middle',
                  'play', 'true',
                  'loop', 'true',
                  'scale', 'showall',
                  'wmode', 'window',
                  'devicefont', 'false',
                  'id', 'layers',
                  'bgcolor', '#ffffff',
                  'name', 'layers',
                  'menu', 'true',
                  'allowFullScreen', 'false',
                  'allowScriptAccess','sameDomain',
                  'movie', 'layers',
                  'salign', ''
          ); //end AC code
</script>
<noscript>
          <object classid="clsid:d27cdb6e-ae6d-11cf-96b8-444553540000"
codebase="http://download.macromedia.com/pub/shockwave/cabs/flash/swflash.cab#version=10,0,0,0" width="550"
height="400" id="layers" align="middle">
          <param name="allowScriptAccess" value="sameDomain" />
          <param name="allowFullScreen" value="false" />
          <param name="movie" value="layers.swf" /><param name="quality" value="high" /><param name="bgcolor"
value="#ffffff" />          <embed src="layers.swf" quality="high" bgcolor="#ffffff" width="550" height="400"
name="layers" align="middle" allowScriptAccess="sameDomain" allowFullScreen="false" type="application/x-
shockwave-flash" pluginspage="http://www.adobe.com/go/getflashplayer" />
          </object>
</noscript>
</body>
</html>
```

Publish a movie for distribution on the web

1. Verify layers.fla is open.

2. Click **File** on the menu bar, then click **Publish**.

   The files layers.html and layers.swf are automatically generated and saved in the same folder as the Flash document.

3. Use your file management program to navigate to the drive and folder where you save your work.

4. Notice the three files that begin with "layers," as shown in Figure 40.

   Layers.fla, the Flash movie; layers.html, the HTML document; layers.swf, the Flash Player file.

5. Double-click **layers.html** to play the movie in the browser.

   Note: Depending on your browser, browser settings and version, you may need to complete additional steps to view the layers.html document.

   TIP Click the browser button on the taskbar if the movie does not open automatically in your browser.

   Notice the animation takes up only a portion of the browser window, as shown in Figure 41. This is because the Stage size is set to 550 x 440, which is smaller than the browser window.

6. Close the browser.

You used the Publish command to create an HTML document (.html) and a Flash Player file (.swf), then you displayed the HTML document in a web browser.

FIGURE 40
The three layers files after publishing the movie

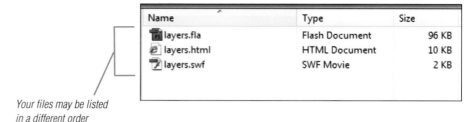

Your files may be listed in a different order

FIGURE 41
The animation played in a browser window

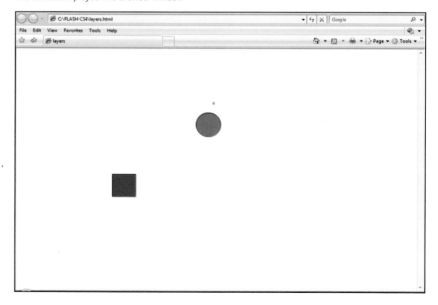

FIGURE 42

Publish Settings dialog box with the Formats tab selected

Create a projector file

1. Return to Flash, click **File** on the menu bar, then click **Publish Settings** to open the Publish Settings dialog box.

2. Verify the Formats tab is selected, as shown in Figure 42.

   Notice the various file formats (and their file names) that can be generated automatically when you publish a Flash document.

3. Click the **Windows Projector (.exe)** (Win) or **Macintosh Projector** (Mac) **check box**.

4. Click **Publish**, then click **OK**.

5. Use your file management program to navigate to the drive and folder where you save your work.

6. Double-click **layers.exe** (Win), or **layers** (Mac), then notice that the application plays in the Flash Player window.

   In this case, the Flash Player window is sized to the dimensions of the Stage.

   Note: You must have the Flash Player installed to view the movie.

7. Close the Flash Player window.

8. Close layers.fla in Flash, saving your changes if prompted.

You created and displayed a stand-alone projector file.

PLAN AN APPLICATION OR A
WEBSITE

What You'll Do

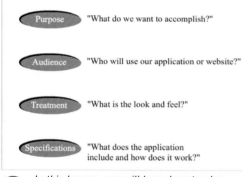

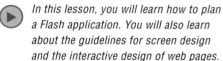

In this lesson, you will learn how to plan a Flash application. You will also learn about the guidelines for screen design and the interactive design of web pages.

Planning an Application or a Website

Flash can be used to develop animations that are part of a product, such as a game or educational tutorial, and delivered via the internet, a CD, a DVD, or a mobile device. You can use Flash to create enhancements to web pages, such as animated logos and interactive navigation buttons. You can also use Flash to create entire websites. No matter what the application, the first step is planning. Often, the temptation is to jump right into the program and start developing movies. The problem is that this invariably results in a more time-consuming process at best; and wasted effort, resources, and money at worst. The larger and more complex the project is, the more critical the planning process becomes. Planning an application or an entire website should involve the following steps:

Step 1: Stating the Purpose (Goals). "What, specifically, do we want to accomplish?"

Determining the goals is a critical step in planning because goals guide the development process, keep the team members on track, and provide a way to evaluate the application or website, both during and after its development.

Step 2: Identifying the Target Audience. "Who will use our application or website?"

Understanding the potential viewers helps in developing an application or a website that can address their needs. For example, children respond to exploration and surprise, so having a dog wag its tail when the mouse pointer rolls over it might appeal to this audience.

Step 3: Determining the Treatment. "What is the look and feel?"

The treatment is how the application or website will be presented to the user, including the tone, approach, and emphasis.

Tone. Will the application or website be humorous, serious, light, heavy, formal, or informal? The tone of a site can often be used to make a statement—projecting a progressive, high-tech, well-funded corporate image, for instance.

Approach. How much direction will be provided to the user? An interactive game might focus on exploration such as when the user points to an object on the screen and the object becomes animated. While an informational website might provide lots of direction and include lists of options in the form of drop-down menus.

Emphasis. How much emphasis will be placed on the various multimedia elements? For example, a company may want to develop an informational application or website that shows the features of its new product line, including video demonstrations and sound narrations of how each product works. The budget might not allow for the expense of creating the videos, so the emphasis would shift to still pictures with text descriptions.

Step 4: Developing the Specifications and Storyboard. "What precisely does the application or website include and how does it work?"

The specifications state what will be included in each screen, including the arrangement of each element and the functionality of each object (for example, what happens when you click the button labeled Skip Intro). Specifications should include the following:

Playback System. The choice of what configuration to target for playback is critical, especially Internet connection speed, browser versions, screen resolution, screen size especially when targeting mobile devices, and plug-ins.

Elements to Include. The specifications should include details about the various elements that are to be included in the site. What are the dimensions for the animations, and what is the frame rate? What are the sizes of the various objects such as photos, buttons, and so on? What fonts, font sizes, and font formatting will be used? Should video or sound be included?

Functionality. The specifications should include the way the program reacts to an action by the user, such as a mouse click. For example, clicking a door (object) might cause a doorbell to ring (sound), the door

Rich media content and accessibility

Flash provides the tools that allow you to create compelling applications and websites by incorporating rich media content, such as animations, sound, and video. Generally, incorporating rich media enhances the user's experience. However, accessibility becomes an issue for those persons who have visual, hearing, or mobility impairments, or have a cognitive disability. Designers need to utilize techniques that help ensure accessibility, such as providing consistency in navigation and layout, labeling graphics, captioning audio content throughout the applications and website, and providing keyboard access.

to open (an animation), an "exit the program" message to appear (text), or an entirely new screen to be displayed.

The **user interface** involves designing the appearance of objects (how each object is arranged on the screen) and the interactivity (how the user navigates through the site).

A **flowchart** is a visual representation of how the contents in an application or a website are organized and how various screens are linked. It provides a guide for the developer and helps to identify problems with the navigation scheme before work begins. Figure 43 shows a simple flowchart illustrating the site organization and links.

A **storyboard** shows the layout of the various screens. It describes the contents and illustrates how text, graphics, animation, and other screen elements will be positioned. It also indicates the navigation process, such as menus and buttons. Figure 44 shows a storyboard. The exact content (such as a specific photo) does not have to be decided, but it is important to show where text, graphics, photos, buttons, and other elements, will be placed. Thus, the storyboard includes placeholders for the various elements.

Using Screen Design Guidelines

The following screen design guidelines are used by application and web developers.

The implementation of these guidelines is affected by the goals of the application or website, the intended audience, and the content.

Balance in screen design refers to the distribution of optical weight in the layout. Optical weight is the ability of an object to attract the viewer's eye, as determined by the object's size, shape, color, and so on. Figure 44 shows a fairly well-balanced layout, especially if the logo has as much optical weight as the text description. In general, a balanced design is more appealing to a viewer. However, for a game application or entertainment site, a balanced layout may not be desired.

FIGURE 43
Sample Flowchart

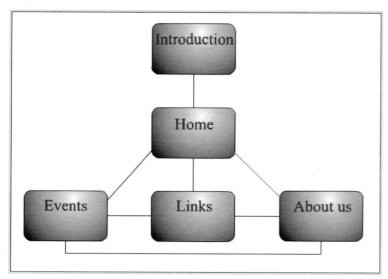

FIGURE 44
Sample Storyboard

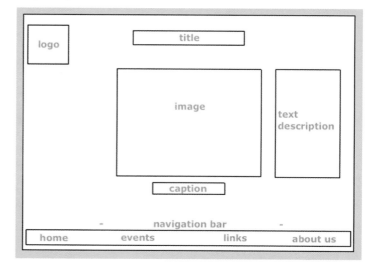

Unity helps the screen objects reinforce each other. **Intra-screen** unity has to do with how the various screen objects relate and how they all fit in. For example, a children's game might only use cartoon characterizations of animals for all the objects—including navigation buttons and sound control buttons, as well as the on-screen characters. **Inter-screen** unity refers to the design that viewers encounter as they navigate from one screen to another, and it provides consistency throughout the application. For example, all navigation buttons are located in the same place on each screen.

Movement refers to the way the viewer's eyes move through the objects on the screen. Different types of objects and various animation techniques can be used to draw the viewer to a location on the screen.

For example, a photo of a waterfall may cause the viewer's eyes to follow the flow of the water down, especially if the waterfall is animated. The designer could then place an object, such as a logo or link, below the waterfall.

Using Interactive Design Guidelines

In addition to screen design guidelines, interactive guidelines determine the interactivity of the application. The following guidelines are not absolute rules but are affected by the goals of the application, the intended audience, and the content:

- Make it simple, easy to understand, and easy to use so that viewers do not have to spend time learning what the application is about and what they need to do.

- Build in consistency in the navigation scheme. Help the users know where they are in the application and help them avoid getting lost.
- Provide feedback. Users need to know when an action, such as clicking a button, has been completed. Changing its color or shape, or adding a sound can indicate this.
- Give the user control. Allow the user to skip long introductions; provide controls for starting, stopping, and rewinding animations, video, and audio; and provide controls for adjusting audio.

Project management

Developing websites or any extensive application, such as a game, involves project management. A project plan needs to be developed that provides the project scope and identifies the milestones, including analyzing, designing, building, testing, and launching. Personnel and resource needs are identified, budgets built, tasks assigned, and schedules developed. Successful projects are a team effort relying on the close collaboration of designers, developers, project managers, graphic artists, programmers, testers, and others. Adobe provides various product suites, such as their Creative Suite 4 (CS4) Web Collection series, that include programs such as Flash, Dreamweaver, Fireworks, Photoshop, and Illustrator. These are the primary tools needed to develop interactive applications and websites. These programs are designed for easy integration. So, a graphic artist can use Photoshop to develop an image that can easily be imported into Flash and used by an animator. In addition, other tools in the suites, such as Adobe Bridge and Adobe Version Cue, help ensure efficient workflow when working in a team environment.

The Flash Workflow Process

After the planning process, you are ready to start work on the Flash documents. The following steps can be used as guidelines in a general workflow process suggested by Adobe.

Step 1: Create and/or acquire the elements to be used in the application. The elements include text, photos, drawings, video, and audio. The elements become the raw material for the graphics, animations, menus, buttons, and content that populate the application and provide the interactivity. You can use the various Flash drawing and text tools to create your own images and text content; or, you can use another program, such as Adobe Photoshop, to develop the elements, and then import them into Flash. Alternately, you can acquire stock clip art and photographs. You can produce video and audio content in-house and import it into Flash or you can acquire these elements from a third party.

Step 2: Arrange the elements and create the animations. Arrange the elements (objects) on the Stage and on the Timeline to define when and how they appear in your application. Once the elements are available, you can create the various animations called for in the specifications.

Step 3: Apply special effects. Flash provides innumerable special effects that can be applied to the various media elements and animations. These include graphic and text filters, such as drop shadows, blurs, glows, and bevels. In addition, there are effects for sounds and animations such as fade-ins and fade-outs, acceleration and deceleration, and morphing.

Step 4: Create the interactivity. Flash provides a scripting feature, ActionScript, which allows you to develop programming code to control how the media elements behave, including how various objects respond to user interactions, such as clicking buttons and rolling over images.

Step 5: Test and publish the application. Testing should be done throughout the development process, including using the Test Movie feature in the Control menu to test the movie using the Flash Player and to publish the movie in order to test it in a browser.

Using the Flash Help feature

Flash provides a comprehensive Help feature that can be very useful when first learning the program. You access the Help feature from the Help menu. The Help feature is organized by categories, including Using Flash CS4 Professional, which have several topics such as Workspace and Managing documents. In addition, the Help feature has a Help Search feature. You use the Help Search feature to search for topics using keywords, such as Timeline. Searching by keywords accesses the Flash Community Help feature, which displays links to content relevant to the search terms. Other resources not affiliated with Adobe are available through the web. You may find some by searching the web for Flash resources.

FIGURE 45

The Flash Help categories

FIGURE 46

The Flash Help Search feature

Search term

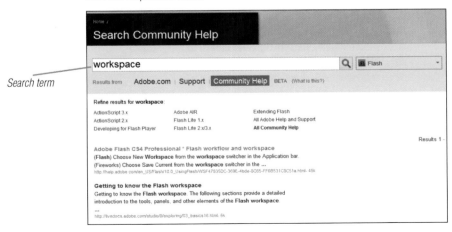

1. Start a new Flash document.

2. Click **Help** on the menu bar, then click **Flash Help**.

   Note: If you see a page not found message, be sure you are connected to the Internet.

3. Click the **Expand button** ⊞ next to Workspace to expand the category, as shown in Figure 45.

4. Click **The Timeline**, then click **About the Timeline**.

5. Read through the text in About the Timeline.

6. Scroll to display the top of the Help window.

7. Click in the **Search text box**, then type **workspace**.

8. Press **[Enter]** (Win) or **[return]** (Mac) to access the Community Help site.

9. Study the various links provided on the site.

   Note: Figure 46 shows the results of one search for workspace. New links are added regularly because this is community-based help. Therefore, your results may differ.

10. Close the Community Help site and the Flash Help site, then exit the Flash program.

You used the Flash Help feature to access information on the Timeline and the workspace.

Start Flash, open a movie, set the magnification and make changes to the workspace.

1. Start Flash, open fl1_2.fla, then save it as **skillsdemo1**. This movie has two layers. Layer 1 contains the heading and the line at the top of the Stage. Layer 2 contains an animation that runs for 75 frames.
2. Change the magnification to 50% using the View menu. (*Hint:* Click View, point to Magnification, then click 50%.)
3. Change the magnification to Fit in Window.
4. Change the Timeline view to Small. (*Hint:* Click the Frame View icon in the upper-right corner of the Timeline title bar.)
5. Hide all panels.
6. Display the Tools panel, Timeline panel, Properties panel, and the Library panel.
7. Group the Library and Properties panels if they are not already grouped.
8. Drag the Library panel from the Properties panel and position it on the Stage.
9. Collapse the Library panel.
10. Close the Library panel to remove it from the screen.
11. Reset the Essentials workspace.

Play and test a movie.

1. Drag the playhead to view the contents of each frame. Use the commands on the Control menu to play and rewind the movie.
2. Press [Enter] (Win) or [return] (Mac) to play and stop the movie.

3. Use the Controller to rewind, play, stop, and start the movie.
4. Test the movie in the Flash Player window, then close the Flash Player window.

Change the document size and background color.

1. Use the Properties panel to display the Document Properties dialog box.
2. Change the document height to 380.
3. Change the background color to a medium gray color (#999999).
4. Close the Document Properties dialog box.
5. Play the movie.

Create an object, create a motion tween animation, and apply effects.

1. Insert a new layer above Layer 2, then select frame 1 of the new layer.
2. Draw a green ball in the middle of the left side of the Stage, approximately the same size as the red ball. (*Hint:* The green gradient color can be used to draw the ball. Several gradient colors are found in the bottom row of the color palette when you click on the Fill Color tool in the Tools panel.)
3. Use the Selection tool to draw a marquee around the green ball to select it, then create a motion tween to animate the green ball so that it moves across the screen from left to right.

4. Use the Selection tool to reshape the motion path to an arc by dragging the middle of the path downward.
5. Play the movie.
6. Use the Undo command to undo the reshape. (*Note:* You may need to use the Undo feature twice.)
7. Use the Selection tool to select frame 75 of the new layer, click the green ball if it is not already selected to select it, then use the Properties panel to change the transparency (alpha) from 100% to 20%. (*Hint:* If the Properties panel COLOR EFFECT option is not displayed, make sure the Properties panel is open and click the green ball to make sure it is selected.)
8. Play the movie, then rewind it.
9. Click frame 75 on Layer 3 and click the green ball to select it.
10. Use the Properties panel to increase the width of the ball to 80.
11. Play the movie.
12. Select frame 1 on Layer 3 and click the green ball to select it.
13. Use the Filters option in the Properties panel to add a drop shadow.
14. Play the movie.
15. Select frame 1 on Layer 2 and click the red ball to select it.
16. Open the Motion Presets panel and add a bounce-smoosh preset.
17. Play the movie.
18. Save the movie.

Change the frame rate and change the view of the Timeline.

1. Change the frame rate to 8 frames per second, play the movie, then change the frame rate to 12.
2. Change the view of the Timeline to display more frames.
3. Change the view of the Timeline to display a preview of the object thumbnails.
4. Change the view of the Timeline to display the Small view.
5. Click frame 1 on Layer 1, use the playhead to display each frame, then compare your screens to Figure 47.
6. Save the movie.

Publish a movie.

1. Click File on the menu bar, then click Publish.
2. Open your browser, then open skillsdemo1.html.
3. View the movie, then close your browser.

Create a projector file.

1. Display the Publish Settings dialog box.
2. Select the appropriate projector setting for your operating system.
3. Publish the movie, then close the Publish Settings dialog box.
4. Use your file management program to navigate to the drive and folder where yousave your work, then open the skillsdemo1 projector file.

5. View the movie, then close the Flash Player window.

6. Save and close the Flash document.
7. Exit Flash.

FIGURE 47
Completed Skills Review

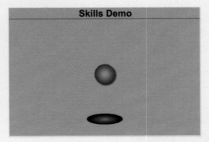

A friend cannot decide whether to sign up for a class in Flash or Dreamweaver. You help her decide by showing her what you already know about Flash. Since you think she'd enjoy a class in Flash, you decide to show her how easy it is to create a simple animation. You decide to animate three objects. The first object is placed on the center of the Stage and pulsates throughout the movie. The second object enters the Stage from the left side and moves across the middle of the Stage and off the right side of the Stage. The third object enters the Stage from the right side and moves across the middle of the Stage and off the left side of the Stage. The motion paths for the two objects that move across the Stage are reshaped so they go above and below the pulsating object in the middle of the Stage.

1. Open a Flash document, then save it as **demonstration**.
2. Change the view to 50%.
3. Use the tools on the Tools panel to create a circle (or object of your choice) and color of your choice on the middle of the Stage.
4. Draw a marquee around the object to select it and apply a pulse motion preset.
5. Insert a new layer, then select frame 1 on the layer.
6. Create a simple shape or design, and place it off the left side of the Stage and halfway down the Stage.

7. Select the object and insert a motion tween that moves the object directly across the screen and off the right side of the Stage.
8. Reshape the motion path so that the object goes in an arc below the center pulsating object.
9. Insert a new layer, then select frame 1 on the layer.
10. Create an object and place it off the right side of the Stage and halfway down the Stage.

11. Draw a marquee to select the object and insert a motion tween that moves the object directly across the screen and off the left side of the Stage.
12. Reshape the motion path so that the object goes in an arc above the center pulsating object.
13. Play the movie.
14. Add a background color.
15. Play the movie and test it.
16. Save the movie, then compare your movie to the sample provided in Figure 48.

FIGURE 48
Sample completed Project Builder 1

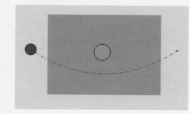

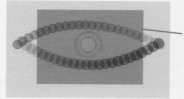

This figure shows the animated objects with outlines of their positions during the animations. Your completed project will not show these outlines.

You've been asked to develop a simple movie about recycling for a day care center. For this project, you will add two animations to an existing movie. You will show three objects that appear on the screen at different times, and then move each object to a recycle bin at different times. You can create the objects using any of the Tools on the Tools panel.

1. Open fl1_3.fla, then save it as **recycle**.
2. Play the movie and study the Timeline to familiarize yourself with the movie's current settings. Currently, there are no animations.

3. Insert a new layer above Layer 2, then draw a small object in the upper-left corner of the Stage.
4. Create a motion tween that moves the object to the recycle bin. (*Hint:* Be sure to select frame 40 on the new layer before creating the motion tween animation.)
5. Reshape the path so that the object moves in an arc to the recycle bin. (*Note:* At this time, the object will appear outside the recycle bin when it is placed in the bin.)
6. Insert a new layer above the top layer, draw a small object in the upper-center of the Stage, then create a motion tween that moves the object to the recycle bin.

7. Insert a new layer above the top layer, draw a small object in the upper-right corner of the Stage, then create a motion tween that moves the object to the recycle bin.
8. Reshape the path so that the object moves in an arc to the recycle bin.
9. Move Layer 1 to the top of all the layers.
10. Play the movie and compare your movie to the sample provided in Figure 49.
11. Save the movie.

FIGURE 49
Sample completed Project Builder 2

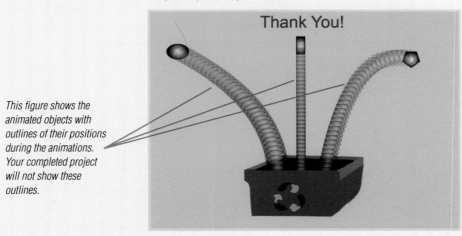

This figure shows the animated objects with outlines of their positions during the animations. Your completed project will not show these outlines.

Figure 50 shows the home page of a website. Study the figure and answer the following questions. For each question, indicate how you determined your answer.

1. Connect to the Internet, then go to *www. argosycruises.com*.

2. Open a document in a word processor or open a new Flash document, save the file as **dpc1**, then answer the following questions. (*Hint*: Use the Flash Text tool if you open a Flash document.)

   - Whose website is this?
   - What is the goal(s) of the site?
   - Who is the target audience?
   - What treatment (look and feel) is used?
   - What are the design layout guidelines being used (balance, movement, etc.)?
   - How can animation enhance this page?
   - Do you think this is an effective design for the company, its products, and its target audience? Why, or why not?
   - What suggestions would you make to improve the design, and why?

FIGURE 50
Design Project

There are numerous companies in the business of developing websites for others. Many of these companies use Flash as one of their primary development tools. These companies promote themselves through their own websites and usually provide online portfolios with samples of their work. Log onto the Internet, then use your favorite search engine and keywords such as Flash developers and Flash animators to locate three of these companies, and generate the following information for each one. A sample website is shown in Figure 51.

1. Company name:
2. Contact information (address, phone, and so on):
3. Website URL:
4. Company mission:
5. Services provided:
6. Sample list of clients:
7. Describe three ways the company seems to have used Flash in its website. Were these effective? Why, or why not?
8. Describe three applications of Flash that the company includes in its portfolio (or showcases or samples). Were these effective? Why, or why not?

9. Would you want to work for this company? Why, or why not?
10. Would you recommend this company to another company that was looking to enhance its website? Why, or why not?

FIGURE 51
Sample website for Portfolio Project

chapter

2

DRAWING OBJECTS IN
ADOBE FLASH

1. Use the Flash drawing tools

2. Select objects and apply colors

3. Work with drawn objects

4. Work with text and text objects

5. Work with layers and objects

2 DRAWING OBJECTS IN
ADOBE FLASH

Introduction

Computers can display graphics in either a bitmap or a vector format. The difference between these formats is in how they describe an image. Bitmap graphics represent the image as an array of dots, called **pixels**, which are arranged within a grid. Each pixel in an image has an exact position on the screen and a precise color. To make a change in a bitmap graphic, you modify the pixels. When you enlarge a bitmap graphic, the number of pixels remains the same, resulting in jagged edges that decrease the quality of the image. Vector graphics represent the image using lines and curves, which you can resize without losing image quality. Also, the file size of a vector image is generally smaller than the file size of a bitmap image, which makes vector images particularly useful for a website. However, vector graphics are not as effective as bitmap graphics for representing photo-realistic images. One of the most compelling features of Flash is the ability to create and manipulate vector graphics.

Images (objects) created using Flash drawing tools have a stroke (border line), a fill, or both. In addition, the stroke of an object can be segmented into smaller lines. You can modify the size, shape, rotation, and color of each stroke, fill, and segment.

Flash provides two drawing modes, called models. In the Merge Drawing Model, when you draw two shapes and one overlaps the other, a change in the top object may affect the object beneath it. For example, if you draw a circle on top of a rectangle and then move the circle off the rectangle, the portion of the rectangle covered by the circle is removed. The Object Drawing Model allows you to overlap shapes which are then kept separate, so that changes in one object do not affect another object. Another way to avoid having changes in one object affect another is to place them on separate layers on the Timeline as you did in Chapter 1.

Tools You'll Use

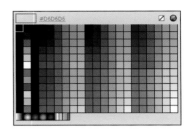

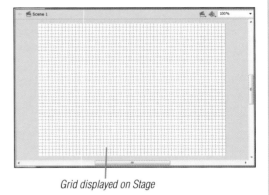

Grid displayed on Stage

USE THE
FLASH DRAWING TOOLS

What You'll Do

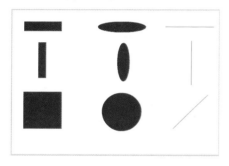

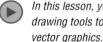 In this lesson, you will use several drawing tools to create various vector graphics.

Using Flash Drawing and Editing Tools

When you point to a tool on the Tools panel, its name appears next to the tool. Figure 1 identifies the tools described in the following paragraphs. Several of the tools have options that modify their use. These options are available in the Options area of the Tools panel when the tool is selected.

Selection—Used to select an object or parts of an object, such as the stroke or fill; and to reshape objects. The options for the Selection tool are Snap to Objects (aligns objects), Smooth (smoothes lines), and Straighten (straightens lines).

Subselection—Used to select, drag, and reshape an object. Vector graphics are composed of lines and curves (each of which is a segment) connected by **anchor points**. Selecting an object with this tool displays the anchor points and allows you to use them to edit the object.

Free Transform—Used to rotate, scale, skew, and distort objects.

Gradient Transform—Used to transform a gradient fill by adjusting the size, direction, or center of the fill.

The Free and Gradient Transform tools are grouped within one icon on the Tools panel.

3D Rotation—Used to create 3D effects by rotating movie clips in 3D space on the Stage.

3D Translation—Used to create 3D effects by moving movie clips in 3D space on the Stage.

The 3D Rotation and the 3D Translation tools are grouped within one icon on the Tools panel.

Lasso—Used to select objects or parts of objects. The Polygon Mode option allows you to draw straight lines when selecting an object.

Pen—Used to draw lines and curves by creating a series of dots, known as anchor points, that are automatically connected. Other tools used to add, delete, and convert the anchor points created by the Pen tool are grouped with the Pen tool. To see the menu containing these tools, hold down the Pen tool until the menu opens.

Text—Used to create and edit text.

Line—Used to draw straight lines. You can draw vertical, horizontal, and 45° diagonal lines by pressing and holding [Shift] while drawing the line.

Rectangle—Used to draw rectangular shapes. Press and hold [Shift] to draw a perfect square.

Oval—Used to draw oval shapes. Press and hold [Shift] to draw a perfect circle.

Primitive Rectangle and Oval—Used to draw objects with properties, such as corner radius or inner radius, that can be changed using the Properties panel.

PolyStar—Used to draw polygons and stars.

The Rectangle, Oval, Primitive and PolyStar tools are grouped within one tool on the Tools panel.

Pencil—Used to draw freehand lines and shapes. The Pencil Mode option displays a menu with the following commands: Straighten (draws straight lines), Smooth (draws smooth curved lines), and Ink (draws freehand with no modification).

Brush—Used to draw (paint) with brush-like strokes. Options allow you to set the size and shape of the brush, and to determine the area to be painted, such as inside or behind an object.

Spray Brush—Used to spray colors and patterns onto objects. Dots are the default pattern for the spray. However, you can use a symbol, such as a flag, to create the pattern.

The Brush and Spray Brush tools are grouped together.

Deco—Used to turn graphic shapes into geometric patterns or create kaleidoscopic-like effects.

Bone—Used to animate a set of objects, such as arms and legs, using a series of linked objects to create character animations.

Bind—Used to adjust the relationships between individual bones.

Paint Bucket—Used to fill enclosed areas of a drawing with color. Options allow you to fill areas that have gaps and to make adjustments in a gradient fill.

Ink Bottle—Used to apply line colors and thickness to the stroke of an object.

The Paint Bucket and Ink Bottle are grouped together.

Eyedropper—Used to select stroke, fill, and text attributes so they can be copied from one object to another.

Eraser—Used to erase lines and fills. Options allow you to choose what part of the object to erase, as well as the size and shape of the eraser.

FIGURE 1
Flash tools

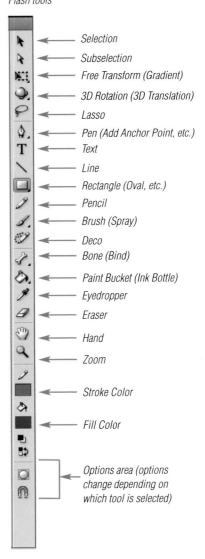

Selection
Subselection
Free Transform (Gradient)
3D Rotation (3D Translation)
Lasso
Pen (Add Anchor Point, etc.)
Text
Line
Rectangle (Oval, etc.)
Pencil
Brush (Spray)
Deco
Bone (Bind)
Paint Bucket (Ink Bottle)
Eyedropper
Eraser
Hand
Zoom
Stroke Color
Fill Color
Options area (options change depending on which tool is selected)

Hand—Used to move the Stage around the Pasteboard by dragging the Stage.

Zoom—Used to change the magnification of an area of the Stage. Clicking an area of the Stage zooms in and holding down [Alt] (Win) or [option] $\mathcal{H}$ (Mac) and clicking zooms out.

Stroke Color—Used to set the stroke color of drawn objects.

Fill Color—Used to set the fill color of drawn objects.

Options—Used to select an option for a tool, such as the type of rectangle (object drawn) or size of the brush when using the Brush tool.

Working with Grouped Tools
To display a list of grouped tools, you click the tool and hold the mouse button until the menu opens. For example, if you want to select the Oval tool and the Rectangle tool is displayed, you click and hold the Rectangle tool. Then, when the menu opens, you click the Oval tool option. You know a tool is a grouped tool if you see an arrow in the lower-right corner of the tool icon.

Working with Tool Options
Some tools have additional options that allow you to modify their use. For example, the brush tool has options to set the brush size and to set where the brush fill will be applied. If additional options for a tool are available, they appear at the bottom of the Tools panel in the Options area when the tool is selected. If the option has a menu associated with it, then the option icon will have an arrow in the lower-right corner. Click and hold the option until the menu opens.

Tools for Creating Vector Graphics
The Oval, Rectangle, Pencil, Brush, Line, and Pen tools are used to create vector objects.

Positioning Objects on the Stage
Flash provides several ways to position objects on the Stage including rulers, gridlines, and guides. The Rulers, Grid, and Guides commands, which are found on the View menu, are used to turn on and off these features. Figure 2 shows ruler lines being used to position an object.

FIGURE 2
Using rulers to position an object

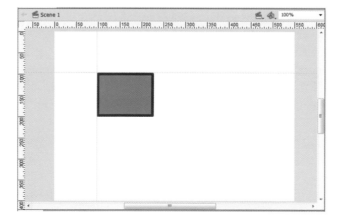

After displaying the rulers, you can drag the lines from the top ruler or the left side ruler to the Stage. To remove a ruler line, you drag the ruler line up to the top ruler or across to the left ruler. You can specify the unit of measure for the rulers.

Figure 3 shows the gridlines displayed and being used to position an object. You can modify the grid size and color. In addition to using rulers and guides to help place objects, you can create a new layer as a Guide layer that you use to position objects on the Stage. When you turn gridlines and guides on, they appear on the Stage. However, they do not appear in the Flash movie when you test or publish it.

Other methods for positioning objects include the align options found on the Align command of the Modify menu, as shown in Figure 4, and the options on the Align panel.

FIGURE 3

Using gridlines to position an object

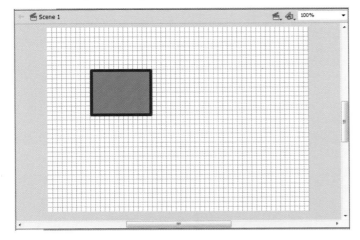

FIGURE 4

The Align command option from the Modify menu

Show gridlines and check settings

1. Open fl2_1.fla from the drive and folder where your Data Files are stored, then save it as **tools**.

2. Click **Window** on the menu bar, point to **Workspace**, then click **Reset 'Essentials'**.

3. Click **View** on the menu bar, point to **Magnification**, then click **Fit in Window**.

4. Click the **Stroke Color tool color swatch** ◢ on the Tools panel, then click the **red color swatch** in the left column of the Color palette.

5. Click the **Fill Color tool color swatch** ◢ on the Tools panel, then click the **blue color swatch** in the left column of the Color palette.

6. Click **View** on the menu bar, point to **Grid**, then click **Show Grid** to display the gridlines.

   A gray grid appears on the Stage.

7. Point to each tool on the Tools panel, then read its name.

8. Click the **Text tool** T , then click **CHARACTER** to open the area if it is not open already.

   Notice the options in the Properties panel including the CHARACTER area, as shown in Figure 5. The Properties panel options change depending on the tool selected. For the Text tool the properties include the character family and the paragraph family.

You opened a document, saved it, set up the workspace, changed the stroke and fill colors, displayed the grid, viewed tool names on the Tools panel, and then viewed the Text tool options in the Properties panel.

FIGURE 5
Tool name on the Tools panel

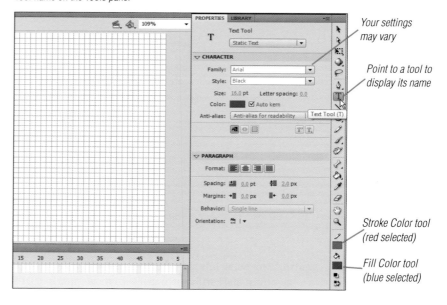

Your settings may vary

Point to a tool to display its name

Stroke Color tool (red selected)

Fill Color tool (blue selected)

FIGURE 6

Objects created with drawing tools

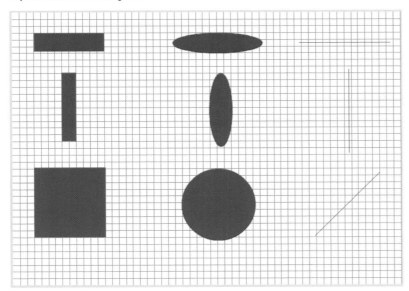

1. Click the **Rectangle tool** ⬛ on the Tools panel.

   Note: If the Rectangle tool is not displayed, click and hold the Oval tool to display the group of tools.

2. Verify that the Object Drawing option ◯ in the Options area of the Tools panel is deselected.

   TIP   When the Object Drawing option is deselected, the object is drawn so that its stroke and fill can be selected separately.

3. Using Figure 6 as a guide, draw the three rectangle shapes.

   TIP   Use the grid to approximate shape sizes and hold down [Shift] to draw a square. To undo an action, click the Undo command on the Edit menu.

   Notice the blue color for the fill and the red color for the strokes (border lines).

4. Click and hold down the **Rectangle tool** ⬛ on the Tools panel, then click the **Oval tool** ◯ .

5. Using Figure 6 as a guide, draw the three oval shapes.

   TIP   Hold down [Shift] to draw a perfect circle.

6. Click the **Line tool** ╲ , then, using Figure 6 as a guide, draw the three lines.

   TIP   Hold down [Shift] to draw a straight line.

You used the Rectangle, Oval, and Line tools to draw objects on the Stage.

Use the Pen, Pencil, and Brush tools

1. Click **Insert** on the menu bar, point to **Timeline**, then click **Layer**.

   A new layer—Layer 2—appears above Layer 1.

2. Click **frame 5** on Layer 2.

3. Click **Insert** on the menu bar, point to **Timeline**, then click **Keyframe**.

   Since the objects were drawn in frame 1 on Layer 1, they are no longer visible when you insert a keyframe in frame 5 on Layer 2. A keyframe allows you to draw in any location on the Stage on the specified frame.

4. Click the **Zoom tool** 🔍 on the Tools panel, click near the upper-left quadrant of the Stage to zoom in, then scroll as needed to see more of the grid.

5. Click the **Pen tool** ✒. on the Tools panel, position it in the upper-left quadrant of the Stage, as shown in Figure 7, then click to set an anchor point.

6. Using Figure 8 as a guide, click the remaining anchor points to finish drawing an arrow.

   | TIP To close an object, be sure to re-click the first anchor point as your last action.

7. Click the **Paint Bucket tool** 🪣 , then click inside the arrow.

8. Click **View** on the menu bar, point to **Magnification**, then click **Fit in Window**.

9. Insert a **new layer**, Layer 3, then insert a **keyframe** in frame 10.

10. Click the **Pencil tool** ✏ on the Tools panel.

11. Click **Pencil Mode** in the Options area of the Tools panel, then click the **Smooth option** ⌇. , as shown in Figure 9.

(continued)

FIGURE 7
Positioning the Pen tool on the Stage

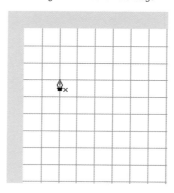

FIGURE 8
Setting anchor points to draw an arrow

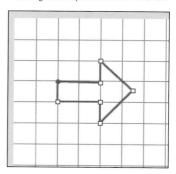

FIGURE 9
Pencil tool options

Click the Pencil Mode Smooth icon to display the 3 options (Note: The Straighten icon might be displayed instead of the Smooth icon.)

Drawing Objects in Adobe Flash

FIGURE 10

Images drawn using drawing tools

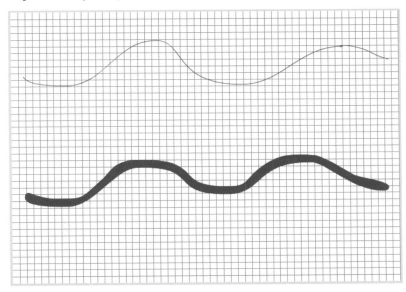

FIGURE 11

The dot pattern indicating the object is selected

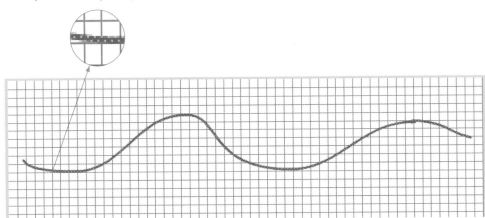

12. Draw the top image, as shown in Figure 10.

13. Click the **Brush tool** ✎ on the Tools panel.

14. Click the **Brush Size Icon** ·. in the Options area of the Tools panel, then click the fifth option from the top.

15. Draw the bottom image, as shown in Figure 10.

    Notice the Pencil tool displays the stroke color and the Brush tool displays the fill color.

You added a layer, inserted a keyframe, then used the Pen tool to draw an arrow; you selected the Smooth option for the Pencil tool and drew an object; you selected a brush size for the Brush tool and drew an object.

Modify an object using tool options

1. Click the **Selection tool** ➤ on the Tools panel, then drag a **marquee** around the top object to select it.

   The line displays a dot pattern, as shown in Figure 11, indicating that it is selected.

2. Click the **Pencil Mode Smooth icon** ς. in the Options area of the Tools panel three times. The line becomes smoother.

3. Use the stroke slider △ in the FILL AND STROKE area of the Properties panel to change the stroke size to **20**.

4. Click the **Style list arrow** in the FILL AND STROKE area, then click **Dotted**.

5. Repeat step 4 and change the line style to **Hairline**.

(continued)

6. Click **View** on the menu bar, point to **Grid**, then click **Show Grid** to remove the gridlines.

7. Save your work.

You smoothed objects using the tool options.

Use the Spray tool with a symbol

1. Click **Insert** on the menu bar, point to **Timeline**, then click **Layer**.

2. Click **frame 15** on Layer 4.

3. Click **Insert** on the menu bar, point to **Timeline**, then click **Keyframe**.

4. Click and hold the **Brush tool** on the Tools panel, then click the **Spray Brush tool**.

5. Display the Properties panel if it is not already displayed, then click the **Edit button** in the SYMBOL area of the Properties panel, as shown in Figure 12.

   Note: If the Properties panel does not display the options for the Spray Brush tool, click the Selection tool, then click the Spray Brush tool.

6. Click **Flag** in the Swap Symbol dialog box, then click **OK**.

7. Click the **Random scaling check box** to select it, then click to deselect the **Rotate symbol check box** and the **Random rotation check box** if they are checked.

8. Display the Brush section of the Properties panel, then set the width and height to **9 px**.

(continued)

FIGURE 12
The properties for the Spray Brush tool

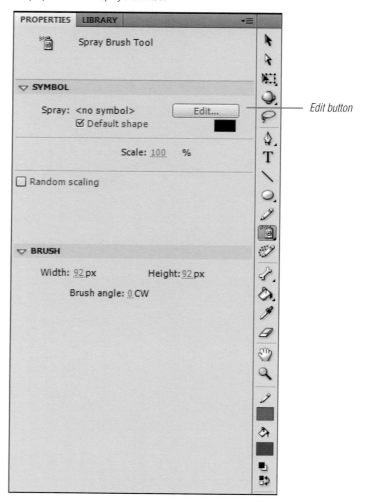

Edit button

FIGURE 13
A design created using the Spray Brush tool

9. Click the **Spray Brush tool** in the Tools panel, then slowly draw the **U** in USA, as shown in Figure 13.

10. Click the **Selection tool** in the Tools panel, click the **Spray Brush tool**, then draw the **S** in USA.

11. Click the **Selection tool** in the Tools panel, click the **Spray Brush tool**, then draw the **A** in USA.

Hint: If you need to redo the drawing use the Selection tool to draw a marquee around the drawing, then delete the selection.

12. Save your work.

You specified a symbol as a pattern and used the Spray Brush tool to complete a drawing.

SELECT OBJECTS
AND APPLY COLORS

What You'll Do

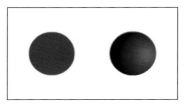

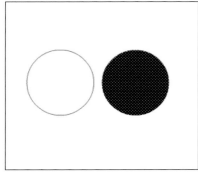

In this lesson, you will use several techniques to select objects, change the color of strokes and fills, and create a gradient fill.

Selecting Objects

Before you can edit a drawing, you must first select the object, or the part of the object, on which you want to work. Objects are made up of a stroke(s) and a fill. Strokes can have several segments. For example, a rectangle will have four stroke segments, one for each side of the object. These can be selected separately or as a whole. Flash highlights objects that have been selected, as shown in Figure 14. When the stroke of an object is selected, a colored line appears. When the fill of an object is selected, a dot pattern appears; and when objects are grouped, a bounding box appears.

Using the Selection Tool

You can use the Selection tool to select part or all of an object, and to select multiple objects. To select only the fill, click just the fill; to select only the stroke, click just the stroke. To select both the fill and the stroke, double-click the object or draw a marquee around it. To select part of an object, drag a marquee that defines the area you wish to select, as shown in Figure 14. To select multiple objects or combinations of strokes

and fills, press and hold [Shift], then click each item. To deselect an item(s), click a blank area of the Stage.

Using the Lasso Tool

The Lasso tool provides more flexibility than the Selection tool when selecting an object(s) or parts of an object on the Stage. You can use the tool in a freehand manner to draw any shape that then selects the object(s) within the shape. Alternately, you can use the Polygon Mode option to draw straight lines and connect them to form a shape that will select any object(s) within the shape.

Drawing Model Modes

Flash provides two drawing modes, called models. In the Merge Drawing Model mode, the stroke and fill of an object are separate. Thus, as you draw an object such as a circle, the stroke and fill can be selected individually as described earlier. When using the Object Drawing Model mode, the stroke and fill are combined and cannot be selected individually. However, you can use the Break Apart option from the Modify menu to separate the stroke and fill so that they can be selected individually. In addition, you can turn off either the stroke or fill when drawing an object in either mode. You can toggle between the two modes by clicking the Object Drawing option in the Options area of the Tools panel.

Working with Colors

Flash allows you to change the color of the stroke and fill of an object. Figure 15 shows the Colors area of the Tools panel. To change a color, you click the color swatch of the Stroke Color tool or the color swatch of the Fill Color tool, and then select a color swatch on the Color palette. The Color palette, as shown in Figure 16, allows you to select a color from the palette or type in a six-character code that represents the values of three colors (red, green, blue), referred to as

RGB. When these characters are combined in various ways, they can represent virtually any color. The values are in a hexadecimal format (base 16), so they include letters and digits (A–F + 0–9 = 16 options), and they are preceded by a pound sign (#). The first two characters represent the value for red, the next two for green, and the last two for blue. For example, #000000 represents black (lack of color); #FFFFFF represents white; and #FFCC66 represents a shade of gold. You do not have to memorize the codes. There are reference manuals with the codes, and many programs allow you to set the values visually by selecting a color from a palette. You can also use the Properties panel to change the stroke and fill colors.

You can set the desired colors before drawing an object, or you can change a

color of a previously drawn object. You can use the Ink Bottle tool to change the stroke color, and you can use the Paint Bucket tool to change the fill color.

Working with Gradients

A gradient is a color fill that makes a gradual transition from one color to another. Gradients can be very useful for creating a 3D effect, drawing attention to an object, and generally enhancing the appearance of an object. You can apply a gradient fill by using the Paint Bucket tool. The position of the Paint Bucket tool over the object is important because it determines the direction of the gradient fill. The Color palette can be used to create and alter custom gradients.

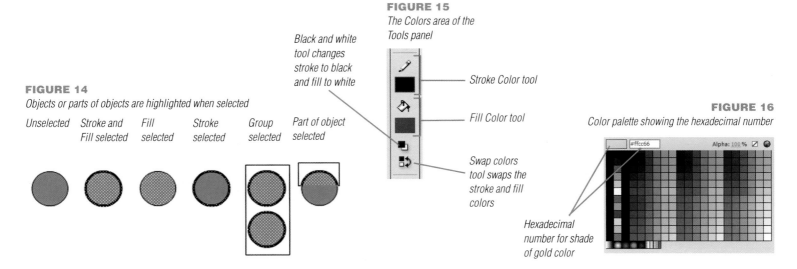

FIGURE 15
The Colors area of the Tools panel

Black and white tool changes stroke to black and fill to white

Stroke Color tool

Fill Color tool

Swap colors tool swaps the stroke and fill colors

FIGURE 14
Objects or parts of objects are highlighted when selected

Unselected | Stroke and Fill selected | Fill selected | Stroke selected | Group selected | Part of object selected

FIGURE 16
Color palette showing the hexadecimal number

#ffcc66   Alpha: 100 %

Hexadecimal number for shade of gold color

Select a drawing using the Selection tool

1. Click **frame 1** on the Timeline.

   TIP The options available to you in the Properties panel differ depending on whether you click a frame number on the Timeline or a frame within a layer.

2. Click the **Selection tool** ➤ on the Tools panel if it is not already selected, then drag a **marquee** around the circle to select the entire object (both the stroke and the fill).

3. Click anywhere on the Stage to deselect the object.

4. Click inside the circle to select the fill only, then click outside the circle to deselect it.

5. Click the stroke of the circle to select it, as shown in Figure 17, then deselect it.

6. Double-click the **circle** to select it, press and hold **[Shift]**, double-click the **square** to select both objects, then deselect both objects.

7. Click the right border of the square to select it, as shown in Figure 18, then deselect it.

   Objects, such as rectangles, have border segments that can be selected individually.

8. Drag a **marquee** around the square, circle, and diagonal line to select all three objects.

9. Click a blank area of the Stage to deselect the objects.

10. Click inside the oval in row 2 to select the fill, then drag it outside the stroke, as shown in Figure 19.

11. Look at the Properties panel.

    Notice the stroke color is none and the fill color is blue. This is because only the object's

    (continued)

FIGURE 17
Using the Selection tool to select the stroke of the circle

FIGURE 18
Using the Selection tool to select a segment of the stroke of the square

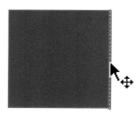

FIGURE 19
Separating the stroke and fill of an object

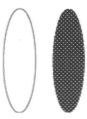

FIGURE 20
Circles drawn with the Oval tool

FIGURE 21
Changing the stroke color

fill is selected. You can use the Properties panel to verify what you have selected when working with the Selection tool.

12. Click **Edit** on the menu bar, then click **Undo Move**.

You used the Selection tool to select the stroke and fill of an object, and to select multiple objects.

Change fill and stroke colors

1. Click **Layer 4**, click **Insert** on the menu bar, point to **Timeline**, then click **Layer**.

2. Click **frame 20** of the new layer, click **Insert** on the menu bar, point to **Timeline**, then click **Keyframe**.

3. Select the **Oval tool** on the Tools panel, then draw two circles similar to those shown in Figure 20.

4. Click the **Fill Color tool color swatch** on the Tools panel, then click the **yellow color swatch** in the left column of the Color palette.

5. Click the **Paint Bucket tool** on the Tools panel, then click the fill of the right circle.

6. Click the **Stroke Color tool color swatch** on the Tools panel, then click the **yellow color swatch** in the left column of the color palette.

7. Click and hold the **Paint Bucket tool** on the Tools panel, click the **Ink Bottle tool**, point to the red stroke line of the left circle, as shown in Figure 21, then click to change the stroke color to yellow.

You used the Paint Bucket and Ink Bottle tools to change the fill and stroke colors of an object.

Create a gradient and make changes to the gradient

1. Click the **Fill Color tool color swatch** on the Tools panel, then click the **red gradient color swatch** in the bottom row of the Color palette, as shown in Figure 22.

2. Click and hold the **Ink Bottle tool** on the Tools panel, click the **Paint Bucket tool**, then click the **yellow circle**.

3. Click different parts of the right circle to view how the gradient changes.

4. Click the right side of the circle, as shown in Figure 23.

5. Click and hold the **Free Transform tool** on the Tools panel, then click the **Gradient Transform tool**.

6. Click the **gradient-filled circle**.

7. Drag each of the four handles shown in Figure 24 to determine the effect of each handle on the gradient, then click the **Stage** to deselect the circle.

8. Click the **Selection tool** on the Tools panel, then click inside the left circle.

9. Click the **Fill Color tool color swatch** in the FILL AND STROKE area of the Properties panel, click the **Hex Edit text box**, type **#006637** (two zeros), then press **[Enter]** (Win) or **[return]** (Mac).

   The Fill color swatch and the fill color for the circle change to a shade of green.

10. Save your work.

You applied a gradient fill, you used the Gradient Transform tool to alter the gradient, and you applied a new color using its Hexadecimal number.

FIGURE 22
Selecting the red gradient

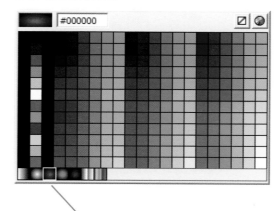

Click red gradient
color swatch to
select it

FIGURE 23
Clicking the right side of the circle

FIGURE 24
Gradient Transform handles

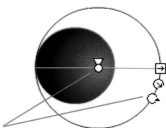

Handles are
used to adjust
the gradient
effect

Work with Object Drawing Model mode

1. Insert a **new layer**, then insert a **keyframe** on frame 25.

2. Select the **Oval tool** ⊙, click the **Stroke Color tool color swatch** , then click the **red swatch**.

3. Click the **Fill Color tool color swatch** , then click the **black swatch**.

4. Click the **Object Drawing option** ⊙ in the Options area of the Tools panel to change the mode to Object Drawing Model.

5. Draw a **circle** as shown in Figure 25.

   Notice that when you use Object Drawing Model mode, objects are automatically selected, and the stroke and fill areas are combined.

6. Click the **Selection tool** ⊀ on the Tools panel, then click a blank area of the Stage to deselect the object.

7. Click once on the **circle**, then drag the circle around the Stage.

   The entire object is selected, including the stroke and fill areas.

8. Click **Modify** on the menu bar, then click **Break Apart**.

   Breaking apart an object drawn in Object Drawing Model mode allows you to select the strokes and fills individually.

9. Click a blank area of the Stage, click the fill area of the circle, drag to the right, then save your work.

   Notice the fill moves but the stroke stays.

You used the Object Drawing Model mode to draw an object, deselect it, and then break it apart to display and then separate the stroke and fill.

FIGURE 25
Circle drawn using the Object Drawing Model mode

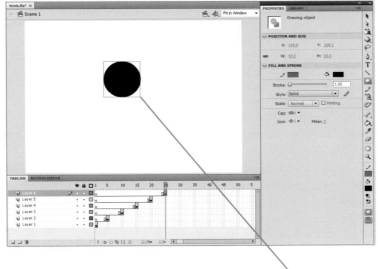

Blue outline indicates
the object is selected

WORK WITH DRAWN
OBJECTS

What You'll Do

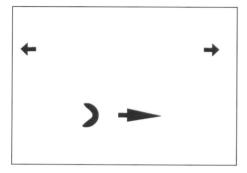

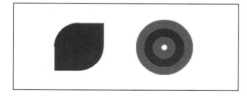

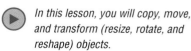 In this lesson, you will copy, move, and transform (resize, rotate, and reshape) objects.

Copying and Moving Objects

To copy an object, select it, and then click the Copy command on the Edit menu. To paste the object, click the Paste command on the Edit menu. You can copy an object to another layer by selecting the frame on the layer prior to pasting the object. You can copy and paste more than one object by selecting all the objects before using the Copy or Paste commands.

You move an object by selecting it and dragging it to a new location. You can position an object more precisely by selecting it and then pressing the arrow keys, which move the selection up, down, left, and right in small increments. In addition, you can change the X and Y coordinates in the Properties panel to position an object exactly on the Stage.

Transforming Objects

You use the Free Transform tool and the Transform panel to resize, rotate, skew, and reshape objects. After selecting an object, you click the Free Transform tool to display eight square-shaped handles used to transform the

object, and a circle-shaped transformation point located at the center of the object. The transformation point is the point around which the object can be rotated. You can also change its location.

Resizing an Object

You enlarge or reduce the size of an object using the Scale option, which is available when the Free Transform tool is selected. The process is to select the object and click the Free Transform tool, and then click the Scale option in the Options area of the Tools panel. Eight handles appear around the selected object. You drag the corner handles to resize the object without changing its proportions. That is, if the object starts out as a square, dragging a corner handle will change the size of the object, but it will still be a square. On the other hand, if you drag one of the middle handles, the object will be reshaped as taller, shorter, wider, or narrower. In addition, you can change the Width and Height settings in the Properties panel to resize an object in increments of one-tenth of one pixel.

Rotating and Skewing an Object

You use the Rotate and Skew option of the Free Transform tool to rotate an object and to skew it. The process is to select the object, click the Free Transform tool, and then click the Rotate and Skew option in the Options area of the Tools panel. Eight square-shaped handles appear around the object. You drag the corner handles to rotate the object, or you drag the middle handles to skew the object, as shown in Figure 26. The Transform panel can be used to rotate and skew an object in a more precise way; select the object, display the Transform panel (available via the Window menu), enter the desired rotation or skew in degrees, and then press [Enter] (Win) or [return] (Mac).

Distorting an Object

You can use the Distort and Envelope options to reshape an object by dragging its handles. The Distort option allows you to reshape an object by dragging one corner without affecting the other corners of the object. The Envelope option provides more than eight handles to allow more precise distortions. These options are accessed through the Transform command on the Modify menu.

Reshaping a Segment of an Object

You use the Subselection tool to reshape a segment of an object. You click an edge of the object to display handles that can be dragged to reshape the object.

You use the Selection tool to reshape objects. When you point to the edge of an object, the pointer displays an arc symbol. Using the Arc pointer, you drag the edge of the object you want to reshape, as shown in Figure 27. If the Selection tool points to a corner of an object, the pointer changes to an L-shape. You drag the pointer to reshape the corner of the object.

Flipping an Object

You use a Flip option on the Transform menu to flip an object either horizontally or vertically. You select the object, click the Transform command on the Modify menu, and then choose Flip Vertical or Flip Horizontal. Other Transform options allow you to rotate and scale the selected object. The Remove Transform command allows you to restore an object to its original state.

FIGURE 26
Using handles to manipulate an object

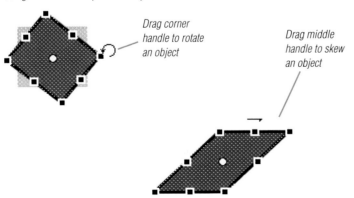

Drag corner handle to rotate an object

Drag middle handle to skew an object

FIGURE 27
Using the Selection tool to distort an object

Copy and move an object

1. Click **frame 5** on the Timeline.

2. Click the **Selection tool** ⟍ on the Tools panel, then draw a **marquee** around the arrow object to select it.

3. Click **Edit** on the menu bar, click **Copy**, click **Edit** on the menu bar, then click **Paste in Center**.

4. Drag the newly copied **arrow** to the upper-right corner of the Stage, as shown in Figure 28.

5. Verify the right arrow object is selected on the Stage, press the **down arrow key** [↓] on the keyboard to move the object in approximately one-pixel increments, and notice how the Y coordinate in the Properties panel changes.

6. Press the **right arrow key** [→] on the keyboard to move the object in one-pixel increments, and notice how the X coordinate in the Properties panel changes.

7. Select the **number** in the X coordinate box in the Properties panel, type **450**, as shown in Figure 29, then press **[Enter]** (Win) or **[return]** (Mac).

8. Point to the **Y coordinate**, when the pointer changes to a double-headed arrow ⇕ drag the ⇕ **pointer** to change the setting to **30**.

9. Select the **left arrow object**, then set the X and Y coordinates to **36** and **30**, respectively.

10. Click a blank area of the Stage to deselect the object.

You used the Selection tool to select an object, then you copied and moved the object.

FIGURE 28
Moving the copied object

X value indicates
position on
Stage

FIGURE 29
Changing the X coordinate in the Properties panel

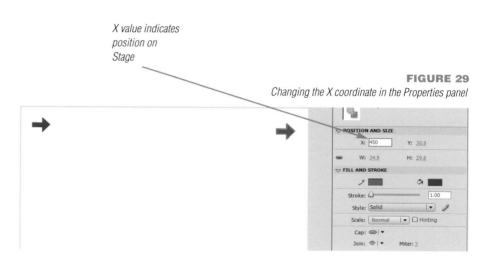

X and Y coordinates

The Stage dimensions are made up of pixels (dots) matching the Stage size. So, a Stage size of 550×400 would be 550 pixels wide and 400 pixels high. Each pixel has a location on the Stage designated as the X (across) and Y (down) coordinates. The location of any object is determined by its position from the upper-left corner of the Stage, which is 0,0. So, an object having coordinates of 450,30 would be positioned at 450 pixels across and 30 pixels down the Stage. The registration point of an object is used to align it with the coordinates. The registration point is initially set at the upper-left corner of an object.

FIGURE 30

Resizing an object using the corner handles

FIGURE 31

Reshaping an object using the middle handles

Transform options

Different transform options, such as rotate, skew, and scale, can be accessed through the Options area on the Tools panel when the Free Transform tool is selected, the Transform command on the Modify menu, and the Transform panel via the Transform command on the Window menu.

Resize and reshape an object

1. Draw a **marquee** around the arrow object on the right side of the Stage to select the object.

2. Select the **Free Transform tool** on the Tools panel.

   Note: You may need to click and hold the Gradient tool to display the Free Transform tool.

3. Select the **Scale option** in the Options area of the Tools panel.

4. Drag each **corner handle** toward and then away from the center of the object, as shown in Figure 30.

   As you drag a corner handle, the object's size is changed, but its proportions remain the same.

5. Click **Edit** on the menu bar, then click **Undo Scale**.

6. Repeat Step 5 until the arrow returns to its original size.

   TIP The object is its original size when the option Undo Scale is no longer available on the Edit menu.

7. Verify the arrow is still selected and the handles are displayed, then select the **Scale option** .

8. Drag each **middle handle** toward and then away from the center of the object, as shown in Figure 31.

   As you drag the middle handles, the object's size and proportions change.

9. Click **Edit** on the menu bar, then click **Undo Scale** as needed to return the arrow to its original size.

You used the Free Transform tool and the Scale option to display an object's handles, and you used the handles to resize and reshape the object.

Rotate, skew, and flip an object

1. Verify that the Free Transform tool and the right arrow are selected (handles displayed), then click the **Rotate and Skew option** ⟳ in the Options area of the Tools panel.

2. Click the **upper-right corner handle**, then rotate the object clockwise.

3. Click the **upper-middle handle**, then drag it to the right.

   The arrow slants down and to the right.

4. Click **Edit** on the menu bar, click the **Undo Skew** command, then repeat, selecting the Undo Rotate command, until the arrow is in its original shape and orientation.

5. Click the **Selection tool** ▸ on the Tools panel, verify that the right arrow is selected, click **Window** on the menu bar, then click **Transform**.

6. Click the **Rotate text box**, type **45**, then press **[Enter]** (Win) or **[return]** (Mac).

   The arrow rotates 45°, as shown in Figure 32.

7. Click **Edit** on the menu bar, then click **Undo Transform**.

8. Close the Transform panel.

9. Draw a **marquee** around the arrow in the upper-left corner of the Stage to select the object.

10. Click **Modify** on the menu bar, point to **Transform**, then click **Flip Horizontal**.

11. Save your work.

You used options on the Tools panel and the Transform panel, as well as commands on the Modify menu to rotate, skew, and flip an object.

FIGURE 32
Using the Transform panel to rotate an object

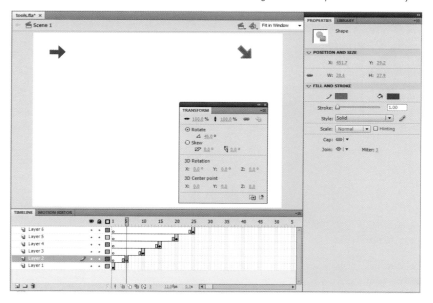

FIGURE 33
Using the Subselection tool to select an object

Click the tip of the
object to display
the handles

FIGURE 34
Using the Subselection tool to drag a handle to reshape the object

FIGURE 35
Using the Selection tool to drag an edge to reshape the object

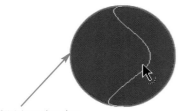

Click here, then drag

Use the Zoom, Subselection, and Selection tools

1. Select the **arrow** in the upper-right corner of the Stage, click **Edit** on the menu bar, click **Copy**, click **Edit** on the menu bar, then click **Paste in Center**.

2. Click the **Zoom tool** 🔍 on the Tools panel, then click the middle of the copied object to enlarge the view.

3. Click the **Subselection tool** 🔧 on the Tools panel, then click the **tip of the arrow** to display the handles, as shown in Figure 33.

   TIP   The handles allow you to change any segment of the object.

4. Click the **handle** at the tip of the arrow, then drag it, as shown in Figure 34.

5. Select the **Oval tool** ⬭ on the Tools panel, then deselect the **Object Drawing option** ⬭ in the Options area of the Tools panel.

6. Verify the Fill color is set to blue, then draw a **circle** to the left of the arrow you just modified.

7. Click the **Selection tool** ▸ on the Tools panel, then point to the left edge of the circle until the Arc pointer ⤵ is displayed.

8. Drag the ⤵ **pointer** to the position shown in Figure 35.

9. Click **View** on the menu bar, point to **Magnification**, then click **100%**.

10. Save your work.

You used the Zoom tool to change the view, and you used the Subselection and Selection tools to reshape objects.

Use the Primitive Rectangle and Oval tools

1. Insert a **new layer** above Layer 6, click **frame 30** on Layer 7, then insert a **Keyframe**.

2. Click and hold down the **Oval tool** ◯ (or the Rectangle tool if it is displayed) to display the menu.

3. Click the **Rectangle Primitive tool** ▢ , then click the **Reset button** in the Properties panel RECTANGLE OPTIONS area to clear all of the settings.

4. Hold down **[Shift]**, point to the middle of the Stage, then draw the **square** shown in Figure 36.

5. Click the **Selection tool** ▸ in the Tools panel, then drag **the upper-right corner handle** toward the center of the object.
   As you drag the corner, the radius of each of the four corners is changed.

6. Click the **Reset button** in the Properties panel to clear the setting.

7. Slowly drag the **slider** ◠ in the RECTANGLE OPTIONS area to the right until the radius changes to 100, then slowly drag the **slider** ◠ to the left until the radius changes to −100.

8. Click the **Reset Button** on the Properties panel to clear the radius settings.

9. Click the **Lock corner radius icon** ⊂⊃ in the Properties panel RECTANGLE OPTIONS area to unlock the individual controls.

10. Type **-60** in the upper-left corner radius text box, then type **-60** in the upper-right corner text box, as shown in Figure 37.

(continued)

FIGURE 36
Drawing an object with the Rectangle Primitive tool

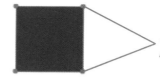

The corner handles can be dragged to change the radius of the corners; in addition, the Properties panel can be used to make changes to the object

FIGURE 37
Setting the corner radius of two corners

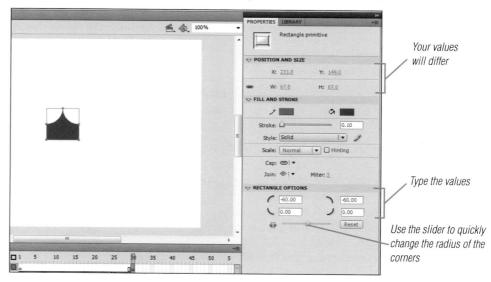

Your values will differ

Type the values

Use the slider to quickly change the radius of the corners

FIGURE 38
Drawing an object with the Oval Primitive tool

FIGURE 39
Setting the stroke value to 12

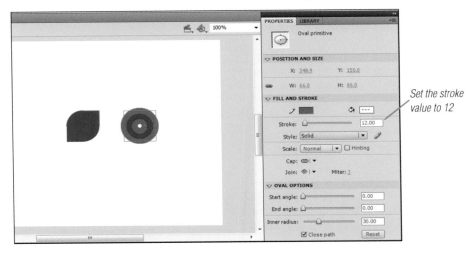

Set the stroke
value to 12

11. Click the **Reset button** in the Properties panel to clear the radius settings.

12. Click the **Lock corner radius icon** ⊖ to unlock the individual controls.

13. Set the upper-left corner radius to **60** and the lower-right corner to **60**.

14. Click a blank area of the Stage to deselect the object.

15. Click and hold the **Rectangle Primitive tool** ▣ , click the **Oval Primitive tool** ◔. on the Tools panel, then hold down **[Shift]** and draw the **circle** shown in Figure 38.

    TIP   Remember some tools are grouped. Click and hold a grouped tool, such as the Oval tool, to see the menu of tools in the group.

16. Click the **Reset button** in the Properties panel OVAL OPTIONS area to clear any settings.

17. Drag the **Start angle slider** ⌂ and the **End angle slider** ⌂ to view their effect on the circle, then drag each **slider** back to 0.

18. Click the **Reset button** to clear the settings.

19. Drag the **Inner radius slider** ⌂ to see the effect on the circle, then set the inner radius to **30**.

20. Display the FILL AND STROKE area of the Properties panel, then set the Stroke value to **12**, as shown in Figure 39.

21. Save your work.

You used the Primitive tools to create objects and the Properties panel to alter them.

WORK WITH TEXT
AND TEXT OBJECTS

What You'll Do

Join Us Now

We have great events
each year including a
Car Rally!

In this lesson, you will enter text using text blocks. You will also resize text blocks, change text attributes, and transform text.

Learning About Text

Flash provides a great deal of flexibility when using text. Among other settings for text, you can specify the typeface (font), size, style (bold, italic), and color (including gradients). You can transform the text by rotating, scaling, skewing, and flipping it. You can even break apart a letter and reshape its segments.

Entering Text and Changing the Text Block

It is important to understand that text is entered into a text block, as shown in Figure 40. You use the Text tool to place a text block on the Stage and to enter and edit text. A text block expands as more text is entered and may even extend beyond the edge of the Stage. You can adjust the size of the text block so that it is a fixed width by dragging the handle in the upper-right corner of the block. Figure 41 shows the process of using the Text tool to enter text and resize the text block. Once you select the Text tool, you click the Stage where you want the text to

appear. An insertion point indicates where the next character will appear in the text block when it is typed. You can reshape the text block by dragging the circle handle. After reshaping the text block, the circle handle changes to a square, indicating that the text block now has a fixed width. Then, when you enter more text, it automatically wraps within the text block. You can resize the text block at any time by selecting it with the Selection tool and dragging a handle.

Changing Text Attributes

You can use the Properties panel to change the font, size, and style of a single character or an entire text block. Figure 42 shows the Properties panel when a text object is selected. You select text, display the Properties panel, and make the changes. You use the Selection tool to select the entire text block by drawing a marquee around it. You use the Text tool to select a single character or string of characters by dragging the I-beam pointer over the text you want to select, as shown in Figure 43.

Working with Paragraphs

When working with large bodies of text, such as paragraphs, Flash provides many of the features found in a word processor. You can align paragraphs (left, right, center, justified) within a text block, set margins (space between the border of a text block and the paragraph text), set indents for the first line of a paragraph, and set line spacing (distance between paragraphs) using the Properties panel.

Transforming Text

It is important to understand that a text block is an object. Therefore, you can apply filters, such as drop shadows, and you can transform (reshape, rotate, skew, and so on) a text block in the same way you transform other objects. If you want to transform individual characters within a text block, you must first break apart the text block. To do this, you use the Selection tool to select the text block, then you click the Break Apart command on the Modify menu. Each character (or a group of characters) in the text block can now be selected and transformed.

FIGURE 40
A text block

This is a text block used to enter text.

FIGURE 41
Using the Text tool

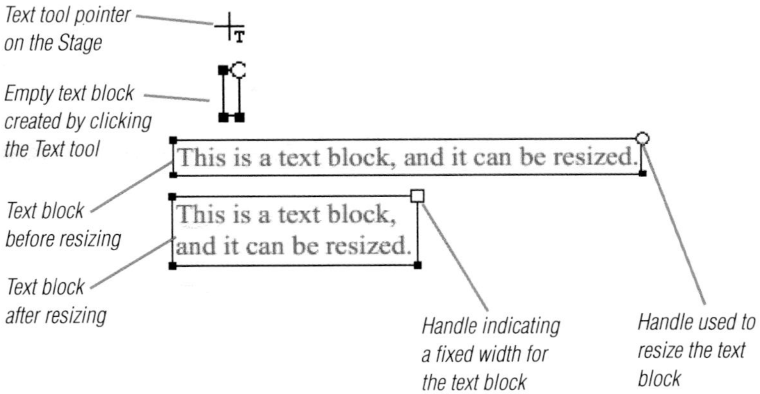

Text tool pointer on the Stage

Empty text block created by clicking the Text tool

This is a text block, and it can be resized.

Text block before resizing

This is a text block, and it can be resized.

Text block after resizing

Handle indicating a fixed width for the text block

Handle used to resize the text block

FIGURE 42
The Properties panel when a text object is selected

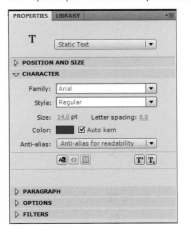

FIGURE 43
Dragging the I-Beam pointer to select text

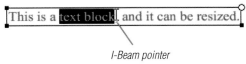

This is a text block, and it can be resized.

I-Beam pointer

Enter text and change text attributes

1. Click **Layer 7**, insert a **new layer**, then insert a **keyframe** in frame 35 of the new layer.

2. Click the **Text tool** T on the Tools panel, click the left-center of the Stage, then type **We have great events each year including a Rally**!

3. Click the **I-Beam pointer** I before the word "Rally," as shown in Figure 44, then type **Car** followed by a space.

4. Verify that the Properties panel is displayed, then drag the I-Beam pointer I across the text to select all the text.

5. Make the following changes in the CHARAC-TER area of the Properties panel: Family: **Arial**; Style: **Black** (Win) or **Bold** (Mac); Size:**16**; Color: **#990000**, then click the **text box**.

   Your Properties panel should resemble Figure 45.

6. Verify the text block is selected, position the **text pointer** ⊹ over the circle handle until the pointer changes to a double arrow ↔, then drag the **handle** to just before the word each, as shown in Figure 46.

7. Select the text using the I-Beam pointer I, then click the **Align center icon** ≣ in the PARAGRAPH area of the Properties panel.

8. Click the **Selection tool** ↖ on the Tools panel, click the **text object**, then drag the **object** to the lower-middle of the Stage.

   TIP The Selection tool is used to select the text block, and the Text tool is used to select and edit the text within the text block.

You entered text and changed the font, type size, and text color; you also resized the text block and changed the text alignment.

FIGURE 44
Using the Text tool to enter text

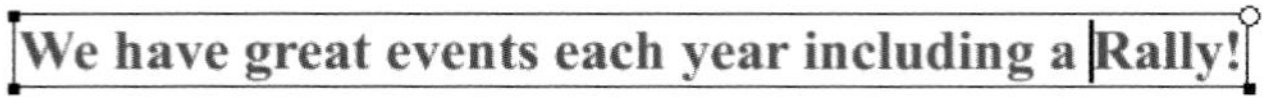

We have great events each year including a |Rally!

FIGURE 45
Changes in the CHARACTER area of the Properties panel

FIGURE 46
Resizing the text block

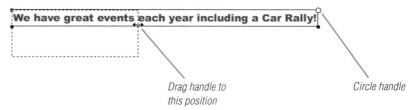

We have great events each year including a Car Rally!

Drag handle to this position

Circle handle

FIGURE 47
The Filters options in the Properties panel

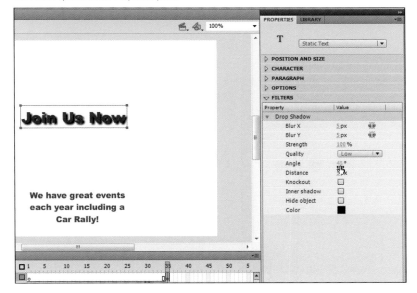

Using filters

You can apply special effects, such as drop shadows, to text using options in the FILTERS area of the Properties panel. The process is to select the desired text, display the FILTERS area of the Properties panel, choose the desired effect, and make any adjustments, such as changing the angle of a drop shadow. You can copy and paste a filter from one object to another using the clipboard icon in the FILTERS area of the Properties panel.

Add a Filter effect to text

1. Click the **Text tool** T on the Tools panel, click the center of the Stage, then type **Join Us Now**. *Hint:* If the text box does not appear, double-click the Stage.
2. Drag the **I-Beam pointer** I across the text to select it, then use the Properties panel to change the Font size to **30** and the Text (fill) color to **#003399**.
3. Click **CHARACTER** on the Properties panel to close the CHARACTER area, then close all areas in the Properties panel except for the FILTERS area.
4. Click the **Selection tool** on the Tools panel, then verify the text block is selected.
5. Click the **Add filter icon** at the bottom of the FILTERS area, then click **Drop Shadow**.
6. Point to the **Angle value** in the FILTERS area of the Properties panel, as shown in Figure 47.
7. When the pointer changes to a double-headed arrow , drag the **pointer** to the right to view the effect on the shadow, then set the Angle to **50**.
8. Click the **Distance value**, when the pointer changes to a double-headed arrow , drag the **pointer** to the right and notice the changes in the drop shadow.
9. Set the Distance to **6**.
10. Use the **Selection tool** to select the text position and position it as needed to match the placement shown in Figure 47, then save your work.

You used the Filter panel to create a drop shadow and then made changes to it.

Skew text and align objects

1. Click the **Text tool** T to select it, click the pointer near the top middle of the Stage twice, then type **Classic Car Club**.

2. Click **CHARACTER** in the Properties panel to display the CHARACTER area.

   The attributes of the new text reflect the most recent settings entered in the Properties panel.

3. Drag the **I-Beam pointer** I to select the text, then use the CHARACTER area of the Properties panel to change the font size to **40** and the fill color to **#990000**.

4. Click the **Selection tool** ↖ on the Tools panel to select the text box, then select the **Free Transform tool** ⚏ on the Tools panel.

5. Click the **Rotate and Skew option** ↻ in the Options area of the Tools panel.

6. Drag the top middle handle to the right, as shown in Figure 48, to skew the text.

7. Click the **Selection tool** ↖ on the Tools panel.

8. Drag a **marquee** around all of the objects on the Stage to select them.

9. Click **Modify** on the menu bar, point to **Align**, verify To Stage has a check mark next to it, then click **Horizontal Center**.

   Note: If the Modify menu closes before you select Horizontal Center, repeat step 9.

10. Click a blank area of the Stage to deselect the objects.

You entered a heading, changed the font size and color, and skewed text using the Free Transform tool, then you aligned the objects on the Stage.

FIGURE 48
Skewing the text

FIGURE 49
Reshaping a letter

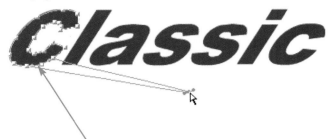

Drag this handle; notice the lines are drawn
from the anchor points on either side of the
anchor point being dragged

FIGURE 50
Applying a gradient fill to each letter

Reshape and apply a gradient to text

1. Click the **Selection tool** , click the **Classic Car Club text block** to select it, click **Modify** on the menu bar, then click **Break Apart**.

   The letters are now individual text blocks.

2. Click **Modify** on the menu bar, then click **Break Apart**.

   The letters are filled with a dot pattern, indicating that they can now be edited.

3. Click the **Zoom tool** on the Tools panel, then click the **"C"** in Classic.

4. Click the **Subselection tool** on the Tools panel, then click the edge of the letter **"C"** to display the object's segment handles.

5. Drag a lower handle on the "C" in Classic, as shown in Figure 49.

6. Click the **Selection tool** , then click a blank area of the Stage to deselect the objects.

7. Click **View** on the menu bar, point to **Magnification**, then click **Fit in Window**.

8. Click the **Fill Color tool color swatch** on the Tools panel, then click the **red gradient color swatch** in the bottom row of the Color palette.

9. Click the **Paint Bucket tool** on the Tools panel, then click the top of each letter to change the fill to a red gradient, as shown in Figure 50.

10. Use the status bar to change the movie frame rate to **3**, click **Control** on the menu bar, click **Test Movie**, watch the movie, then close the Flash Player window.

11. Save your work, then close the movie.

You broke apart a text block, reshaped text, and added a gradient to the text.

WORK WITH LAYERS
AND OBJECTS

What You'll Do

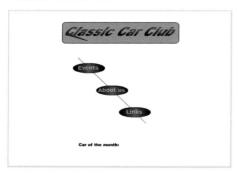

 In this lesson, you will create, rename, reorder, delete, hide, and lock layers. You will also display objects as outlines on layers, use a Guide layer, distribute text to layers, and create a Folder layer.

Learning About Layers

Flash uses two types of spatial organization. First, there is the position of objects on the Stage, and then there is the stacking order of objects that overlap. An example of overlapping objects is text placed on a banner. Layers are used on the Timeline as a way to organize objects. Placing objects on their own layer makes them easier to work with, especially when reshaping them, repositioning them on the Stage, or rearranging their order in relation to other objects. In addition, layers are useful for organizing other elements such as sounds, animations, and ActionScript.

There are five types of layers, as shown in the Layer Properties dialog box displayed in Figure 51 and discussed next.

Normal—The default layer type. All objects on these layers appear in the movie.

Mask—A layer that hides and reveals portions of another layer.

Masked—A layer that contains the objects that are hidden and revealed by a Mask layer.

Folder—A layer that can contain other layers.

Guide (Standard and Motion)—A Standard Guide layer serves as a reference point for positioning objects on the Stage. A Motion Guide layer is used to create a path for animated objects to follow.

Motion Guide, Mask, and Masked layer types are covered in a later chapter.

Working with Layers

The Layer Properties dialog box, accessed through the Timeline command on the Modify menu, allows you to specify the type of layer. It also allows you to name, show (and hide), and lock them. Naming a layer provides a clue to the objects on the layer. For example, naming a layer Logo might indicate that the object on the layer is the company's logo. Hiding a layer(s) may reduce the clutter on the Stage and make it easier to work with selected objects from the layer(s) that are not hidden. Locking a layer(s) prevents the objects from being accidentally edited. Other options in the Layer Properties dialog box allow you to view layers as outlines and change the outline color.

Outlines can be used to help you determine which objects are on a layer. When you turn on this feature, each layer has a colored box that corresponds with the color of the objects on its layer. Icons on the Layers area of the Timeline, as shown in Figure 52, correspond to features in the Layer Properties dialog box.

FIGURE 51
The Layer Properties dialog box

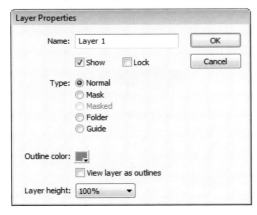

FIGURE 52
The Layers area of the Timeline

Show or Hide All Layers

Lock or Unlock All Layers

Show All Layers as Outlines

Lock or Unlock This Layer

Padlock indicates this layer is locked

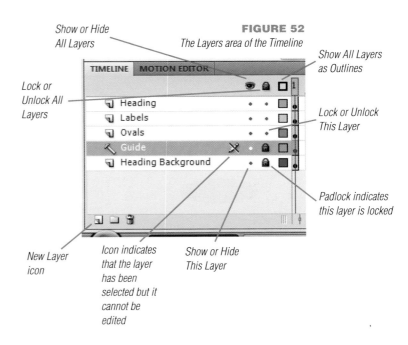

New Layer icon

Icon indicates that the layer has been selected but it cannot be edited

Show or Hide This Layer

Using a Guide Layer

Guide layers are useful in aligning objects on the Stage. Figure 53 shows a Guide layer that has been used to align three buttons along a diagonal path. The buttons are on one layer and the diagonal line is on another layer, the Guide layer. The process is to insert a new layer above the layer containing the objects to be aligned, you use the Layer Properties command from the Timeline option on the Modify menu to display the Layer Properties dialog box, select Guide as the layer type, and then draw a path that will be used as the guide to align the objects. You then verify the Snap to Guides option from the Snapping command on the View menu is turned on, and drag the desired objects to the Guide line. Objects have a transformation point that is used when snapping to a guide. By default, this point is at the center of the object. Figure 54 shows the process.

FIGURE 53
A Guide layer used to align objects on the Stage

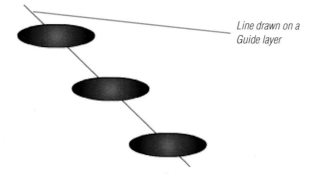

Line drawn on a
Guide layer

FIGURE 54
The transformation point of an object

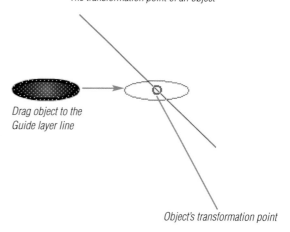

Drag object to the
Guide layer line

Object's transformation point

WORKING WITH SYMBOLS
AND INTERACTIVITY

1. Create symbols and instances

2. Work with libraries

3. Create buttons

4. Assign actions to frames and buttons

5. Importing graphics

3 WORKING WITH SYMBOLS
AND INTERACTIVITY

Introduction

An important benefit of Flash is its ability to create movies with small file sizes. This allows the movies to be delivered from the web more quickly. One way to keep the file size small is to create reusable graphics, buttons, and movie clips. Flash allows you to create a graphic (drawing) and then make unlimited copies, which you can use throughout the current movie and in other movies. Flash calls the original drawing a **symbol** and the copied drawings **instances**. Flash stores symbols in the Library panel—each time you need a copy of the symbol, you can open the Library panel and drag the symbol to the Stage, which creates an instance (copy) of the symbol. Using instances reduces the movie file size because Flash stores only the symbol's information (size, shape, color), but Flash does not save the instance in the Flash movie. Rather, a link is established between the symbol and an instance so that the instance has the same properties (such as color and shape) as the symbol.

What is especially valuable about this process is that you can change the properties for each instance. For example, if your website is to contain drawings of cars that are similar, you can create just one drawing, convert it to a symbol, insert as many instances of the car as needed, and then change an individual instance as desired.

There are three categories of symbols: graphic, button, and movie clip. A graphic symbol is useful because you can reuse a single image and make changes in each instance of the image. A button symbol is useful because you can create buttons for interactivity, such as starting or stopping a movie. A movie clip symbol is useful for creating complex animations because you can create a movie within a movie. Symbols can be created from objects you draw using the Flash drawing tools. In addition, you can import graphics into a Flash document that can then be converted into symbols.

Tools You'll Use

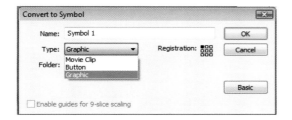

CREATE SYMBOLS
AND INSTANCES

What You'll Do

 In this lesson, you will create graphic symbols, turn them into instances, and then edit the instances.

Creating a Graphic Symbol

You can use the New Symbol command on the Insert menu to create and then draw a symbol. You can also draw an object and then use the Convert to Symbol command on the Modify menu to convert the object to a symbol. The Convert to Symbol dialog box, shown in Figure 1, allows you to name the symbol and specify the type of symbol you want to create (Movie Clip, Button, or Graphic). When naming a symbol, it's a good idea to use a naming convention that allows you to quickly identify the type of symbol and to group like symbols together. For example, you could identify all graphic symbols by naming them g_*name* and all buttons as b_*name*. In Figure 1, the drawing on the Stage is being converted into a graphic symbol, which will be named g_ball.

After you complete the Convert to Symbol dialog box, Flash places the symbol in the Library panel, as shown in Figure 2. In Figure 2, an icon identifying the symbol as a graphic symbol and the symbol name are listed in the Library panel, along with a preview of the selected symbol. To create an instance of the symbol, you simply drag a symbol from the Library panel to the Stage. To edit a symbol, you select it from the Library panel or you use the Edit Symbols command on the Edit menu. This displays the symbol in an edit window, where changes can be made to it. When you edit a symbol, the changes are reflected in all instances of that symbol in your movie. For example, you can draw a car, convert the car to a symbol, and then create several instances of the car. You can uniformly change the size of all the cars by double-clicking the car symbol in the Library panel to open the edit window, and then rescaling it to the desired size.

Working with Instances

You can have as many instances as needed in your movie, and you can edit each one to make it somewhat different from the others. You can rotate, skew (slant), and resize graphic and button instances. In addition, you can change the color, brightness, and transparency. However, there are some limitations. An instance is a single object with no segments or parts, such as a stroke and a fill. You cannot select a part of an instance. Therefore, any changes to the color of the instance are made to the entire object. Of course, you can use layers to stack other objects on top of an instance to change its appearance. In addition, you can use the Break Apart command on the Modify menu to break the link between an instance and a symbol. Once the link is broken, you can make any changes to the object, such as changing its stroke and fill color. However, because the link is broken,

the object is no longer an instance; if you make any changes to the original symbol, then the object is not affected.

The process for creating an instance is to open the Library panel and drag the desired symbol to the Stage. Once the symbol is on the Stage, you select the instance by using the Selection tool to drag a marquee around it. A blue border indicates that the object is selected. Then, you can use the Free Transform tool options (such as Rotate and Skew, or Scale) to modify the

entire image, or you can use the Break Apart command to break apart the instance and edit individual strokes and fills.

QUICKTIP

You need to be careful when editing an instance. Use the Selection tool to drag a marquee around the instance, or click the object once to select it. Do not double-click the instance when it is on the Stage; otherwise, you will open an edit window that is used to edit the symbol, not the instance.

FIGURE 1

Using the Convert to Symbol dialog box to convert an object to a symbol

FIGURE 2

A graphic symbol in the Library panel

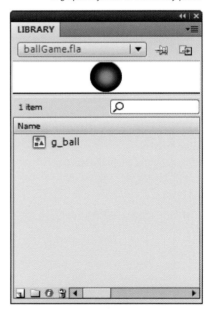

Create a symbol

1. Open fl3_1.fla from the drive and folder where your Data Files are stored, then save it as **coolCar**. This document has one object, a car, that was created using the Flash drawing tools.

2. Verify the Properties panel, the Library panel, and the Tools panel are displayed.

3. Set the magnification to **100%**.

4. Click the **Selection tool** ➤ on the Tools panel, then drag a **marquee** around the car to select it.

5. Click **Modify** on the menu bar, then click **Convert to Symbol**.

6. Type **g_car** in the Name text box.

7. Click the **Type list arrow** to display the symbol types, as shown in Figure 3.

8. Click **Graphic**, then click **OK**.

9. Click the **Library panel tab**, then study the Library panel, as shown in Figure 4, and notice it displays the symbol (red car) in the Item Preview window, an icon 🖼 indicating that this is a graphic symbol, and the name of the symbol (g_car).

   The symbol is contained in the library, and the car on the Stage is now an instance of the symbol.

You opened a file with an object, converted the object to a symbol, and displayed the symbol in the Library panel.

FIGURE 3
Options in the Convert to Symbol dialog box

FIGURE 4
Newly created symbol in the Library panel

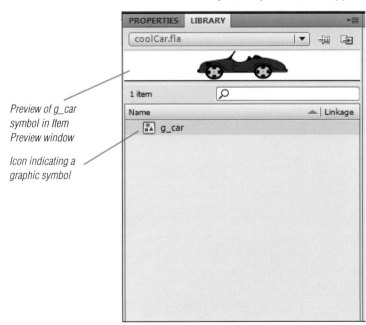

Preview of g_car symbol in Item Preview window

Icon indicating a graphic symbol

FIGURE 5
Creating an instance

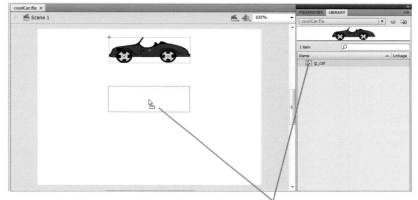

Drag the symbol from the Library
panel to below the original
instance to create a second
instance of the symbol

This area may
not be open

FIGURE 6
The alpha set to 50%

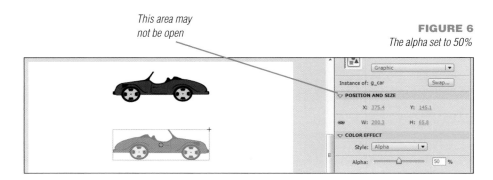

Create and edit an instance

1. Point to the **car image** in the Item Preview window of the Library panel, then drag the **image** to the Stage beneath the first car, as shown in Figure 5.

   TIP You can also drag the name of the symbol from the Library panel to the Stage. Both cars on the Stage are instances of the graphic symbol in the Library panel.

2. Verify the bottom car is selected, click **Modify** on the menu bar, point to **Transform**, then click **Flip Horizontal**.

3. Display the Properties panel, then display the COLOR EFFECT area if it is not already showing.

4. Click the **Style list arrow**, then click **Alpha**.

5. Drag the **Alpha slider** to 50%.

   Notice how the transparency changes. Figure 6 shows the transparency set to 50%.

6. Click a blank area of the Stage to deselect the object.

   Changing the alpha setting gives the car a more transparent look.

You created an instance of a symbol and edited the instance on the Stage.

Edit a symbol in the edit window

1. Display the Library panel, double-click the **g_car symbol icon** 🖼 in the Library panel to display the edit window, then compare your screen to Figure 7.

   The g_car symbol appears in the edit window, indicating that you are editing the g_car symbol.

   | TIP   You can also edit a symbol by clicking Edit on the menu bar, then clicking Edit Symbols.

2. Click a blank area of the window to deselect the car.

3. Verify the Selection tool ▸ is selected, then click the **light gray hubcap** inside the front wheel to select it.

4. Press and hold **[Shift]**, then click the **hubcap** inside the back wheel so both hubcap fills are selected.

5. Set the **Fill Color** 🖌 to the **blue gradient color swatch** in the bottom row of the color palette, deselect the image, then compare your image to Figure 8.

6. Click **Scene 1** at the top left of the edit window to exit the edit window and return to the main Timeline and main Stage.

   Changes you make to the symbol affect every instance of the symbol on the Stage. The hubcap fill becomes a blue gradient in the Library panel and on the Stage.

   You edited a symbol in the edit window that affected all instances of the symbol.

FIGURE 7
Edit window

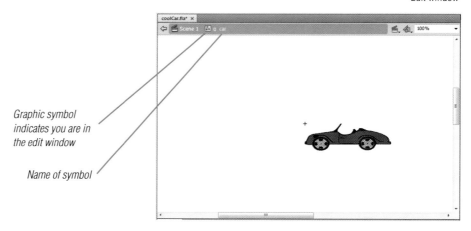

Graphic symbol indicates you are in the edit window

Name of symbol

FIGURE 8
Edited symbol

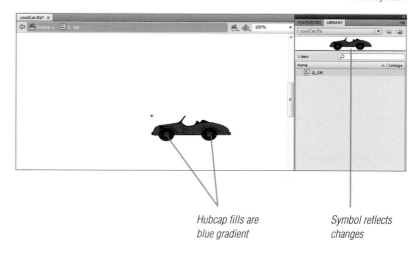

Hubcap fills are blue gradient

Symbol reflects changes

FIGURE 9
The car with the maroon body selected

FIGURE 10
Changing the symbol affects only the one instance of the symbol

Instance of the
symbol

Object that is no
longer an instance
of the symbol

Break apart an instance

1. Drag a **marquee** around the bottom car to select it if it is not selected.

2. Click **Modify** on the menu bar, then click **Break Apart**.

   The object is no longer linked to the symbol, and its parts (strokes and fills) can now be edited.

3. Click a blank area of the Stage to deselect the object.

4. Click the **blue front hubcap**, press and hold **[Shift]**, then click the **blue back hubcap** so both hubcaps are selected.

5. Set the **Fill Color** to the **light gray color swatch (#999999)** in the left column of the color palette.

6. Double-click the **g_car symbol icon** in the Library panel to display the edit window.

7. Click the **maroon front body** of the car to select it, press and hold **[Shift]**, then click the **maroon back body** of the car, as shown in Figure 9.

8. Set the **Fill Color** to the **red gradient color swatch** in the bottom row of the color palette.

9. Click **Scene 1** at the top left of the edit window, then compare your image to Figure 10.

   The body color of the car in the original instance is a different color, but the body color of the car to which you applied the Break Apart command remains unchanged.

10. Save your work.

You used the Break Apart command to break the link of the instance to its symbol, you edited the object, and then you edited the symbol.

WORK WITH LIBRARIES

What You'll Do

In this lesson, you will use the Library panel to organize the symbols in a movie.

Understanding the Library

The library in a Flash document contains the symbols and other items such as imported graphics, movie clips, and sounds. The Library panel provides a way to view and organize the items, and allows you to change the item name, display item properties, and add and delete items. Figure 11 shows the Library panel for a document. Refer to this figure as you read the following descriptions of the parts of the library.

Title tab—Identifies this as the Library panel.

List box—The list box below the title tab can be used to select an open document and display the Library panel associated with that open document. This allows you to use the items from one movie in another movie. For example, you may have developed a drawing in one Flash movie and need to use it in the movie you are working on. With both documents open, you simply use the list box to display the library with the desired drawing, and then drag it to the Stage of the current movie. This will automatically place the drawing in the library for the current movie. In addition to the movie libraries, you can create permanent libraries that are available whenever you start Flash. Flash also has sample libraries that contain buttons and other objects. The permanent and sample libraries are accessed through the Common Libraries command on the Window menu. All assets in all of these libraries are available for use in any movie.

Options menu—Shown in Figure 12; provides access to several features used to edit symbols (such as renaming symbols) and organize symbols (such as creating a new folder).

Item Preview window—Displays the selected item. If the item is animated or a sound file, a control button appears, allowing you to preview the animation or play the sound.

Toggle Sorting Order icon—Allows you to reorder the list of folders and items within folders.

Name text box—Lists the folder and item names. Each item type has a different icon

associated with it. Clicking an item name or icon displays the item in the Item Preview window.

New Symbol icon—Displays the Create New Symbol dialog box, allowing you to create a new symbol.

New Folder icon—Allows you to create a new folder.

Properties icon—Displays the Properties dialog box for the selected item.

Delete Item icon—Deletes the selected item or folder.

To make changes to an item, you can double-click the item icon in the Library panel to display the edit window.

FIGURE 11
The Library panel

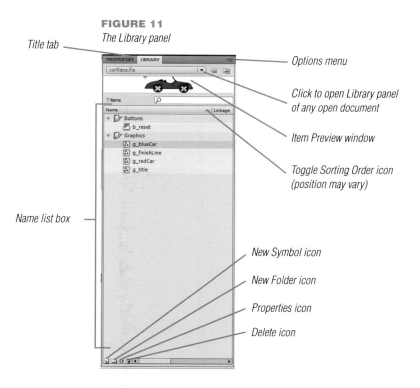

Title tab

Name list box

Options menu

Click to open Library panel of any open document

Item Preview window

Toggle Sorting Order icon (position may vary)

New Symbol icon

New Folder icon

Properties icon

Delete icon

FIGURE 12
The Options menu

Create folders in the Library panel

1. Open fl3_2.fla, then save it as **carRace**.

2. Verify the Properties panel, the Library panel, and the **Tools panel** are displayed.

3. Set the magnification to **100%**.

   This movie has eight layers containing various objects such as text blocks, lines, and a background. Two layers contain animations of cars.

4. Test the movie, then close the Flash Player window.

5. Click the **Show or Hide All Layers icon** 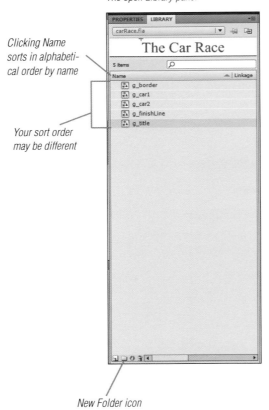 on the Timeline to hide all of the layers.

6. Click the **Show or Hide This Layer icon** for each layer to show the contents of each layer.

   Note: The reset layer shows an empty Stage. This is because the word Reset is located in frame 65 at the end of the movie and does not appear in frame 1.

7. Click each item in the Library panel to display it in the Item Preview window. Notice that there is one button symbol (b_reset) and five graphic symbols.

   Note: The g_finishLine graphic will look like a black line because the preview window is small.

8. Click the **New Folder icon** in the Library panel, as shown in Figure 13.

9. Type **Graphics** in the Name text box, then press **[Enter]** (Win) or **[return]** (Mac).

   (continued)

FIGURE 13
The open Library panel

Clicking Name sorts in alphabetical order by name

Your sort order may be different

New Folder icon

FIGURE 14
The Library panel with the folders added

Buttons folder

Graphics folder

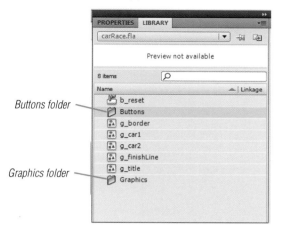

FIGURE 15
The Library panel after moving the symbols to the folders

Your folders might
be expanded

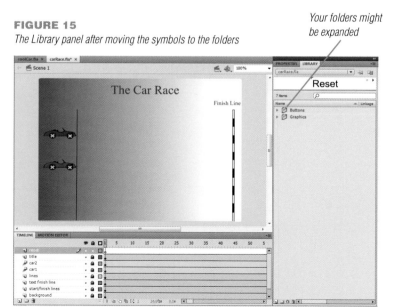

10. Click the **New Folder icon** 🗀 on the Library panel.

11. Type **Buttons** in the Name text box, then press [**Enter**] (Win) or [**return**] (Mac).

Your Library panel should resemble Figure 14.

You opened a Flash movie and created folders in the Library panel.

Organize items within Library panel folders

1. Click **Name** on the Name list box title bar and notice how the items are sorted.

2. Repeat step 1 and notice how the items are sorted.

3. Drag the **g_title symbol** in the Library panel to the Graphics folder.

4. Drag the other graphic symbols to the Graphics folder.

5. Drag the **b_reset symbol** to the Buttons folder, then compare your Library panel to Figure 15.

6. Click the **Graphics folder expand list arrow** ▶ to open it and display the graphic symbols.

7. Click the **Buttons folder expand list arrow** ▶ to open it and display the button symbol.

8. Click the **Graphics folder collapse list arrow** ▼ to close the folder.

9. Click the **Buttons folder collapse list arrow** ▼ to close the folder.

Note: To remove an item from a folder, drag the item down to a blank area of the Library panel.

You organized the symbols within the folders and opened and closed the folders.

Display the properties of symbols, rename symbols, and delete a symbol

1. Click the **expand list arrow** ▶ for the Graphics folder to display the symbols.

2. Click the **g_car1 symbol**, then click the **Properties icon** 🛈 at the bottom of the Library panel to display the Symbol Properties dialog box.

3. Type **g_redCar** in the Name text box, as shown in Figure 16, then click **OK**.

4. Repeat Steps 2 and 3 renaming the g_car2 symbol to **g_blueCar**.

> TIP Double-click the name to rename it without opening the Symbol Properties dialog box.

5. Click **g_border** in the Library panel to select it.

6. Click the **Delete icon** 🗑 at the bottom of the Library panel.

> TIP You can also select an item and press [Delete], or you can use the Options menu in the Library panel to remove an item from the library. The Undo command in the Edit menu can be used to undelete an item.

You used the Library panel to display the properties of symbols, rename symbols, and delete a symbol.

FIGURE 16
Renaming a symbol

FIGURE 17
The carRace.fla document and the coolCar.fla Library panel

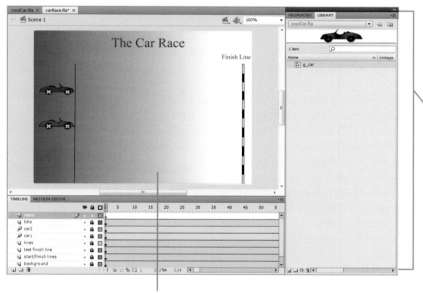

The Library panel for the coolCar.fla document

The carRace.fla document

Use multiple Library panels

1. Click the **Library panel list arrow** near the top of the Library panel to display a list of open documents.

2. Click **coolCar.fla**, then click **g_car**.

   The Library panel for the coolCar document is displayed. However, the carRace document remains open, as shown in Figure 17.

3. Click **frame 1** on the reset layer, then drag the **car** from the Library panel to the center of the Stage.

   The reset layer is the only unlocked layer. Objects cannot be placed on locked layers.

4. Click the **Library panel list arrow** to display the open documents.

5. Click **carRace.fla** to view the carRace document's Library panel.

   Notice the g_car symbol is automatically added to the Library panel of the carRace document.

6. Click the **g_car symbol** in the Library panel.

7. Click the **Delete icon** 🗑 at the bottom of the Library panel.

   You deleted the g_car symbol from the carRace library but it still exists in the coolCar library. The car was also deleted from the Stage.

8. Save your work.

9. Click the **coolCar.fla tab** at the top of the workspace to display the document.

10. Close the coolCar document and save the document if asked.

You used the Library panel to display the contents of another library and added an object from that library to the current document.

Lesson 2   Work with Libraries

FLASH 3-15

CREATE
BUTTONS

What You'll Do

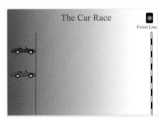

 In this lesson, you will create a button, edit the four button states, and test a button.

Understanding Buttons

Button symbols are used to provide inter-activity. When you click a button, an action occurs, such as starting an animation or jumping to another frame on the Timeline. Any object, including Flash drawings, text blocks, and imported graphic images, can be made into buttons. Unlike graphic symbols, buttons have four states: Up, Over, Down, and Hit. These states correspond to the use of the mouse and recognize that the user requires feedback when the mouse is pointing to a button and when the button has been clicked. This is often shown by a change in the button (such as a differ-ent color or different shape). An example of a button with different colors for the four different states is shown in Figure 18. These four states are explained in the fol-lowing paragraphs.

Up—Represents how the button appears when the mouse pointer is not over it.

Over—Represents how the button appears when the mouse pointer is over it.

Down—Represents how the button appears after the user clicks the mouse.

Hit—Defines the area of the screen that will respond to the click. In most cases, you will want the Hit state to be the same or similar to the Up state in location and size.

When you create a button symbol, Flash automatically creates a new Timeline. The Timeline has only four frames, one for each button state. The Timeline does not play; it merely reacts to the mouse pointer by displaying the appropriate button state and performing an action, such as jumping to a specific frame on the main Timeline.

The process for creating and previewing buttons is as follows:

Create a button symbol—Draw an object or select an object that has already been created and placed on the Stage. Use the Convert to Symbol command on the Modify menu to convert the object to a button symbol and to enter a name for the button.

Edit the button symbol—Select the button and choose the Edit Symbols command on the Edit menu or double-click the button symbol in the Library panel. This displays the button Timeline, shown in Figure 19, which allows you to work with the four button states. The Up state is the original button symbol. Flash automatically places it in frame 1. You need to determine how the original object will change for the other states. To change the button for the Over state, click frame 2 and insert a keyframe. This automatically places a copy of the

button that is in frame 1 into frame 2. Then, alter the button's appearance for the Over state by, for instance, changing the fill color. Use the same process for the Down state. For the Hit state, you insert a keyframe on frame 4 and then specify the area on the screen that will respond to the pointer. If you do not specify a hit area, the image for the Up state is used for the hit area. You add a keyframe to the Hit frame only if you are going to specify the hit area.

Return to the main Timeline—Once you've finished editing a button, you

choose the Edit Document command on the Edit menu, or click Scene 1 above the edit window, to return to the main Timeline.

Preview the button—By default, Flash disables buttons so that you can manipulate them on the Stage. You can preview a button by choosing the Enable Simple Buttons command on the Control menu. You can also choose the Test Movie command on the Control menu to play the movie and test the buttons.

FIGURE 18
The four button states

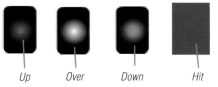

Up   Over   Down   Hit

FIGURE 19
The button Timeline

Create a button

1. Insert a new layer above the top layer in the Timeline, then name the layer **signal**.

2. Select the **Rectangle Primitive tool** ⬛ , click the **Stroke Color tool** 🖊 on the Tools panel, then click the **No Stroke icon** ☑ in the upper-right corner of the color palette.

3. Set the **Fill Color** 🖊 to the **red gradient Color swatch** in the bottom row of the color palette.

4. Display the Properties panel, click the **Reset button** in the RECTANGLE OPTIONS area, then set the corner radius to **5**.

5. Draw the **rectangle** shown in Figure 20.

6. Click the **Zoom tool** 🔍 on the Tools panel, then click the **rectangle** to enlarge it.

7. Select the **Gradient Transform tool** 🔲 on the Tools panel, then click the **rectangle**.

   You may need to click and hold the Free Transform tool first.

8. Drag the **diagonal arrow** toward the center of the rectangle as shown in Figure 21 to make the red area more round.

9. Click the **Selection tool** ▸ on the Tools panel, then drag a **marquee** around the rectangle to select it.

10. Click **Modify** on the menu bar, then click **Convert to Symbol**.

11. Type **b_signal** in the Name text box, click the **Type list arrow**, click **Button**, then click **OK**.

12. Display the Library panel, drag the **b_signal symbol** to the Buttons folder.

You created a button symbol on the Stage and dragged it to the Buttons folder in the Library panel.

FIGURE 20
The rectangle object

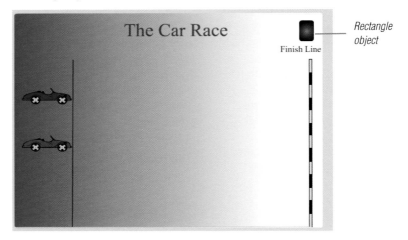

Rectangle object

FIGURE 21
Adjusting the gradient

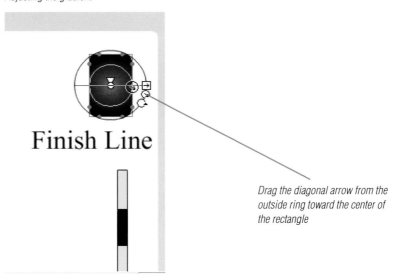

Drag the diagonal arrow from the outside ring toward the center of the rectangle

FIGURE 22
Specifying the hit area

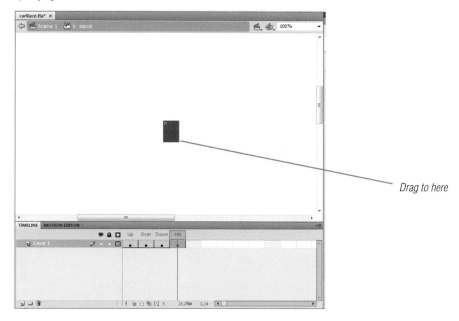

Drag to here

1. Open the Buttons folder, right-click (Win) or control-click (Mac) **b_signal** in the Library panel, then click **Edit**.

   Flash displays the edit window showing the Timeline with four button states.

2. Click the blank **Over frame** on Layer 1, then insert a keyframe.

   TIP   The [F6] key inserts a keyframe in the selected frame (Win).

3. Set the **Fill Color** to the **gray gradient color swatch** on the bottom of the color palette.

4. Insert a **keyframe** in the Down frame on Layer 1.

5. Set the **Fill Color** to the **green gradient color swatch** on the bottom of the color palette.

6. Insert a **keyframe** in the Hit frame on Layer 1.

7. Select the **Rectangle tool** on the Tools panel, set the **Fill Color** to the **blue color swatch** in the left column of the color palette.

8. Draw a **rectangle** slightly larger than the button, as shown in Figure 22, then release the mouse button.

   TIP   The Hit area will not be visible on the Stage.

9. Click **Scene 1** above the edit window to return to the main Timeline.

You edited a button by changing the color of its Over and Down states, and you specified the Hit area.

Test a button

1. Click the **Selection tool** ✎ , then click a blank area of the Stage.

2. Click **Control** on the menu bar, then click **Enable Simple Buttons**.

   This command allows you to test buttons on the Stage without viewing the movie in the Flash Player window.

3. Point to the **signal button** on the Stage, then compare your image to Figure 23.

   The pointer changes to a hand 🖑 , indicating that the object is clickable, and the button changes to a gray gradient, the color you selected for the Over State.

4. Press and hold the **mouse button**, then notice that the button changes to a green gradient, the color you selected for the Down state, as shown in Figure 24.

   (continued)

FIGURE 23
The button's Over state

FIGURE 24
The button's Down state

The button Hit area

All buttons have an area that responds to the mouse pointer, including rolling over the button and clicking it. This hit area is usually the same size and shape as the button itself. However, you can specify any area of the button to be the hit area. For example, you could have a button symbol that looks like a target with just the bulls-eye center being the hit area.

FIGURE 25
The button's Up state

FIGURE 26
View options from the View list

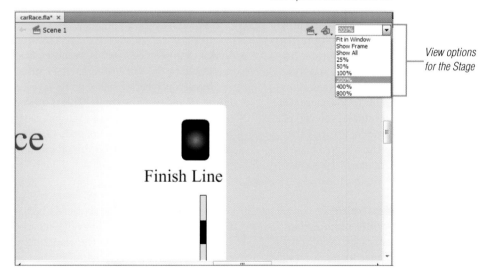

View options
for the Stage

5. Release the mouse and notice that the button changes to a gray gradient, the color you selected for the Over state.

6. Move the mouse away from the signal button, and notice that the button returns to a red gradient, the Up state color, as shown in Figure 25.

7. Click **Control** on the menu bar, then click **Enable Simple Buttons** to turn off the command.

8. Click the **View list arrow** above the Stage, as shown in Figure 26, then click **Fit in Window**.

   This shortcut allows you to change the magnification view without using the Magnification command on the View menu or the Zoom tool in the Tools panel.

9. Save your work.

You used the mouse to test a button and view the button states.

ASSIGN ACTIONS
TO FRAMES AND BUTTONS

What You'll Do

In this lesson, you will use ActionScripts to assign actions to frames and buttons.

Understanding Actions

In a basic movie, Flash plays the frames sequentially, repeating the movie without stopping for user input. However, you may often want to provide users with the ability to interact with the movie by allowing them to perform actions, such as starting and stopping the movie or jumping to a specific frame in the movie. One way to provide user interaction is to assign an action to the Down state of a button. Then, whenever the user clicks the button, the action occurs. Flash provides a scripting language, called ActionScript, that allows you to add actions to buttons and frames within a movie. For example, you can place a stop action in a frame that pauses the movie, and then you can assign a play action to a button that starts the movie when the user clicks the button.

Analyzing ActionScript

ActionScript is a powerful scripting language that allows those with even limited programming experience to create complex actions. For example, you can create order

forms that capture user input or volume controls that display when sounds are played. A basic ActionScript involves an event (such as a mouse click) that causes some action to occur by triggering the script. The following is an example of a basic ActionScript:

```
on (release) {
        gotoAndPlay(10);
}
```

In this example, the event is a mouse click (indicated by the word release) that causes the movie's playback head to go to frame 10 and play the frame. This is a simple example of ActionScript code and is easy to follow. Other ActionScript code can be quite complex and may require programming expertise to understand.

ActionScript 2.0 and 3.0

Adobe has identified two types of Flash CS4 users, designers and developers. Designers focus more on the visual features of a Flash movie, including the user interface design, drawing objects, and acquiring and editing additional assets (such as sound clips). Whereas, developers focus more on the programming aspects of a Flash movie, including creation of complex animations and writing the code that specifies how the movie responds to user interactions. In many cases, designers and developers work together to create sophisticated Flash applications. In other cases, designers work without the benefit of a developer's programming expertise. In order to accommodate the varying needs of these two types of uses, Flash CS4 provides two versions of ActionScript, 2.0 and 3.0, called AS2 and AS3. ActionScript 3.0 is used by developers because it provides a programming environment that is more familiar to them and can be used to create movies that download more quickly. However, the differences between AS2 and AS3 are transparent to designers who do not have programming expertise. AS2 allows the new Flash user to create compelling applications while not having to have a background in programming. At the same time it provides an introduction to ActionScript that can be the basis for learning ActionScript 3.0. ActionScript 2.0 will be used in this chapter. You can specify ActionScript 2.0 when creating a new document or you can use the Flash section of the Publish Settings command found on the File menu to specify AS2.

An advantage of using AS2 is a feature called Script Assist, which provides an easy way to use ActionScript without having to learn the scripting language. The Script Assist feature within the Actions panel allows you to assign basic actions to frames and objects, such as buttons. Figure 27 shows the Actions panel displaying an ActionScript indicating that when the user clicks the selected object (a button, in this example, b_signal), the movie goes to frame 2.

FIGURE 27
The Actions panel displaying an ActionScript

Event
on (release)

Action
gotoAndPlay(2)

Action assigned
to this smbol

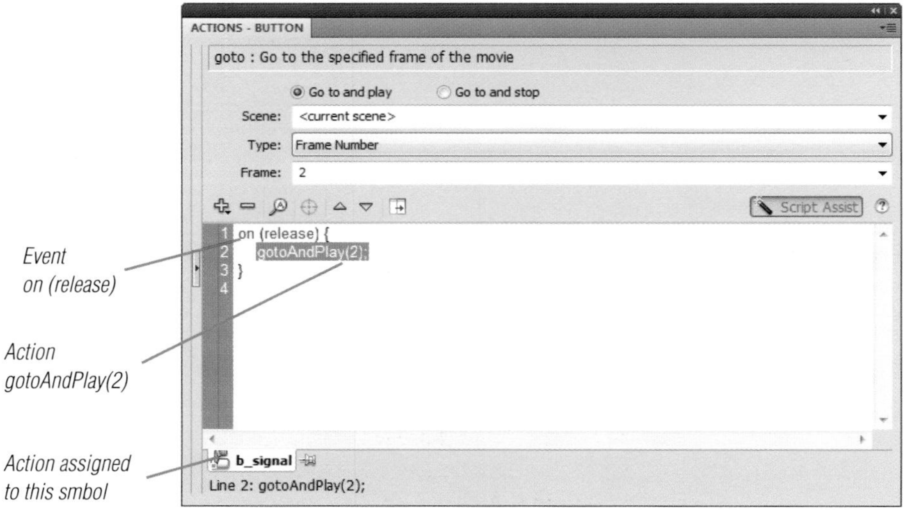

The process for assigning actions to buttons, shown in Figure 28, is as follows:

- Select the button on the Stage that you want to assign an action to.
- Display the Actions panel, using the Window menu.
- Select the Script Assist button to display the Script Assist panel within the ActionScript panel.
- Click the Add a new item to the script icon to display a list of Action categories.
- Select the appropriate category from a drop-down list. Flash provides several Action categories. The Timeline Control category within the Global Functions menu allows you to create scripts for controlling movies and navigating within movies. You can use these actions to start and stop movies, jump to specific frames, and respond to user mouse movements and keystrokes.
- Select the desired action, such as goto.
- Specify the event that triggers the action, such as on (release). This step in the process is not shown in Figure 28.

Button actions respond to one or more mouse events, including:

Release—With the pointer inside the button Hit area, the user presses and releases (clicks) the mouse button. This is the default event.

Key Press—With the button displayed, the user presses a predetermined key on the keyboard.

Roll Over—The user moves the pointer into the button Hit area.

Drag Over—The user holds down the mouse button, moves the pointer out of the button Hit area, and then back into the Hit area.

Using Frame Actions—In addition to assigning actions to buttons, you can assign actions to frames. Actions assigned to frames are executed when the playhead reaches the frame. A common frame action is stop, which is often assigned to the first and last frame of a layer on the Timeline.

FIGURE 28
The process for assigning actions to buttons

3. Click the Add a new item to the script icon

Hide/Display arrow; click at any time and as needed to hide or display the Toolbox pane

1. Select the button

2. Click the Script Assist button to toggle between on (seen here) and off

4. Select the Actions category and the action

Understanding the Actions panel—The Actions panel has two panes. The left pane (also called the Toolbox pane) uses folders to display the Action categories. The right pane, called the Script pane, is used with the Script Assist feature and it displays the ActionScript code as the code is being generated. When using the Script Assist feature, it is best to close the left pane. This is done by clicking the Hide/Display arrow as shown in Figure 29. The lower-left corner of the Script pane displays the symbol name or the frame to which the action(s) will apply. Always verify that the desired symbol or frame is displayed.

Using Frame Labels—Buttons are often used to move the playhead to a specific location on the Timeline. For example, clicking a Start button might cause the playhead to jump from frame 1 to frame 10 to start an animation. In addition to referencing frame numbers, like 10, you can reference frame labels in the ActionScript code. Frame labels have an advantage over frame numbers, especially in large and complex applications, because adding or deleting frames will not disrupt the navigation to a frame reference you already have in actions, since the label remains attached to the frame even if the frame moves. The process is to select a frame and use the Properties panel to specify a name. Then use the name in the ActionScript code instead of the frame number. Figure 30 shows the Timeline with a frame label and the Actions panel with the code that references the label.

FIGURE 29
The Actions panel

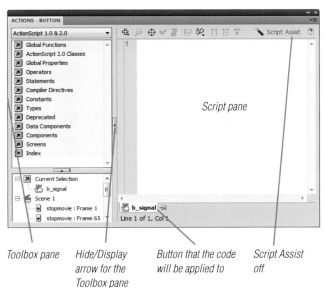

Toolbox pane   Hide/Display arrow for the Toolbox pane   Button that the code will be applied to   Script Assist off

FIGURE 30
The Timeline with a frame label

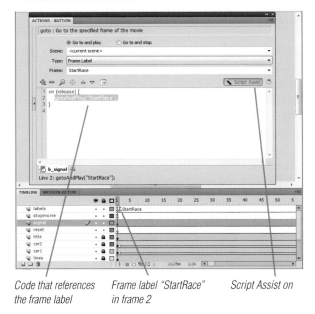

Code that references the frame label   Frame label "StartRace" in frame 2   Script Assist on

Assign a stop action to frames

1. Click **Control** on the menu bar, then click **Test Movie**.

   The movie plays and continues to loop.

2. Close the Flash Player window.

3. Insert a **new layer**, name it **stopmovie**, then click **frame 1** on the layer to select the frame.

4. Click **Window** on the menu bar, then click **Actions** to display the Actions panel.

5. Study the Actions panel. If the Toolbox pane is displayed as shown in Figure 31, then click the **Hide/Display arrow** to hide the pane.

6. Click the **Script Assist button** to turn on the Script Assist feature.

7. Verify stopmovie:1 (indicating the layer and frame to which the action will be applied) is displayed in the lower-left corner of the Script pane.

8. Click the **Add a new item to the script button** ➕ to display the Script categories, point to **Global Functions**, point to **Timeline Control**, then click **stop**, as shown in Figure 32.

9. Move the Actions panel as needed to see the Timeline, then click **frame 65** on the stopmovie layer.

10. Insert a **keyframe** in frame 65 on the stopmovie layer, then repeat Step 8. Compare your screen to Figure 33. Test the movie.

    The movie does not play because there is a stop action assigned to frame 1.

11. Close the Flash Player window.

You inserted a layer and assigned a stop action to the first and last frames on the layer.

FLASH 3-26

FIGURE 31
The Actions panel Toolbox pane

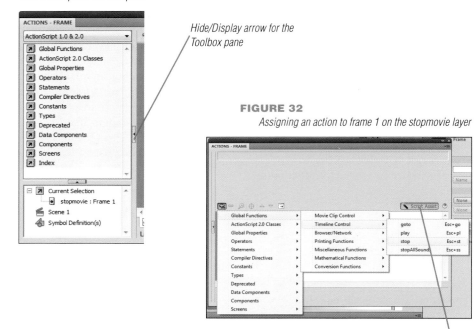

Hide/Display arrow for the Toolbox pane

FIGURE 32
Assigning an action to frame 1 on the stopmovie layer

Script Assist on

FIGURE 33
Script for the stopmovie layer

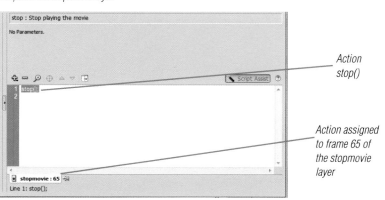

Action stop()

Action assigned to frame 65 of the stopmovie layer

FIGURE 34
Assigning an event and an action to a button

Button selected

Action assigned
to the button
named b_signal

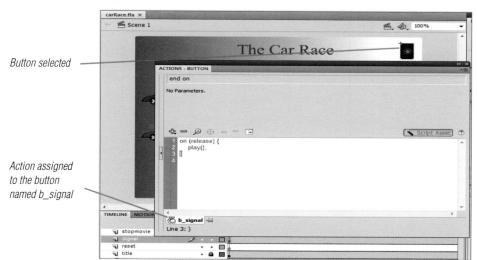

1. Click **frame 1** on the Signal layer.
2. Move the **Actions panel** to view the signal button on the Stage (if necessary).

    TIP You can collapse the Actions panel to view more of the Stage, then expand the Actions panel when needed. Alternately, you can drag the bottom of the Actions panel up to make the panel smaller.

3. Click the **Selection tool** ▸ on the Tools panel, then click the **button** on the Stage.
4. Verify b_signal is displayed in the lower left of the Actions panel.

    This ensures that the actions specified in the Actions panel will apply to the b_signal button.

5. Click ⊹ to display the Script categories, point to **Global Functions**, point to **Timeline Control**, then click **play**.

    Release is the default event, as shown in Figure 34.

6. Click **Control** on the menu bar, then click **Test Movie**.
7. Click the **signal button** to play the animation.
8. Close the Flash Player window.

You used the Actions panel to assign a play action to a button.

Lesson 4   Assign Actions to Frames and Buttons

Assign a goto frame action to a button

1. Click **Control** on the menu bar, then click **Test Movie**.

2. Click the **signal button**.

   The movie plays and stops, and the word Reset, which is actually a button, appears.

3. Click the **Reset button** and notice nothing happens because it does not have an action assigned to it.

4. Close the Flash Player window.

5. Click **frame 65** on the reset layer to display the Reset button on the Stage.

   Note: You many need to move the Actions panel to view the Reset button on the Stage.

6. Click the **Reset button** on the Stage to select it.

7. Verify b_reset is displayed in the lower left of the Actions panel.

8. Verify Script Assist is active, click ✥, point to **Global Functions**, point to **Timeline Control**, click **goto**, then verify Frame 1 is specified, as shown in Figure 35.

9. Click **Control** on the menu bar, then click **Test Movie**.

10. Click the **signal button** to start the movie, then when the movie stops, click the **Reset button**.

11. Close the Flash Player window.

You used the Actions panel to assign an action to a button.

FIGURE 35

Assigning a goto action to a button

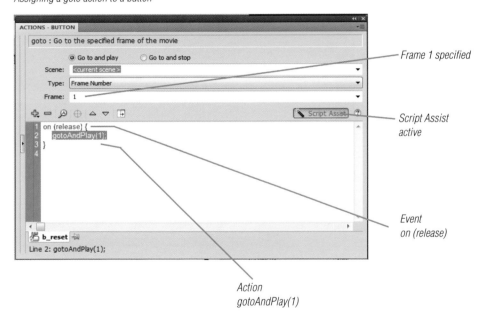

Frame 1 specified

Script Assist active

Event on (release)

Action gotoAndPlay(1)

FIGURE 36

Assigning a keypress action to a button

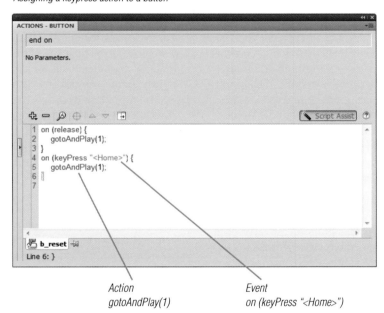

Action
gotoAndPlay(1)

Event
on (keyPress "<Home>")

1. Click the **right curly bracket** (}) in the Actions panel to highlight the bracket in Step 3 of the ActionScript.

2. Click ⬚ in the Script Assist window, point to **Global Functions**, point to **Movie Clip Control**, then click **on**.

   The Script Assist window displays several event options. Release is selected.

3. Click the **Release check box** to deselect the option.

4. Click the **Key Press check box** to select it, then press the [**Home**] **key** on the keyboard.

   TIP If your keyboard does not have a [Home] key, use [fn]+[◀—] (Mac) or one of the function keys (Win) to complete the steps.

5. Click ⬚ in the Script Assist window, point to **Global Functions**, point to **Timeline Control**, then click **goto**.

   The ActionScript now indicates that pressing the [Home] key will cause the playhead to go to frame 1, as shown in Figure 36.

   The Reset button can now be activated by clicking it or by pressing the [Home] key.

6. Click **File** on the menu bar, point to **Publish Preview**, then click **Default – (HTML)**.

   The movie opens in your default browser.

   Note: If a warning message opens, follow the messages to allow blocked content.

7. Click the **signal button** to start the movie, then when the movie stops, press the [**Home**] **key**.

8. Close the browser window.

9. Close the Actions panel, then save and close the movie.

You added an event that triggers a goto frame action.

IMPORTING
GRAPHICS

What You'll Do

▶ *In this lesson, you will import and work with bitmap and vector graphics.*

Understanding Graphic Types

Flash provides excellent drawing tools that allow you to create various objects that can be changed into symbols. In addition, you can import graphics and other assets, such as photographs and sounds. There are two types of graphic files, bitmap graphics and vector graphics. They are distinguished by the way in which the image is represented.

Bitmap images are made up of a group of tiny dots of color called **pixels** (picture elements). Bitmap graphics are often used with photographic images because they can represent subtle gradients in color. However, one disadvantage of bitmap graphics is the inability to enlarge the graphic without distorting the image. This is because both the computer screen's resolution (pixels per inch) and the number of pixels making up the image are a fixed number. So, when you enlarge an image each pixel must increase in size to fill the larger image dimensions. This causes the pixels to display jagged edges as shown in Figure 37.

Vector graphics represent an image as a geometric shape made up of lines and arcs that are combined to create various shapes, such as circles and rectangles. This is similar to Flash drawings that include strokes and fills. Flash drawing tools create vector graphics. An advantage of vector graphics is that they can be resized without distorting the image. The reason is that the geometric shapes are based on mathematical models that are recalculated when the image is resized. Figure 38 shows an example of a vector graphic before and after resizing. Vector graphics are best used for drawings rather than for images requiring photographic quality.

There are several programs that allow you to create and edit graphics including Adobe Illustrator, Fireworks, and Photoshop. There are also clip art and stock photograph collections that are available online. Filename extensions identify the file type. For example, .jpg, .tif, .bmp, and .gif are file formats for bitmap graphics; while .ai is a vector file format.

Importing and Editing Graphics

Once you have identified the graphic you would like to include in a Flash document, you can use the Import feature to bring the graphic into Flash. The process for importing is to select the Import command from the File menu and specify where to import (Stage or library). Then you navigate to the location where the file is stored and select it. After importing a vector graphic you can work with it as you would any graphic. Because bitmap graphics are not easy to edit in Flash, you may want to use another program, like Photoshop, to obtain the desired size, color, and other enhancements before importing the graphic.

FIGURE 37
Bitmap graphic enlarged

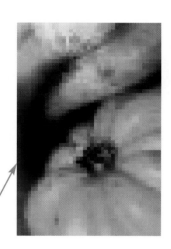

FIGURE 38
Vector graphic enlarged

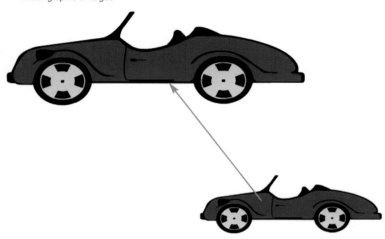

Importing graphics

1. Start a new Flash document, then save it as **sailing.fla**.

2. Click **File** on the menu bar, point to **Import**, then click **Import to Library**.

3. Navigate to the folder where your Data Files are stored, click **islandview.jpg**, then click **Open** (Win) or **Import to Library** (Mac).

   Islandview.jpg is a digital photo that was edited in Photoshop and saved as a .jpg file.

4. Display the Library panel and notice the icon used for bitmap graphics.

5. Drag the **islandview icon** to the Stage, then lock the layer.

6. Click **File** on the menu bar, point to **Import**, then click **Import to Library**.

7. Navigate to the folder where your Data Files are stored, then click **sailboat.ai**.

   This graphic was created using Adobe Illustrator and is made up of several layers.

8. Click **Open** (Win) or **Import to Library** (Mac).

   A dialog box appears asking you to choose the layers to import. All layers are selected by default.

9. Click **OK**.

   The graphic is added to the Library panel as a symbol.

10. Add a new layer to the Timeline, click **frame 1** on the layer, then drag the **sailboat icon** to the Stage, as shown in Figure 39.

(continued)

FIGURE 39
Positioning the sailboat image on the Stage

Working with Symbols and Interactivity

FIGURE 40
Changing the color of the sail

FIGURE 41
Rotating and skewing the sailboat image

11. Click **Modify** on the menu bar, click **Break apart**, then repeat this step until the dotted pattern that indicates the image is no longer a symbol appears.

12. Click the **Selection tool** , then click a blank area of the Pasteboard.

13. Click the **left sail**, then change the color to a rainbow pattern, as shown in Figure 40.

    Hint: The rainbow color is found at the bottom of the palette for the Fill Color tool.

14. Use the **Selection tool** to drag a **marquee** around the entire sailboat to select it, then convert the image to a graphic symbol named **sailboat**.

15. Change the width of the boat to **60** on the Properties panel.

16. Click the **Zoom tool** on the Tools panel, click the **sailboat** twice, then scroll as needed to view both sailboats.

    Notice how the bitmap photograph becomes distorted, while the vector sailboat does not.

17. Change the magnification to **Fit in Window**.

18. Use the **Free Transform tool** to rotate and skew the sailboat slightly to the left as shown in Figure 41.

19. Test the movie, close the Flash Player window, then save your work and exit Flash.

You imported bitmap and vector graphics, and edited the vector graphic.

Create a symbol.

1. Start Flash, open fl3_3.fla, then save it as **skillsdemo3**. This document consists of a single object that was created using the Flash drawing tools.
2. Use the Selection tool to drag a marquee around the ball to select it.
3. Convert the ball to a graphic symbol with the name g_beachball.
4. Double-click the g_beachball symbol on the Library panel to open the edit window, change the fill color to a rainbow gradient, add a text block that sits on top of the ball with the words **BEACH BALL** (see Figure 42), change the font color to white, then click Scene 1 to return to the main Timeline.
5. With the ball selected, create a motion tween animation that moves the ball from the left edge of the Stage to the right edge of the Stage.
6. Use the Selection tool to drag the middle of the motion path up to near the middle of the Stage to create an arc.
7. Select the last frame of the animation on the Timeline and set Rotate to 1 time in the Rotation area of the Properties panel.
8. Play the movie.
   The ball should move across the Stage in an arc and spin at the same time.
9. Lock the beachball-spin layer.

Create and edit an instance.

1. Insert a new layer and name it **redBall**.
2. Click frame 1 on the redBall layer, then drag the g_beachball symbol from the Library panel so it is on top of the ball on the Stage.
3. Use the arrow keys to align the ball so that it covers the ball on the Stage.
4. With the ball selected, break apart the object.
5. Change the fill color of the ball to a red gradient and change the text to **RED BALL**.
6. Insert a new layer and name it **greenBall**.
7. Click frame 12 on the greenBall layer, then insert a keyframe.
8. Drag the g_beachball symbol from the Library panel so it is on top of the ball that is near the middle of the Stage.
   (*Note:* Align only the balls, not the text.)
9. With the ball selected, break apart the object and change the fill color of the ball to a green gradient and the text to **GREEN BALL**.
10. Move the beachball-spin layer to above the other layers.
11. Insert a new layer and name it **title**.
12. Click frame 1 on the title layer, create a text block at the top middle of the Stage with the words **Beachball Spin** using Arial as the font, blue as the color, and 20 as the font size.
13. Insert a new layer above the title layer and name it **titlebkgnd**.
14. Draw a primitive rectangle with a corner radius of 10, a medium gray fill (#999999) and no stroke that covers the Beachball Spin title text.
15. Verify the rectangle is selected, convert it to a graphic symbol, then name it **g_bkgnd**.
16. Move the title layer so it is above the title-bkgnd layer.
17. Play the movie, then save your work.

Create a folder in the Library panel.

1. Click the New Folder button at the bottom of the Library panel to create a new folder.
2. Name the folder **Graphics**.
3. Move the two graphic symbols to the Graphics folder.
4. Expand the Graphics folder.
5. Save your work.

Work with the Library panel.

1. Rename the g_bkgnd symbol to **g_title-bkgnd** in the Library panel.
2. Collapse and expand the folder.
3. Save your work.

Create a button.

1. Insert a new layer above the title layer and name it **startButton**.
2. Drag the g_title-bkgnd symbol from the Library panel to the bottom center of the Stage.
3. Create a text block with the word **Start** formatted with white, bold, 22-pt Arial, then position the text block on top of the g_title-bkgnd object. Center the text block on top of the g_title-bkgnd object.
4. Select the rectangle and the text. (*Hint*: Drag a marquee around both objects or click the Selection tool, press and hold [Shift], then click each object.)

5. Convert the selected objects to a button symbol and name it **b_start**.
6. Create a new folder named **Buttons** in the Library panel and move the b_start button symbol to the folder.
7. Display the edit window for the b_start button.
8. Insert a keyframe in the Over frame.
9. Select the text and change the color to gray.
10. Insert a keyframe in the Down frame.
11. Select the text and change the color to blue.
12. Insert a keyframe in the Hit frame.
13. Draw a rectangular object that covers the button area for the Hit state.
14. Click Scene 1 to exit the edit window and return to the main Timeline.
15. Save your work.

Test a button.

1. Turn on Enable Simple Buttons.
2. Point to the button and notice the color change.
3. Click the button and notice the other color change.

Stop a movie.

1. Insert a new layer and name it **stopmovie**.
2. Insert a keyframe in frame 24 on the new layer.
3. With frame 24 selected, display the Actions panel.
4. Assign a stop action to the frame.
5. Click frame 1 on the stopmovie layer.
6. Assign a stop action to frame 1.
7. Save your work.

Assign a goto action to a button.

1. Click Control on the menu bar, then click Enable Simple Buttons to turn off this feature.
2. Use the Selection tool to select the Start button on the Stage.
3. Use Script Assist in the Actions panel to assign an event and a goto action to the button. (*Hint*: Refer to the section on assigning a goto action as needed.)
4. Test the movie.

FIGURE 42
Completed Skills Review

Import a graphic.

1. Import BeachScene.jpg from the drive and folder where your Data Files are stored to the Library panel.
2. Insert a new layer and name the layer **background**.
3. Select frame 1 on the background layer, then drag the BeachScene image to the Stage.
4. Move the background layer to the bottom of the Timeline.
5. Test the movie.
6. Save your work, then compare your image to Figure 42.
7. Exit Flash.

Working with Symbols and Interactivity

The Ultimate Tours travel company has asked you to design a sample navigation scheme for its website. The company wants to see how its home page will link with one of its main categories (Treks). Figure 43 shows a sample home page and Treks screen. Using the figures or the home page you created in Chapter 2 as a guide, you will add a Treks screen and link it to the home page. (*Hint*: Assume that all of the drawings on the home page are on frame 1, unless noted.)

1. Open ultimatetours2.fla (the file you created in Chapter 2 Project Builder 1), then save it as **ultimatetours3**.
2. Insert a layer above the Subheading layer and name it **logo**.
3. Import the UTLogo.jpg file from the drive and folder where your Data Files are stored to the Library panel.
4. Select frame 1 on the logo layer and drag the logo image to the upper-left corner of the Stage.

5. Select the logo and convert it to a graphic symbol with the name **g_utlogo**.
6. Lock the **logo layer**.
7. Select the layer that the Ultimate Tours text block is on, then insert a keyframe on a frame at least five frames farther along the Timeline.
8. Insert a new layer, name it **treks headings**, insert a keyframe on the last frame of the movie, then create the Treks screen shown in Figure 43, except for the home graphic. (*Note:* The underline was created using the Line tool.)
9. Convert the Treks graphic on the home page to a button symbol named **b_treks**, then edit the symbol so that different colors appear for the different states.
10. Assign a goto action that jumps the playhead to the Treks screen when the Treks button is clicked. (*Hint:* You need to use ActionScript 2.0 to complete the steps that follow. You can set the ActionScript version by selecting Publish Settings from the File menu, clicking the Flash tab and specifying ActionScript 2.0.)

11. Insert a new layer and name it **stopmovie**. Add stop actions that cause the movie to stop after displaying the home page and after displaying the Treks page. Make sure there is a keyframe in the last frame of the stopmovie layer.
12. Insert a new layer and name it **homeButton**, insert a keyframe on the last frame of the movie, then draw the home button image with the Home text.
13. Convert the image to a button symbol named **b_home**, then edit the symbol so that different colors appear for the different states. Assign a goto action for the button that jumps the movie to frame 1.
14. Select the last frame of the movie on the **logo layer** and insert a keyframe. (*Note:* You do this so that the logo appears on the home page and on the Treks page.)
15. Test the movie.
16. Save your work, then compare your web pages to the samples shown in Figure 43.

FIGURE 43

Sample completed Project Builder 1

Home page

Convert to a button
symbol

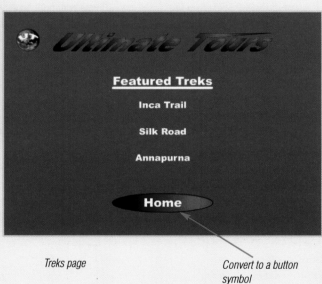

Treks page

Convert to a button
symbol

You have been asked to assist the International Student Association (ISA). The association sponsors a series of monthly events, each focusing on a different culture from around the world. The events are led by a guest speaker who makes a presentation, followed by a discussion. The events are free and they are open to everyone. ISA would like you to design a Flash movie that will be used with its website. The movie starts by providing information about the series, and then provides a link to the upcoming event.

1. Open a new Flash ActionScript 2.0 document and save it as **isa3**.
2. Create an initial Information screen with general information about the association's series.
3. Assign an action to frame 1 that stops the movie.
4. Create two more screens: a next event screen that presents information about the next event and a series screen that lists the series (all nine events for the school year—September through May).
5. Add a button on the general information screen that jumps the movie to the next event screen, and add a second button on the information screen that jumps the movie to the series screen.
6. On the next event and series screens, add a Return button that jumps the movie back to the general information screen.
7. On the next event screen, create a second button that jumps the movie to the series screen.
8. On the series screen, create a second button that jumps the movie to the event screen.
9. For each button you create, specify different colors for each state of each button.
10. Add an action that stops the movie on the next event screen, and another action that stops the movie on the series screen. (*Hint:* Place the stop actions on the same layer as the stop action created in step 3.)
11. Test the movie.
12. Save your work, then compare your movie to the sample shown in Figure 44.

FIGURE 44
Sample completed Project Builder 2

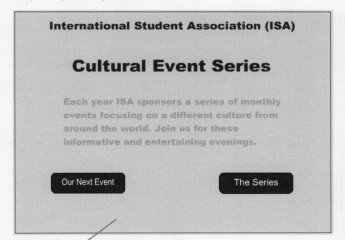

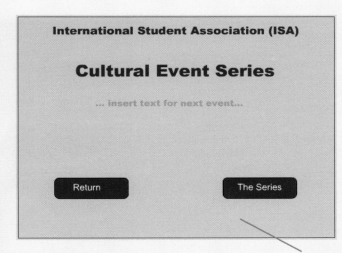

*Sample general
information screen*

*Sample next
event screen*

*Sample series
screen*

Figure 45 shows the home page of a website. Study the figure and complete the following questions. For each question, indicate how you determined your answer.

1. Connect to the Internet and go to *www.zoo.org*. Notice that this website has images that change as you visit the website.

2. Open a document in a word processor or open a new Flash document, save the file as **dpc3**, then answer the following questions. (*Hint*: Use the Text tool in Flash.)

   ■ Whose website is this?

   ■ What is the goal(s) of the site?

   ■ Who is the target audience?

   ■ What treatment ("look and feel") is used?

   ■ What are the design layout guidelines being used (balance, movement, and so on)?

   ■ What may be animated in this home page?

   ■ Do you think this is an effective design for the company, its products, and its target audience? Why or why not?

   ■ What suggestions would you make to improve the design, and why?

FIGURE 45
Design Project

This is a continuation of the Chapter 2 Portfolio Project, which is the development of a personal portfolio. The home page has several categories, including the following:

- Personal data
- Contact information
- Previous employment
- Education
- Samples of your work

In this project, you will create a button that will be used to link the home page of your portfolio to the animations page. Next, you will create another button to start the animation.

1. Open portfolio2.fla (the file you created in Portfolio Project, Chapter 2), then save it as **portfolio3**. (*Hint*: When you open the file, you may receive a warning message that the font is missing. You can replace this font with the default, or with any other appropriate font on your computer.)
2. Unlock the layers as needed.
3. Insert a new layer, name it **sampleAnimations**, then insert a keyframe on frame 2.
4. Create a Sample Animations screen that has a text block with an oval background and the words **Sample Animations** at the top of the Stage, then add another text block and oval background with the word **Tweened**. (*Note*: This screen will have several animation samples added to it later.)

5. Insert a new layer, name it **home button**, then insert a keyframe on frame 2.
6. Add another text block with an oval background that says **Home** at the bottom of the Stage.
7. Insert a new layer, name it **tweened Animation**, then insert a keyframe on frame 3.
8. Create an animation(s) of your choice using objects you draw or import, or objects from the Library panel of another document. (*Note*: To create a motion tween animation when starting in a frame other than frame 1, you need to specify the ending frame of the animation by inserting a keyframe before repositioning the object on the Stage.) (*Hint*: To create more than one animation that plays at the same time, put each animation on its own layer.)
9. Insert a new layer, name it **animationHeading**, then insert a keyframe on frame 3.
10. Add a heading to the screen used for the animation(s).
11. On the Sample Animations screen, convert the Tweened and Home text blocks into button symbols, then edit each symbol so that different colors appear for the different states. For the Tweened button, assign an action that jumps to the frame that plays an animation. For the Home button, assign an action to the Home button that jumps to the frame that displays My Portfolio. (*Hint*: You need to use ActionScript 2.0. You can set the ActionsScript version by selecting Publish

Settings from the File menu, clicking the Flash tab and specifying ActionScript 2.0.)
12. Change the Animations graphic on the home page to a button, then edit the symbol so that different colors appear for the different states. Assign an action to the Animations button that jumps to the Sample Animations screen.
13. Insert a new layer, then name it **stopmovie**. Insert keyframes and assign stop actions to the appropriate frames.
14. Test the movie.
15. Save your work, then compare your movie to the sample shown in Figure 46.

FIGURE 46
Sample completed Portfolio Project

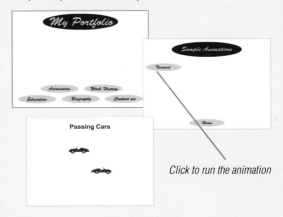

Click to run the animation

chapter

4

CREATING
ANIMATIONS

1. Create motion tween animations

2. Create classic tween animations

3. Create frame-by-frame animations

4. Create shape tween animations

5. Create movie clips

6. Animate text

4 CREATING ANIMATIONS

Introduction

Animation can be an important part of your application or website, whether the focus is on e-commerce (attracts attention and provides product demonstrations), education (simulates complex processes such as DNA replication), or entertainment (provides interactive games).

How Does Animation Work?

The perception of motion in an animation is actually an illusion. Animation is like a motion picture in that it is made up of a series of still images. Research has found that our eye captures and holds an image for one-tenth of a second before processing another image. By retaining each impression for one-tenth of a second, we perceive a series of rapidly displayed still images as a single, moving image. This phenomenon is known as persistence of vision and provides the basis for the frame rate in animations. Frame rates of 10–12 frames-per-second (fps) generally provide

an acceptably smooth computer-based animation. Lower frame rates result in a jerky image, while higher frame rates may result in a blurred image. Flash uses a default frame rate of 12 fps.

Flash Animation

Creating animation is one of the most powerful features of Flash, yet developing basic animations is a simple process. Flash allows you to create animations that can move and rotate an object around the Stage, and change its size, shape, or color. You can also use the animation features in Flash to create special effects, such as an object zooming or fading in and out. You can combine animation effects so that an object changes shape and color as it moves across the Stage. Animations are created by changing the content of successive frames. Flash provides two animation methods: frame-by-frame animation and tweened animation. Tweened animations can be motion, classic, or shape tweens.

Tools You'll Use

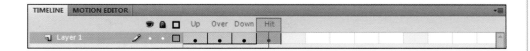

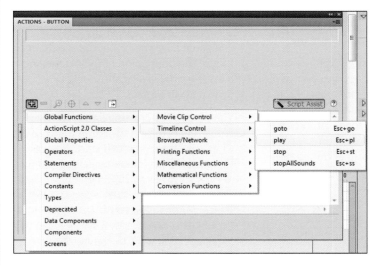

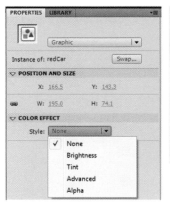

CREATE MOTION TWEEN
ANIMATIONS

What You'll Do

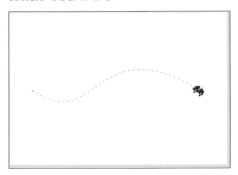

In this lesson, you will create and edit motion tween animations.

Understanding Motion Tween Animations

An animation implies some sort of movement in an object. However, the concept of animation is quite a bit more broad. Objects have specific properties such as position, size, color, and shape. Any change in a property of an object over time (i.e., across frames in the Timeline) can be considered an animation. So, having an object start at the left of the screen in frame 1 and then having it move across the screen and end up at the right side in frame 10 would be a change in the position property of the object. Each of the in-between frames (2-9) would show the position of the object as it moves across the screen. In a motion tween animation, you specify the position of the object in the beginning and ending frames and Flash fills in the in-between frames, a process known as tweening. Fortunately, you can change several properties with one motion tween. For example, you could have a car move across the screen and, at the same time, you could have the size of the car change to give the impression of the car moving away from the viewer. Motion tweens are new to Flash CS4.

The process for creating a motion tween animation is to select the frame and layer where the animation will start. If necessary, insert a keyframe (by default, frame 1 of each layer has a keyframe). Select the object on the Stage, then select the Motion Tween command from the Insert menu. If the object is not already a symbol, you will be asked if you want to convert it to a symbol. You must convert the object to a symbol if prompted, because only symbols can have a motion tween applied. Then you select the ending frame and make any changes to the object, such as moving it to another location or resizing it. When you create a motion tween, a tween span appears on the Timeline.

Tween Spans

Figure 1 shows a motion tween animation of a car that starts in frame 1 and ends in frame 30. The Onion Skin feature is enabled so that outlines of the car are displayed for each frame of the animation in the figure. Notice a blue highlight appears on the Timeline for the frames of the animation. The blue highlighted area is called the tween or motion span. By default the number of frames in a tween span is equal to the number of frames in one second of the movie. So, if the frame rate is 12 frames per second, then the span is 12 frames. You can increase or decrease the number of frames in the span by dragging the end of the span. In addition, you can move the span to a different location on the Timeline, and you can copy the span to have it apply to another object.

Motion Path

The animation shown in Figure 2 includes a position change (from frame 1 to frame 30); a motion path showing the position change is displayed on the Stage. Each symbol on the path corresponds to a frame on the Timeline and indicates the location of the object (in this example, the car) when the frame is played. A motion path can be altered by dragging a point on the path

FIGURE 1
Sample motion tween animation

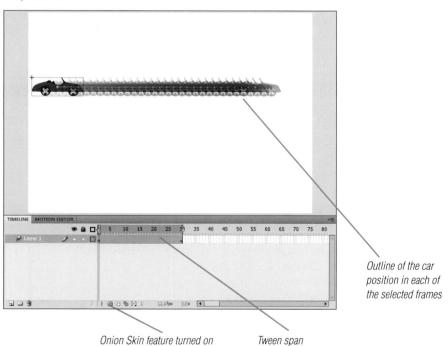

Outline of the car position in each of the selected frames

Onion Skin feature turned on   *Tween span*

using the Selection and Subselection tools or by manipulating Bezier handles as shown in Figure 3. Entire paths can be moved around the Stage and reshaped using the Free Transform tool.

Property Keyframes
A keyframe indicates a change in a Flash movie, such as the start or ending of an animation. Motion tween animations use property keyframes that are specific to each property such as a position keyframe, color keyframe, or rotation keyframe. In most cases these are automatically placed on the Timeline as the motion tween animation is created.

Keep in mind:
- Only one object on the Stage can be animated in each tween span.
- You can have multiple motion tween animations playing at the same time, if they are on different layers.
- A motion tween is, in essence, an object animation because while several changes can be made in the object's properties, only one object is animated for each motion tween.
- The types of objects that can be tweened include graphic, button, and movie clip symbols, as well as text fields.
- You can remove a motion tween animation by clicking the tween span on the Timeline and choosing Remove Tween from the Insert menu.

FIGURE 2
The motion path

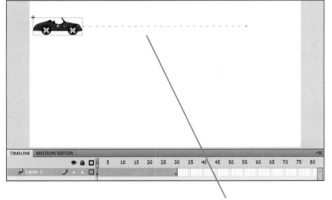

Motion path with symbols corresponding to a frame in the Timeline and showing the location of the car when the frame is played

FIGURE 3
Bezier handles used to alter the path

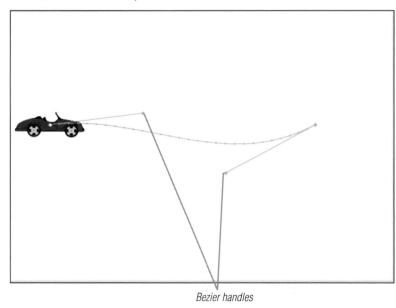

Bezier handles

FIGURE 4
Positioning the car object

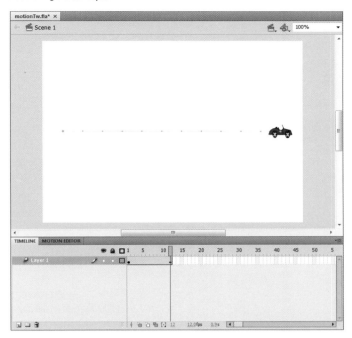

FIGURE 5
Change the end of the tween span

Drag pointer
to here

Create a motion tween animation

1. Open fl4_1.fla from the drive and folder where your Data Files are stored, then save it as **motionTw**.

   This document has one drawn object—a car that has been converted to a symbol.

2. Click the **Selection tool** ↖ on the Tools panel, then click the **car** to select it.

3. Click **Insert** on the menu bar, then click **Motion Tween**.

   Notice the tween span appears on the Timeline. The number of frames in the span equals the frames per second for the movie.

4. Verify the playhead is on the last frame of the tween span, then drag the **car** to the right side of the Stage, as shown in Figure 4.

   A motion path appears on the Stage with dots indicating the position of the object for each frame. A diamond symbol appears in frame 12. This is a position keyframe automatically inserted at the end of the motion path. This assumes the document frame rate is set to 12.

   Note: To see the diamond symbol more clearly, move the playhead.

5. Point to the end of the tween span, when the pointer changes to a double arrow ↔, drag the **tween span** to frame 40, as shown in Figure 5.

6. Click **frame 1** on the Timeline, then press the **period key** to move the playhead one frame at a time and notice the position of the car for each frame.

7. Play the movie, then save your work.

You created a motion tween animation, extended the length of the animation, and viewed the position of the animated object in each frame of the animation.

Edit a motion path

1. Click the **Selection tool** ↖ on the Tools panel, then click a blank area of the Stage.

2. Click **frame 1** on Layer 1.

3. Point to the middle of the motion path, as shown in Figure 6.

4. When the pointer changes to a pointer with an arc ↖⌣, drag the ↖⌣ **pointer** down, as shown in Figure 7.

(continued)

FIGURE 6
Pointing to the middle of the path

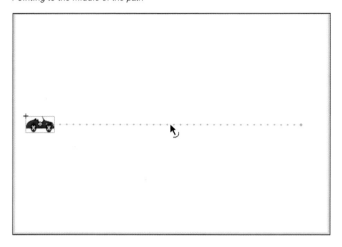

FIGURE 7
Dragging the motion path down

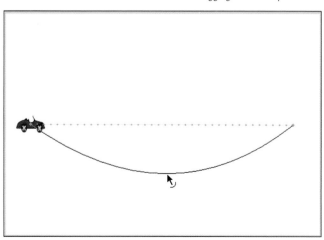

Creating Animations

FIGURE 8
Displaying the Bezier handles

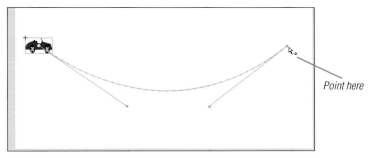

Point here

*Drag pointer
to here*

FIGURE 9
Using the handles to alter the shape of the path

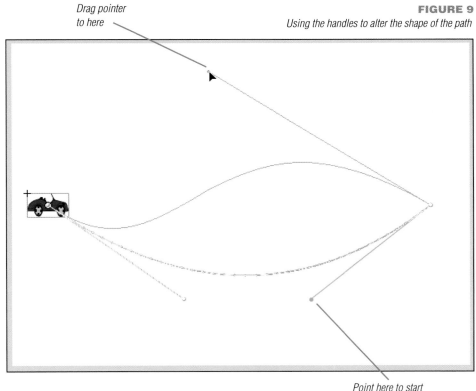

Point here to start

5. Play the movie, then click **frame 1** on Layer 1.

6. Click the **Subselection tool** on the Tools panel, point to the end of the motion path, when the pointer changes into an arrow with a small square, click the end of path to display Bezier handles, as shown in Figure 8.

7. Point to the **lower right handle**, when the pointer changes into a delta symbol ▶, drag the handle up and toward the center of the Stage to form a horizontal S shape, as shown in Figure 9.

8. Play the movie, then save your work.

You edited a motion path by using the Selection tool to drag the path and by using the Subselection tool to display and reposition Bezier handles.

Change the ease value of an animation

1. Play the movie and notice that the car moves at a constant speed.

2. Display the **Properties panel**, then click **frame 1** on Layer 1.

3. Point to the **Ease value**, when the pointer changes to a hand with a double arrow 🖐, drag the 🖐 **pointer** to the right to set the value at **100**, as shown in Figure 10.

4. Play the movie.

   The car starts moving fast and slows down near the end of the animation. Notice the word "out" is displayed next to the ease value in the Properties panel indicating that the object will ease out, slow down, at the end of the animation.

5. Click **frame 1** on Layer 1.

6. Point to the **Ease value** in the Properties panel, then drag the 🖐 **pointer** to the left to set the value to **−100**.

7. Play the movie.

   The car starts moving slowly and speeds up near the end of the animation. Notice the word "in" is displayed next to the ease value in the Properties panel. Also, notice the dots are grouped closer together at the beginning of the motion path indicating that the object does not move very far in that section of the path.

8. Set the ease value to **0**.

9. Save your work.

You changed the ease out and ease in values of the animation.

FIGURE 10
Changing the ease value

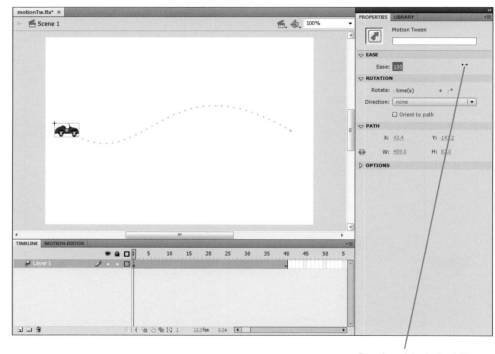

Drag the pointer to the right

FIGURE 11
Changing the width of the object

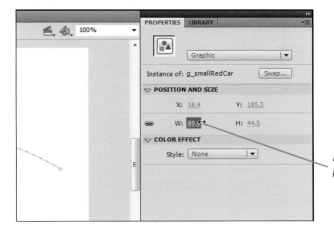

*Point here and drag the
pointer to change the width*

FIGURE 12
Using the Free Transform tool to skew the object

*Point to the middle handle and
drag the pointer to the right*

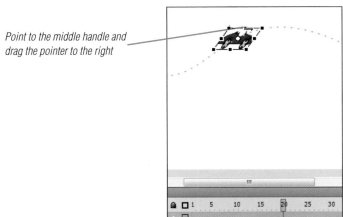

Resize and reshape an object

1. Click **frame 1** on Layer 1.
2. Click the **Selection tool** ▸ , then click the **car**.
3. Point to the **width (W:)** value in the Properties panel, when the pointer changes to a hand with a double arrow 🖐 , drag the 🖐 **pointer** to the right to set the value to **80**, as shown in Figure 11.
4. Play the movie.
5. Click **frame 40** on Layer 1, then click the **car**.
6. Point to the **width (W:)** value in the Properties panel, when the pointer changes to a hand with a double arrow 🖐 , drag the 🖐 **pointer** to the left to set the value to **30**.
7. Play the movie.

   The car starts out large and ends up small.
8. Click **frame 20** on Layer 1.
9. Click the **Free Transform tool** ⊞ in the Tools panel, then verify the Rotate and Skew option ⟳ is selected.
10. Point to the **top middle handle**, when the pointer changes to a double line ⇌, drag the ⇌ **pointer** to the right to skew the object, as shown in Figure 12.

    A skew keyframe appears in frame 20.
11. Play the movie, use the Undo command on the Edit menu to undo the skew, then save the movie.

    Note: You may have to click the Undo command more than one time to undo the skew.

    The skew keyframe is removed from frame 20.

You resized and skewed a motion tween object.

Create a color effect

1. Click the **Selection tool** ↖ in the Tools panel.
2. Click **frame 40** on Layer 1.
3. Click the **car** to select it.
4. Click the **Style list arrow** in the COLOR EFFECTS area of the Properties panel.
5. Click **Alpha**, then drag the **slider** △ to set the value to **0%**, as shown in Figure 13.
6. Play the movie.

   Notice the car slowly becomes transparent.
7. Reset the Alpha to **100%**.
8. Click **frame 40** on Layer 1.
9. Click the **car** to select it.
10. Click the **Style list arrow** in the COLOR EFFECT area of the Properties panel.
11. Click **Advanced**, then set the x R + value for Red to **100**, as shown in Figure 14.
12. Play the movie.

    Notice the car slowly changes to a shade of red. Because the car is a symbol, it is one part (not a composite of pieces). As a result changes made to the color value affect the entire car.
13. Set the x R + value back to **0**, then save your work.

You changed the alpha and advanced color option for an object.

FIGURE 13
Setting the Alpha (transparency) value

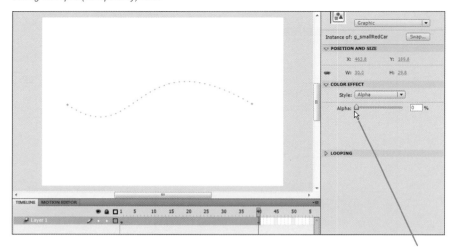

Drag the slider to the left

FIGURE 14
Changing a color value for the object

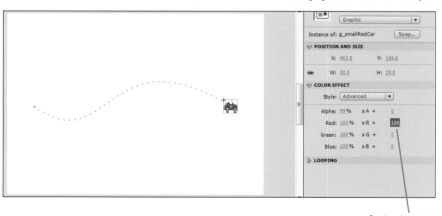

Setting the red value

FIGURE 15
Aligning the car to the path

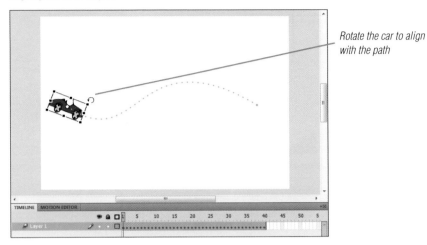

Rotate the car to align
with the path

FIGURE 16
Aligning the car to the end of the motion path

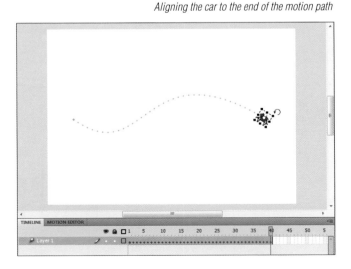

Orient an object to a path

1. Play the movie.

   Notice the car follows the path but it is not oriented to the path.

2. Click **frame 1** on Layer 1.

3. Click the **Orient to path check box** in the ROTATION area of the Properties panel.

4. Click the **Free Transform tool** ✥ on the Tools panel, then verify the Rotate and Skew option ↻ near the bottom of the Tools panel is selected.

5. Point to the upper-right corner of the car, when the pointer changes into a circular arrow ↻ , rotate the front of the car so that it aligns with the path, as shown in Figure 15.

6. Click **frame 40** on Layer 1, then rotate the back of the car so that it aligns with the path, as shown in Figure 16.

7. Play the movie.

   The car is oriented to the path.

   Notice the diamond symbol in each Layer 1 frame. These are rotation keyframes that indicate the object will change in each frame as it rotates to stay oriented to the path.

8. Save your work, then close the document.

You oriented an object to a motion path and aligned the object with the path in the first and last frames of the motion tween.

Copy a motion path

1. Open fl4_2.fla, save it as **tweenEdits**, then play the movie.

2. Insert a **new layer** and name it **biker2**, then click **frame 1** on the biker2 layer.

3. Verify the Selection tool ![arrow] is selected, drag the **g_biker symbol** from the Library panel to the Stage, as shown in Figure 17.

4. Click any frame on the tween span on the biker layer.

5. Click **Edit** on the menu bar, point to **Timeline**, then click **Copy Motion**.

6. Click the new instance of the biker, click **Edit** on the menu bar, point to **Timeline**, then click **Paste Motion**.

7. Play the movie, then hide the biker layer.

8. Click **frame 1** on the biker2 layer, click the **Free Transform tool** ![icon] on the Tools panel, then click the **path** to select it, as shown in Figure 18.

(continued)

FIGURE 17
Dragging the biker symbol to the Stage

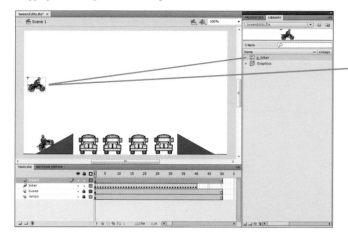

Drag g_biker symbol from the Library panel and position it on the Stage

FIGURE 18
Selecting the path with the Free Transform tool

Click the path to select it and display the handles

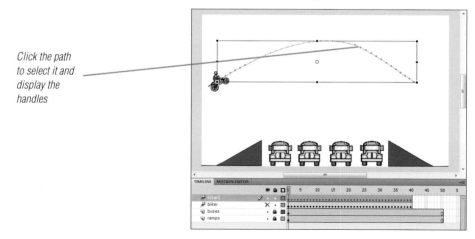

Creating Animations

FIGURE 19
Positioning the path

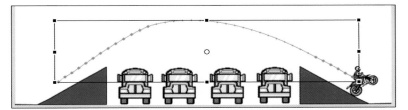

FIGURE 20
Aligning the biker to the path

9. Click **Modify** on the menu bar, point to **Transform**, then click **Flip Horizontal**.

10. Use the arrow keys on the keyboard to position the path, as shown in Figure 19.

11. Click the **biker object**, click **Modify** on the menu bar, point to **Transform**, then click **Flip Horizontal**.

12. Use the Free Transform tool ▓ and the arrow keys to align the biker, as shown in Figure 20.

13. Play the movie, then save your work.

You copied a motion path to another object.

Rotate an object

1. Click **frame 1** on the biker2 layer, then display the Properties panel.

2. Point to the **Rotate times value** in the ROTATION area of the Properties panel, when the pointer changes to a hand with a double arrow 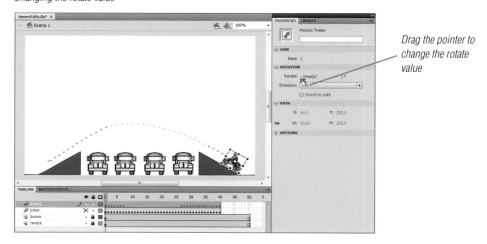, drag the 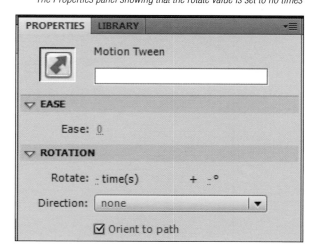 **pointer** to the right to set the count to **1**, as shown in Figure 21.

3. Verify the Direction is set to **CW (Clockwise)**, then play the movie.

   The biker object rotates one time in a clockwise direction. Look at the Timeline. Notice some of the keyframes have been removed from the motion tween span. This is because, as the biker rotates, he is no longer oriented to the path. Motion tweens do not allow an object to be rotated and oriented to a path simultaneously since orienting an object to a path rotates the object in each frame along the path. You can use a classic tween to rotate and orient an object to a path at the same time. The remaining keyframes at the beginning and ending of the tween span were used to align the original biker to the ramp.

4. Click **frame 1** on the biker2 layer, set the rotation count to **2**, click the **Direction list arrow**, click **CCW** (Counter Clockwise), then play the movie.

5. Click **Orient to path** to select it.

   The rotate value is automatically set to no times (indicated by a -), as shown in Figure 22.

6. Play the movie, then save your work.

You caused an object to rotate by setting the rotate value and specifying a rotation direction.

FIGURE 21
Changing the rotate value

Drag the pointer to change the rotate value

FIGURE 22
The Properties panel showing that the rotate value is set to no times

FIGURE 23

Timeline showing the motion tween removed

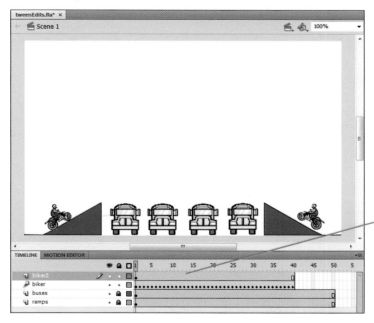

Removal of motion tween in the biker2 layer removes the blue highlight in the Timeline

1. Unhide the **biker layer**, then play the movie.
2. Click anywhere on the tween span on the biker2 layer to select the path.
3. Click **Insert** on the menu bar, then click **Remove Tween**.
4. Click a blank area of the Stage, then notice that the blue highlight on the biker2 layer is gone, as shown in Figure 23.
5. Play the movie and notice that the biker on the biker2 layer is visible but it does not move.
6. Use the Undo command in the Edit menu to undo the Remove Tween process.

   Note: You may need to select the Undo command more than one time.
7. Click **biker2** on the Timeline to select the layer.
8. Click the **Delete icon** at the bottom of the Timeline to delete the biker2 layer that includes the motion tween.
9. Test the movie, then close the Flash Player window.
10. Save your work.

You removed an object's motion tween, undid the action, then deleted a layer containing a motion tween and undid the action.

Work with multiple motion tweens

1. Click **frame 40** on the biker layer, then click the **biker** on the Stage.

2. Lock the **biker layer**, then add a **new layer** above the biker layer and name it **bikeOffStage**.

3. Click **frame 40** on the bikeOffStage layer.

4. Click **Insert** on the menu bar, point to **Timeline**, then click **Keyframe**.

5. Drag an instance of the **g_biker symbol** from the Library panel so it is on top of the biker on the Stage, as shown in Figure 24.

6. Use the the Free Transform tool and the arrow keys on the keyboard to align the two biker objects.

7. Click **frame 41** on the **bikeOffStage** layer, then insert a **keyframe**.

8. Use the **arrow keys** on the keyboard and the **Free Transform tool** to align the biker with the bottom of the ramp, as shown in Figure 25.

(continued)

FIGURE 24
Placing an instance of the g_biker symbol on top of the object on the Stage

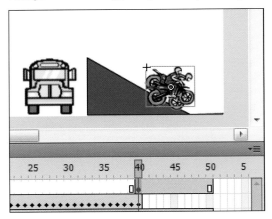

FIGURE 25
Aligning the biker with the ramp

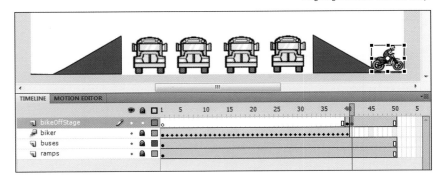

Creating Animations

FIGURE 26

Dragging the biker object off the Stage

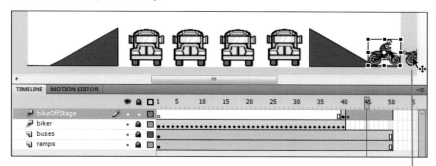

Drag the object off
the Stage

9. Click the **Selection tool** , then click the **biker**.

10. Click the **View list arrow**, then click **100%**.

11. Click **Insert** on the menu bar, then click **Motion Tween**.

12. Click **frame 45** on the bikeOffStage layer, then drag the **biker** off the Stage, as shown in Figure 26.

13. Test the movie, close the Flash Player window, save your work, then close the document.

You created a second motion tween for the movie.

CREATE CLASSIC TWEEN
ANIMATIONS

What You'll Do

In this lesson, you will create a motion guide and attach an animation to it.

Understanding Classic Tweens

Classic tweens are similar to motion tweens in that you can create animations that change the properties of an object over time. Motion tweens are easier to use and allow the greatest degree of control over tweened animations. Classic tweens are a bit more complex to create, however, they provide certain capabilities that some developers desire. For example, with a motion tween, you can alter the ease value so that an object starts out fast and ends slow, but with a classic tween, you can alter the ease value so that an object starts out fast, slows down, and then speeds up again. You can do this because a motion tween consists of one object over the tween span, but a classic tween can have more than one instance of the object over the tween span. The process for creating a classic tween animation that moves an object is to select the starting frame and, if necessary, insert a keyframe. Next, insert a keyframe at the ending frame, and click anywhere on the layer between the keyframes. Then select classic tween from the Insert menu, select the ending

frame, and move the object to the position you want it to be in the ending frame. While all prior versions of Flash used classic tweening only, you now have a choice between classic tweens and motion tweens.

Understanding Motion Guides

When you use motion tweening to generate an animation that moves an object, a motion path that shows the movement is automatically created on the Stage. When you use classic tweening, the object moves in a straight line from the beginning location to the ending location on the Stage. There is no path displayed. You can draw a path, called a **motion guide**, that can be used to alter the path of a classic tween animation as shown in Figure 27. A motion guide is drawn on the motion guide layer with the classic tween animation placed on its own layer beneath the motion guide layer, as shown in Figure 28. The process for creating a motion guide and attaching it to a classic tween animation is:

■ Create a classic tween animation.
■ Insert a new layer above the classic tween animation layer and change the

layer properties to a Guide layer. Drag the classic tween animation layer to the guide layer so that it indents, as shown in Figure 28. This indicates that the classic tween animation layer is associated with the motion guide layer.

- Draw a path using the Pen, Pencil, Line, Circle, Rectangle, or Brush tools.
- Attach the object to the path by clicking the first keyframe of the layer that contains the animation, and then dragging the object by its transformation point to the beginning of the path. Select the end keyframe and then repeat the steps to attach the object to the end of the path.

Depending on the type of object you are animating and the path, you may need to orient the object to the path.

The advantages of using a motion guide are that you can have an object move along any path, including a path that intersects itself, and you can easily change the shape of the path, allowing you to experiment with different motions. A consideration when using a motion guide is that, in some instances, orienting the object along the path may result in an unnatural-looking animation. You can fix this by stepping through the animation one frame at a time until you reach the frame where the object is positioned poorly. You can then insert a keyframe and adjust the object as desired.

Transformation Point and Registration Point

Each symbol has a transformation point in the form of a circle (O) that is used to orient the object when it is being animated. For example, when you rotate a symbol, the transformation point is the pivot point around which the object rotates. The transformation point is also the point that snaps to a motion guide, as shown in Figure 27. When attaching an object to a path, you can drag the transformation point to the path. The default position for a transformation point is the center of the object. You can reposition the transformation point while in the symbol edit mode by dragging the transformation point to a different location in the object. Objects also have a registration point (+) that is used to position the object on the Stage using ActionScript code. The transformation and registration points can overlap—this is displayed as a plus sign within a circle ⊕.

FIGURE 27

A motion guide with an object (motorbike) attached

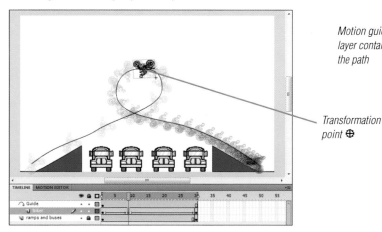

Transformation point ⊕

FIGURE 28

A motion guide layer

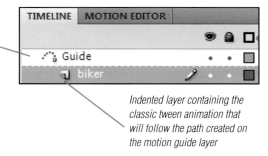

Motion guide layer containing the path

Indented layer containing the classic tween animation that will follow the path created on the motion guide layer

Create a classic tween animation

1. Open fl4_3.fla, then save it as **cTween**.

2. Insert a **new layer**, then name it **biker**.

3. Click **frame 1** on the biker layer, then drag the **biker symbol** from the Library panel to the Stage, as shown in Figure 29.

4. Click **frame 30** on the biker layer, click **Insert** on the menu bar, point to **Timeline**, then click **Keyframe**.

5. Drag the **biker** to the position shown in Figure 30.

6. Click **frame 2** on the biker layer, click **Insert** on the menu bar, then click **Classic Tween**.

   An arrow appears on the Timeline indicating that this is a classic tween.

7. Play the movie.

You created an animation using a classic tween.

Add a motion guide and orient the object to the guide

1. Insert a **new layer**, then name it **Guide**.

2. Click **Modify** on the menu bar, point to **Timeline**, then click **Layer Properties**.

3. Click the **Guide option button**, click **OK**, then drag the **biker layer** up to the Guide layer, as shown in Figure 31.

   The biker layer indents below the Guide layer.

4. Click **frame 1** on the Guide layer, click the **Pencil tool** ✎ on the Tools panel, then set the stroke color to **black**.

   (continued)

FIGURE 29
Dragging the biker symbol to the Stage

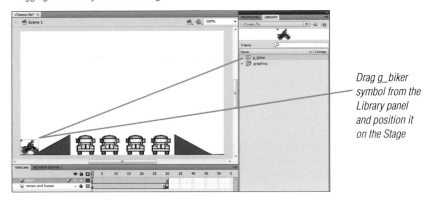

Drag g_biker symbol from the Library panel and position it on the Stage

FIGURE 30
Repositioning the biker

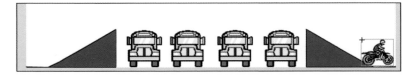

FIGURE 31
Dragging the biker layer up to the Guide layer

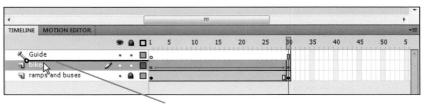

Drag biker layer up to but not above the Guide layer

FIGURE 32
Drawing a guide path on a Guide layer

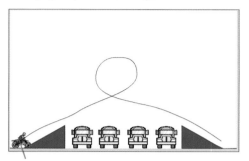

Point to the middle of the biker object

FIGURE 33
Aligning the object with the guide path

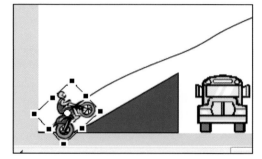

FIGURE 34
Aligning the object with the end of the guide path

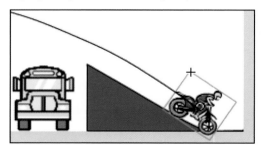

5. Point to the middle of the biker, then draw a line with a loop similar to the one shown in Figure 32.

6. Click **frame 30** on the biker layer, click the **Selection tool** ↖ , then drag the **biker** so that it snaps to the end of the line.

   Hint: Use the Zoom tool to zoom in on the biker to make it easier to see you have placed the transformation point on the path.

7. Play the movie.

8. Click **frame 1** on the biker layer, then click the **biker** to select the object.

9. Click the **Free Transform tool** ⧉ on the Tools panel, then rotate the **biker**, as shown in Figure 33.

10. Click **frame 30** on the biker layer, then rotate the **biker**, as shown in Figure 34.

11. Click the **Selection tool** ↖ , then click **frame 1** on the biker layer.

12. Display the Properties panel, then click the **Orient to path check box**.

13. Play the movie.

14. Click **frame 1** on the biker layer, then set the Ease value in the Properties panel to **100**.

15. Insert a **keyframe** on the frame on the biker layer that displays the highest point in the animation, then set the ease value to **100**.

16. Test the movie, save your work, then close the document.

You added a motion guide, oriented the animated object to the guide, and set an ease value.

CREATE FRAME-BY-FRAME
ANIMATIONS

What You'll Do

▶ *In this lesson, you will create frame-by-frame animations.*

Understanding Frame-by-Frame Animations

A frame-by-frame animation (also called a frame animation) is created by specifying the object that is to appear in each frame of a sequence of frames. Figure 35 shows three images that are variations of a cartoon character. In this example, the head and body remain the same, but the arms and legs change to represent a walking motion. If these individual images are placed into succeeding frames (with keyframes), an animation is created.

Frame-by-frame animations are useful when you want to change individual parts of an image. The images in Figure 35 are simple—only three images are needed for the animation. However, depending on the complexity of the image and the desired movements, the time needed to display each change can be substantial. When creating a frame-by-frame animation, you need to consider the following points:

■ The number of different images. The more images there are, the more effort is needed to create them. However, the

greater the number of images, the less change you need to make in each image and the more realistic the movement in the animation may seem.

■ The number of frames in which each image will appear. Changing the number of frames in which the object appears may change the effect of the animation. If each image appears in only one frame, the animation may appear rather jerky, since the frames change very rapidly. However, in some cases, you may want to give the impression of a rapid change in an object, such as rapidly blinking colors. If so, you could make changes in the color of an object from one frame to another.

■ The movie frame rate. Frame rates below 10 may appear jerky, while those above 30 may appear blurred. The frame rate is easy to change, and you should experiment with different rates until you get the desired effect.

Keyframes are critical to the development of frame animations because they signify a change in the object. Because frame animations are created by changing the object, each frame in a frame animation may need to be a keyframe. The exception is when you want an object displayed in several frames before it changes.

Creating a Frame-by-Frame Animation

To create a frame animation, select the frame on the layer where you want the animation to begin, insert a keyframe, and then place the object on the Stage. Next, select the frame where you want the change to occur, insert a keyframe, and then change the object. You can also add a new object in place of the original one. Figure 36 shows the first three frames of an animation in which three different objects are placed one on top of the other in succeeding frames. In the figure, the movement is shown as shadows. These shadows are visible because the Onion Skin feature is turned on. In this movie, the objects stay in place during the animation. However, a frame animation can also involve movement of the object around the Stage.

Using the Onion Skin Feature

Normally, Flash displays one frame of an animation sequence at a time on the Stage. Turning on the Onion Skin feature allows you to view an outline of the object(s) in any number of frames. This can help in positioning animated objects on the Stage.

FIGURE 35
Three images used in an animation

FIGURE 36
A frame-by-frame animation of 3 figures appearing to walk in place

Onion Skin feature is turned on so that all of the objects in frames 1-3 are viewable even though the playhead is on frame 1

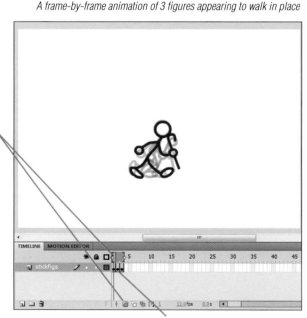

The 3 objects placed on top of each other on the Stage, each in its own frame on the Timeline

---

Lesson 3   Create Frame-by-Frame Animations

Create an in-place frame-by-frame animation

1. Open fl4_4.fla, then save it as **frameAn**.

2. Insert a **new layer**, name it **stickfigs**, click **frame 1** of the stickfigs layer, then drag **stickfig1** from the Library panel to the center of the Stage so it touches the white walkway.

3. Click **frame 2** of the stickfigs layer to select it, click **Insert** on the menu bar, point to **Timeline**, then click **Keyframe**.

4. Drag **stickfig2** so it is on top of stickfig1, as shown in Figure 37, use the arrow keys on the keyboard to align the heads, then click a blank area of the Stage to deselect stickfig2.

5. Select **stickfig1** by clicking the foot that points up, as shown in Figure 38, then press **[Delete]**.

6. Click **frame 3** on Layer 1 to select it, insert a **keyframe**, drag **stickfig3** so it is on top of stickfig2, then use the **arrow keys** on the keyboard to align the heads.

7. Click a blank area of the Stage to deselect stickfig3.

8. Select **stickfig2** by clicking the foot that points down, as shown in Figure 39, then press **[Delete]**.

9. Play the movie.

You created a frame-by-frame animation.

FIGURE 37
Dragging stickfig2 on top of stickfig1

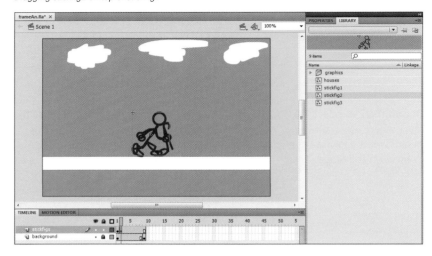

FIGURE 38
Selecting stickfig1

FIGURE 39
Selecting stickfig2

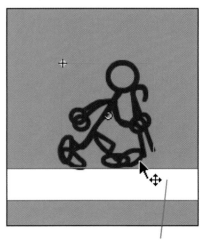

Click foot that points up

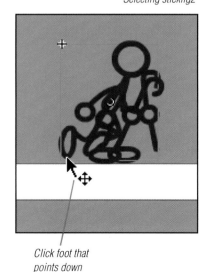

Click foot that
points down

FIGURE 40
Moving the houses layer to below the stickfigs layer

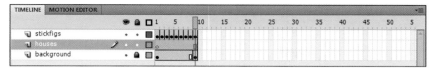

FIGURE 41
Positioning the houses symbol on the Stage

FIGURE 42
Repositioning the houses object

Copy frames and add a moving background

1. Click **frame 1** of the stickfigs layer, hold down **[Shift]**, then click **frame 3**.

2. Click **Edit** on the menu bar, point to **Timeline**, then click **Copy Frames**.

3. Click **frame 4** of the stickfigs layer, click **Edit** on the menu bar, point to **Timeline**, then click **Paste Frames**.

4. Click **frame 7**, then repeat step 3.

5. Click **frame 10** of the stickfigs layer, hold down **[Shift]**, then click **frame 13**.

6. Click **Edit** on the menu bar, point to **Timeline**, then click **Remove Frames**.

7. Insert a **new layer**, name the layer **houses**, then drag the **houses layer** below the stickfigs layer, as shown in Figure 40.

8. Click **frame 1** of the houses layer, then drag the **houses symbol** from the Library panel to the Stage, position the house, as shown in Figure 41.

9. Play the movie.

10. Click **frame 1** of the houses layer, click **Insert** on the menu bar, then click **Motion Tween**.

11. Click **frame 9** on the houses layer, then drag the **houses object** to the left, as shown in Figure 42.

12. Test the movie, close the Flash Player window, save your work, then close the document.

You copied frames and added a motion tween to a movie with an in-place frame-by-frame animation.

Create a frame-by-frame animation of a moving object

1. Open fl4_5.fla, then save it as **frameM**.

   This document has a background layer that contains a row of houses and clouds.

2. Insert a **new layer**, then name it **stickfigs**.

3. Click **View** on the menu bar, point to **Magnification**, then click **50%**.

4. Click **frame 5** on the stickfigs layer, then insert a **keyframe**.

5. Drag **stickfig1** from the Library panel to the left edge of the Stage, as shown in Figure 43.

6. Click **frame 6** on the stickfigs layer, then click **Insert** on the menu bar, point to **Timeline**, then click **Blank Keyframe**.

   A blank keyframe keeps the object in the previous frame from appearing in the current frame.

7. Click the **Edit Multiple Frames button** ⬚ on the Timeline status bar to turn it on.

   This allows you to view the contents of more than one frame at a time.

8. Drag **stickfig2** to the right of stickfig1, as shown in Figure 44.

9. Click **frame 7** on the stickfigs layer, then insert a **Blank Keyframe**.

10. Drag **stickfig3** to the right of stickfig2, as shown in Figure 45.

(continued)

FIGURE 43
Positioning stickfig1 on the Stage

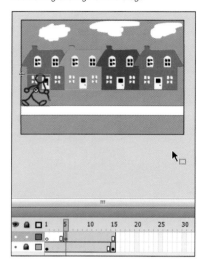

FIGURE 45
Positioning stickfig3 on the Stage

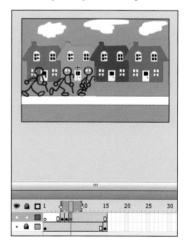

FIGURE 44
Positioning stickfig2 on the Stage

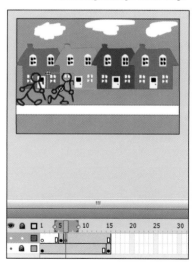

FIGURE 46

Adding stickfig3 as the final object

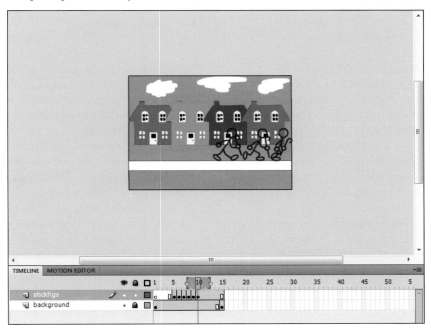

11. Click **frame 8** on the stickfigs layer, insert a **Blank Keyframe**, then drag **stickfig1** from the Library panel to the right of stickfig3.

12. Click **frame 9** on the stickfigs layer, insert a **Blank Keyframe**, then drag **stickfig2** to the right of stickfig1.

13. Click **frame 10** on the stickfigs layer, insert a **Blank Keyframe**, then drag **stickfig3** to the right of stickfig2.

   Your screen should resemble Figure 46.

14. Click **frame 11** on the stickfigs layer, then insert a **Blank Keyframe**.

15. Click the **Edit Multiple Frames button** on the Timeline status bar to turn it off.

16. Test the movie, then close the Flash Player window.

17. Change the frame rate to **6** fps.

18. Test the movie, then close the Flash Player window.

19. Save the movie, then close the document.

You created a frame-by-frame animation that causes objects to appear to move across the screen.

CREATE SHAPE TWEEN
ANIMATIONS

What You'll Do

 In this lesson, you will create a shape tween animation and specify shape hints.

Shape Tweening

In previous lessons, you learned that you can use motion tweening to change the shape of an object. You accomplish this by selecting the Free Transform tool and then dragging the handles to resize and skew the object. While this is easy and allows you to include motion along with the change in shape, there are two drawbacks. First, you are limited in the type of changes (resizing and skewing) that can be made to the shape of an object. Second, you must work with the same object throughout the animation. When you use **shape tweening**, however, you can have an animation change the shape of an object to any form you desire, and you can include two objects in the animation with two different shapes. As with motion tweening, you can use shape tweening to change other properties of an object, such as the color, location, and size.

Using Shape Tweening to Create a Morphing Effect

Morphing involves changing one object into another, sometimes unrelated, object.

For example, you could turn a robot into a man, or turn a football into a basketball. The viewer sees the transformation as a series of incremental changes. In Flash, the first object appears on the Stage and changes into the second object as the movie plays. The number of frames included from the beginning to the end of this shape tween animation determines how quickly the morphing effect takes place. The first frame in the animation displays the first object and the last frame displays the second object. The in-between frames display the different shapes that are created as the first object changes into the second object.

When working with shape tweening, you need to keep the following points in mind:

- Shape tweening can be applied only to editable graphics. To apply shape tweening to instances, groups, symbols, text blocks, or bitmaps, you must break apart the object to make it editable. To do this, you use the Break Apart command on the Modify menu. When you break apart an instance of a symbol, it is no longer linked to the original symbol.

- You can shape tween more than one object at a time as long as all the objects are on the same layer. However, if the shapes are complex and/or if they involve movement in which the objects cross paths, the results may be unpredictable.
- You can use shape tweening to move an object in a straight line, but other options, such as rotating an object, are not available.
- You can use the settings in the Properties panel to set options (such as the ease value, which causes acceleration or deceleration) for a shape tween.
- Shape hints can be used to control more complex shape changes.

Properties Panel Options

Figure 47 shows the Properties panel options for a shape tween. The options allow you to adjust several aspects of the animation, as described in the following:

- Adjust the rate of change between frames to create a more natural appearance during the transition by setting an ease value. Setting the value between -1 and -100 will begin the shape tween gradually and accelerate it toward the end of the animation. Setting the value between 1 and 100 will begin the shape tween rapidly and decelerate it toward the end of the animation. By default, the rate of change is set to 0, which causes a constant rate of change between frames.
- Choose a blend option. The Distributive option creates an animation in which the in-between shapes are smoother and more irregular. The Angular option preserves the corners and straight lines and works only with objects that have these features. If the objects do not have corners, Flash defaults to the Distributive option.

Shape Hints

You can use shape hints to control the shape's transition appearance during animation. Shape hints allow you to specify a location on the beginning object that corresponds to a location on the ending object. Figure 48 shows two shape animations of the same objects, one using shape hints and the other not using shape hints. The figure also shows how the object being reshaped appears in one of the in-between frames. Notice that with the shape hints, the object in the in-between frame is more recognizable.

FIGURE 47
The Properties panel options for a shape tween

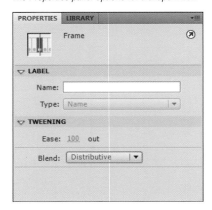

FIGURE 48
Two shape animations with and without shape hints

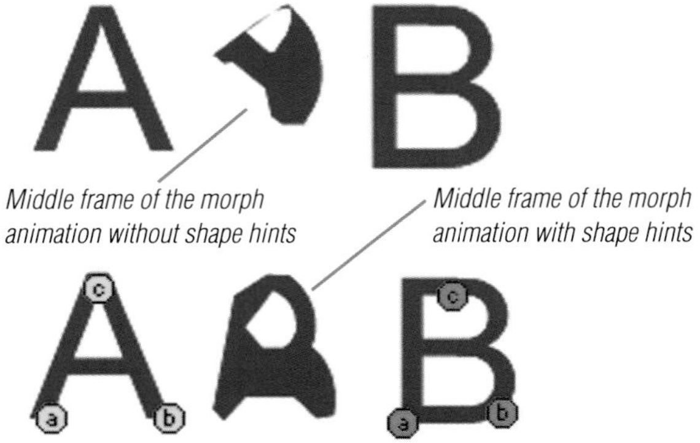

Middle frame of the morph animation without shape hints

Middle frame of the morph animation with shape hints

Create a shape tween animation

1. Open fl4_6.fla, then save it as **antiqueCar**.

2. Set the view to **Fit in Window**.

   | TIP This chapter assumes you always set the magnification to Fit in Window.

3. Click **frame 30** on the shape layer, then insert a **keyframe**.

4. Click the **Selection tool** ▸ on the Tools panel, then click a blank area of the pasteboard to deselect the car.

5. Point to the right side of the top of the car, then use the arc pointer ↳ to drag the **car top** to create the shape shown in Figure 49.

6. Click anywhere on the shape layer between frames 1 and 30.

7. Click **Insert** on the menu bar, then click **Shape Tween**.

8. Click **frame 1** on the shape layer, then play the movie.

9. Click **frame 30** on the shape layer.

10. Click the **Selection tool** ▸ on the Tools panel, then drag a **marquee** around the car to select it if it is not already selected.

11. Drag the **car** to the right side of the Stage.

12. Play the movie, then save and close it.

You created a shape tween animation, causing an object to change shape as it moves over several frames.

FIGURE 49
The reshaped object

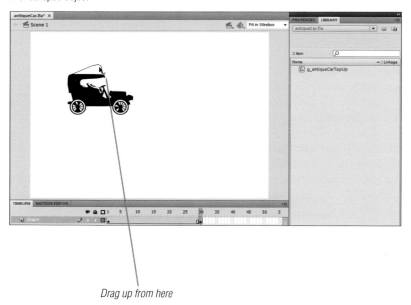

Drag up from here

Create a morphing effect

1. Open fl4_7.fla, then save it as **morphCar**.

2. Click **frame 40** on the morph layer.

3. Click **Insert** on the menu bar, point to **Timeline**, then click **Blank Keyframe**.

   TIP Inserting a blank keyframe prevents the object in the preceding keyframe from automatically being inserted into the blank keyframe.

4. Click the **Edit Multiple Frames button** on the Timeline.

   Turning on the Edit Multiple Frames feature allows you to align the two objects to be morphed.

5. Display the Library panel.

6. Drag the **g_antiqueCarTopDown graphic** symbol from the Library panel directly on top of the car on the Stage, as shown in Figure 50.

   TIP Use the arrow keys to move the object in small increments as needed.

7. Make sure the **g_antiqueCarTopDown** object is selected, click **Modify** on the menu bar, then click **Break Apart**.

8. Click the **Edit Multiple Frames button** to turn off the feature.

9. Click anywhere between frames 1 and 40 on the morph layer, click **Insert** on the menu bar, then click **Shape Tween**.

10. Click **frame 1** on the Timeline, then play the movie.

    The first car morphs into the second car.

11. Save the movie.

You created a morphing effect, causing one object to change into another.

FIGURE 50
Positioning the car instance on the Stage

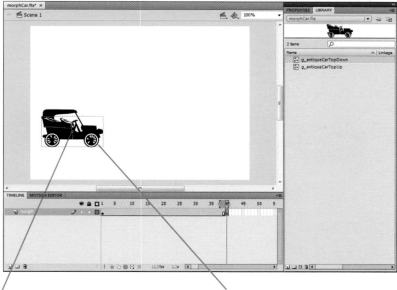

Transformation point appears when the mouse is released

Line up both cars so it appears that there is only one car; use the spokes on the wheels to help you know when the two objects are aligned

Adjust the rate of change in a shape tween animation

1. Click **frame 40** on the morph layer.

2. Click the **Selection tool** ➤ on the Tools panel, then drag a **marquee** around the car to select it (if necessary).

3. Drag the **car** to the right side of the Stage.

4. Click **frame 1** on the morph layer.

5. Set the ease value on the Properties panel to **–100**, as shown in Figure 51.

6. Click the **Stage**, then play the movie.

   The car starts out slow and speeds up as the morphing process is completed.

7. Repeat Steps 4 and 5, but change the ease value to **100**.

8. Click **frame 1** on the Timeline, then play the movie.

   The car starts out fast and slows down as the morphing process is completed.

9. Save your work, then close the movie.

You added motion to a shape tween animation and changed the ease value.

FIGURE 51
Setting the ease value of the morph

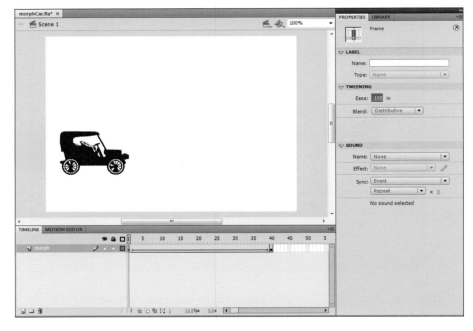

FIGURE 52

Positioning a shape hint

FIGURE 53

Adding shape hints

FIGURE 54

Matching shape hints

1. Open fl4_8.fla, then save it as **shapeHints**.

2. Play the movie and notice how the L morphs into a Z.

3. Click **frame 15** on the Timeline, the midpoint of the animation, then notice the shape.

4. Click **frame 1** on the hints layer to display the first object.

5. Make sure the object is selected, click **Modify** on the menu bar, point to **Shape**, then click **Add Shape Hint**.

6. Drag the **Shape Hint icon** 🅐 to the location shown in Figure 52.

7. Repeat Steps 5 and 6 to set a second and third Shape Hint icon, as shown in Figure 53.

8. Click **frame 30** on the hints layer.

   The shape hints are stacked on top of each other.

9. Drag the **Shape Hint icons** to match Figure 54.

10. Click **frame 15** on the hints layer, then notice how the object is more recognizable now that the shape hints have been added.

11. Click **frame 1** on the Timeline, then play the movie.

12. Save your work, then close the movie.

You added shape hints to a morph animation.

CREATE MOVIE CLIPS

What You'll Do

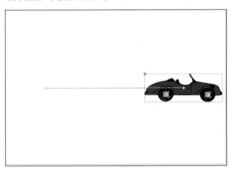

In this lesson, you will create, edit, and animate a movie clip.

Understanding Movie Clip Symbols

Until now you have been working with two kinds of symbols, graphic and button. A third type is a **movie clip symbol**, which provides a way to create more complex types of animations. A movie clip is essentially a movie within a movie. Each movie clip has its own Timeline, which is independent of the main Timeline. This allows you to nest a movie clip that is running one animation within another animation or in a scene on the main Timeline. Because a movie clip retains its own Timeline, when you insert an instance of the movie clip symbol into a Flash document, the movie clip continues in an endless loop even if the main Timeline stops.

The wheels on a car rotating while the car is moving across the screen is an example of a movie clip with an animation that is nested in another animation. To create the animated movie clip, a drawing of a wheel separate from the car is converted into a movie clip symbol. Then the movie clip symbol is opened in the edit window, which includes a Timeline that is unique to the movie clip. In the edit window, an animation is created that causes the wheel to rotate. After exiting the edit window and returning to the main Timeline, an instance of the movie clip symbol is placed on each wheel of the car. Finally, the car, including the wheels, is animated on the main Timeline. As the car is moving across the screen, the wheels are rotating according to their own Timeline. This process is shown in Figure 55.

In addition to allowing you to create more complex animations, movie clips help to organize the different reusable pieces of a movie and provide for smaller movie file sizes. This is because only one movie clip symbol needs to be stored in the Library panel while an unlimited number of instances of the symbol can be used in the Flash document. An animated movie clip can be viewed in the edit window that is displayed when you double-click on the movie clip symbol in the Library panel; and it can be viewed when you test or publish the movie that contains the movie clip. It is important to note that an animated movie clip cannot be viewed simply by playing the movie on the main Timeline.

In this lesson, you will learn how to create a movie clip symbol from a drawn object, edit the movie clip to create an animation, and nest the movie clip in another animation.

FIGURE 55

The process of nesting a movie clip within an animation

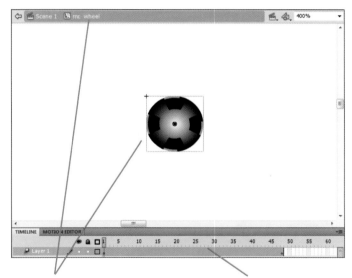

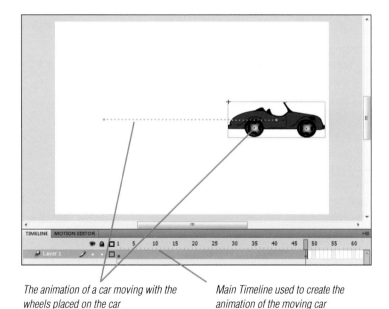

The movie clip of a wheel that has been animated to rotate shown in the edit window

Timeline in the edit window used to create the animation of the rotating wheel

The animation of a car moving with the wheels placed on the car

Main Timeline used to create the animation of the moving car

Break apart a graphic symbol and select parts of the object to separate from the graphic

1. Open fl4_9.fla, then save it as **mClip**.

   This document has one graphic symbol—a car that has been placed on the Stage.

2. Click the **Selection tool** ↖ on the Tools panel, then click the **car** to select it.

3. Click **Modify** on the menu bar, then click **Break Apart**.

4. Click a blank area of the Stage to deselect the object.

5. Click the **Zoom tool** 🔍 on the Tools panel, then click the **front wheel** two times to zoom in on the wheel.

6. Click the **Selection tool** ↖ on the Tools panel.

7. Click the **gray hubcap**, hold down **[Shift]**, then click the rest of the wheel, as shown in Figure 56.

   Hint: There are several small parts to the wheel, so click until a dot pattern covers the entire wheel, but do not select the tire. Use the Undo command if you select the tire.

8. Drag the **selected area** down below the car, as shown in Figure 57.

9. Compare your selected wheel to Figure 57, if your wheel does not match the figure, use the Undo command to move the wheel back to its original position, and repeat step 7.

You broke apart a graphic symbol and selected parts of the object to separate from the graphic.

FIGURE 56
Selecting the wheel

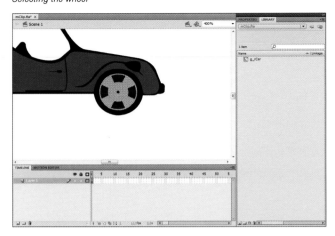

FIGURE 57
Separating the wheel from the car

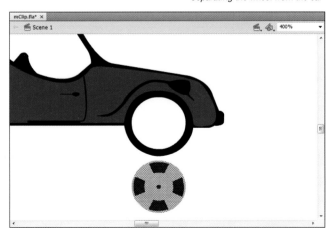

Creating Animations

FIGURE 58
Selecting the gray area of the wheel

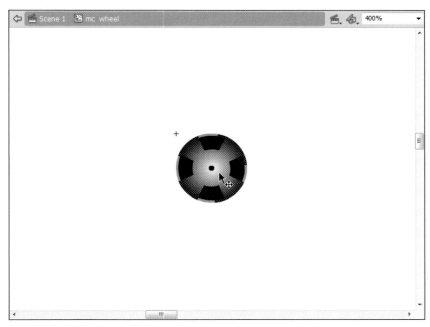

Create and edit a movie clip

1. Verify the wheel is selected, click **Modify** on the menu bar, then click **Convert to Symbol**.

2. Type **mc_wheel** for the name, select **Movie Clip** for the Type, then click **OK**.

   The mc_wheel movie clip appears in the Library panel.

3. Double-click the **mc_wheel icon** in the Library panel to display the edit window.

4. Click the **Zoom tool** 🔍 on the Tools panel, then click the **wheel** twice to zoom in on the wheel.

   The movie clip has been broken apart as indicated by the dot pattern.

5. Click the **Selection tool** ▸ , click a blank area of the Stage to deselect the object, then click the **gray area** of the wheel to select it, as shown in Figure 58.

6. Click the **Fill color tool color swatch** 🎨 on the Tools panel, then click the **gray gradient color swatch** in the bottom row of the palette.

You created a movie clip symbol and edited it to change the color of the object.

Animate a movie clip

1. Use the Selection tool ▸ to drag a marquee around the entire wheel to select it.

2. Click **Insert** on the menu bar, click **Motion Tween**, then click **OK** for the Convert selection to symbol for tween dialog box.

3. Point to the end of the tween span on Layer 1 of the Timeline, when the pointer changes to a double-headed arrow ↔ , drag the span to **frame 48**, as shown in Figure 59.

4. Click **frame 1** on Layer 1.

5. Display the Properties panel.

6. Change the rotate value to **4** times and verify the Direction is **CW (Clockwise)**, as shown in Figure 60.
   Hint: If you don't see the Rotate option, click the Selection tool, then drag a marquee around the object.

7. Verify the frame rate in the Timeline status bar is **12**, test the movie, then close the Flash Player window.

8. Click **Scene 1** near the top left side of the edit widow to exit the edit window.

9. Drag the **wheel** on the Stage and position it so it is on top of the front wheel of the car.

10. Click **View** on the menu bar, point to **Magnification**, then click **Fit in Window**.

11. Drag the **mc_wheel movie clip** from the Library panel and position it using the arrow keys as needed so it is on the back wheel.
    Hint: Use the Zoom tool as needed to zoom in on the wheel.

(continued)

FIGURE 59
Increasing the tween span on the Timeline

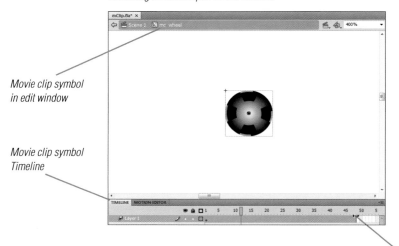

Movie clip symbol
in edit window

Movie clip symbol
Timeline

Drag the tween
span to frame 48

FIGURE 60
Changing the rotate value

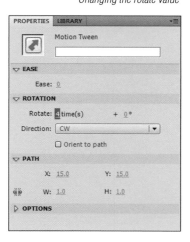

Creating Animations

FIGURE 61
Repositioning the car

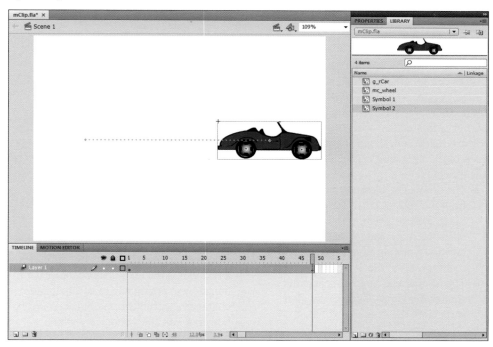

12. Test the movie and notice how the wheels turn, then close the Flash Player window.

13. Use the Selection tool ▶ to drag a marquee around the car to select it and the wheels.

14. Click **Insert** on the menu bar, click **Motion Tween**, then click **OK**.

15. Drag the tween span on Layer 1 to **frame 48**.

16. Click **frame 48** on Layer 1, then drag the **car** to the right side of the Stage, as shown in Figure 61.

17. Test the movie, then close the Flash Player window.

18. Save your work, then close the document.

You edited a movie clip to create an animation, then nested the movie clip in an animation on the main Timeline.

ANIMATE TEXT

What You'll Do

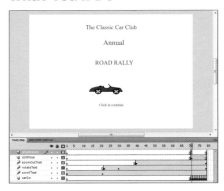

 In this lesson, you will animate text by scrolling, rotating, zooming, and resizing it.

Animating Text

You can motion tween text block objects just as you do graphic objects. You can resize, rotate, reposition, and change their colors. Figure 62 shows three examples of animated text with the Onion Skin feature turned on. When the movie starts, each of the following occurs one after the other:

- The Classic Car Club text block scrolls in from the left side to the top center of the Stage. This is done by creating the text block, positioning it off the Stage, and creating a motion-tweened animation that moves it to the Stage.
- The Annual text block appears and rotates five times. This occurs after you create the Annual text block, position it in the middle of the Stage under the heading, and use the Properties panel to specify a clockwise rotation that repeats five times.
- The ROAD RALLY text block slowly zooms out and appears in the middle of the Stage. This occurs after you create the text block and use the Free Transform tool handles to resize it to a small block at the beginning of the animation. Then, you resize the text block to a larger size at the end of the animation.

Once you create a motion animation using a text block, the text block becomes a symbol and you are unable to edit individual characters within the text block. You can, however, edit the symbol as a whole.

Creating Animations

FIGURE 62
Three examples of animated text

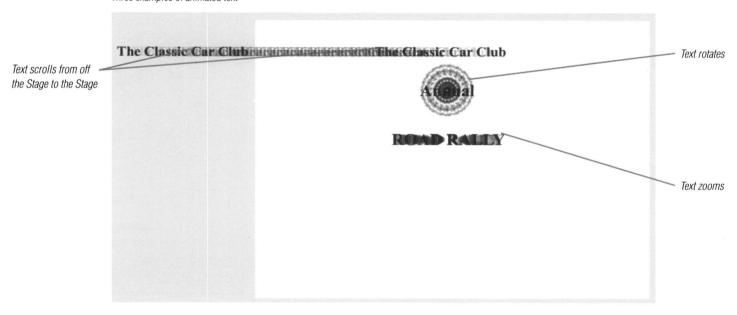

Text scrolls from off
the Stage to the Stage

Text rotates

Text zooms

The Classic Car Club ... The Classic Car Club
Annual
ROAD RALLY

Select, copy, and paste frames

1. Open fl4_10.fla, then save the movie as **textAn**.

   This document has a frame-by-frame animation of a car where the front end rotates up and down, and then the car moves off the screen.

2. Play the movie, then click **frame 1** on the Timeline.

3. Press the **period [.] key** to move through the animation one frame at a time and notice the changes to the object in each frame.

4. Change the view to **Fit in Window**.

5. Click **frame 9** on the carGo layer, press and hold **[Shift]**, then click **frame 1** to select all the frames, as shown in Figure 63.

6. Click **Edit** on the menu bar, point to **Timeline**, then click **Cut Frames**.

7. Click the **Frame View icon** ▾≡ near the upper right of the Timeline, then click **Small**.

8. Click **frame 71** on the carGo layer.

9. Click **Edit** on the menu bar, point to **Timeline**, then click **Paste Frames**.

10. Click **frame 1** on the carGo layer.

11. Point to the **vertical line** on the Timeline until the ◀▶ appears, then drag it to the left until frame 80 appears on the Timeline, as shown in Figure 64 (if necessary).

12. Change the view to **100%**.

13. Play the movie, then save your work.

You selected frames and moved them from one location on the Timeline to another location on the Timeline.

FIGURE 63
Selecting a range of frames

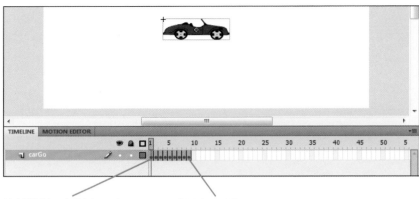

Hold [Shift] and click frame 1 to select the range of frames   Click frame 9 first

FIGURE 64
Expanding the view of the Timeline

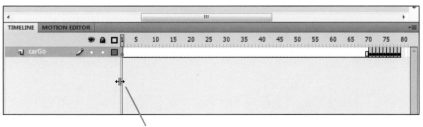

Drag the pointer to the left

FIGURE 65
Positioning the Text tool pointer outside the Stage

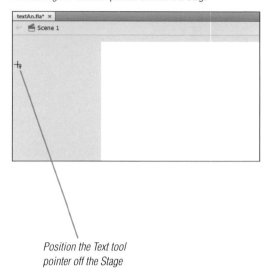

Position the Text tool
pointer off the Stage

FIGURE 66
Positioning the text block

This will be the position of the text
block at the end of the animation

Create animated text

1. Insert a **new layer**, then name it **scrollText**.
2. Click **frame 1** on the scrollText layer.
3. Click the **Text tool** T on the Tools panel, click the ⊤ **pointer** outside the Stage in the upper-left corner of the pasteboard, as shown in Figure 65, then click to display a text box.

   TIP   You may need to scroll the Stage to make room for the text box.
4. Click the **Family list arrow** in the Properties panel, then click **Times New Roman** if it is not already selected.
5. Change the Character size to **20**.
6. Click the **Text (fill) color swatch** ▮ , then click the **blue color swatch** on the left column of the color palette.
7. Type **The Classic Car Club**.
8. Click the **Selection tool** ▶ , click **Insert** on the menu bar, then click **Motion Tween**.
9. Click **frame 20** on the scrollText layer, then insert a **keyframe**.
10. Drag the **text block** horizontally to the top center of the Stage, as shown in Figure 66.
11. Click **frame 1** on the Timeline, then play the movie.

    The text moves to center Stage from offstage left.

You created a text block object and applied a motion tween animation to it.

Create rotating text

1. Insert a **new layer**, then name it **rotateText**.

2. Insert a **keyframe** in frame 21 on the rotateText layer.

3. Click the **Text tool** T on the Tools panel, position the pointer beneath the "a" in "Classic," then click to display a blank text box.

4. Change the Character size in the Properties panel to **24**, type **Annual**, then compare your image to Figure 67.

5. Click the **Selection tool** ↖ on the Tools panel, verify Annual is selected, click **Insert** on the menu bar, then click **Motion Tween**.

6. Set the Rotate value in the Properties panel to **2** times with a **CW** (clockwise) direction.

   TIP You may need to click the frame in the Timeline to have the rotate setting appear.

7. Point to the end of the tween span (frame 79) until the pointer changes to ↔ , then drag the ↔ **pointer** to frame 30, as shown in Figure 68.

8. Click **frame 79** on the rotateText layer, then insert a **keyframe**.

9. Click **frame 1** on the Timeline, then play the movie.

   The Annual text rotates clockwise two times.

You inserted a new layer, created a rotating text block, applied a motion tween to text, and used the Properties panel to rotate the text box.

FIGURE 67
Positioning the Annual text block

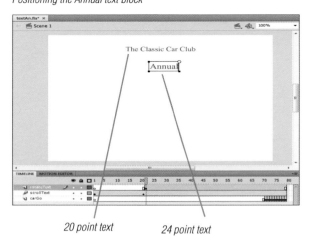

20 point text   24 point text

FIGURE 68
Resizing the tween span from frame 79 to frame 30

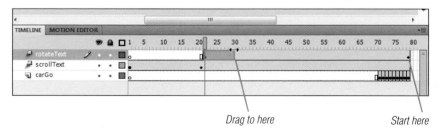

Drag to here   Start here

FIGURE 69
Using the Text tool to type ROAD RALLY

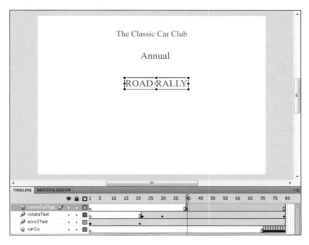

Resize and fade in text

1. Insert a **new layer**, name it **zoomOutText**, then insert a **keyframe** in frame 40 on the layer.

2. Click the **Text tool** T , position the pointer beneath the Annual text box, aligning it with the "h" in "The," then type **ROAD RALLY**, as shown in Figure 69.

3. Click the **Selection tool** , click **frame 40** on the zoomOutText layer, click **Insert** on the menu bar, then click **Motion Tween**.

4. Click **frame 40** on the zoomOutText layer, click the **Free Transform tool** , then click the **Scale button** in the Options area of the Tools panel.

5. Drag the upper-left corner handle inward to resize the text block, as shown in Figure 70.

6. Click **frame 79** on the ZoomOutText layer, verify the Scale option in the Options area of the Tools panel is selected, then drag the upper-left corner handle outward to resize the text block to its original size.

7. Test the movie, then close the Flash Player window.

You created a motion animation that caused a text block to zoom out.

FIGURE 70
Resizing the Text block

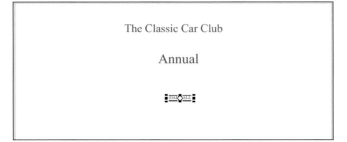

Make a text block into a button

1. Insert a **new layer**, then name it **continue**.

2. Insert a **keyframe** in frame 71 on the continue layer.

3. Click the **Text tool** T on the Tools panel, position the **Text tool pointer** beneath the back wheel of the car, then type **Click to continue**.

4. Drag the **pointer** over the text to select it, change the character size in the Properties panel to **12**, click the **Selection tool** on the Tools panel, then compare your image to Figure 71.

5. Verify that the text box is selected, click **Modify** on the menu bar, click **Convert to Symbol**, type **b_continue** in the Name text box, set the Type to **Button**, then click **OK**.

6. Double-click the **text block** to edit the button.

7. Insert a **keyframe** in the Over frame, set the fill color to the **black color swatch** in the left column of the color palette.

8. Insert a **keyframe** in the Down frame, set the fill color to the **bright green color swatch** in the left column of the color palette.

9. Insert a **keyframe** in the Hit frame, select the **Rectangle tool** on the Tools panel, then draw a **rectangle** that covers the text block, as shown in Figure 72.

10. Click **Scene 1** at the top left of the edit window to return to the main Timeline.

You made the text block into a button.

FIGURE 71
Adding a button

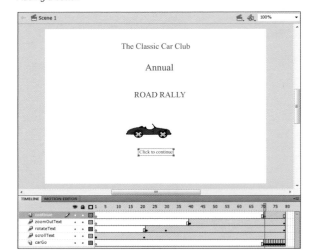

FIGURE 72
The rectangle that defines the hit area

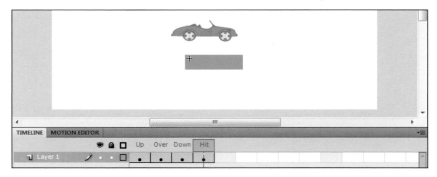

Creating Animations

FIGURE 73
Adding a play action

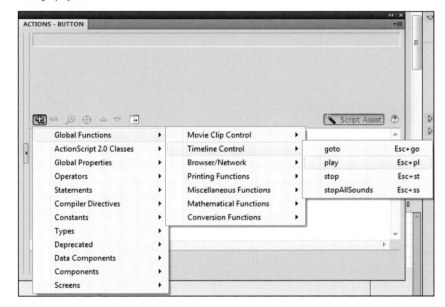

ACTIONS - BUTTON

Global Functions ▶	Movie Clip Control ▶	
ActionScript 2.0 Classes ▶	Timeline Control ▶	goto Esc+go
Global Properties ▶	Browser/Network ▶	play Esc+pl
Operators ▶	Printing Functions ▶	stop Esc+st
Statements ▶	Miscellaneous Functions ▶	stopAllSounds Esc+ss
Compiler Directives ▶	Mathematical Functions ▶	
Constants ▶	Conversion Functions ▶	
Types ▶		
Deprecated ▶		
Data Components ▶		
Components ▶		
Screens ▶		

Script Assist

Add an action to the button

1. Display the Actions panel.
2. Click the **Selection tool** ▶ on the Tools panel, then click the **Click to continue button** on the Stage.
3. Verify the Script Assist button is turned on, then verify the button symbol and b_continue are displayed in the lower-left corner of the Actions panel.

   Note: You need to have ActionScript 2.0 active. You can check your ActionScript version by choosing Publish Settings on the Edit menu, then selecting the Flash tab.
4. Click the **Add a new item to the script button** ⊞ in the Script Assist window, point to **Global Functions**, point to **Timeline Control**, then click **play**, as shown in Figure 73.
5. Insert a **new layer**, name it **stopmovie**, then insert a **keyframe** in frame 71 on that layer.
6. Verify that stopmovie:71 is displayed in the lower-left corner of the Actions panel.
7. Click the **Add a new item to the script button** ⊞ in the Script Assist window, point to **Global Functions**, point to **Timeline Control**, then click **stop**.
8. Click **Control** on the menu bar, click **Test Movie**, then click the **Click to continue button** when it appears.

   The movie plays the animated text blocks, then plays the animated car when you click the Click to continue button.
9. Close the Flash Player movie window, save and close the movie, then exit Flash.

You inserted a play button and added a play action to it, then inserted a stop action on another layer.

Create a motion tween animation.

1. Start Flash, open fl4_11.fla, then save it as **skillsdemo4**.
2. Insert a keyframe in frame 20 on the ballAn layer.
3. Display the Library panel, then drag the g_vball graphic symbol to the lower-left corner of the Stage.
4. Click frame 20 on the ballAn layer, then insert a motion tween.
5. Point to the end of frame 20, when the pointer changes to a double-headed arrow, drag the pointer to frame 40 to set the tween span from frames 20 to 40.
6. With frame 40 selected, drag the object to the lower-right corner of the Stage.
7. Change the view of the Timeline to Small so more frames are in view.
8. Insert a blank keyframe in frame 41.
9. Play the movie, then save your work.

Edit a motion tween.

1. Click frame 20, use the Selection tool to alter the motion path to form an arc, then play the movie.
2. Use the Subsection tool to display the Bezier handles, use them to form a curved path, then play the movie.
3. Select frame 20, use the Properties panel to change the ease value to **100**, then play the movie.
4. Select frame 20, change the ease value to **-100**, then play the movie.

5. Select frame 40, select the object, use the Properties panel to change the width of the object to **30**, then play the movie. (*Hint:* Verify the Lock width and height values together chain is unbroken. This will ensure that when one value is changed, the other value changes proportionally.)
6. Select frame 35, select the object, use the Free transform tool to skew the object, then play the movie.
7. Select frame 40, select the object, use the Properties panel to change the alpha setting to **0**, then play the movie.
8. Change the alpha setting back to **100**.
9. Select frame 40, select the object, then use the Advanced Style option in the COLOR EFFECT area of the Properties panel to create a red color.
10. Lock the ballAn layer.
11. Play the movie, then save your work.

Create a classic tween.

1. Insert a new layer and name it **v-ball**.
2. Insert a keyframe in frame 76 on the v-ball layer.
3. Insert a keyframe in frame 41 on the v-ball layer.
4. Drag an instance of the g_vball symbol from the Library panel to the lower-left corner of the Stage.
5. Insert a keyframe in frame 50 on the v-ball layer and drag the ball to the lower-right corner of the Stage.

6. Click on any frame between 41 and 50 on the v-ball layer and insert a Classic tween.
7. Insert a blank keyframe at frame 51 on the v-ball layer.
8. Play the movie, then save your work.

Create a motion guide.

1. Insert a new layer above the v-ball layer and name it **path**.
2. Insert a keyframe in frame 76 on the path layer.
3. Change the path layer to a Guide layer.
4. Insert a keyframe at frame 41 on the path layer.
5. Select the pencil tool, point to the middle of the ball and draw a path with a loop.
6. Insert a keyframe in frame 50 on the path layer.
7. Drag the v-ball layer up to the path layer so that it indents below the path layer.
8. Click frame 41 on the v-ball layer and attach the ball to the path.
9. Click frame 50 on the v-ball layer and attach the ball to the path.
10. Click frame 41 on the v-ball layer and use the Properties panel to orient the ball to the path.
11. Lock the v-ball and path layers.
12. Hide the path layer.
13. Play the movie, then save the movie.

Create a frame animation.

1. Insert a new layer and name it **corner-ball**.
2. Insert a keyframe in frame 76 on the corner-ball layer.

3. Insert a keyframe in frame 51 on the corner-ball layer, then drag the g_vball graphic from the Library panel to the lower-left corner of the Stage.

4. Insert a blank keyframe in frame 55 on the corner-ball layer, then drag g_vball graphic from the Library panel to the upper-left corner of the Stage.

5. Insert a blank keyframe in frame 59 on the corner-ball layer, then drag the g_vball graphic from the Library panel to the upper-right corner of the Stage.

6. Insert a blank keyframe in the frame 63 on the corner-ball layer, then drag the g_vball graphic from the Library panel to the lower-right corner of the Stage.

7. Insert a blank keyframe in frame 66 on the corner-ball layer.

8. Lock the corner-ball layer.

9. Change the movie frame rate to 3 frames per second, then play the movie.

10. Change the movie frame rate to 12 frames per second, play the movie, then save your work.

Create a movie clip.

1. Insert a new layer and name it **spin-ball**.

2. Insert a keyframe at frame 76 on the spin-ball layer.

3. Insert a keyframe at frame 51 on the spin-ball layer.

4. Drag an instance of the g_vball symbol from the Library panel to the center of the Stage.

5. Select the ball and convert it to a movie clip with the name **mc_ball**.

6. Display the edit window for the mc_ball movie clip.

7. Create a motion tween that rotates the ball 6 times counterclockwise in 12 frames.

8. Exit the edit window.

9. Insert a blank keyframe in frame 66 of the spin-ball layer.

10. Lock the spin-ball layer.

11. Test the movie, close the Flash Player window, then save your work.

Animate text.

1. Insert a new layer above the spin-ball layer and name it **heading**.

2. Insert a keyframe in frame 76 on the heading layer.

3. Click frame 1 on the heading layer.

4. Use the Text tool to type **Having fun with a** in a location off the top-left of the Stage.

5. Change the text to Arial, 20 point, light gray (#CCCCCC), and boldface.

6. Select frame 1 on the heading layer and insert a motion tween.

7. Click frame 10 on the heading layer, insert a keyframe, then use the Selection tool to drag the text to the top-center of the Stage.

8. Play the movie and save your work.

9. Lock the heading layer.

10. Insert a new layer and name it **zoom**.

11. Insert a keyframe in frame 76 on the zoom layer.

12. Insert a keyframe in frame 11 on the zoom layer.

13. Use the Text tool to type **Volleyball** below the heading, then center it as needed.

14. Select frame 11 on the zoom layer and create a motion tween.

15. Insert a keyframe in frame 20 on the zoom layer.

16. Click frame 11 on the zoom layer and select the text block.

17. Use the Free Transform tool to resize the text block to approximately one-fourth its original size.

18. Select frame 20 on the zoom layer, and resize the text block to approximately the size shown in Figure 74.

19. Lock the zoom layer.

20. Test the movie, close the Flash Player window, save your work.

Morph text.

1. Insert a new layer above the heading layer and name it **morph**.

2. Insert a keyframe in frame 66 on the morph layer.

3. Drag the g_vball symbol to the center of the Stage.

4. Use the Properties panel to resize the width to **60** px. (*Hint*: Verify the Lock width and height values together chain is unbroken. This will ensure that when one value is changed, the other value changes proportionally.)

Creating Animations

5. Break apart the object.
6. Insert a blank keyframe in frame 76 on the morph layer.
7. Turn on the Edit Multiple Frames feature.
8. Drag the g_vball symbol to the Stage and use the Properties panel to resize the width to **60** px. *(Hint:* Verify the Lock width and height values together chain is unbroken.

This will ensure that when one value is changed, the other value changes proportionally).
9. Center the football on top of the volleyball.
10. Break apart the football object.
11. Turn off the Edit Multiple Frames feature.
12. Click frame 66 on the morph layer and insert a shape tween.

13. Test the movie, then close the Flash Player window.
14. Add shape hints to the volleyball and the football.
15. Lock the morph layer.
16. Test the movie, close the Flash Player window, then save your work.
17. Exit Flash.

FIGURE 74
Completed Skills Review

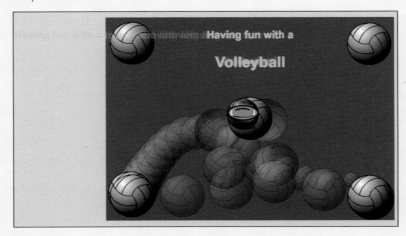

The Ultimate Tours travel company has asked you to design several sample animations for its website. Figure 75 shows a sample home page and the Cruises screen. Using these (or one of the home pages you created in Chapter 3) as a guide, complete the following:

(Tip: If you need to insert frames, select the frame where the inserted frame is to go and press [F5] (Win) or use the Timeline command from the Insert menu (Win) (Mac). To insert several frames, select a range of frames and press [F5] (Win), or use the Timeline command from the Insert menu (Win) (Mac). To move the contents of a frame, you can select the frames you want to move, then use the Cut and Paste commands from the Edit menu to move the contents.)

1. Open ultimatetours3.fla (the file you created in Chapter 3 Project Builder 1) and save it as **ultimatetours4**.

2. Animate the heading Ultimate Tours on the home page so that it zooms out from a transparent text block.

3. Have the logo appear next.

4. After the heading and logo appear, make the subheading We Specialize in Exotic Adventures appear.

5. Make each of the buttons (Treks, Tours, Cruises) scroll from the bottom of the Stage to its position on the Stage. Stagger the buttons so they scroll onto the Stage one after the other.

6. Assign a stop action after the home page appears.

7. Add a new layer, name it **cruises headings**, then add the text blocks shown in Figure 75 (Featured Cruises, Panama Canal, Caribbean, Galapagos).

8. Insert keyframes in the ending frames for the Ultimate Tours title, logo, and home button so that they appear on the cruises screen.

9. Import the graphic file ship.gif from the drive and folder where your Data Files are stored to the Library panel, then rename the graphic file **g_ship**. (*Hint*: To import a graphic to the Library panel, click File on the menu bar, point to Import, then click Import to Library. Navigate to the drive and folder where your Data Files are stored, then select the desired file and click Open (Win) or Import to Library (Mac).)

10. Create a motion tween animation that moves the ship across the screen, then alter the motion path to cause a dip in it, similar to the path shown in Figure 75.

11. Orient the boat to the motion path.

12. Assign a goto action to the Cruises button so it jumps to the frame that has the Cruises screen.

13. Test the movie, then compare your movie to the example shown in Figure 75.

FIGURE 75
Sample completed Project Builder 1

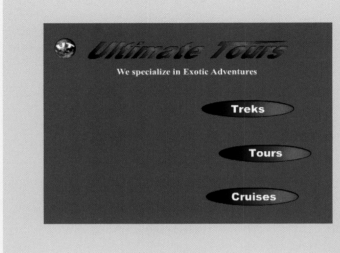

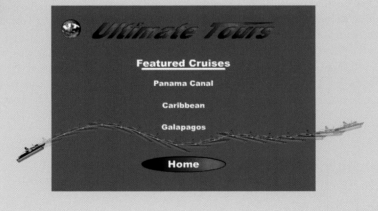

You have been asked to demonstrate some of the animation features of Flash. You have decided to create a movie clip that includes a frame-by-frame animation and then use the movie clip in a motion tween animation. Figure 76 shows the stick figure that will walk across the screen and jump up at each line on the sidewalk. The movement across the screen is a motion tween. The jumping up is a movie clip.

To complete this project, do the following:

1. Start a new Flash document and name it **jumper4**.

2. Add a background color, sidewalk with lines, and houses or other graphics of your choice, adding layers as needed and naming them appropriately. (*Note:* You can open a previous movie that used the stick figures, such as frameAn, then with your movie open, click the list arrow under the Library panel tab. This displays a list of all open documents. Click the name of the file that has the stick figures to display its Library panel. Then drag the symbols you need to the Stage of your movie. This will place the objects in the jumper4 Library panel.)

3. Create a new movie clip. (*Note:* You can create a new movie clip by selecting New Symbol from the Insert menu, then you can drag objects from the Library panel to the movie clip edit window.)

4. Edit the clip to create a frame-by-frame animation of the stick figures walking in place. In the movie clip, place the stick figures one after the other, but have one of the stick figures in the sequence placed above the others to create a jumping effect. You will use each stick figure two times in the sequence.

5. Exit the edit window and place the movie clip on the Stage, then create a motion tween that moves the movie clip from the left side to the right side of the Stage.

6. Test the movie. (*Note:* Movie clips do not play from the Stage, you must use the Test Movie command.)

7. Close the Flash Player movie, then save the movie.

FIGURE 76
Sample completed Project Builder 2

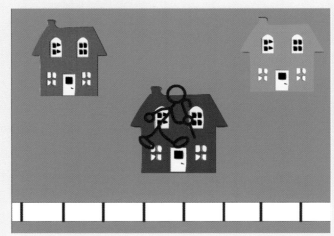

Figure 77 shows a website for kids. Study the figure and complete the following. For each question, indicate how you determined your answer.

1. Connect to the Internet, then go to *www.smokeybear.com/kids*.
2. Open a document in a word processor or open a new Flash document, save the file as **dpc4**, then answer the following questions. (*Hint*: Use the Text tool in Flash.)

   ■ What seems to be the purpose of this site?
   ■ Who would be the target audience?
   ■ How might a frame animation be used in this site?
   ■ How might a motion tween animation be used?
   ■ How might a motion guide be used?
   ■ How might motion animation effects be used?
   ■ How might the text be animated?

FIGURE 77
Design Project

This is a continuation of the Portfolio Project in Chapter 3, which is the development of a personal portfolio. The home page has several categories, including the following:

- Personal data
- Contact information
- Previous employment
- Education
- Samples of your work

In this project, you will create several buttons for the sample animations screen and link them to the animations.

1. Open portfolio3.fla (the file you created in Portfolio Project, Chapter 3) and save it as **portfolio4**. (*Hint*: When you open the file, you may receive a missing font message, meaning a font used in this document is not available on your computer. You can choose a substitute font or use a default font. If you have to use a default font or if you substitute a font, the resulting text may not look as intended.)

2. Display the Sample Animation screen and change the heading to Sample Animations.

3. Add layers and create buttons with labels, as shown in Figure 78, for the tweened animation, frame-by-frame animation, motion path animation, and animated text.

4. Create a tween animation or use the passing cars animation from Chapter 3, and link it to the appropriate button on the Sample

Animations screen by assigning a go to action to the button.

5. Create a frame-by-frame animation, and link it to the appropriate button on the Sample Animations screen.

6. Create a motion path animation, and link it to the appropriate button on the Sample Animations screen.

FIGURE 78
Sample completed Portfolio Project

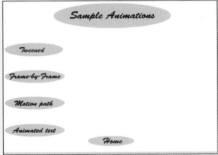

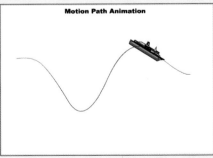

7. Create several text animations, using scrolling, rotating, and zooming; then link them to the appropriate button on the Sample Animations screen.

8. Add a layer and create a Home button that links the Sample Animations screen to the Home screen.

9. Create frame actions that cause the movie to return to the Sample Animations screen after each animation has been played.

10. Test the movie.

11. Save your work, then compare sample pages from your movie to the example shown for two of the screens in Figure 78.

chapter

5

CREATING SPECIAL
EFFECTS

1. Create a mask effect

2. Add sound

3. Add video

4. Create an animated navigation bar

5. Create character animations using inverse kinematics

6. Create 3D effects

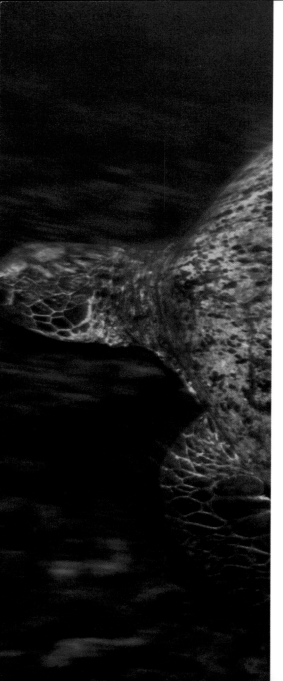

5 CREATING SPECIAL EFFECTS

Introduction

Now that you are familiar with the basics of Flash, you can begin to apply some of the special features that can enhance a movie. Special effects can provide variety and add interest to a movie, as well as draw the viewer's attention to a location or event in the movie. One type of special effect is a spotlight that highlights an area(s) of the movie or reveals selected content on the Stage. You can use sound effects to enhance a movie by creating moods and dramatizing events. In addition, you can add sound to a button to provide feedback to the viewer when the button is clicked. Video can be incorporated into a Flash movie and effects such as fading in and out can be applied to the display of the video.

Another type of special effect is an animated navigation bar, for example, one that causes a drop-down menu when the user rolls over a button. This effect can be created using masks and invisible buttons.

Two new features of Adobe Flash CS4 are Inverse Kinematics and 3D Effects. Inverse Kinematics allows you to easily create character animations and even allows users to interact with the character when viewing the Flash movie. The 3D tools allow you to create 3D effects such as objects moving and rotating through 3D space.

Tools You'll Use

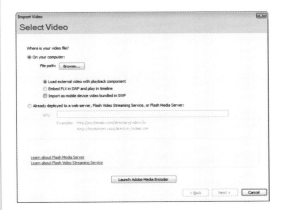

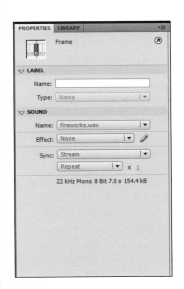

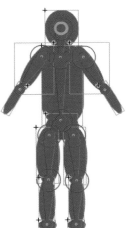

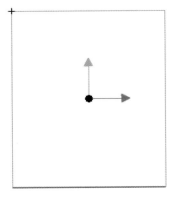

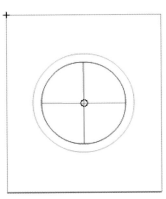

CREATE A
MASK EFFECT

What You'll Do

Cla ssic Car lub

 In this lesson, you will apply a mask effect.

Understanding Mask Layers

A **mask layer** allows you to cover up the objects on one or more layers and, at the same time, create a window through which you can view objects on those layer(s). You can determine the size and shape of the window and specify whether it moves around the Stage. Moving the window around the Stage can create effects such as a spotlight that highlights certain content on the Stage, drawing the viewer's attention to a specific location. Because the window can move around the Stage, you can use a mask layer to reveal only the area of the Stage and the objects you want the viewer to see.

You need at least two layers on the Timeline when you are working with a mask layer. One layer, called the mask layer, contains the window object through which you view the objects on the second layer below. The second layer, called the masked layer, contains the object(s) that are viewed through the window. Figure 1 shows how a mask layer works: The top part of the figure shows the mask layer with the window in the shape of a circle. The next part of the figure shows the layer to be masked. The last part of the figure shows the result of applying the mask. Figure 1 illustrates the simplest use of a mask layer. In most cases, you want to have other objects appear on the Stage and have the mask layer affect only a certain portion of the Stage.

The process for using a mask layer follows:
- Select an original layer that will become the masked layer—it contains the objects that you want to display through the mask layer window.
- Insert a new layer above the masked layer that will become the mask layer. A mask layer always masks the layer(s) immediately below it.
- Draw a filled shape, such as a circle, or create an instance of a symbol that will become the window on the mask layer. Flash will ignore bitmaps, gradients, transparency colors, and line styles on a mask layer. On a mask layer, filled areas become transparent and non-filled areas become opaque when viewed over a masked layer.

- Select the new layer and open the Layer Properties dialog box using the Timeline option from the Modify menu, then select Mask. Flash converts the layer to the mask layer.
- Select the original layer and open the Layer Properties dialog box using the Layer command on the Modify menu, and then choosing Masked. Flash converts the layer to the masked layer.
- Lock both the mask and masked layers.
- To mask additional layers: Drag an existing layer beneath the mask layer, or create a new layer beneath the mask layer and use the Layer Properties dialog box to convert it to a masked layer.
- To unlink a masked layer: Drag it above the mask layer, or select it and select Normal from the Layer Properties dialog box.

FIGURE 1
A mask layer with a window

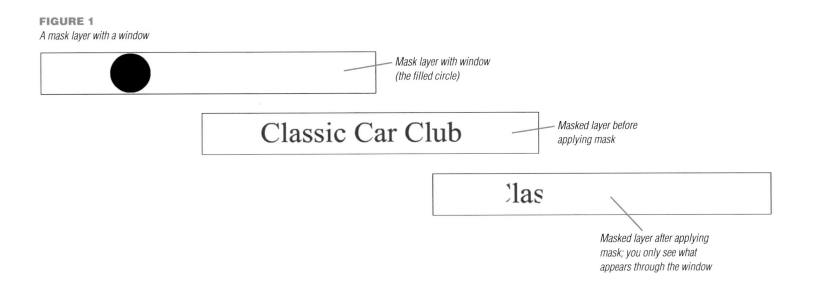

Mask layer with window
(the filled circle)

Classic Car Club

Masked layer before
applying mask

ʹlas

Masked layer after applying
mask; you only see what
appears through the window

Create a mask layer

1. Open fl5_1.fla, then save it as **classicCC**.

2. Insert a **new layer**, name it **mask**, then click **frame 1** on the mask layer.

3. Select the **Oval tool** on the Tools panel, set the **Stroke Color** to **No Stroke** on the top row of the color palette.

4. Set the **Fill Color** to the **black color swatch** in the left column of the color palette.

5. Draw the **circle** shown in Figure 2, click the **Selection tool** on the Tools panel, then drag a **marquee** around the circle to select it.

6. Click **Insert** on the menu bar, click **Motion Tween**, then click **OK** to convert the drawing into a symbol so that it can be tweened.

7. Click **frame 40** on the mask layer, then drag the **circle** to the position shown in Figure 3.

8. Click **mask** on the Timeline to select the mask layer, click **Modify** on the menu bar, point to **Timeline**, then click **Layer Properties**.

9. Verify that the Show check box is selected in the Name section, click the **Lock check box** to select it, click the **Mask option button** in the Type section, then click **OK**.

   The mask layer has a shaded mask icon next to it on the Timeline.

10. Play the movie from frame 1 and notice how the circle object covers the text on the heading layer as it moves across the Stage.

    Note: The circle object will not become transparent until a masked layer is created beneath it.

You created a mask layer containing a circle object that moves across the Stage.

FIGURE 2
Object to be used as the window on a mask layer

FIGURE 3
Repositioning the circle

Create a masked layer

1. Click **heading** on the Timeline to select the heading layer, click **Modify** on the menu bar, point to **Timeline**, then click **Layer Properties** to open the Layer Properties dialog box.

2. Verify that the Show check box is selected in the Name section, click the **Lock check box** to select it, click the **Masked option button** in the Type section, compare your dialog box to Figure 4, then click **OK**.

   The text on the Stage seems to disappear. The heading layer title appears indented and has a shaded masked icon next to it on the Timeline.

3. Play the movie and notice how the circle object acts as a window to display the text on the heading layer.

4. Click **Control** on the menu bar, then click **Test Movie**.

5. View the movie, then close the Flash Player window.

6. Save your work, then close the movie.

You used the Layer Properties dialog box to create a masked layer.

FIGURE 4
The completed Layer Properties dialog box

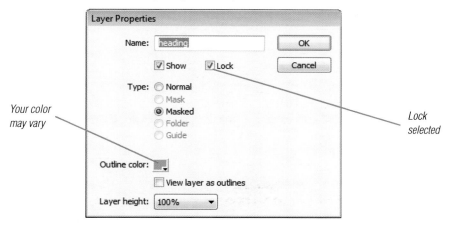

Your color may vary

Lock selected

ADD SOUND

What You'll Do

In this lesson, you will add sound to an animation.

Incorporating Animation and Sound

Sound can be extremely useful in a Flash movie. Sounds are often the only effective way to convey an idea, elicit an emotion, dramatize a point, and provide feedback to a user's action, such as clicking a button. How would you describe in words or show in an animation the sound a whale makes? Think about how chilling it is to hear the footsteps on the stairway of a haunted house. Consider how useful it is to hear the pronunciation of "buenos dias" as you are studying Spanish. All types of sounds can be incorporated into a Flash movie: for example, CD-quality music that might be used as background for a movie; narrations that help explain what the user is seeing; various sound effects, such as a car horn beeping; and recordings of special events, such as a presidential speech or a rock concert.

The process for adding a sound to a movie follows:

- Import a sound file into a Flash movie; Flash places the sound file into the movie's library.
- Create a new layer.
- Select the desired frame on the new layer where you want the sound to play and drag the sound symbol to the Stage.

You can place more than one sound file on a layer, and you can place sounds on layers with other objects. However, it is recommended that you place each sound on a separate layer so that it is easier to identify and edit. In Figure 5, the sound layer shows a wave pattern that extends from frame 1 to frame 24. The wave pattern gives some indication of the volume of the sound at any particular frame. The higher spikes in the pattern indicate a louder sound. The wave pattern also gives some indication of the pitch. The denser the wave pattern,

the lower the pitch. You can alter the sound by adding or removing frames. However, removing frames may create undesired effects. It is best to make changes to a sound file using a sound-editing program.

You can use options in the Properties panel, as shown in Figure 6, to synchronize a sound to an event (such as clicking a button) and to specify special effects (such as fade in and fade out). You can import the following sound file formats into Flash:

- ASND (Windows or Macintosh)
- WAV (Windows only)
- AIFF (Macintosh only)
- MP3 (Windows or Macintosh)

If you have QuickTime 4 or later installed on your computer, you can import these additional sound file formats:
- AIFF (Windows or Macintosh)
- Sound Designer II (Macintosh only)
- Sound Only QuickTime Movies (Windows or Macintosh)
- Sun AU (Windows or Macintosh)
- System 7 Sounds (Macintosh only)
- WAV (Windows or Macintosh)

FIGURE 5

A wave pattern displayed on a sound layer

FIGURE 6

Sound Effect options in the Properties panel

Add sound to a movie

1. Open fl5_2.fla, then save it as **rallySnd**.

2. Play the movie and notice that there is no sound.

3. Click the **stopmovie layer**, insert a **new layer**, then name it **carSnd**.

4. Insert a **keyframe** in frame 72 on the carSnd layer.

5. Click **File** on the menu bar, point to **Import**, then click **Import to Library**.

6. Use the Import to Library dialog box to navigate to the drive and folder where your Data Files are stored, click the **CarSnd.wav file**, then click **Open** (Win) or **Import to Library** (Mac).

7. Display the Library Panel if it is not displayed.

8. Click **frame 72** on the CarSnd layer.

9. Drag the **CarSnd sound symbol** ◀€ to the Stage, as shown in Figure 7.

   After releasing the mouse button, notice the wave pattern that has been placed on the carSnd layer starting in frame 72.

   | TIP The wave pattern may not appear on the layer until the movie is played one time.

10. Click **Control** on the menu bar, then click **Test Movie**.

11. Click the **Click to continue button** to test the sound.

12. Close the Flash Player window.

You imported a sound and added it to a movie.

FIGURE 7
Dragging the CarSnd symbol to the Stage

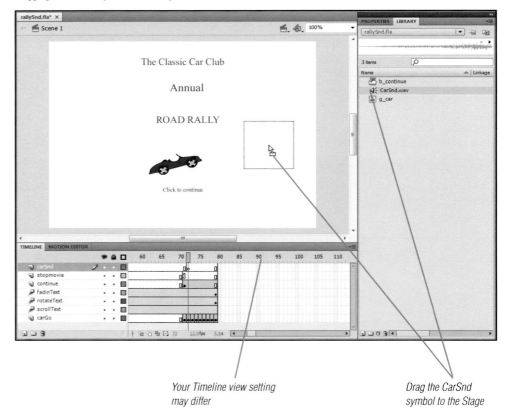

Your Timeline view setting
may differ

Drag the CarSnd
symbol to the Stage

FIGURE 8
The Timeline for the button with the sound layer

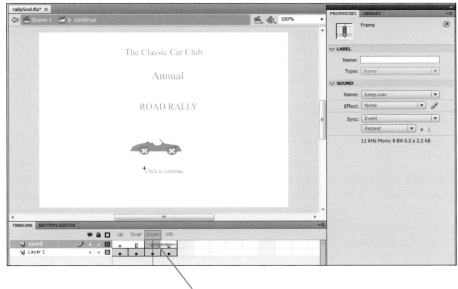

Sound wave pattern appears
in the selected frame

1. Click **frame 71** on the carSnd layer.

2. Click the **Selection tool** ↖ on the Tools panel, drag a **marquee** around "Click to continue" to select the button, then double-click the **selection** to display the button's Timeline.

3. Insert a **new layer** above Layer 1, then name it **sound**.

4. Click the **Down frame** on the sound layer, click **Insert** on the menu bar, point to **Timeline**, then click **Blank Keyframe**.

5. Click **File** on the menu bar, point to **Import**, then click **Import to Library**.

6. Use the Import to Library dialog box to navigate to the drive and folder where your Data Files are stored, click the **beep.wav file**, then click **Open** (Win) or **Import to Library** (Mac).

7. Display the Properties panel, click the **Name list arrow** in the SOUND area, then click **beep.wav**.

8. Click the **Sync list arrow** in the Properties panel, click **Event**, then compare your screen to Figure 8.

9. Click **Scene 1** on the upper left of the edit window title bar to display the main Timeline.

10. Test the movie.

11. Click the **Click to continue button** and listen to the sounds, then close the Flash Player window.

12. Save your work, then close the movie.

You added a sound layer to a button, imported a sound, then attached the sound to the button.

ADD
VIDEO

What You'll Do

 In this lesson, you will import a video, add actions to video control buttons, and then synchronize sound to a video clip.

Incorporating Video

Adobe Flash allows you to import FLV (Flash video) files that then can be used in a Flash document. Flash provides several ways to add video to a movie, depending on the application and, especially, file size. Video content can be embedded directly into a Flash document, progressively downloaded, or streamed.

Embedded video becomes part of the SWF file similar to other objects, such as sound and graphics. A placeholder appears on the Stage and is used to display the video during playback. If the video is imported as a movie clip symbol, then the placeholder can be edited, including rotating, resizing, and even animating it. Because embedded video becomes part of the SWF file, the technique of embedding video is best used for small video clips in order to keep the file size small. The process for embedding video is to import a video file using the Import Video Wizard. Then, you place the video on the Stage and add controls as desired. Figure 9

shows a video placeholder for an embedded video. The video file (fireworks.mov) is in the Library panel and the video layer in the Timeline contains the video object.

Progressive downloading allows you to use ActionScript to load an external FLV file into a SWF file; the video then plays when the SWF file is played. With progressive downloading, the FLV file resides outside the SWF file. Therefore, the SWF file size can be kept smaller than when the video is embedded in the Flash document. The video begins playing soon after the first part of the file has been downloaded.

Streaming video provides a constant connection between the user and the video delivery. Streaming has several advantages over the other methods of delivering video, including starting the video quicker and allowing for live video delivery. However, streaming video requires the Flash Media Server, an Adobe software product designed specifically for streaming video content.

Using the Adobe Media Encoder

The Adobe Media Encoder is an application used by Flash to convert various video file formats, such as .mov, .avi, and .mpeg, to the FLV (Flash Video) format so the videos can be used with Flash. The Encoder allows you to, among other things, choose the size of the placeholder the video will play in, to edit the video, and to insert cue points that can be used to synchronize the video with animations and sound. Figure 10 shows the Encoder ready to convert the fireworks.mov video (Source Name) to fireworks.flv (Output File). The Start Queue button is used to start the process. When the conversion is complete, a green check mark is displayed in the Status column. The Adobe Media Encoder can be accessed through the Import Video Wizard.

Using the Import Video Wizard

The Import Video Wizard is used to import FLV files into Flash documents. The Wizard, in a step-by-step process, leads you through a series of windows that allows you to select the file to be imported and the deployment method (embed, progressive, streaming). In addition, you can specify whether or not to have the video converted to a movie clip symbol which allows you to animate the placeholder. The Wizard appears when you choose the Import Video command from the Import option on the File menu.

FIGURE 9
An embedded video

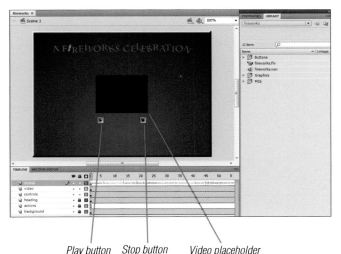

Play button   Stop button   Video placeholder

FIGURE 10
The Adobe Media Encoder

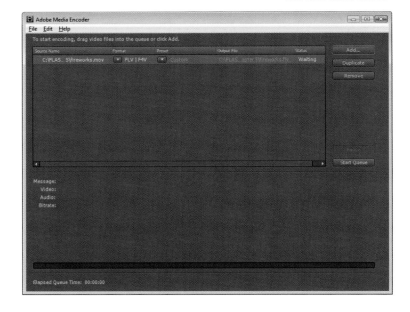

Import a video

1. Open fl5_3.fla, then save it as **fireworks**.

   Note: If the Missing Font Warning message appears, click Use Default.

   The movie has four layers and 85 frames. The actions layer has a stop action in frame 1. The heading layer contains the text object. The controls layer contains start and stop buttons that will be used to control the video. The background layer contains a blue gradient background object. The Library panel contains the two button symbols and a sound file as well as graphics and movie clip files.

2. Insert a **new layer** above the controls layer, name it **video**, then click **frame 1** on the video layer.

3. Click **File** on the menu bar, point to **Import**, then click **Import Video**.

   The Import Video Wizard begins by asking for the path to the video file and the desired method for importing the file, as shown in Figure 11.

4. Click the **Embed FLV in SWF and play in timeline option button**.

5. Click **Browse**, navigate to the drive and folder where your Data Files are stored, click **fireworks.mov**, then click **Open**.

   A message appears indicating that the video format is not valid for embedding video. You must convert the file to the FLV format.

   (continued)

FIGURE 11
The Import Video Wizard

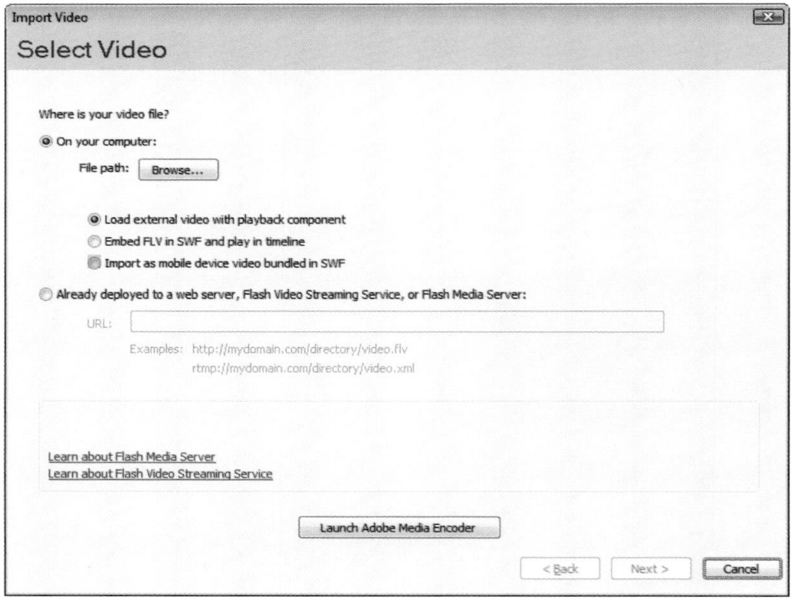

FIGURE 12
The embed video options

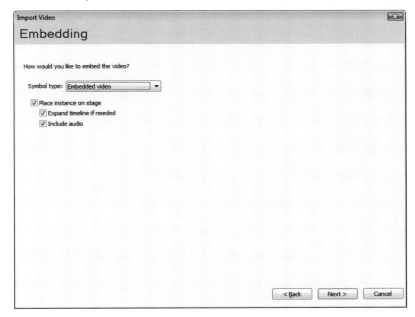

6. Click **OK**, then click the **Launch Adobe Media Encoder button**.

   Note: If a message about browsing to the file after it is converted opens, click OK.

   After several moments the encoder opens.

   Note: Click the Adobe Media Encoder button on the taskbar if the encoder does not open automatically in its own window.

7. Click **Start Queue**, when the process is done as indicated by a green check mark, close the encoder window.

8. Click **OK** to close the message window if one opens, then click the **Browse button**.

9. Click **fireworks.flv**, then click **Open**.

   Note: If you do not see fireworks.flv, navigate to the drive and folder where your solution file is stored.

   The Select Video screen now displays the path to the fireworks.flv file.

10. Click **Next** (Win) or **Continue** (Mac) in the Wizard.

    The Embedding window opens, which allows you to specify how you would like to embed the video.

11. Verify your settings match those in Figure 12.

12. Click **Next** (Win) or **Continue** (Mac).

13. Read the Finish Video Import screen, then click **Finish**.

    The video is encoded and placed on the Stage and in the Library panel.

You imported a video and then *specified the embed and encoding type.*

Attach actions to video control buttons

1. Test the movie, then click the **control buttons**.

   Nothing happens because there is a stop action in frame 1 and no actions have been assigned to the buttons.

2. Close the Flash Player window.

3. Open the Actions panel.

4. Click the **play button** on the Stage, then verify the playback – play button symbol appears at the lower left of the Script pane.

5. Turn on Script Assist if it is off.

6. Click the **Add a new item to the script button** ⊕, point to **Global Functions**, point to **Timeline Control**, then click **play** as shown in Figure 13.

7. Click the **Stop button** on the Stage, then verify the playback - stop button symbol appears at the lower left of the Script pane.

8. Click the **Add a new item to the script button** ⊕, point to **Global Functions**, point to **Timeline Control**, then click **stop**.

9. Close the Actions panel.

10. Test the movie, click the **play button**, then click the **stop button**.

    The video plays, however there is no sound.

11. Close the Flash Player window.

You assigned play and stop actions to video control buttons.

FIGURE 13
Using Script Assist to assign a play action to a button

Script Assist on

Play button selected

FIGURE 14

The completed Properties panel

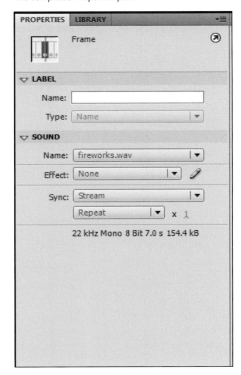

1. Insert a **new layer** above the video layer, then name it **sound**.

2. Click **frame 1** on the sound layer.

3. Display the Properties panel, then display the SOUND area options.

4. Click the **Name list arrow** in the SOUND area, then click **fireworks.wav**.

5. Click the **Sync sound list arrow** in the SOUND area, click **Stream**, then compare your screen to Figure 14.

6. Test the movie, click the **play button**, then click the **stop button**.

7. Close the Flash Player window, save your work, then close the file.

You inserted a layer, then you synchronized a sound to the video clip.

CREATE AN ANIMATED
NAVIGATION BAR

What You'll Do

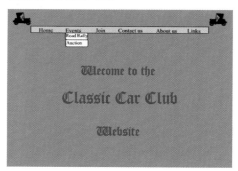

In this lesson, you will work through the process to create one drop-down menu. A navigation bar has been provided as well as the necessary buttons.

Understanding Animated Navigation Bars

A common navigation scheme for a website is a navigation bar with drop-down menus, such as the one shown in Figure 15. Using a navigation bar has several advantages. First, it allows the developer to provide several menu options to the user without cluttering the screen, thereby providing more screen space for the website content. Second, it allows the user to go quickly to a location on the site without having to navigate several screens to find the desired content. Third, it provides consistency in function and appearance, making it easy for users to learn and work with the navigation scheme.

There are various ways to create drop-down menus using the animation capabilities of Flash and ActionScript. One common technique allows you to give the illusion of a drop-down menu by using masks that reveal the menu. When the user points to (rolls over) an option in the navigation bar, a list or "menu" of buttons is displayed ("drops down"). Then the user can click a button to go to another location in the website or trig-

ger some other action. The dropping down of the list is actually an illusion created by using a mask to "uncover" the menu options.

The process is as follows:
- Create a navigation bar. This could be as basic as a background graphic in the shape of a rectangle with navigation bar buttons.
- Position the drop-down buttons. Add a layer beneath the navigation bar layer. Next, select an empty frame adjacent to the frame containing the navigation bar. Place the buttons on the Stage below their respective menu items on the navigation bar. If the navigation bar has an Events button with two choices, Road Rally and Auction, that you want to appear as buttons on a drop-down menu, position these two buttons below the Events button on the drop-down buttons layer.
- Add the animated mask. Add a mask layer above the drop-down buttons layer and create an animation of an object that starts above the drop-down buttons

and moves down to reveal them. Then change the layer to a mask layer and the drop-down buttons layer to a masked layer.

- Assign actions to the drop-down buttons. Select each drop-down button and assign an action, such as "on (release) gotoAndPlay."
- Assign a roll over action to the navigation bar button. The desired effect is to have the drop-down buttons appear when the user points to a navigation bar button. Therefore, you need to assign an "on rollOver" action to the navigation bar button that causes the playhead to go to the frame that plays the animation on the mask layer. This can be done using the Script Assist feature.
- Create an invisible button. When the user points to a navigation bar button,

the drop-down menu appears showing the drop-down buttons. There needs to be a way to have the menu disappear when the user points away from the navigation bar button. This can be done by creating a button on a layer below the masked layer. This button is slightly larger than the drop-down buttons and their navigation bar button, as shown in Figure 16. A rollOver action is assigned to this button so that when the user rolls off the drop-down or navigation bar buttons, he or she rolls onto this button and the action is carried out. This button should be made transparent so the user does not see it.

Using Frame Labels

Until now, you have worked with frame numbers in ActionScript code when creat-

ing a goto action. Frame labels can also be used in the code. You can assign a label to a frame as an identifier. For example, you could assign the label home to frame 10 and then create a goto home action that will cause the playhead to jump to frame 10. One advantage of using frame labels is that if you insert frames in the Timeline, the label adjusts for the added frames. So, you do not have to change the ActionScript that uses the frame label. Another advantage is that the descriptive labels help you identify parts of the movie as you work with the Timeline. You assign a frame label by selecting the desired frame and typing a label in the Frame text box in the Properties panel.

FIGURE 15
A website with a navigation bar with drop-down menus

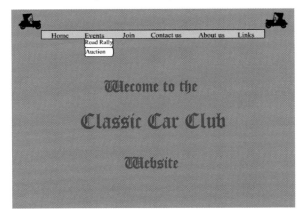

FIGURE 16
A button that will be assigned a rollOver action

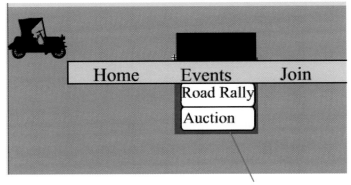

When the user rolls over the blue button with the pointer, a script is executed that causes the drop-down menu to disappear

Position the drop-down buttons

1. Open fl5_4.fla, then save it as **navBar**.

2. Click the **homeBkgrnd layer**, insert a **new layer**, then name it **roadRally**.

3. Click **frame 2** on the roadRally layer, then insert a **keyframe**.

4. Display the Library panel, open the Buttons folder, then drag the **b_roadRally button** to the position just below the Events button on the Navigation bar, as shown in Figure 17.

5. Insert a **new layer** above the homeBkgrnd layer, then name it **auction**.

6. Click **frame 2** on the auction layer, then insert a **keyframe**.

7. Drag the **b_auction button** from the Library panel and position it below the b_roadRally button.

8. Click the **Zoom tool** 🔍 on the Tools panel, then click the **Events button** on the Stage to enlarge the view.

9. Click the **Selection tool** ↖ on the Tools panel, then click each button and use the arrow keys to position them, as shown in Figure 18.

   The top line of the Road Rally button must overlap the bottom border of the navigation bar, and the bottom border of the Road Rally button must overlap the top border of the Auction button.

You placed the drop-down buttons on the Stage and repositioned them.

FIGURE 17
Positioning the b_roadRally button

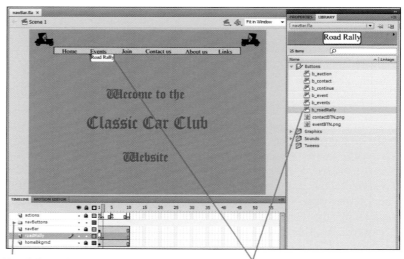

The expand icon indicates that this is a folder layer. In this case, all of navigation bar buttons are within this folder. Clicking the arrow reveals the contents of the folder.

Drag from library to here

FIGURE 18
Positioning the buttons

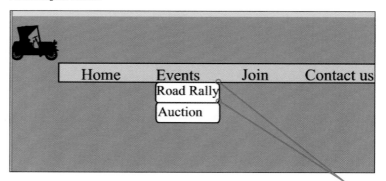

Make sure the button borders overlap

FIGURE 19
The drawn rectangle that covers the buttons

FIGURE 20
Dragging the rectangle above the buttons

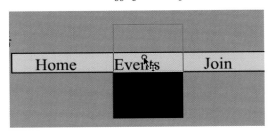

FIGURE 21
The rectangle positioned over the buttons

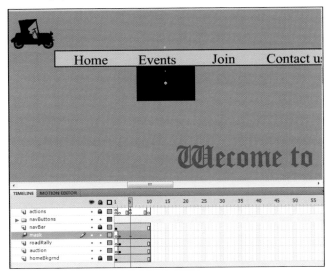

Lesson 4   Create an Animated Navigation Bar

Add a mask layer

1. Click the **roadRally layer**, insert a **new layer** above the roadRally layer, then name it **mask**.

2. Click **frame 2** on the mask layer, then insert a **keyframe**.

3. Select the **Rectangle tool** ⬛ on the Tools panel, set the **Stroke Color** to **none** ⊘ , then set the **Fill Color** to **black**.

4. Draw a **rectangle** that covers the buttons, as shown in Figure 19.

5. Click the **Selection tool** ➤ on the Tools panel, then drag the **rectangle** to above the buttons, as shown in Figure 20.

6. Verify the rectangle is selected, click **Insert** on the menu bar, click **Motion Tween**, then click **OK**.

7. Click **frame 5** on the mask layer, then insert a **keyframe**.

8. Use the **Selection tool** ➤ to move the **rectangle**, as shown in Figure 21.

9. Click **mask** on the Timeline, click **Modify** on the menu bar, point to **Timeline**, click **Layer Properties**, click the **Mask option button**, then click **OK**.

10. Click **roadRally** on the Timeline.

11. Click **Modify** on the menu bar, point to **Timeline**, click **Layer Properties**, click the **Masked option button**, then click **OK**.

12. Click **auction** on the Timeline, then repeat step 11.

13. Drag the **playhead** along the Timeline, notice how the mask hides and reveals the buttons.

You added a mask that animates to hide and reveal the menu buttons.

Assign an action to a drop-down button

1. Click **frame 2** on the roadRally layer, then click the **Road Rally button** to select it.

2. Open the **Actions panel** and verify the Script Assist button is selected and b_roadRally is displayed, as shown in Figure 22.

   b_roadRally in the lower-left corner of the Script pane indicates that the b_roadRally button symbol is selected on the Stage and that the ActionScript you create will apply to this object.

3. Click the **Add a new item to the script icon** ⚘ , point to **Global Functions**, point to **Timeline Control**, then click **goto**.

4. Click the **Scene list arrow**, point to **Scene 2** as shown in Figure 23, then click.

   Scenes are a way to organize large movies. In this case Scene 2 contains the Road Rally screen for the website.

5. Verify the Type is set to Frame Number and the Frame is set to 1.

6. Collapse the Actions panel.

You used the Script Assist window to assign a goto action to a menu button.

FIGURE 22
The Actions panel with the b_roadRally button selected

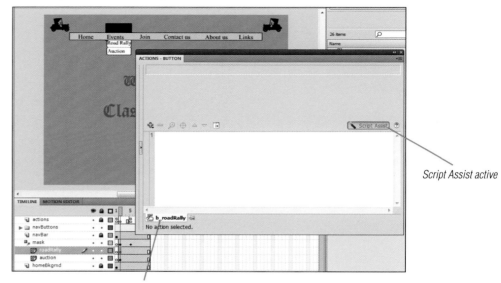

Script Assist active

b_roadRally button indicating the action to be created will be assigned to the button

FIGURE 23
Selecting the scene to go to

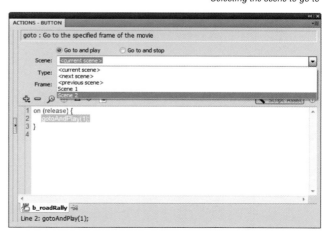

Creating Special Effects

FIGURE 24

Specifying a frame label

FIGURE 25

The completed Actions panel

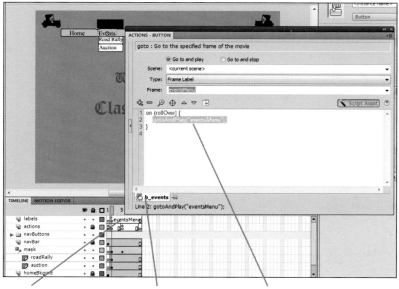

Frame label

b_event button symbol indicating the action will be assigned to the button

gotoAndPlay("eventsMenu");

Add a frame label and assign a rollover action

1. Insert a **new layer** at the top of the Timeline, name it **labels**, then insert a **keyframe** in frame 2 on the labels layer.

2. Display the Properties panel, click inside the **Name text box** in the LABEL area, then type **eventsMenu**, as shown in Figure 24.

3. Click the **Events button** on the Stage to select it.

4. Expand the Actions panel, then verify b_events is displayed in the lower-left corner of the Script pane.

5. Click the **Add a new item to the script icon** ⤴, point to **Global Functions**, point to **Movie Clip Control**, then click **on**.

6. Click the **Release check box** to deselect it, then click the **Roll Over check box** to select it.

7. Click the **Add a new item to the script icon** ⤴, point to **Global Functions**, point to **Timeline Control**, then click **goto**.

8. Click the **Type list arrow**, then click **Frame Label**.

9. Click the **Frame list arrow**, then click **eventsMenu**.

   Your screen should resemble Figure 25.

10. Click **Control** on the menu bar, then click **Test Movie**.

11. Point to **Events**, then click **Road Rally**.

12. Close the Flash Player window, collapse the Actions panel, then save your work.

You added a frame label and assigned a rollOver action using the frame label.

Add an invisible button

1. Click **Control** on the menu bar, click **Test Movie**, move the pointer over Events on the navigation bar, then move the pointer away from Events.

   Notice that when you point to Events, the drop-down menu appears. However, when you move the pointer away from the menu, it does not disappear.

2. Close the Flash Player window.

3. Insert a **new layer** above the homeBkgrnd layer, then name it **rollOver**.

4. Insert a **keyframe** in frame 2 on the rollOver layer.

5. Select the **Rectangle tool** 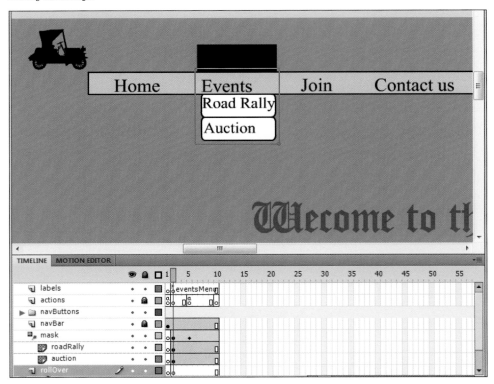 on the Tools panel, verify that the Stroke Color is set to **none**, then set the **Fill Color** to **blue**.

6. Draw a **rectangle**, as shown in Figure 26.

7. Click the **Selection tool** on the Tools panel, then click the **blue rectangle** to select it.

8. Click **Modify** on the menu bar, then click **Convert to Symbol**.

9. Type **b_rollOver** for the name, click the **Type list arrow**, click **Button**, then click **OK**.

10. Expand the Actions panel.

   (continued)

FIGURE 26
Drawing the rectangle

FIGURE 27

FIGURE 27

The Actions panel displaying Actionscript assigned to the b_rollOver button symbol

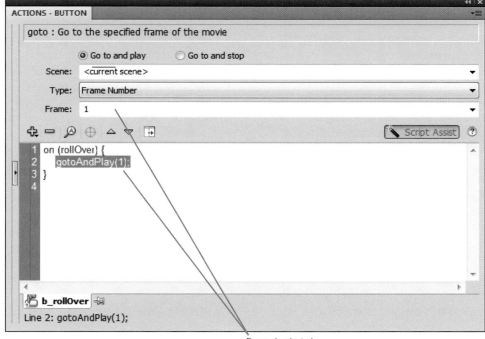

Frame 1 selected

11. Verify the rollOver button is selected and b_rollOver is displayed in the lower-left corner of the Script pane.

12. Click the **Add a new item to the script icon** , point to **Global Functions**, point to **Movie Clip Control**, then click **on**.

13. Click the **Release check box** to deselect it, then click the **Roll Over check box** to select it.

14. Click the **Add a new item to the script icon** , point to **Global Functions**, point to **Timeline Control**, then click **goto**.

15. Verify Frame 1 is specified, as shown in Figure 27.

16. Close the Actions panel.

17. Click the **Style list arrow** in the COLOR EFFECT area of the Properties panel, click **Alpha**, then set the percentage to **0**.

18. Click **Control** on the menu bar, then click **Test Movie**.

19. Point to **Events** to display the drop-down menu, then move the pointer away from Events.

The drop-down menu disappears.

20. Close the Flash Player window, then save and close the movie.

21. Exit Flash.

You added a button and assigned a rollOver action to it, then made the button transparent.

CREATE CHARACTER ANIMATIONS
USING INVERSE KINEMATICS

What You'll Do

In this lesson, you will use the bone tool to create a character animation and create a movie clip that can be manipulated by the viewer.

Understanding Inverse Kinematics

One way to create character animations is to use the frame-by-frame process in which you place individually drawn objects into a series of successive frames. You did this with the stick figure graphics in an earlier chapter. Those graphics were simple to draw. However, if you have more complex drawings, such as fill shapes that are more realistic, and if you want to create animations that show an unlimited number of poses, the time required to develop all of the necessary drawings would be considerable.

Flash provides a process that allows you to create a single image and add a structure to the image that can be used to animate the various parts of the image. The process is called **Inverse Kinematics (IK)** and involves creating an articulated structure of bones that allow you to link the parts of an image. Once the bone structure is created, you can animate the image by changing the position of any of

its parts. The bone structure causes the related parts to animate in a natural way. For example, if you draw an image of a person, create the bone structure, and then move the person's right foot, then all parts of the leg (lower leg, knee, upper leg) respond. This makes it easy to animate various movements.

Figure 28 shows a drawing of a character before and after the bone structure is added. Figure 29 shows how moving the right foot moves the entire leg. The image is made up of several small drawings, each one converted to a graphic symbol. These include a head, torso, upper and lower arms, upper and lower legs, hips, and feet.

Creating the Bone Structure

The bone structure can be applied to a single drawn shape, such as an oval created with the Flash drawing tools. More often it is applied to an image, such as a character, made up of several drawings. When this is the case, each drawing is converted to a graphic symbol or a movie clip symbol and then assembled to form the desired image. If you import a graphic, it needs to be broken apart using the Modify menu and the individual parts of the imported graphic converted to graphic symbols or movie clip symbols. If the imported graphic has only one part (such as a bitmap), it needs to be broken apart and treated as a single drawn shape.

Once the image is ready, you use the Bone tool to create the bone structure, called the armature, by clicking and dragging the Bone tool pointer to link one part of the image to another. You continue adding bones to the structure until all parts of the image are linked. For a human form you would link the head to the torso and the torso to the upper left arm and the upper left arm to the lower left arm, and so on. The bones in an armature are connected to each other in a parent-child hierarchy, so that adjusting the child adjusts the parent.

Animating the IK Object

As you are creating the bone structure, a layer named Armature_1 is added to the Timeline, and the image with the bone structure is placed in frame 1 on the layer. This new layer is called a **pose layer**. Each pose layer can contain only one armature and its associated image. Animating the image is done on this layer. When animating using inverse kinematics, you simply specify the start and end positions of the image. Flash interpolates the position of the parts of the image for the in-between frames. So, you can insert a keyframe in any frame after frame 1 on the Armature_1 layer and then change the position of one or more of the bones. This is referred to as creating a pose. When one bone moves, the other connected bones move in relation to it. Additional poses can be set along the Timeline by inserting keyframes and adjusting the bone structure. Animations of IK objects, other than those within movie clips, only allow you to change the shape, position, and ease in the animation.

FIGURE 28
Drawings showing before and after the bone structure is added

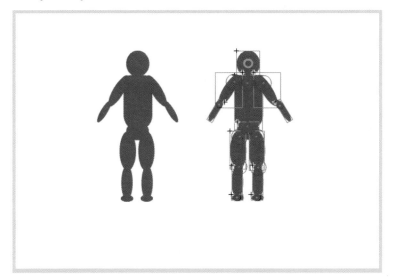

FIGURE 29
Moving the foot moves the other parts of the leg

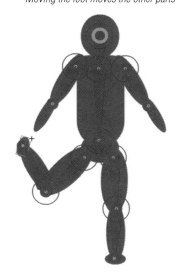

Creating a Movie Clip with an IK Object

Movie clips provide a great deal of flexibility when animating IK objects. You can change properties such as the color effect and you can nest one movie clip within another. So, you could have a movie clip of a character walking and nest another movie clip within it to have its mouth move. In addition, you can apply a motion tween to a movie clip. So, you could have a movie clip of a character walking and have it play within a motion tween which causes the character (movie clip) to jump over an obstacle.

Runtime Feature

Flash provides a runtime feature for manipulation of an IK object. That is, you can allow the user to click on the object and adjust the image. This is useful if you are creating a game or just wanting to provide some interaction on a website. The process is to click a frame on the Armature layer, then use the Properties panel to set the Type to Runtime. The runtime feature only works with IK structures connected to drawn shapes or movie clip symbols, not graphic or button symbols. In addition, only one pose can used. At the time this book was published, some browsers, such as Firefox, supported the runtime feature, but other browsers did not.

IK Objects

As you are working with IK objects, keep in mind the following:

- The Undo feature can be used to undo a series of actions such as undoing a mistake made when creating the bone structure.
- The bone structure may disappear as you are working on it. This could be caused by going outside the image as you are connecting the parts of the image. If the bone structure disappears, use the Undo feature to Undo your last action.
- To delete an individual bone and all of its children, click the bone and press [Delete]. You can select multiple bones to delete by holding down [Shift] and clicking each bone.
- To delete all bones, select the image and choose the Break Apart command from the Modify menu.
- To create IK animations, ActionScript 3.0 and Flash Player 10 need to be specified in the Publish Settings dialog box, which is displayed by choosing Publish Settings from the File menu.

FIGURE 30
Connecting the head and torso

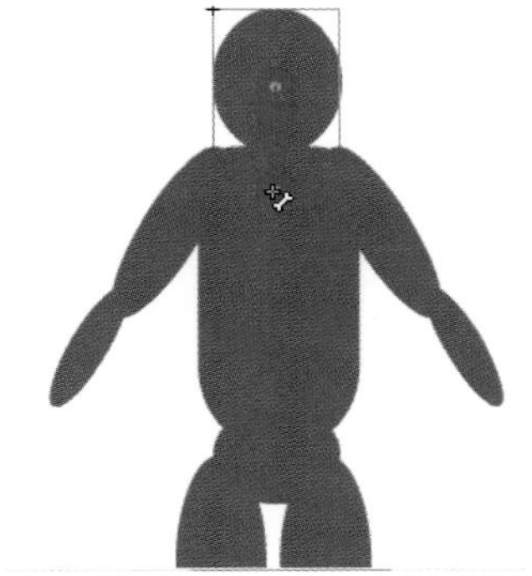

FIGURE 31
Connecting the torso and the upper arm

FIGURE 32
Connecting the upper and lower arms

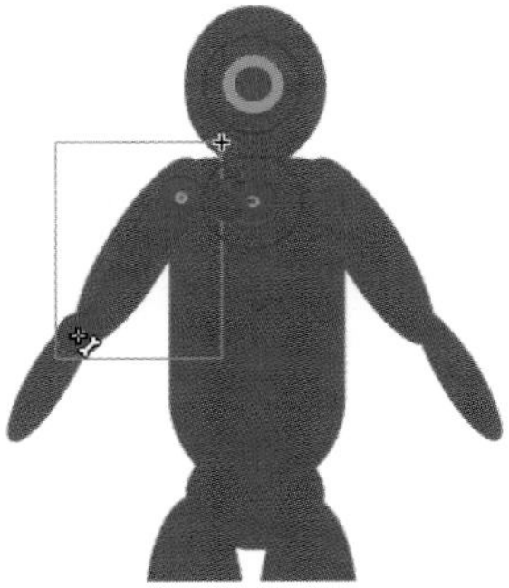

Note: If the bone structure disappears as you are working on it, use the Undo feature to undo your last action.

FIGURE 33
The completed bone structure

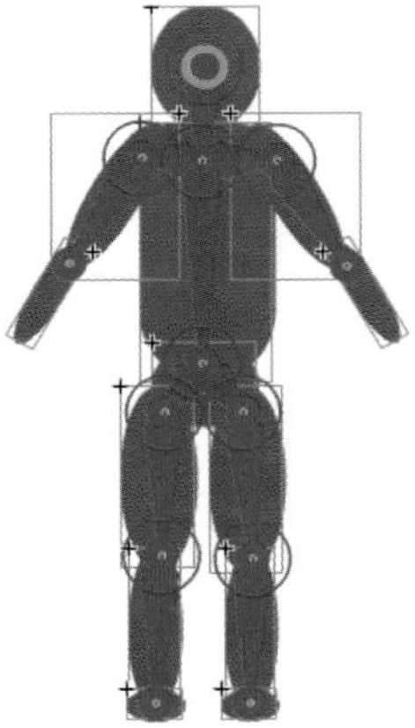

Create the bone structure

1. Open fl5_5.fla, then save it as **kicker**.
   This document has a graphic symbol made up of 13 individual drawings to form a character shape.
2. Use the **Selection tool** to drag a marquee around the image to select it.
   Notice the separate objects.
3. Click a blank area of the Stage to deselect the image.
4. Click the **Zoom tool**, then click the image to zoom in on it.
5. Scroll the Stage to view the head, then click the **Bone tool** on the Tools panel.
6. Point to the middle of the head, when the pointer changes to a bone with a cross, drag the **pointer** down to the torso as shown in Figure 30, then release the mouse button.
7. Point to the bottom of the bone, when the pointer changes to a bone with a cross, drag the **pointer** to the left as shown in Figure 31.
8. Point to the left end of the bone, when the pointer changes to a bone with a cross, drag the **pointer** down as shown in Figure 32.
   Notice that a bone connects two overlapping objects, such as the bone used to connect the upper arm and lower arm.
9. Using Figure 33 as a guide, complete the drawing of the other bones.
   Hint: Use the Undo command as needed if your connections do not match Figure 33.
10. Save your work.

You created a bone structure by connecting objects on the Stage with the Bone tool.

Animate the character

1. Change the view to **Fit in Window**.

2. Click **frame 10** on the Armature_1 layer, then insert a **keyframe**.

3. Click the **Selection tool** ↖ , then click a blank area of the Stage to deselect the object if it is selected.

4. Point to the **right foot**, when the pointer changes to a bone with a delta symbol ↘, drag the ↘ **pointer** to position the foot as shown in Figure 34.

5. Point to the **right arm**, then use the ↘ **pointer** to position it as shown in Figure 35.

6. Use the ↘ **pointer** to position the left arm and left foot as shown in Figure 36.

   Hint: To position the left foot, move the left knee first, then move the left foot.

7. Click **frame 20** on the Armature_1 layer, then insert a **keyframe**.

8. Adjust the arms and legs as shown in Figure 37.

   Hint: Move the right leg to the position shown to create a kicking motion.

9. Click the **Free Transform tool** on the Tools panel, then drag a **marquee** around the image to select it.

10. Point to the **upper-right handle**, when the pointer changes to an arc ↻ , drag the ↻ **pointer** to the left as shown in Figure 38.

11. Test the movie, close the Flash Player window, then save the movie.

You animated the character by adjusting the armatures of the various bones.

FIGURE 34
Positioning the right foot

FIGURE 35
Positioning the right arm

FIGURE 36
Positioning the left arm and left foot

right leg

FIGURE 37
Positioning the left arm and left leg

right leg

FIGURE 38
Rotating the object

Creating Special Effects

FIGURE 39
Increasing the length of the tween span

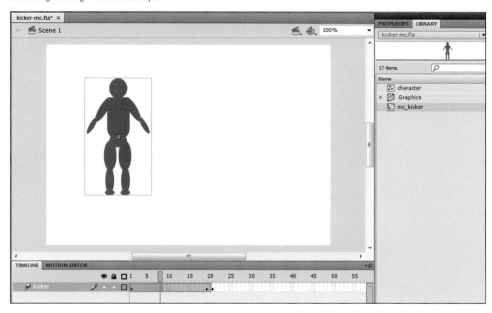

Create a movie clip of the IK

1. Click **File** on the menu bar, click **Save as**, type **kicker-mc**, then click **OK** [Win] or **Save as** [Mac].

2. Click **frame 1** on the Armature_1 layer.

3. Use the **Selection tool** ➤ to drag a marquee around the entire image to select it.

4. Click **Modify** on the menu bar, then click **Convert to Symbol**.

5. Type **mc_kicker** for the name, select **Movie Clip** for the Type, then click **OK**.

6. Click **Armature_1** on the Timeline, then click the **Delete icon** 🗑 .

7. Click **frame 1** on the kicker layer, display the Library panel, then drag the **mc_kicker** symbol to the Stage.

8. Insert a **Motion Tween**.

9. Drag the **tween span** on the Timeline to **frame 20**, as shown in Figure 39.

10. Click **frame 10** on the kicker layer.

11. Verify the object is selected, then press the **up arrow** [↑] on the keyboard 10 times.

12. Click **frame 20**, then press the **down arrow** [↓] on the keyboard 10 times.

13. Test the movie, close the Flash Player window, then save your work.

You created a movie clip and applied a motion tween to it.

Apply an ease value

1. Double-click the **mc_kicker symbol** in the Library panel to display the edit window, then scroll as needed to see the entire object.
2. Display the Properties panel.
3. Click **frame 10** on the Armature_2 layer.
4. Set the Ease Strength to **−100**.
5. Click the **Type list arrow** in the EASE area, then click **Simple (Fastest)**, as shown in Figure 40.

   Frame 10 is the start of the motion tween where the right leg begins to kick downward. Setting the ease value to −100 will cause the leg motion to start out slow and accelerate as the leg follows through to the end of the kicking motion. This is a more natural way to represent the kick than to have the leg speed constant throughout the downward motion and follow through.

6. Click **Scene 1** on the edit window title bar to return to the main Timeline.
7. Test the movie, close the Flash Player window, save your work, then close the file.

You added an ease value to the movie clip.

FIGURE 40
Setting the ease value

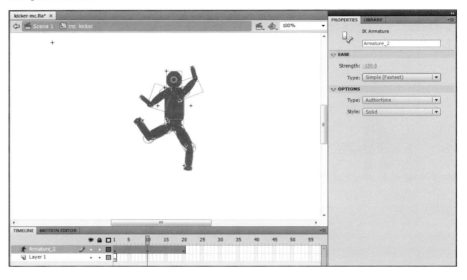

Creating Special Effects

FIGURE 41
The completed armature structure

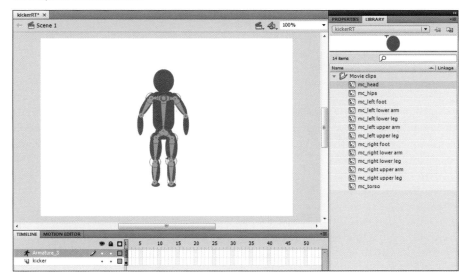

1. Open fl5_6.fla, then save it as **kickerRT**.

   This is the same character used in the kicker movie, however it has been created using movie clips instead of graphic symbols. Also, only one pose is used.

2. Use the **Bone tool** to create the armature structure as shown in Figure 41.

3. Click **frame 1** on the Armature_3 layer, click the **Type list arrow** in the OPTIONS area of the Properties panel, then click **Runtime**.

4. Click **File**, point to **Publish Preview**, then click **Default -(HTML)** to display the movie in a browser, then drag the parts of the character, such as an arm or a leg.

   Hint: Press [F12] (Win) to display the movie in a browser.

5. Close your browser.

6. Save your work, then close the document.

You created an animated character, set the play to runtime and manipulated the character in a browser.

CREATE 3D EFFECTS

What You'll Do

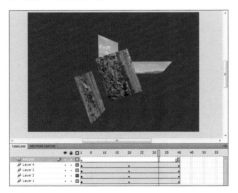

In this lesson, you will create a movie with 3D effects.

Flash allows you to create 3D effects by manipulating objects in 3D space on the Stage. Until now you have been working in two dimensions, width and height. The default settings for the Stage are 550 pixels wide and 400 pixels high. These are represented by an x axis (across) and a y axis (down). Any position on the Stage can be specified by x and y coordinates. The upper-left corner of the Stage has an x value of 0 and a y value of 0, and the lower-right corner has an x value of 550 and a y value of 400, as shown in Figure 42. In 3D space there is also a z axis that represents depth. Flash provides two tools, 3D Translation and 3D Rotation that can be used to move and rotate objects using all three axes. In addition, Flash provides two other properties that can be adjusted to control the view of an object. The Perspective Angle property controls the angle of the object and can be used to create a zooming in and out effect. The Vanishing Point property more precisely controls the direction of an object as it moves away from the viewer.

The Perspective Angle and the Vanishing Point settings are found in the Properties panel.

The 3D Tools

The 3D tools are available on the Tools panel. By default the 3D Rotation tool is displayed on the Tools panel. To access the 3D Translation tool, click and hold the 3D Rotation tool to open the menu. Toggle between these two 3D tools as needed.

The process for creating 3D effects is to create a movie clip (only movie clips can have 3D effects applied to them), place the movie clip on the Stage and then click it with either of the 3D tools. When you click an object with the 3D Translation tool, the three axes, X, Y, and Z appear on top of the object, as shown in Figure 43. Each has its own color: red (X), green (Y), and blue (Z). The X and Y axes have arrows and the Z axis is represented by a dot. You point to an arrow or the black dot and drag it to reposition the object.

When you click the object with the 3D Rotation tool, the three axes, X, Y, and Z appear on top of the object, as shown in Figure 44. Dragging the X axis (red) will flip the object horizontally. Dragging the Y axis (green) will flip the object vertically. Dragging the Z axis (blue) will spin the object. A forth option, the orange circle, rotates the object around the X and Y axes at the same time.

Using a Motion Tween with a 3D Effect

Creating 3D effects requires a change in the position of an object. A motion tween is used to specify where on the Timeline the effect will take place. This allows you to create more than one effect by selecting various frames in the tween span and making adjustments as desired. If you are animating more than one object, each object should be on its own layer.

FIGURE 42
The x and y coordinates on the Stage

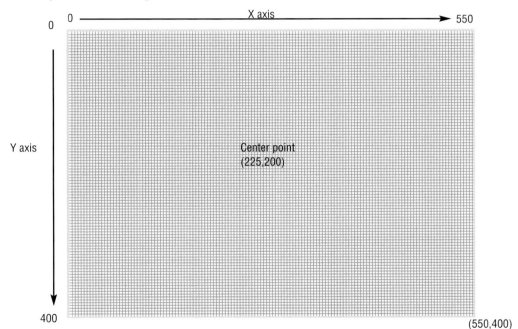

FIGURE 43
The 3D Translation tool

FIGURE 44
The 3D Rotation tool

Create a 3D animation

1. Open fl5_7.fla, then save it as **puzzle**.

   Note: The document opens with the ruler feature turned on and showing the vertical and horizontal lines that intersect at the center of the Stage.

2. Click **frame 1** on Layer 1, insert a **motion tween**, then drag the tween span to **frame 40**.

3. Click **frame 20** on Layer 1, then select the **3D Translation tool** 🔧 from the Tools panel.

4. Click the image in the upper-right corner of the Stage, point to the **green arrow**, then use the ➤ **pointer** to drag the image down to the horizontal ruler line.

5. Click the **red arrow**, then use the ➤ **pointer** to drag the image to the left, as shown in Figure 45.

6. Select the **3D Rotation tool** 🔵, point to the **green line Y axis** on the right side of the object, then drag the ➤ **pointer** down and to the left to flip the image horizontally.

7. Click **frame 40** on Layer 1, then use the **3D Translation tool** 🔧 to move the image to the position shown in Figure 46.

8. Use the **3D Rotation tool** 🔵 to drag the solid green line down and to the right, which flips the image again.

9. Click **frame 1** on Layer 2, insert a **motion tween**, then drag the tween span to **frame 40**.

10. Click **frame 20** on Layer 2, select the **3D Translation tool** 🔧, then drag the image to the position shown in Figure 47.

(continued)

FIGURE 45
Using the 3D Translation tool to position an object

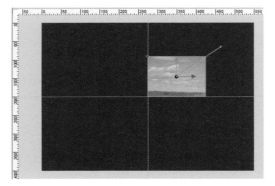

FIGURE 46
Using the 3D Translation tool to position the object again

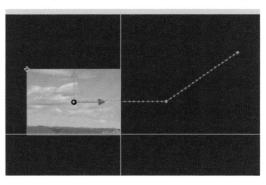

FIGURE 47
Using the 3D Translation tool to position a second object

You have been asked to develop a website illustrating the signs of the zodiac. The introductory screen should have a heading with a mask effect and 12 zodiac signs, each of which could become a button. Clicking a sign button displays an information screen with a different graphic to represent the sign and information about the sign, as well as special effects such as sound, mask effect, and character animation (inverse kinematics). Each information screen would be linked to the introductory screen. (*Note:* Using the inverse kinematics feature requires ActionScript 3.0, therefore, you will start with a movie that has the ActionScript for the buttons and stop actions already developed.)

1. Open fl5_11.fla, save it as **zodiac5**, then change the frame rate to **12 fps**.
2. Test the movie and then study the Timeline to understand how the movie works.
3. Refer to Figure 55 as you complete the introductory screen with the following:
    - A new layer above the signs layer named **heading** with the heading, **Signs of the** that appears from frame 1 through frame 31
    - A new layer named **masked** that contains the word **Zodiac** and that appears from frame 1 through frame 31
    - A mask layer that passes across the heading Zodiac

(*Notes:* Use a fill color that can be seen on the black background. After creating the motion tween, drag the end of the tween span on the Timeline to frame 31. Be sure to set the Layer Properties for the mask and masked layers.)
    - A new layer that displays the word **Zodiac** in frame 31 only
(*Note:* Remove frames 32–80 from the layer by using the Remove Frames option from the Timeline command of the Edit menu.)
    - A new layer with a sound that plays from frame 1 through frame 31 as the mask is revealing the contents of the masked layer
4. Refer to Figure 55 as you complete the scorpio screen with the following:
(*Notes:* The scorpio screen starts in frame 51. Remove frames in other layers containing content that you do not want displayed after frame 31, such as the Zodiac heading.)
    - A new layer with the three-line heading
    - An inverse kinematics animation that moves the tail (*Note:* Be sure to connect the head to the tail.)
5. Test the movie, then save it.
6. Save the movie as **zodiac5-mc**.
7. Select frame 51 on the Armature1 layer and convert the IK animation to a movie clip.
8. Delete the Armature1 layer, then select frame 51 on the scorpio layer and drag the movie clip to the Stage.
9. Create a motion tween to animate the movie clip so the scorpion moves across the screen.

10. Test the movie, compare your screens to Figure 55, close the Flash Player window, then save the movie.

FIGURE 55
Sample completed Project Builder 2

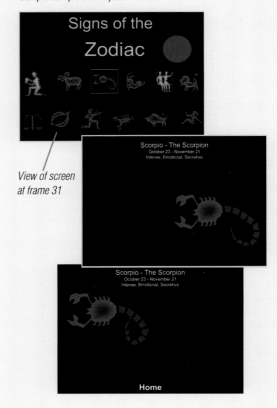

View of screen at frame 31

Figure 56 shows the home page of a website. Study the figure and complete the following questions. For each question, indicate how you determined your answer.

1. Connect to the Internet, then go to *www.nikeid.com*.

   TIP: Use Figure 56 to answer the questions. Go to the site and explore several links to get a feeling for how the site is constructed.

2. Open a document in a word processor or open a new Flash document, save the file as **dpc5**, then answer the following questions. (*Hint*: Use the Text tool in Flash.)

   - Who's site is this and what seems to be the purpose of this site?
   - Who would be the target audience?
   - How might a character animation using inverse kinematics be used?
   - How might video be used?
   - How might a mask effect be used?
   - How might sound be used? How might 3D be used?
   - What suggestions would you make to improve the design and why?

FIGURE 56
Design Project

This is a continuation of the Portfolio Project in Chapter 4, which is the development of a personal portfolio. The home page has several categories, including the following:

- Personal data
- Contact information
- Previous employment
- Education
- Samples of your work

In this project, you will create several buttons for the Sample Animations screen and link them to their respective animations.

1. Open portfolio4.fla (the file you created in Portfolio Project, Chapter 4) and save it as **portfolio5**. (*Hint*: When you open the file, you may receive a missing font message, meaning a font used in this document is not available on your computer. You can choose a substitute font or use a default font.)

2. Display the Sample Animations screen. You will be adding buttons to this screen that play various animations. In each case, have the animation return to the Sample Animations screen at the end of the animation.

3. Add a button for a character animation so it appears on the Sample Animations screen, add a new layer and create a character animation (inverse kinematics) on that layer,

then link the character animation button to the character animation.

4. Add a button for a mask effect so it appears on the Sample Animations screen, add new layers to create a mask effect (such as to the words My Portfolio) on that layer, add a sound that plays as the mask is revealing the contents of the masked layer, then link the mask effect button to the mask effect animation.

5. Add a button for an animated navigation bar so it appears on the Sample Animations screen, add a new layer and create an animated navigation bar on that layer, then link

the navigation bar button to the animated navigation bar.

6. Test the movie, then compare your Sample Animation screen to the example shown in Figure 57.

7. Close the Flash Player window, then save your work.

FIGURE 57
Sample completed Portfolio Project

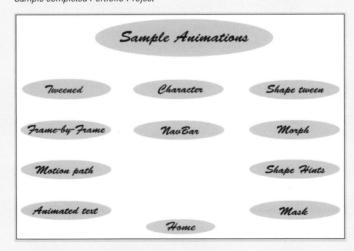

chapter 1

GETTING STARTED
WITH ADOBE
FIREWORKS

1. Understand the Fireworks work environment

2. Work with new and existing documents

3. Work with layers and images

4. Create shapes

5. Create and modify text

1 GETTING STARTED
WITH ADOBE FIREWORKS

Understanding Fireworks

Fireworks is a graphics program intended specifically for creating web images and media. Both web enthusiasts and professionals can create, edit, and optimize files, and then add animation and JavaScript-enabled interactivity to those optimized files. Fireworks is perfectly suited to prototyping a website and optimizing both graphics and designs created in other applications. Many Fireworks tasks are compartmentalized so that graphic artists can enhance or create designs without disturbing the programming added by developers, and vice versa.

Fireworks is an integral component of Adobe Creative Suite 4 Web Standard,

Web Premium, and Master Collection editions. It integrates seamlessly with other Adobe Web suite applications, including Flash, Dreamweaver, InDesign, Photoshop, and Illustrator. Fireworks is the default image editor for some file types and you can edit images using the Fireworks interface from within the host application. You can also open native Photoshop and Illustrator files in Fireworks; layers and filters are preserved and editable.

In this chapter, you will learn about the interface and learn to use the tools and apply the concepts that make Fireworks a comprehensive web graphics program.

Tools You'll Use

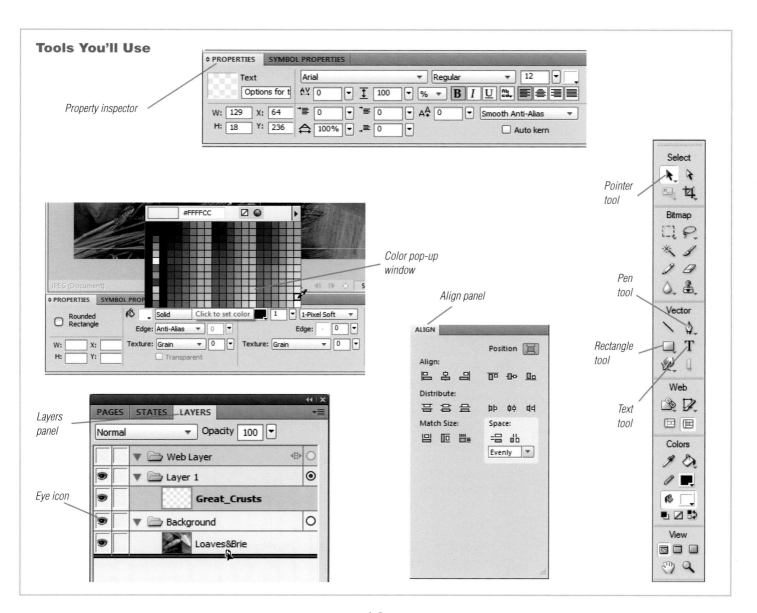

Property inspector

Color pop-up window

Align panel

Layers panel

Eye icon

Pointer tool

Pen tool

Rectangle tool

Text tool

UNDERSTAND THE FIREWORKS WORK ENVIRONMENT

What You'll Do

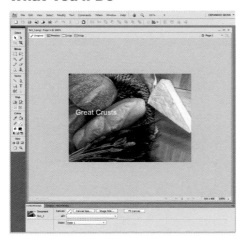

In this lesson, you will start Fireworks, open a file, and adjust panels, including undocking and collapsing them.

Viewing the Fireworks Window

The Fireworks window, shown in Figures 1 and 2, contains the space where you work with documents, tools, and panels. The main area of the **Document window** contains the canvas, which is where you work with all the elements in your document. When you open or create a document, the Document window contains four display buttons: Original, Preview, 2-Up, and 4-Up. You can work in your document when you click the Original button; the other three are document preview buttons. The 2-Up and 4-Up buttons allow you to select different optimization settings and evaluate them side by side. When you open multiple documents and the Document window is maximized, each open document's title appears on a separate tab.

QUICKTIP

The bottom of each Document window contains frame control buttons for playing animation.

Tools are housed in the **Tools panel**. The Tools panel is organized into **tool groups**: Select, Bitmap, Vector, Web, Colors, and View, so you can easily locate the tool you need. You can modify selected objects and set tool properties and other options using the **Property inspector**. Depending on the action you are performing, information in the Property inspector changes. For example, when you select a tool or an object, or click the canvas, properties specific to the selection appear in the Property inspector.

Opening Windows-specific toolbars

If you are using Windows, you can open the Main toolbar from the Toolbars command on the Window menu. The Main toolbar includes buttons for common tasks.

You can rearrange panels in the Fireworks window using the **panels dock** to maximize your onscreen real estate based on your work preferences. You can modify your workspace panel view by clicking an option on the **Application bar**. By default, Expanded Mode appears, but you can also select Iconic Mode or Iconic Mode With

Panel Names. Fireworks allows you to dock, undock, regroup, collapse, expand, and close panels or panel groups. To open or close a panel, click the panel name on the Window menu on the Application bar. To expand or collapse a panel or panel group, click the gray title bar. To undock a panel group, drag the gray bar, and to undock a

single panel, drag the panel name in the title bar.

QUICKTIP

You can quickly hide or show all open panels by pressing [Tab] or [F4].

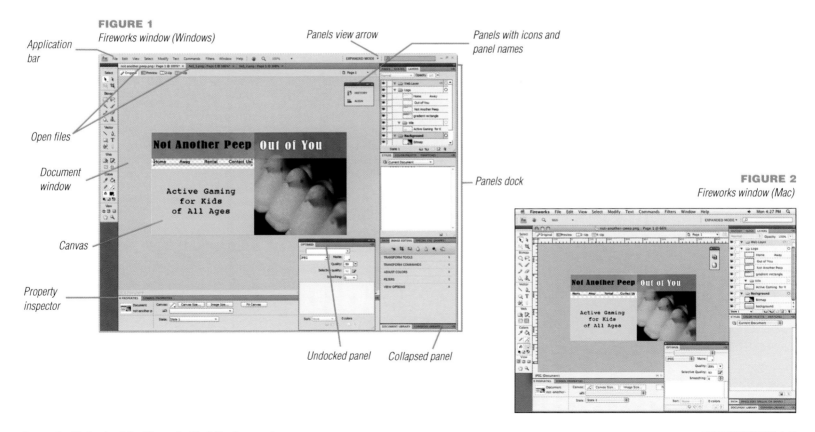

FIGURE 1
Fireworks window (Windows)

Application bar

Open files

Document window

Canvas

Property inspector

Panels view arrow

Panels with icons and panel names

Panels dock

Undocked panel

Collapsed panel

FIGURE 2
Fireworks window (Mac)

Start Fireworks and open a Fireworks document

1. Windows users, click the **Start button** 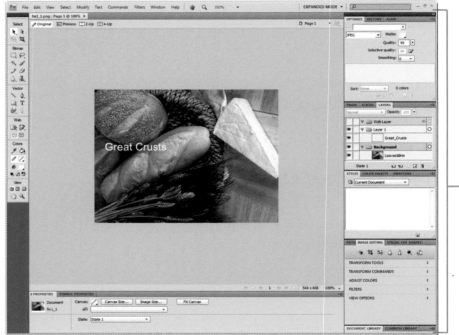 on the taskbar, point to **All Programs**, click **Adobe Web Premium CS4**, then click **Adobe Fireworks CS4** (Win).

   | TIP   The name of your Adobe suite may differ.

2. Mac users, click **Finder** on the Dock, click **Applications**, click the **Adobe Fireworks CS4 folder**, then double-click the **Fireworks CS4 application** [Fw]. After Fireworks is running, [control]-click [Fw] the Fireworks CS4 icon in the Dock, then click **Keep In Dock** (if necessary).

   The application opens with the Start page displayed. Previously opened documents appear on the left, the button to open a new document appears on the left, along with other options for training and obtaining plug-ins.

   | TIP   The name of some panels differ on a Mac.

3. Click **File** on the Application bar, then click **Open**.

   | TIP   You can also press [Ctrl][O](Win) or [⌘][O](Mac) to open a file, or you can click Open on the Start page. To disable the Start page, click the Don't show again check box.

4. Navigate to where you store your Data Files, click **fw1_1.png**, then click **Open**.

5. Compare your Fireworks window to Figure 3.

You started Fireworks and opened a file.

FIGURE 3
Newly opened document

Your open or collapsed panels might differ

Icon changes to
Expand Panels
arrow

Icon view of
panels

Drag the title bar
in the Fireworks
window

FIGURE 6

Resized Document window

Drag corner to
resize Document
window

Open and adjust panels in the Fireworks window

1. Click the **Collapse to Icons arrow** ▶▶ at the top of the panels dock to collapse the panels.

   The panels are collapsed to Icon view, as shown in Figure 4. You can also open panels by clicking Window on the Application bar and then clicking a panel name, or by double-clicking a panel name tab in a collapsed group.

2. Click the **Expand Panels arrow** ◀◀ at the top of the panels dock.

   The Main toolbar may appear beneath the Application bar (Win).

   > TIP To increase the size of a panel, place the cursor in between panels, then drag ↕ up or down.

3. Drag the **gray title bar** on the Document window down, as shown in Figure 5.

   The Document window is in Restore Down view.

4. Drag the **bottom-right corner** of the Document window to approximate the size shown in Figure 6.

5. Click **File** on the Application bar, then click **Close**.

   > TIP You can also press [Ctrl][W](Win) or ⌘ [W](Mac) to close a file.

You adjusted panels in the Fireworks window, and closed a document.

WORK WITH NEW AND
EXISTING DOCUMENTS

What You'll Do

In this lesson, you will set document properties, use Help, add a layer, and copy an object between documents.

Working with Files

Fireworks files are known as **documents**. When you create a new document, you can set properties such as the document's size, resolution, and canvas color. Fireworks will retain the changes you make to document properties as the default settings for new documents. A Fireworks document consists of many **layers**, which you can use to organize the elements of your document. A layer can contain multiple objects, all of which are managed in the Layers panel. By default, the **Layers panel** has the Web layer, which stores HTML objects such as slices and hotspots, for use in Dreamweaver. You can also create a **sub layer**, which helps you better organize related objects in a layer in the Layers panel. A layer group can contain multiple sub layers.

Working with Pages

By default, each Fireworks document contains one page, but you can create several different pages. A **page** stores all the layers in a document, or you can create new pages that store only certain layers, which is useful when you want to view different versions of a design or of a web page. You can also create a **Master Page** containing repetitive elements, and share pages across layers. Using a Master Page can serve as a design template for your design.

Although you can open or import a wide range of file formats, the files you create in Fireworks are PNG files and have a .png extension. PNG files have unique characteristics that afford you considerable flexibility in working with images. Different file formats support images differently. You can divide a document or image into parts and then individually optimize and export them in the format that best supports the image. For example, you can save a photograph in your document as a JPEG and a cartoon illustration as a GIF. JPEG format compresses color efficiently and is thus best suited for photographs, whereas GIF format is suitable for line art.

You can also open an existing file or import a file into a Fireworks document. You can copy and paste or drag and drop images, graphics, or text into a Fireworks document from other documents or applications, or from a scanner or digital camera. Figure 7 shows an object copied from a source document to a target document.

Accessing Help

In Windows, you access the Fireworks Help system by clicking Help on the Application bar, and then clicking Fireworks Help. In the Adobe Fireworks CS4 * Home window, you can find what you need by exploring a topic in a category or by typing a word or phrase in the Search text box. You can also click the Community Help link to access materials such as tutorials, articles, and blogs about Fireworks.

Commands on the Help menu link you to online support, such as Fireworks Exchange, where you can download useful and creative add-ins for Fireworks and other Adobe applications. You can also link to the Fireworks Support Center and Adobe Online Forums and Adobe Training.

Using Filters on Bitmap Images

Filters enhance the appearance of objects by transforming pixels in the image. You can apply a filter to any Fireworks object, although not all filters can be applied to bitmap images. You'll learn more about filters in the next chapter.

FIGURE 7
Object copied between documents

Open documents

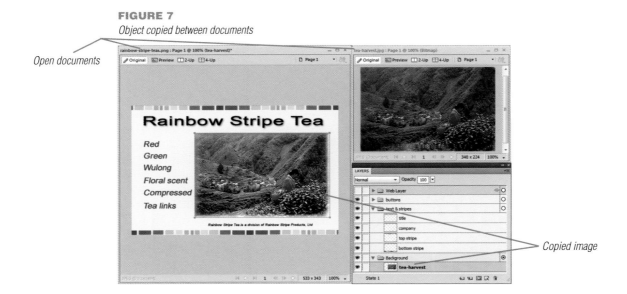

Copied image

Create and save a new document

1. Click **File** on the Application bar, then click **New** to open the New Document dialog box.

    TIP You can also press [Ctrl][N](Win) or ⌘[N](Mac) to open a new file, or you can click Fireworks Document (PNG) on the Start page.

2. Type **325** in the Width text box, double-click the value in the Height text box, type **275**, then verify that the resolution is **72**.

3. Click the **Custom canvas option** in the Canvas color section of the New Document dialog box, then click the **Canvas Color box** ■.

4. Select the value in the Swap colors text box, type **#0099FF**, as shown in Figure 8, press **[Enter]** (Win) or **[return]** (Mac), then click **OK**.

    A new Document window appears in the Fireworks window.

    TIP You can also select a canvas color by clicking a color swatch in the color pop-up window. The canvas color appears in the Default colors box.

5. Click **File** on the Application bar, click **Save As**, type **my_blue_heaven** in the File name text box (Win) or Save As text box (Mac), click the **Save in list arrow** (Win) or **Where box list arrow** (Mac) to choose your destination drive and folder, then click **Save**.

6. Compare your document to Figure 9.

You set the size and color of the canvas for a new document, and then saved it.

FIGURE 8

Selecting a canvas color in the New Document dialog box

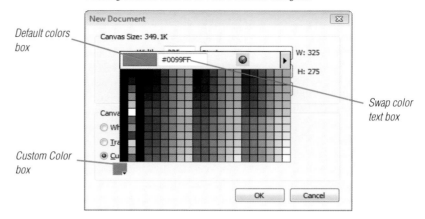

Default colors box

Custom Color box

Swap color text box

FIGURE 9

Newly created document with custom canvas

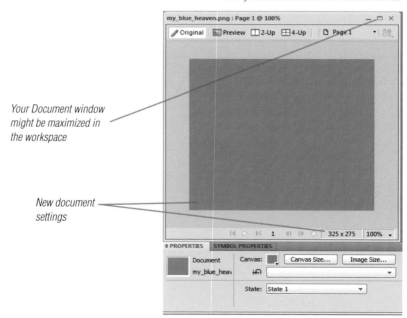

Your Document window might be maximized in the workspace

New document settings

Getting Started with Adobe Fireworks

FIGURE 10
Using Help in Fireworks

Your browser might differ

Type keywords here

Click to expand topic

Select check box

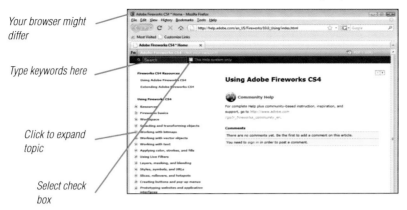

FIGURE 11
Help search results

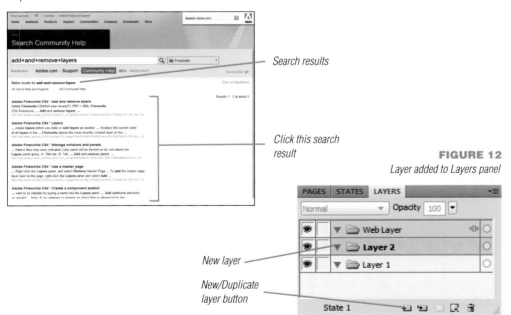

Search results

Click this search result

FIGURE 12
Layer added to Layers panel

New layer

New/Duplicate layer button

Get Help and add a layer

1. Click **Help** on the Application bar, click **Fireworks Help**, then click **?Fireworks help (web)** in the list of links at the right.

   The Adobe Fireworks CS4 * Home window opens, as shown in Figure 10. Because web sites are updated constantly, your page might differ.

   TIP   You can also open the Help system by pressing [F1](Win).

2. Type **add and remove layers** in the Search text box at the top of the Help window, click the **This Help system only check box** to select it, then press **[Enter]** (Win) or **[return]** (Mac).

   Search results appear in the pane, as shown in Figure 11.

3. Click **Adobe Fireworks CS4* Add and remove layers**, read the instructions on adding a layer, then click the **Help window Close button**.

4. Click **Layers** in the Panels dock to open the Layers panel (if necessary), click the **New/Duplicate Layer button** in the Layers panel, then compare your Layers panel to Figure 12.

   A new layer, Layer 2, appears in the Layers panel above the active layer.

   TIP   Expand the Layers panel (if necessary) to see all the layers.

You used Help to get instructions for adding a layer in Fireworks, and then used that information to add a layer in the Layers panel.

Drag and drop an object

1. Click **File** on the Application bar, navigate to where you store your Data Files, click **pool.png**, click **Open**, drag the **pool.png tab** in the Document window until it appears as a separate Document window, then resize both windows as shown in Figure 13.

   The documents first appear on separate tabs in the same Document window, and then appear side by side.

2. Make sure that the **Pointer tool** is selected in the Tools panel.

3. Click the mouse anywhere on the pool image, drag it to the my_blue_heaven document, then compare your image to Figure 14.

   > TIP You can also select the object, click Edit on the Application bar, click Copy, position the pointer in the target document, click Edit on the Application bar, then click Paste.

4. Close pool.png without saving changes.

5. Click the **Align panel** at the top of the panels dock.

6. Click the **Position button** so it is darkened (To canvas), click the **Align horizontal center icon**, then click the **Align vertical center icon** in the Align section.

   The image is centered on the canvas horizontally and vertically. See Figure 15.

7. Collapse the Align panel, click **File** on the Application bar, then click **Save**.

You copied an object from one document to another, and then aligned the object on the canvas.

FIGURE 13
Viewing open documents in separate Document windows

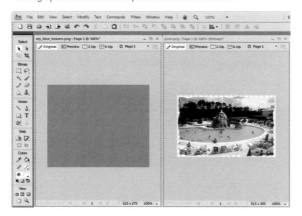

FIGURE 14
Copying an object from one document to another

Copied object

FIGURE 15
Object aligned to canvas

To Canvas option (darkened)

Align vertical center icon

Align horizontal center icon

FIGURE 16
Applying an Inner Shadow filter

*Filter applied
to image*

*Inner Shadow
pop-up window*

FIGURE 18
Filters applied to image

FIGURE 17
Photoshop Live Effects dialog box

*Bevel and Emboss
check box*

Effect settings

Apply filters to an image

1. Verify that the bitmap image is selected, then click the **Pointer tool** in the Tools panel (if necessary).

2. Click the **Add live filters button** in the Property inspector, point to **Shadow and Glow**, click **Inner Shadow**, then compare your screen to Figure 16.

   The Inner Shadow pop-up window opens, where you can adjust settings for the filter.

3. Press **[Enter]** (Win) or **[return]** (Mac) to close the pop-up window and apply the filter.

4. Click the **Add live filters button** in the Property inspector, click **Photoshop Live Effects**, click the **Bevel and Emboss check box**, then click **Bevel and Emboss** (Mac), to view Bevel and Emboss options.

   The Photoshop Live Effects dialog box opens, as shown in Figure 17.

5. Click the **Style list arrow**, click **Outer Bevel**, then click **Ok**.

   The Outer Bevel effect is applied to the image.

6. Click a blank part of the Document window, then compare your screen to Figure 18.

7. Save your work, then close my_blue_heaven.png.

You applied native Fireworks and Photoshop filters to an image.

WORK WITH
LAYERS AND IMAGES

What You'll Do

 In this lesson, you will modify a bitmap image and create and lock a layer.

Understanding the Layers Panel

Although *layer* is a common term in graphic design applications, a layer's function varies depending on the program. In other applications, such as Adobe Photoshop, you use layers to manipulate **pixels**, discrete squares of color values that can be drawn in a document. In Fireworks, you use layers to position **objects**, which are the individual elements in your document. You can arrange the elements in your document in a logical design order. For example, you can place related elements on the same layer, such as the design elements of a logo, or all the buttons for a web page. The position of objects/layers in the Layers panel affects their appearance in your document.

Each object is akin to an image on a clear piece of acetate—you can stack them on top of each other. The artwork on the bottom may be obscured by the layers above it but you can adjust visibility by making some pieces more transparent.

You can place as many objects as you want on a layer, arrange them in any order, and select one or more of them at a time. A document can easily accumulate numerous layers and objects, which can make it difficult to quickly find the ones you want. Figure 19 shows components of the Layers panel. You can collapse layers, lock layers to prevent any inadvertent editing, duplicate layers, create sub layers, and hide or show layers.

Customizing your view of the Layers panel

You can select the size of the thumbnails that are displayed in the Layers panel or choose not to display them at all. To change thumbnail size, click the Options menu button in the Layers panel, click Thumbnail Options, then select the size you want.

Understanding Bitmap Images and Vector Objects

Fireworks allows you to work with both bitmap and vector graphic images in your document. A **bitmap graphic** represents a picture image as a matrix of dots, or pixels, on a grid. Bitmaps allow your computer screen to realistically depict the pixel colors in a photographic image. In contrast, **vector graphics** are mathematically calculated objects composed of anchor points and straight or curved line segments, which you can fill with color or a pattern and outline with a stroke.

Because a bitmap image is defined pixel by pixel, when you scale a bitmap graphic, you lose the sharpness of the original image. **Resolution** refers to the number of pixels in an image, which affects an image's clarity and fineness of detail. On-screen resolution is usually 72 or 96 pixels per inch (ppi). (Print graphics require higher resolution.)

Bitmap images are resolution-dependent—resizing results in a loss of image quality. The most visible evidence is the all-too-familiar jagged appearance in the edges of a resized image.

Because they retain their appearance regardless of how you resize or skew them, vector graphics offer far more flexibility than bitmap images. They are resolution-independent—enlarging retains a crisp edge. Figure 20 compares the image quality of enlarged vector and bitmap images.

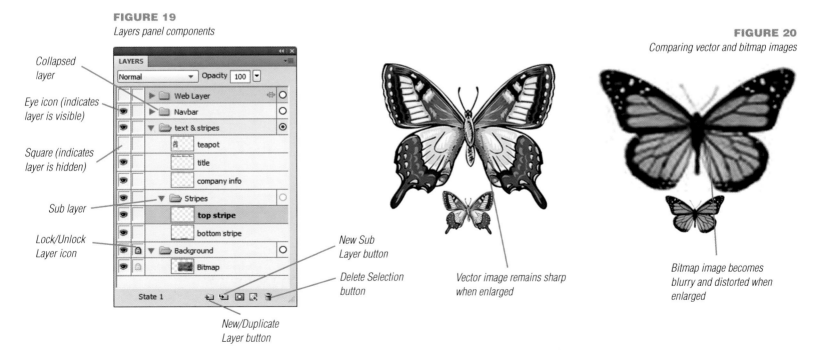

FIGURE 19
Layers panel components

Collapsed layer

Eye icon (indicates layer is visible)

Square (indicates layer is hidden)

Sub layer

Lock/Unlock Layer icon

New Sub Layer button

Delete Selection button

New/Duplicate Layer button

FIGURE 20
Comparing vector and bitmap images

Vector image remains sharp when enlarged

Bitmap image becomes blurry and distorted when enlarged

Open a document and display the Layers panel

1. Open fw1_1.png, then save it as **breads**.

2. Make sure that the Layers panel is displayed and expanded to show all the layers.

3. Click the **Eye icon** 👁 next to the Great_Crusts object in Layer 1 in the Layers panel to hide the layer.

   Notice that the Show/Hide Layer icon toggles between an eye icon and a blank box, depending on whether the layer is hidden or visible.

4. Compare your image to Figure 21, then click the **Show/Hide Layer icon** ☐ next to the Great_Crusts object in Layer 1.

5. Click the **Great_Crusts object** in Layer 1 in the Layers panel, then drag it beneath the Loaves&Brie object in the Background layer until a flashing double line (Win) or dark black line (Mac) appears beneath the Loaves&Brie object, as shown in Figure 22.

   The Great_Crusts object is now beneath or behind the Loaves&Brie object in the Background layer, so it is no longer visible, although you can still see its blue selection line.

6. Verify that the Great_Crusts object is still selected, then click the **Delete Selection button** 🗑 in the Layers panel.

You hid and displayed an object in a layer in the Layers panel and moved and deleted an object. Moving an object in the Layers panel affects its visibility in the document.

FIGURE 21
Hiding a layer in the Layers panel

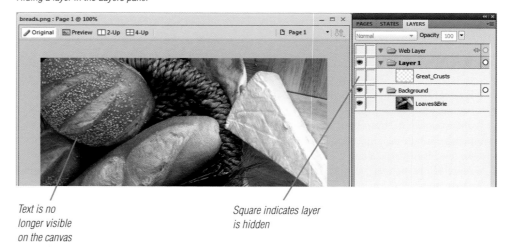

Text is no longer visible on the canvas

Square indicates layer is hidden

FIGURE 22
Moving an object to a different layer

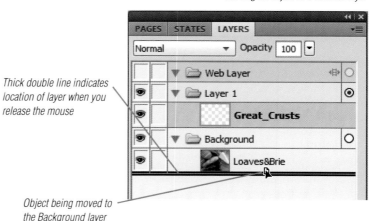

Thick double line indicates location of layer when you release the mouse

Object being moved to the Background layer

FIGURE 23
Brightness/Contrast dialog box

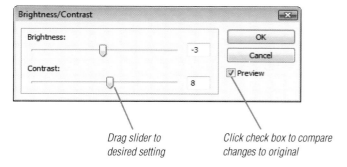

Drag slider to
desired setting   Click check box to compare
                       changes to original

FIGURE 24
Layer locked in Layers panel

Click square in lock
column to lock layer

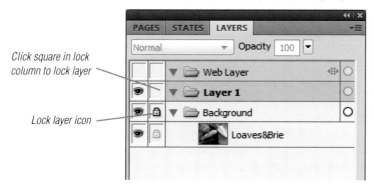

Lock layer icon

Edit a bitmap image and lock a layer

1. Click the **Loaves&Brie object** on the Background layer to select it (if necessary).

2. Click **Filters** on the Application bar, point to **Adjust Color**, then click **Brightness/Contrast**.

    Brightness adjusts the relative lightness or darkness of an image. Contrast adjusts the relative differences in intensity between the darkest and brightest parts of an image.

3. Drag the Brightness slider to **–3**, then drag the Contrast slider to **8**.

    You cannot delete or modify a filter you apply from the Application bar. You can, however, undo the action in the current editing session.

    TIP   You can also enter values in the text boxes.

4. Compare your Brightness/Contrast dialog box to Figure 23, then click **OK**.

    The colors in the image appear richer.

5. Click the **blank box** ☐ in the column in between the eye icon 👁 and the Background folder icon to lock the layer.

    The Lock layer icon 🔒 replaces ☐ in the column. You can lock entire layers or individual objects.

    TIP   While it is locked, you cannot edit a layer or its objects.

6. Compare your Layers panel to Figure 24.

7. Click **File** on the Application bar, then click **Save**.

You adjusted the brightness and contrast of the Loaves&Brie object, locked the layer, and saved the file.

CREATE
SHAPES

What You'll Do

▶ *In this lesson, you will display rulers and guides, and create and modify a vector object.*

Using Rulers, Guides, and the Grid

Rulers, guides, and the grid are design aids that help you precisely align and position objects in your document. Because Fireworks graphics are web-oriented, where the rule of measurement is in pixels, ruler units are always in pixels. You insert guides from the rulers by dragging them onto your canvas. Guides do not print or export, although you can save them in the original .png document. If you want to specify an exact location, you can double-click a guide and then enter a position in the Move Guide dialog box. You can adjust the grid to snap objects directly to guides and the grid.

> QUICKTIP
>
> To change guide and grid settings, click Edit on the Application bar, click Preferences, click Guides and Grids, then make desired changes.

Sizing and Repositioning Objects

You can use the Property inspector to view information about the position of the pointer on the canvas and selected objects. When an object is selected, its position on the canvas is shown in the left corner of the Property inspector. The W and H values show the object's size, while the X and Y values show the object's position on the canvas. You can use the coordinate values to create, resize, or move an object to a precise location. You can also resize and move objects by dragging their sizing handles and moving them on the canvas.

Using the Tools Panel

The Tools panel contains selection, drawing, and editing tools. Although you can use many tools on both bitmap and vector graphics, graphic mode-specific tools are housed in separate sections of the Tools panel. You can also select a tool by pressing its keyboard shortcut, shown in Figure 25.

Some tools have multiple tools associated with them. A small arrow in the lower-right corner of a tool button indicates that more tools are available in that tool group. To select additional tools, click and hold the tool, then click the tool you want from the list, as shown in Figure 25. The properties associated with a selected tool are displayed in the Property inspector, although not all tools have properties associated with them. For example, when you select any of the basic tools or Auto Shapes, such as the Ellipse tool or the Arrow Auto Shape, you can adjust the object's fill and stroke settings in the Property inspector.

Based on the object, layer, or tool, Fireworks automatically determines

whether you are editing a bitmap or a vector graphic, and activates or nullifies the tool appropriately. Figure 26 shows the Blur tool (a bitmap tool) actively blurring the floral bitmap image, but the tool can't blur the text because text is a vector object. Bitmap selection tools modify the pixels in a bitmap image, which makes them useful for retouching photographic images.

You can create vector shapes using the tools in the Vector portion of the Tools panel. The shape tool group is divided into two groups: basic shape tools (Ellipse, Rectangle, and Polygon tools) and Auto Shapes. You can adjust the height, width, and overall size of basic shapes by dragging their sizing handles. You can also use the

Subselection tool to adjust individual points in any shape.

Understanding Auto Shapes

You can create basic shapes or Auto Shapes by selecting the shape and then dragging the mouse pointer on the canvas. For Auto Shapes, you can also click the canvas to create a presized Auto Shape. Auto Shapes are complex vector shapes that you can manipulate by dragging control points. A **control point** is the yellow diamond that appears when you select an Auto Shape on the canvas. When you roll the mouse pointer over a control point, a tool tip appears,

FIGURE 25

Selecting tools in the Tools panel

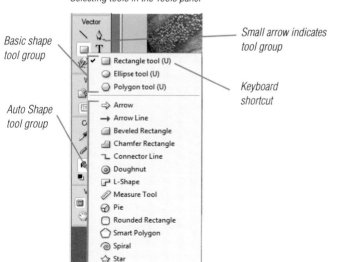

Basic shape tool group

Auto Shape tool group

Small arrow indicates tool group

Keyboard shortcut

FIGURE 26

Using a bitmap tool on different graphic types

Blur tool is inactive on text vector object

Blur tool pointer is active on bitmap image

giving you information on how to adjust the Auto Shape. You can adjust individual aspects specific to each shape, such as tips, corners, roundness, the number of points or sectors, and so on. Figure 27 shows the control points for an Auto Chamfer Rectangle and for an Auto Polygon. You can modify an Auto Shape by dragging the control point or by pressing a keyboard shortcut key, such as [Shift], [Alt], and [Ctrl] (Win); or [Shift], [option], and [⌘] (Mac).

Figure 28 shows how you can radically alter the appearance of an Auto Shape by dragging control points and using the Subselection tool.

QUICKTIP

To access additional Auto Shapes in Fireworks, open the Shapes panel, and then drag one of the displayed Auto Shapes to the canvas. To download Auto Shapes from the Adobe Exchange website, click the Options menu button in the Shapes panel, and then click Get More Auto Shapes.

Applying Fills and Strokes

You can fill an object with a solid color, texture, or pattern. When you apply a **fill**, you can adjust the following attributes: its color and category (such as solid, gradient, or pattern), and the type and amount of edge of the fill. You can apply a border, known as a **stroke**, to an object's edge. You can set several stroke attributes, including color, tip size (the size of the stroke), softness, and texture.

Anti-aliasing blends the edges of a stroke or text with surrounding pixels so that the edges appear to smooth into the background. Anti-aliasing reduces the contrast between the edge and the background by adding pixels of intermediate color.

QUICKTIP

Aliasing can occur when an analog image is represented in a digital mode, such as a graphic image viewed on a computer. The edges of the graphic are rectangles and squares, which do not always illustrate a curve well.

FIGURE 27
Control points for Auto Shapes

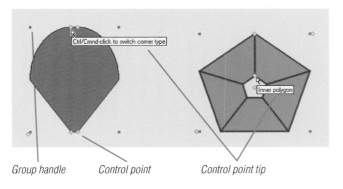

Group handle   Control point   Control point tip

FIGURE 28
Auto Shape variants

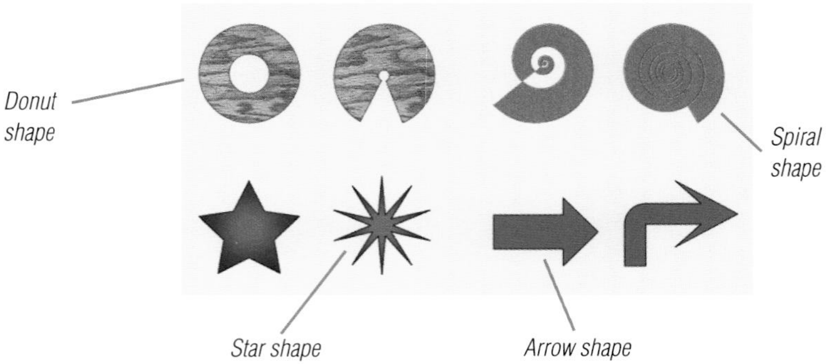

Donut shape

Spiral shape

Star shape   Arrow shape

FIGURE 29
Guides displayed in Document window

Renamed layer

Guide

Display the guides

1. Verify that Layer 1 is active, then click the **New/Duplicate Layer button** ⬕ in the Layers panel to create a new layer, Layer 2.

2. Double-click **Layer 2**, type **AdCopy** in the Layer name text box, then press **[Enter]** (Win) or **[return]**(Mac).

3. Click **View** on the Application bar, point to **Guides**, then click **Show Guides** (if necessary).

   Horizontal and vertical guides appear in the Document window, as shown in Figure 29.

You created and named a layer, and displayed guides in the Document window.

Create a vector object

1. Click and hold the **Rectangle tool** ▢ in the Tools panel, then click the **Rounded Rectangle tool** ▢.

   TIP The basic Rectangle shape has a Rectangle roundness setting on the Property inspector, which you can use to create a rounded rectangle basic shape.

2. Click the **Fill category list arrow** in the Property inspector, click **Solid** (if necessary), then click the **Fill Color box** 🖑 ▢ to open the color pop-up window.

(continued)

3. Click the **far-right swatch** in the second row from the bottom (#FFFFCC) , as shown in Figure 30.

4. Click the **Edge of fills list arrow**, click **Anti-Alias** (if necessary), click the **Texture name list arrow**, click **Grain** (if necessary), click the **Amount of texture list arrow**, then drag the slider to **10**, then click the **Transparent check box**.

   | TIP   Fireworks automatically applies the last selected stroke and fill to an object.

5. Use the guides to position the pointer ✛ at the start coordinates shown in Figure 31, click, then drag the pointer until **220** appears in the Selection width box in the Property inspector and **110** appears in the Selection height box.

6. Click **Edit** on the Application bar, then click the **Undo Shape Tool** (Win) or **Undo Auto Shape Tool** (Mac).

   The rectangle disappears.

   | TIP   You can also press [Ctrl][Z](Win) or [⌘][Z](Mac) to undo a command.

7. Click **Edit** on the Application bar, click **Redo Shape Tool** (Win) or **Redo Auto Shape Tool** (Mac), then compare your image to Figure 31.

   | TIP   You can also press [Ctrl][Y](Win) or [⌘][Y](Mac) to redo a command.

You set properties for the Rounded Rectangle tool, created a rounded rectangle shape, and then practiced undo and redo commands.

FIGURE 30
Selecting a fill color

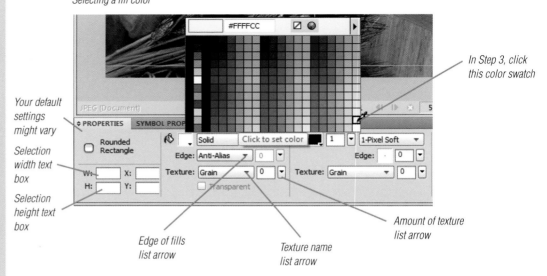

In Step 3, click this color swatch

Your default settings might vary

Selection width text box

Selection height text box

Edge of fills list arrow

Texture name list arrow

Amount of texture list arrow

FIGURE 31
Newly created rounded rectangle shape

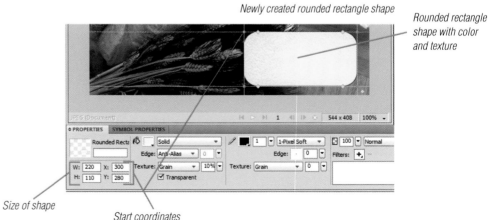

Rounded rectangle shape with color and texture

Size of shape

Start coordinates

FIGURE 32
Stroke properties

*Stroke
category*

Tip size

*Edge
softness*

*Texture
name*

*Amount of
texture*

Apply a stroke to an object

1. Click the **Stroke Color box** ✎ ■ in the Property inspector, type **#FF9900** in the Swap colors text box, then press **[Enter]** (Win) or **[return]** (Mac).

   TIP   If Grain is not selected as the Texture, click the Texture list arrow, then click Grain.

2. Click the **Stroke category list arrow**, point to **Charcoal**, then click **Creamy**.

3. Click the **Tip size list arrow**, then drag the slider to **6**.

4. Enter the remaining stroke values shown in Figure 32.

5. Click **View** on the Application bar, point to **Guides**, then click **Show Guides** to turn off guides.

6. Click **Select** on the Application bar, click **Deselect** (if necessary), then compare your image to Figure 33.

7. Save your work.

You fine-tuned stroke properties to add a border to an object that suits the style and mood you want to create. You selected stroke properties, applied a stroke to the rectangle, and turned off the guides. You used the Deselect command so that you could see the results of your work without seeing the selection bounding box.

FIGURE 33
Stroke settings applied to rounded rectangle

CREATE AND
MODIFY TEXT

What You'll Do

In this lesson, you will create text and a path, attach the text to the path, save your document, and then exit the program.

Using Text in a Document
The text features in Fireworks are typical of most desktop publishing programs—after you select the Text tool, you can preview the font family and modify properties, including size, color, style, kerning, leading, alignment, text flow, offset, and anti-alias properties. **Kerning** adjusts the spacing between adjacent letters, **tracking** affects a block of text or a range of letters, and **leading** adjusts the amount of space between lines of text. You can set other text attributes, such as indent, alignment, the space before and after a paragraph, and baseline shift, in the Property inspector. Figure 34 shows Text tool properties in the Property inspector. You can automatically preview in your document the changes you make to Text tool properties.

After you create text, you can edit the text block as a whole, or edit just a range of text. When you create text, you can create auto-sizing or fixed-width text blocks. **Auto-sizing** means that the text block expands to accommodate the text you enter. If you delete text, the text block contracts. You can spell check text at any time, including selecting multiple text blocks to check their spelling.

> **QUICK**TIP
> You can change the orientation of any selected text block by clicking the Set text orientation button in the Property inspector, and then selecting a vertical or horizontal text orientation.

Using text blocks
Fireworks creates auto-sized text blocks by default. The text block expands or contracts as you add or delete text. To create a fixed-width text block, select the Text tool, then drag to create a text block on the canvas. As you type, the text will wrap to fit the text block.

Attaching Text to a Path

You can manipulate text by creating a path, and then attaching text to it. A **path** is an open or closed vector consisting of a series of anchor points. **Anchor points** join path segments—they delineate changes in direction, whether a corner or a curve. To create a path, you use the Pen tool to define points in your document, and then attach the text to it. You can edit text after you've attached it to a path. You can also edit the path, but only if it is not attached to text. Figure 35 shows text attached to paths.

QUICKTIP

You can also attach text to paths created with a basic shape tool or to paths of Auto Shapes that you've modified with the Freeform tool or the Reshape Area tool.

To edit a path, you adjust the anchor points. To adjust the anchor points, select the path, select the Subselection tool in the Tools panel, and then drag points to new locations on the path as desired. You can also modify the appearance of text on a path by changing its alignment, orientation, and direction. By combining the shape of the path with the text alignment, orientation, and direction, you can create unique-looking text objects that convey the exact message you want.

FIGURE 34
Text options in the Property inspector

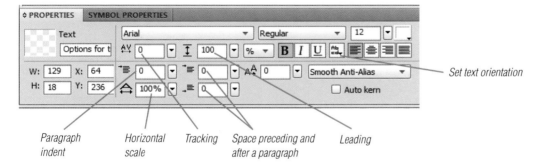

Paragraph indent

Horizontal scale

Tracking

Space preceding and after a paragraph

Leading

Set text orientation

FIGURE 35
Stroke settings applied to rounded rectangle

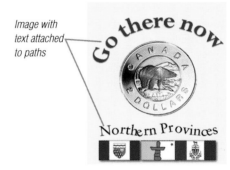

Image with text attached to paths

Paths visible with text attached

Create text using the Text tool

1. Click the **Text tool** T in the Tools panel.

2. Click the **Font Family list arrow** in the Property inspector, click **Times New Roman**, verify that Regular appears as the Font Style, double-click the **Size text box**, then type **36**.

3. Click the **Fill Color box** ☐ in the Property inspector, type **#663300** in the Swap colors text box, then press **[Enter]** (Win) or **[return]** (Mac).

4. Click the **Faux Bold button** B in the Property inspector to select it.

5. Click the **Faux Italic button** *I* to select it.

6. Click the **Auto kern check box** to select it.

7. Verify that the Center alignment button ☰ and Smooth Anti-Alias options are selected, then compare your Property inspector to Figure 36.

(continued)

FIGURE 36
Setting Text tool properties

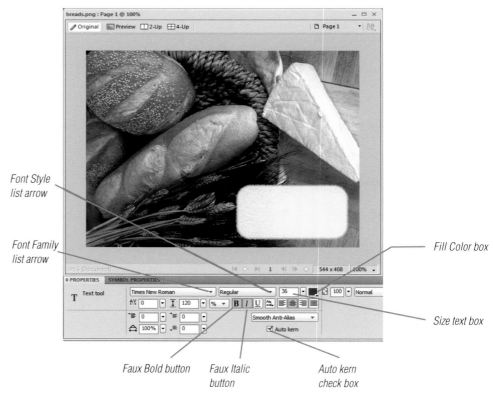

Font Style list arrow

Font Family list arrow

Fill Color box

Size text box

Faux Bold button

Faux Italic button

Auto kern check box

FIGURE 37
Formatted and aligned text

8. Click the top middle of the rectangle, type **Upper Crust**, press **[Enter]** (Win) or **[return]** (Mac), then type **Shoppe**.

   Text objects are automatically named with matching text in the Layers panel.

9. Expand the Align panel (if necessary), then make sure the Position button is not selected.

10. Click the **Pointer tool** 🔖 in the Tools panel, press and hold **[Shift]**, click the **rectangle** on the canvas, click the **Align horizontal center icon** ≜ in the Align panel, then click the **Align vertical center icon** ⬓.

    Both the rectangle and the text objects are selected and aligned to each other.

11. Click **Select** on the Application bar, then click **Deselect**.

    TIP   You can also press [Ctrl][D](Win) or ⌘[A](Mac) to deselect an object.

12. Compare your screen to Figure 37, then save your work.

Spell check text

1. Click the **Text tool** T in the Tools panel, double-click the **Size text box** in the Property inspector, type **24**, then verify that the Bold B and Italic *I* buttons are selected.

2. Click the **Fill Color box** in the Property inspector, type **#FFFFCC** in the Swap colors text box, then press **[Enter]** (Win) or **[return]** (Mac).

3. Click the basket at the top of the image, type **Baked the way you expcet**.

    The word "expcet" is intentionally mispelled.

4. Click **Text** on the Application bar, click **Check Spelling**, then click **Change**.

    The word "expect" is now spelled correctly, as shown in Figure 38.

    TIP If prompted to continue checking the current document, click Cancel. If prompted to select a dictionary, choose an appropriate language. If you have not used the spell checker in Fireworks before now, perform Spelling Setup.

5. Save your work.

You added text and then checked the spelling of the new text.

FIGURE 38
Results of spell checking

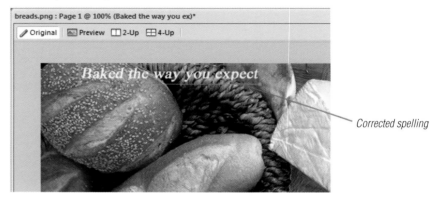

breads.png : Page 1 @ 100% (Baked the way you ex)*

Original Preview 2-Up 4-Up

Corrected spelling

FIGURE 39
Creating a path with the Pen tool

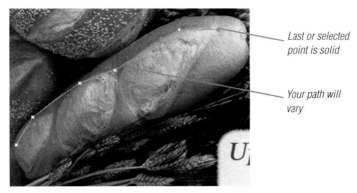

Last or selected
point is solid

Your path will
vary

FIGURE 40

Text attached to path

Create a path, attach text to it, then exit Fireworks

1. Click the **Pen tool** in the Tools panel.

2. Click the **Fill category list arrow** in the Property inspector, click **None** (if necessary), click the **canvas** in the locations shown in Figure 39, then double-click when you reach the last point.

   A path appears in the document and the path is complete.

3. Click the **Pointer tool** in the Tools panel, press and hold **[Shift]**, then click the **Baked the way you expect text** to select both the path and the text.

   TIP To select multiple objects on the canvas at once, press and hold [Shift] while selecting each object.

4. Click **Text** on the Application bar, then click **Attach to Path**.

   The text is attached to the path, but does not fill the entire path.

5. Double-click the **Horizontal scale text box** in the Property inspector, type **125**, then press **[Enter]** (Win) or **[return]** (Mac).

   The text fills the path.

6. Click a blank part of the Document window, then compare your image to Figure 40.

7. Save your work.

8. Click **File** on the Application bar, then click **Exit** (Win); or click **Fireworks**, then click **Quit Fireworks** (Mac).

You created a path using the Pen tool, attached text to it, then saved the document and exited the program.

Start Fireworks and open a document.

1. Start Fireworks.
2. Open fw1_2.png.
3. Undock the Layers panel (Win).
4. Collapse and expand the Layers panel.
5. Close fw1_2.png without saving changes.

Create a new document and use Help.

1. Create a new document and set the Width to 200, the Height to 145, and the Canvas Color to #804A0F.
2. Save the document as **pasta_1.png**.
3. Access Help and search for "master pages."
4. Read the topic on Working with Fireworks pages, then close the Help window.
5. Open the Pages panel, then open the Layers panel.
6. Open gnocchi.png.
7. Drag the object to pasta_1.png. (*Hint*: You might need to separate and resize the Document windows.)
8. Center the object on the canvas.
9. Close gnocchi.png without saving changes.
10. Deselect objects, then compare your image to Figure 41.
11. Save and close pasta_1.png.

Work with the Layers panel and edit a bitmap image.

1. Open fw1_2.png.
2. Save the file as **pasta_2.png**.
3. Select the Varieties object on the Background layer of the Layers panel, then apply the Auto Levels filter from the Adjust Color menu on the Filter menu.
4. Hide and display the Varieties object in the Layers panel.
5. Move the Ingredients object from Layer 1 above the Varieties object so that it is now in the Background layer.
6. Delete the Ingredients object.
7. Select the Varieties object.
8. Open the Brightness/Contrast dialog box, and set the Brightness to 5 and the Contrast to 8. (*Hint*: Use the Adjust Color command on the Filters menu.)
9. Lock the Background layer.
10. Save your work.

Create a vector object.

1. Display the guides.
2. Create a new layer above Layer 1.
3. Rename the newly created layer **Proper_Names**. (*Hint*: Double-click the layer name.)
4. Select the Smart Polygon tool.
5. Enter the following fill color properties in the Property inspector: Color: #66CC00, Fill category: Solid, Edge: Feather, Feather amount: 2, Texture: Burlap, and Texture amount: 20%.
6. Position the pointer at the top-left corner of the rectangle formed by the guides on the left jar.
7. Drag the pointer until the polygon is approximately W: 80 and H: 80.
8. Apply a stroke with the following properties: Color: #339900, Tip size: 2, Stroke Category: Air Brush Basic, Edge: 100, and Texture amount: 0.
9. Hide the guides, then save your work.

Create and modify text.

1. Select the Text tool.
2. Enter the following properties in the Property inspector: Font: Times New Roman, Size: 22 pt, Color: #000000, Bold, and Left alignment.

3. Click the pointer in the polygon, then type **Rotelie**.
4. Center the text in the rectangle (if necessary), then deselect it.
5. Make sure that the Text tool is selected, then enter the following properties: Font: Impact, Size: 66 pt, Color: #990000, Bold, and Justified alignment.
6. Click the pointer on top of the jars, then type **Pasta Pasta Pasta**.
7. Deselect the Pasta Pasta Pasta text.
8. Select the L-Shape tool in the Tools panel, then create an L shape that is W: 140 and H: 250.
9. Select Subselection tool in the Tools panel, click the L-shape, then select the shape and the text. (*Hint*: The Subselection tool is next to the Pointer tool.)
10. Attach the Pasta Pasta Pasta text to the path.
11. Move the text on a path to the top and right side of the canvas.
12. Compare your document to Figure 42, then deselect the text on the path.
13. Save your work.

FIGURE 41
Completed Skills Review

FIGURE 42
Completed Skills Review

You are in charge of new services at Crystal Clear Consulting. You're preparing to roll out a new Crisis Solutions division, designed to help companies that are experiencing management or financial difficulties. You plan to brief your coworkers on the services at an upcoming company lunch. Each department head—including you—is going to submit a sample introductory web ad announcing the division. You'll use your Fireworks skills to design a simple ad.

1. Obtain images that symbolize the new consulting service. You will import and copy these images to a layer in the document. You can take your own photos, use scanned media, or obtain an image from your computer or from the Internet. When downloading from the Internet, you should always assume the work is protected by copyright. Be sure to check the website's terms of use to determine if you can use the work for educational, personal, or noncommercial purposes. Always check the copyright information on any media you download.

2. Create a new document and save it as **crystal.png**.

3. Import or open one of the images you obtained in Step 1 so that it serves as the background.

4. Rename Layer 1 **Background**.

5. Create a new layer and give it an appropriate name based on your images.

6. Open another image that you obtained in Step 1 and copy it to the document.

7. Create at least one vector object and apply a fill and stroke to it.

8. Create a new layer and name it **Text Objects**.

9. Create at least two text objects.

10. Attach at least one text object to a path, then rename the object in the Layers panel, if necessary.

11. Save your work, then examine the sample shown in Figure 43.

FIGURE 43
Sample Completed Project Builder 1

You've just completed your first class in Fireworks. Afterward, you meet with your boss to summarize some of the interesting ways you can attach text to a path. She asks you to prepare a few samples for the next staff meeting.

1. Create a new document and name it **meandering_paths.png**.
2. Create a text object that is at least 15 characters long (you can use the font of your choice and as many words as you want). (*Hint*: You can also apply Orientation commands on the Text menu to the text on the path.)
3. Duplicate the text object two times, then drag the text objects to distribute them on the canvas. (*Hint*: Drag the text layer on top of the New/Duplicate layer button in the Layers panel.)
4. Create a basic shape, then attach one of the text objects to it.
5. Create an Auto Shape, then attach a text object to it. (*Hint*: To select the path of an Auto Shape, select the Subselection tool next to the Pointer tool in the Tools panel, then click the Auto Shape.)
6. Create a simple path using the Pen tool, then attach the third text object to it.
7. Rename the layers to identify the Pen tool or the shape you used as a path.
8. Save your work, then examine the sample shown in Figure 44.

FIGURE 44

Sample Completed Project Builder 2

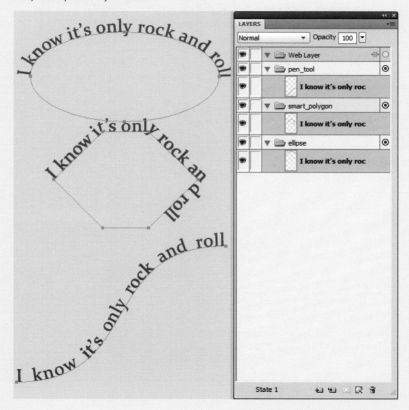

You can develop your design and planning skills by analyzing websites. Figure 45 shows the home page of the Florida Keys National Marine Sanctuary website. Study the image and answer the following questions. Because dynamic websites are updated frequently to reflect current trends, this page might be different from Figure 45 when you open it online.

1. Connect to the Internet and go to *http://floridakeys.noaa.gov/*.
2. Open a document in a word processor, or open a new Fireworks document, then save the file as **floridakeys**.
3. Explore the site and answer the following questions. (*Hint*: If you work in Fireworks, use the Text tool.) For each question, indicate how you determined your answer.
   - What vector shapes does the page contain?
   - What fills or strokes have been added to vector shapes?
   - Do objects appear to have been manipulated in some manner? If so, how?
   - Do objects or text overlap? If so, list the order in which the objects could appear in the Layers panel. List from top to bottom.
   - Has text been attached to a path?
   - What is the overall effect of the text?

FIGURE 45
Sample Completed Design Project

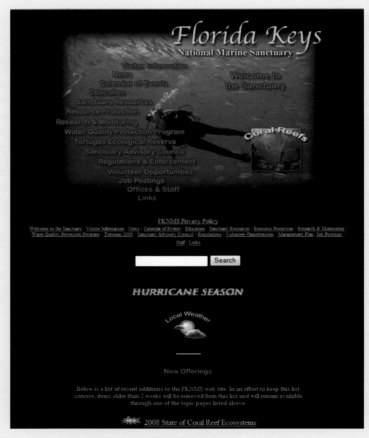

Florida Keys National Marine Sanctuary — http://floridakeys.noaa.gov/

You volunteer to help the Education Committee for Cultural Consequence, a cultural anthropology group. The group is constructing a website that examines facial expressions and moods in people around the world. The committee is in charge of developing emoticons—a shorthand method of expressing moods—for the website. The images will be in the style of the smiley face. You can use the facial expression of your choice in developing the emoticon.

1. Choose an emotion and the emoticon that conveys that feeling.
2. Obtain at least two images for the expression you've chosen. You can take your own photos, or obtain images from your computer or from the Internet. When downloading from the Internet, you should always assume the work is protected by copyright. Be sure to check the website's terms of use to determine if you can use the work for educational, personal, or noncommercial purposes. Always check the copyright information on any media you download.
3. Create a new document, then save it as **emoticon.png**.
4. Choose a canvas color other than white.
5. Create a new layer named **Faces** and copy the images you've obtained to the new layer.
6. Create a new layer and name it with the emotion you selected in Step 1.

7. Create the emoticon on the layer created in Step 6 using tools in the Tools panel, and apply fills and strokes to them as desired. (*Hint*: The emoticon in the sample was created with the Ellipse tool and the Pencil tool.)
8. Create a text object that identifies the expression. (*Hint*: The text in the sample is Pristina.)
9. Save your work, then examine the sample shown in Figure 46.

FIGURE 46
Sample Completed Portfolio Project

2

WORKING WITH
OBJECTS

1. Work with vector tools

2. Modify multiple vector objects

3. Modify color

4. Apply filters to objects and text

5. Apply a style to text

2 WORKING WITH
OBJECTS

Understanding Vector Objects

Fireworks offers a number of vector tools you can use to create vector objects. There are many benefits to working with vector objects. For example, you can modify the properties of a vector path at any time—its shape, size, fill, and stroke—without affecting the quality of the image. This editability makes vector objects easy to work with and adds flexibility to your Web graphics.

After you create an object, you can use a variety of features to transform it into a visually interesting graphic. Many of the tools in Fireworks let you alter or enhance the object. You can combine multiple objects to create entirely new shapes using

various Combine Path commands. You can also modify a graphic's appearance by adjusting the alignment and grouping of multiple objects. You can change a path's color by filling it with a solid color, gradient color, or a texture, or by adjusting the stroke appearance.

The Stroke, Fill, and Filters sections in the Property inspector maximize your ability to experiment. You can create various combinations of strokes, fills, and filters, and turn them on or off in your document at will. An object's overall appearance varies depending on the order in which effects appear in the Filters list in the Property inspector.

Tools You'll Use

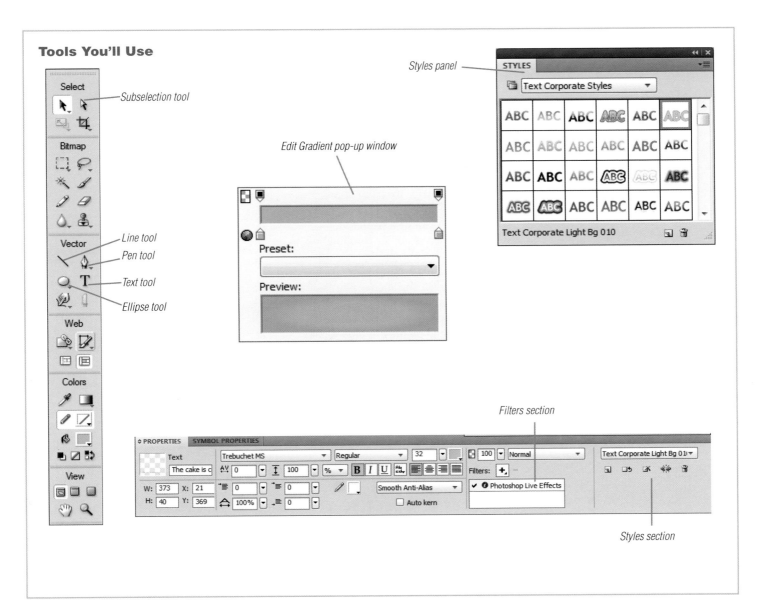

Subselection tool

Select

Bitmap

Vector
— Line tool
— Pen tool
— Text tool
— Ellipse tool

Web

Colors

View

Edit Gradient pop-up window

Preset:

Preview:

Styles panel

STYLES

Text Corporate Styles

Text Corporate Light Bg 010

Filters section

Styles section

◇ PROPERTIES   SYMBOL PROPERTIES

Text

Trebuchet MS   Regular   32   100   Normal   Text Corporate Light Bg 01

The cake is c   AV 0   100   %   **B** *I* U   Filters: +

W: 373   X: 21   0   0   Smooth Anti-Alias   ✓ ❶ Photoshop Live Effects

H: 40   Y: 369   100%   0   Auto kern

WORK WITH
VECTOR TOOLS

What You'll Do

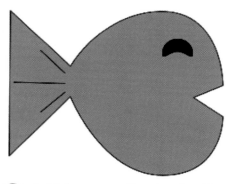

In this lesson, you will create and modify paths and objects using vector tools.

Understanding Vector Tools and Paths

A vector object can be a straight or curved path, or a group or combination of open, closed, straight, or curved paths. When you create a vector object, path segments connect the anchor points of a path. Paths can be open or closed. The points of an open path do not connect; the start and end points of a closed path do connect.

QUICKTIP

The basic Rectangle shape has a Rectangle roundness setting in the Property inspector, which you can use to create a rounded rectangle basic shape. You can choose between pixels or a percentage as your unit of measurement for the corners' curve.

You can draw free-form paths using the Vector Path and Pen tools. The Pen tool creates a path one point at a time.

Making additional points with the Pen tool and Subselection tool

To create a path with the Pen tool, you click the canvas to create corner points. You can create a curve point as you draw the path by dragging the mouse pointer as you click the canvas. If the newly created path is still selected, you can convert a corner point to a curve point by dragging the point with the Pen tool to create a curve point handle. If you want to convert a corner point that is on an existing path, select the path with the Subselection tool and then drag the point until curve point handles are visible.

The Vector Path tool creates paths in one motion. Fireworks automatically inserts anchor points as you drag the pointer on the canvas. Regardless of its initial shape, a vector object's path is always editable.

If the path of an object has curves, such as a circle, ellipse, or rounded rectangle, the circular points are known as **curve points**. If the path has angles or is linear, such as a square, star, or straight line, the square points are known as **corner points**. Figure 1 shows points selected for various objects. When you edit a vector object, you add, delete, or move points along the path; adjust the point handles; or change the shape of the path segment.

Using the Pen Tool and the Subselection Tool

You can add or delete points on a segment using the Pen tool. Modifying the number of points on a path allows you to manipulate it until you have created the exact shape you want. For example, adding points allows you to maneuver the path with greater precision, whereas deleting points simplifies the path's editability. If you want to move points on a path, you can use the **Subselection tool**. You can also use the Subselection tool to select the points of an individual object that has been grouped or to create a curved point.

QUICKTIP
To connect two unconnected paths, select the Pen tool, click the end point of one path, and then click the end point of the other path.

Each anchor point has one or more **point handle**; point handles are visible when you edit a curved path segment, but not when you edit a straight path segment. You can modify the size and angle of a curve by adjusting the length and position of the point handles. You can use both the Pen tool and the Subselection tool to create and modify point handles on curved paths, or to convert curve points into corner points and vice versa.

FIGURE 1
Points on paths

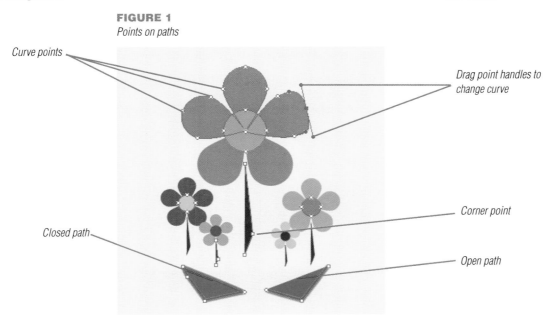

Curve points

Drag point handles to change curve

Corner point

Closed path

Open path

The two-dimensional curves in a vector object are known as **Bézier curves**, named after the French engineer who developed the mathematical formulas to represent three-dimensional (3D) automobile shapes. Figure 2 shows how you can manipulate a vector object by dragging its curve handles.

As you become more familiar with using vector objects, you can experiment with more intricate vector modifications. In the Pen tool group, you can use the Vector Path tool to draw a path with a selected stroke category and attributes; and the Redraw Path tool lets you extend or redraw a selected path. In the Freeform tool group, you can bend or reshape entire areas of a vector object by pushing and pulling the path; the Reshape Area tool distorts and stretches a path based on the size and strength of the brush tip; and, if you have

created a path that has a pressure-sensitive stroke, such as Air Brush Basic or Textured, or Calligraphy Bamboo, you can alter the stroke of a path. You can use the Knife tool to slice a path into multiple objects.

FIGURE 2
Modifying a Bezier curve on a vector path

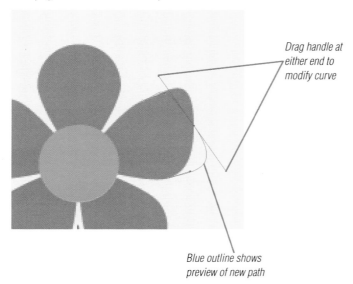

Drag handle at either end to modify curve

Blue outline shows preview of new path

FIGURE 3
Modified vector path

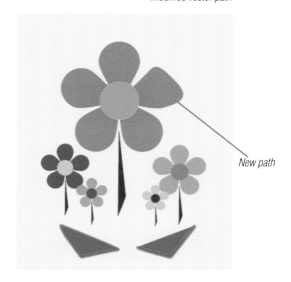

New path

FIGURE 4
Selecting a stroke category

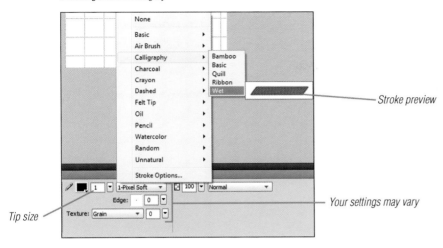

Tip size — Stroke preview — Your settings may vary

FIGURE 5
Creating a shape using the Pen tool

Use any anchor point as your starting and end points

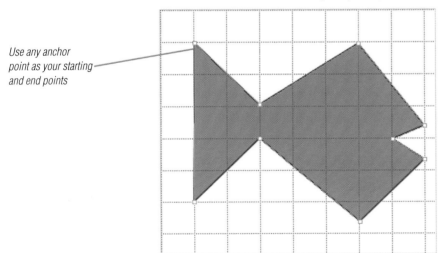

Create an object using the Pen tool

1. Create a new document, set the Width to **300**, set the Height to **275**, verify that the resolution is 72, the canvas color is white, then save it as **fish.png**.

2. Click **View** on the Application bar, point to **Grid**, then click **Show Grid**.

   TIP   You can use the grid to help align objects on the canvas.

3. Click the **Pen tool** in the Tools panel.

4. Click the **Fill Color box** in the Property inspector, type **#3399FF** in the Swap colors text box, then press **[Enter]** (Win) or **[return]** (Mac).

5. Click the **Stroke Color box** in the Property inspector, type **#000000** in the Swap colors text box, then press **[Enter]** (Win) or **[return]** (Mac).

6. Click the **Stroke category list arrow**, point to **Calligraphy**, point to **Wet**, compare your screen to Figure 4, then click **Wet**.

   TIP   You can preview stroke graphics in the Stroke category list.

7. Click the **canvas** in the locations shown in Figure 5.

   TIP   Close the path by clicking your first anchor point.

You created a new document, set properties for the Pen tool, and created a closed path.

Use the Pen tool and the Line tool to modify a path

1. Position the **Pen tool** 🖋 over the top corner point, then click and drag the point to the left to create a smooth curve, as shown in Figure 6.

   The sharp point smoothes into a curve, and the curve point handles are visible.

   | TIP   Undo your changes if you're not satisfied with the results.

2. Repeat Step 1, but click and drag the bottom corner point to the right then click a blank part of the Fireworks window to deselect the vector object.

   | TIP   To reselect the object, click the Subselection tool ▸ in the Tools panel.

3. Press and hold the **Rectangle tool** 🔲 in the Tools panel, then click the **Ellipse tool** ⬭.

   | TIP   If the Rectangle tool is not visible, click the selected tool.

4. In the Property inspector, verify that the **Stroke Color box** 🖋 ■ is black, click the **Fill Color box**, then click the **top-left black color swatch** in the color pop-up window.

5. Press and hold **[Shift]**, then draw the circle shown in Figure 7.

   | TIP   Pressing and holding [Shift] draws a perfect square or circle.

6. Click the **Line tool** ＼ in the Tools panel, then drag the pointer on the canvas to create the lines shown in Figure 8.

You modified an object using the Pen tool and the Line tool.

FIREWORKS 2-8

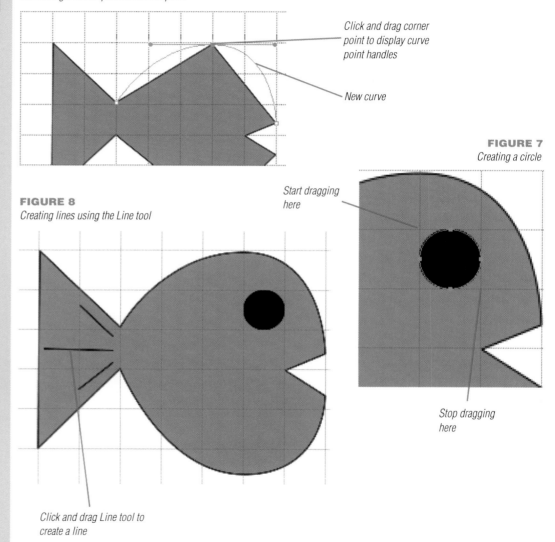

FIGURE 6
Converting a corner point to a curve point

Click and drag corner point to display curve point handles

New curve

FIGURE 7
Creating a circle

Start dragging here

Stop dragging here

FIGURE 8
Creating lines using the Line tool

Click and drag Line tool to create a line

FIGURE 9
Newly created document with custom canvas

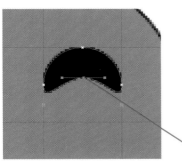

Drag curve handle up

FIGURE 10
Modified vector objects

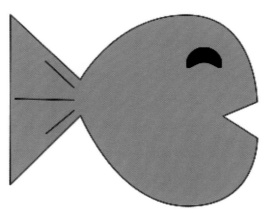

Use the Subselection tool to modify an object

1. Click the **Subselection tool** in the Tools panel, position the pointer over the bottom curve handle of the black circle, then click the **point**.

   TIP Click View on the Application bar, then click Zoom in if you want a larger view while you work.

2. Press and hold **[Shift]**, drag the **point** to the position shown in Figure 9, then click a blank part of the Document window to deselect the object.

   Pressing and holding [Shift] constrains the movement to a straight line.

3. Click **View** on the Application bar, point to **Grid**, then click **Show Grid** to turn off the grid.

4. Compare your image to Figure 10, then save your work.

5. Close fish.png.

You modified an object using the Subselection tool, and then closed the document.

MODIFY MULTIPLE
VECTOR OBJECTS

What You'll Do

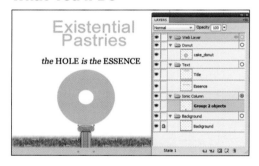

 In this lesson, you will create, copy, and align objects, and combine paths of vector objects using the Punch command. You will also group objects.

Aligning and Grouping Objects

Using vector shapes allows you to work with many individual objects at the same time. The Align commands on the Modify menu allow you to align two or more objects with each other: left, centered vertically, and so on. You can open the Align panel to further align, distribute, size, and space multiple objects or to align a vector object's anchor points.

You can also use the Group command on the Modify menu to configure objects on the canvas. The Group command allows you to combine two or more objects to make a single object. You can group any objects in your document: vector images, bitmap images, text, and so on. Fireworks preserves each individual object's shape and its placement in relation to the other objects. After you group objects, you can modify properties of the group as a whole; for example, by changing fill color or by applying a stroke. If you want to change any one of the objects, you can ungroup the objects, apply the change, and then regroup them. For example, if you want to change the stroke of one object in a group of vector shapes, you must first ungroup the objects before you can modify the individual stroke. However, if the grouped object consists of text and another vector object or bitmap image, you do not need to ungroup the objects to edit the text.

Combining the Paths of Multiple Objects

Fireworks offers six commands for combining paths: Join, Split, Union, Intersect, Punch, and Crop. Each command produces a different result. You must select two or more ungrouped vector objects before you can apply a combination command to them. The Combine Paths commands are described next, and most are illustrated in Figure 11. You can access combine path commands and additional path commands from the Path panel.

Join—The Join command allows you to combine the paths of two or more objects to create a single merged object that includes all the points of both paths. If the two objects are both closed, the new path is a **composite path**; if the objects are open, the new path is a **continuous path**. You can also use the Join command to join two open selected points. The first example in Figure 11 shows all three objects joined.

Split—You can split apart the paths of two or more objects that had been combined using the Join command. The Split command breaks a composite path in two, creating two or more simple objects and paths. Because the Split command is based on the joined path, and not the original objects, it is not the same as performing Undo.

Union—The Union command creates a path that is the sum total of all the selected paths.

If two paths overlap, the nonintersecting areas are also included. If the selected paths have different fill, stroke, or effects properties, the new path assumes the properties of the lowest object in the stacking order, or the lowest layer on the Layers panel. The union example in Figure 11 shows all three objects combined, with the same properties as the blue rectangle.

FIGURE 11
Sample Combine Path commands

Shapes used in Join and Union examples

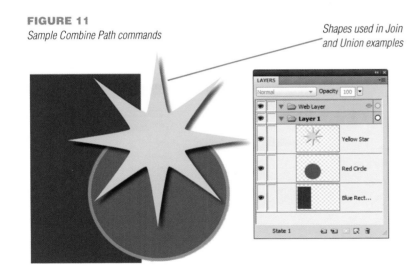

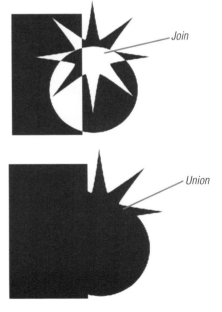

Join

Union

Intersect—The Intersect command creates an object consisting of the area that is common to the selected paths. If the selected paths have different fill, stroke, or effects properties, the new path assumes the properties of the lowest object in the stack (the bottom layer in the Layers panel). In the intersect example shown in Figure 11, the intersection is the area shared by the star and the circle. The shape is where the star overlaps on the circle, but the properties are the same as the circle's.

Punch—The outline of the top object carves through all of the lower selected images. In Figure 11, the *shape* of the star appears to slice through the circle below it. If the rectangle was also selected, the star would punch through that shape where it overlapped, as well. The fill, stroke, and effects properties are unaffected in the areas not being punched. In this example, Punch seems to produce the opposite effect than Intersect.

Crop—The shape of the top path is used to define the areas of the paths beneath it. While the area of the top object defines the object's shape, the fill, stroke, and filter properties of the objects placed further back are retained. In the crop example in Figure 11, the shape of the top object, the star, has the properties of both selected paths beneath it, the circle and the rectangle. When cropping multiple paths, you create two separate objects, as shown in the Layers panel in Figure 11.

QUICKTIP

Use the Group command if you want your objects to maintain independent fill, stroke, and filter settings. If you want to be able to manipulate the paths of two or more objects after you combine them, use the Join command instead of the Group command.

FIGURE 11
Sample Combine Path commands (continued)

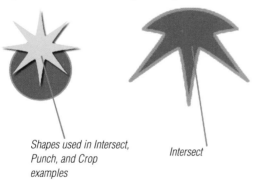

Shapes used in Intersect, Punch, and Crop examples

Intersect

Punch

Crop

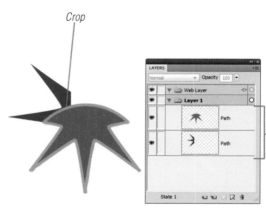

Results of Crop command create two paths with properties of original shapes

FIGURE 12
New layer added to Layers panel

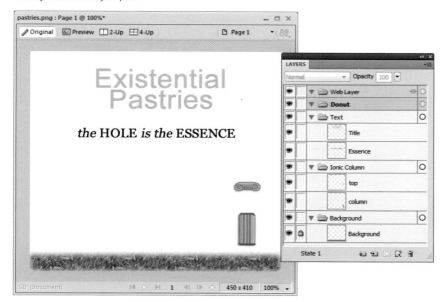

FIGURE 13
Viewing fill color settings

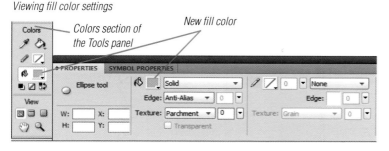

Colors section of the Tools panel

New fill color

1. Open fw2_1.png from where you store your Data Files, then save it as **pastries.png**.

2. Insert a layer above the Text layer on the Layers panel, double-click the **layer name**, type **Donut**, press [**Enter**] (Win) or [**return**] (Mac), then compare your screen to Figure 12.

3. Click the **Ellipse tool** ◯ in the Tools panel.

   TIP   You can modify the fill and stroke properties in the Property inspector or the Tools panel.

4. Click the **Stroke Color box** ✏ ▨ in the Tools panel, then click the **Transparent button** ▨ on the top of the color pop-up window, if necessary.

5. Click the **Fill Color box** ❧ ▭ in the Tools panel, type **#E5B900** in the Swap colors text box, then press [**Enter**] (Win) or [**return**] (Mac).

   TIP   If Solid does not appear as the fill option, click the Fill Options button, click the Fill Category list arrow, then click Solid.

6. Make sure that the Property inspector is open, that the Edge and Texture values in the Fill section are 0, then compare your Property inspector to Figure 13.

7. Click **View** on the Application bar, click **Rulers**, click **View** on the Application bar, then click **Tooltips**.

   Rulers appear at the top and left side of the Document window. Selecting Tooltips allows you to see measurements on the canvas as you create and edit objects.

(continued)

8. Position the pointer + on the canvas at approximately 130 H/180 V on the Rulers, press and hold **[Shift]**, then drag the pointer until W and H values display **165**, as shown in Figure 14.

An orange-yellow circle appears on the canvas and in the Donut layer in the Layers panel.

> TIP You can also enter 165 in the width and height text boxes in the Property inspector.

You created a new layer and a circle, and set the layer's properties and diameter.

Copy an object

1. Verify that the ellipse is selected, click **Edit** on the Application bar, then click **Copy**.

2. Click **Edit** on the Application bar, then click **Paste**.

A duplicate ellipse appears on the Layers panel and on the canvas.

> TIP You can also press [Ctrl][C] and [Ctrl][V] (Win) or ⌘[C] and ⌘[V] (Mac) to copy and paste a selection.

3. Click the **Fill Color box** ⬧ ☐ in the Property inspector, then click the **top-left black color swatch** in the color pop-up window.

4. Double-click the **W text box** in the Property inspector, type **44**, repeat for the H text box, then press **[Enter]** (Win) or **[return]** (Mac).

5. Compare your image to Figure 15.

You copied an object and changed its properties.

FIGURE 14
Creating a shape in a specific size and location

Rulers

Size

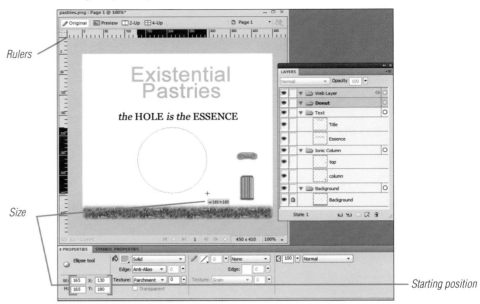

Starting position

FIGURE 15
Copied object

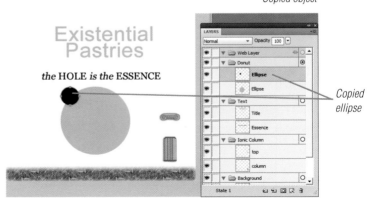

Copied ellipse

FIGURE 16
Aligned objects

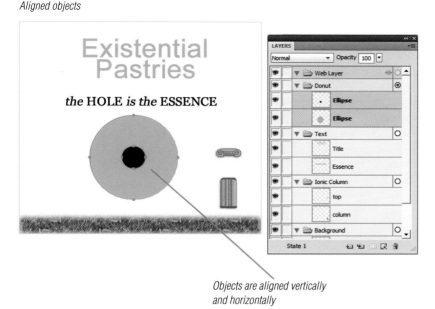

Objects are aligned vertically and horizontally

Align objects and combine paths

1. Click the **Pointer tool** in the Tools panel, then verify that the black circle is selected.

2. Press and hold **[Shift]**, then click the **orange circle** to select both objects.

3. Click **Modify** on the Application bar, point to **Align**, then click **Center Vertical**.

   TIP You can also press [Ctrl][Alt][2] (Win) or ⌘ [option][2] (Mac) to center objects vertically. You can press [Ctrl][Alt][5] (Win) or ⌘ [option][5] (Mac) to center objects horizontally.

4. Click **Modify** on the Application bar, point to **Align**, click **Center Horizontal**, then compare your image to Figure 16.

   The black circle is perfectly centered on the orange-yellow circle.

   (continued)

Cloning, copying, and duplicating

You can replicate any object using the Copy/Paste, Clone, or Duplicate commands on the Edit menu, or by pressing and holding [Alt] (Win) or [option] (Mac) and then dragging the object on the canvas. Each menu command creates an identical object and places it above the original on the Layers panel. The Copy/Paste and Clone commands replicate the object directly on top of the original object on the canvas. The Copy command places a copy of the object on the clipboard, which you can use to paste the object in other open files or in other programs. You can also use Copy/Paste commands to copy items on the Frames or Layers panels. The Duplicate command offsets the copied object 10 pixels down and to the right of the original.

5. Click **Modify** on the Application bar, point to **Combine Paths**, click **Union**, then notice the combined object.

   The black circle is no longer visible.

6. Click **Edit** on the Application bar, then click **Undo Union Paths**.

7. Click **Modify** on the Application bar, point to **Combine Paths**, click **Punch**, then compare your image to Figure 17.

   The paths combine to form a donut shape.

8. Double-click the **Composite Path layer** in the Layers panel, type **cake_donut**, press [**Enter**] (Win) or [**return**] (Mac), then compare your Layers panel to Figure 18.

   The object is renamed to a more intuitive name in the Layers panel and in the Path text box in the Property inspector.

   TIP   You can rename layers in the Layers panel or the Property inspector.

You aligned two objects and then combined their paths. You also undid a Combine Paths command and renamed the composite object.

FIGURE 17
Objects combined by the Punch command

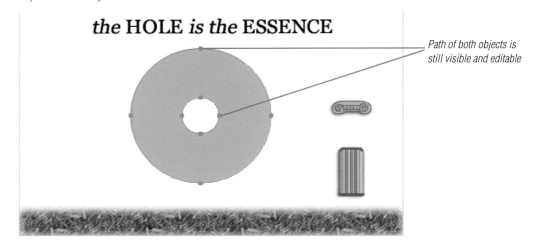

Path of both objects is still visible and editable

FIGURE 18
Renaming an object

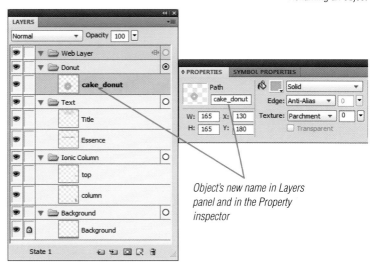

Object's new name in Layers panel and in the Property inspector

Working with Objects

FIGURE 19
Moved object

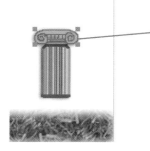

Top object selected as it
is being moved

FIGURE 20
Grouped objects

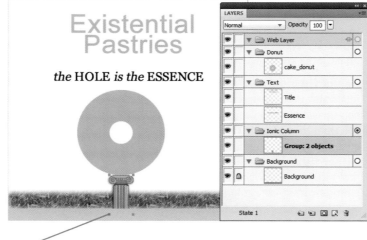

Grouped object has
single set of selection
handles

Group objects

1. Verify that the Pointer tool 🖰 is selected, then click the **top object** in the Ionic Column layer on the Layers panel.

2. Drag the **top object** on top of the column object, as shown in Figure 19.

3. Press and hold [**Shift**], then click the **column object** to select both objects.

   The selection handles for both objects are visible.

4. Click **Modify** on the Application bar, click **Group**, then notice that the object on the Layers panel is renamed Group: 2 objects.

   TIP   You can also press [Ctrl][G] (Win) or ⌘ [G] (Mac) to group objects.

5. Drag the **grouped object** under the circle, as shown in Figure 20.

   The selection handles for a single object are visible.

6. Change the name Group: 2 objects to **full_column**.

7. Save your work.

You grouped and moved objects.

MODIFY COLOR

What You'll Do

In this lesson, you will apply a gradient fill to the cake_donut object, and then modify the fill.

Understanding Fills and Gradients

After you create a vector shape, you can modify its appearance by changing its interior, or **fill**. The Property inspector provides powerful tools for enhancing fills in objects. You can apply several kinds of fills to an object, including solid, gradient, Web dither, and pattern. Some of the available fill patterns are shown in Figure 21.

A **solid fill** is the color swatch or hexadecimal value that you specify in the color pop-up window or in the Color Mixer. If you want to ensure that the colors in your document are Web-safe, you can use a **Web Dither fill.** A Web Dither fill approximates the color of a non-Web-safe color by combining two Web-safe colors. **Pattern fills** are bitmap images that have complex color schemes and textures. Fireworks offers dozens of preset patterns from which to choose, or you can create a pattern in Fireworks or another program and then add it to the list. A **gradient** consists of two or more colors that blend into each other in a fixed design. You can select from

several preset gradient fills, which you can apply to an object by choosing a fill category or by selecting the Gradient tool in the Tools panel. The Gradient tool, located as a tool option under the Paint Bucket tool, fills an object with the selected gradient, just as the Paint Bucket tool fills an object with the selected color.

> QUICKTIP
>
> You can transform or skew a fill's pattern or gradient by adjusting the width, position, rotation, and angle of the fill handles. The gradient adjusts to the contour of the path.

Whether you select a pattern or gradient as a fill, it becomes the active fill color visible in the Tools panel and in the Property inspector. There may be times when you apply a pattern or a gradient and instantly attain the look you want. You can also experiment by modifying the pattern or gradient by adding a transparent gradient, adding an edge or texture, and adjusting the respective amounts of each. The sophisticated styling you add to objects when you choose a pattern fill type can mimic real-world lighting, surface, and depth, and can have quite a dramatic result, as shown in Figure 22.

You can change gradient colors, including preset gradient colors, at any time without affecting the appearance of the gradient. The Edit Gradient pop-up window allows you to modify gradient colors and the transition from one color to the next by manipulating the color swatches beneath the **color ramp**. The color ramp creates and displays the range of colors in a gradient, including their transparency.

QUICKTIP

You can add a color to a gradient by clicking an area beneath the color ramp; to delete a color, drag it off the color ramp. To adjust gradient transparency, modify the opacity swatches above the color ramp.

FIGURE 21
Pattern categories

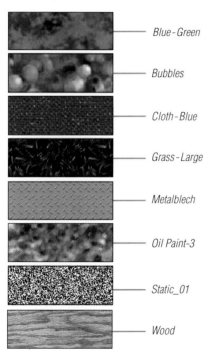

Blue - Green

Bubbles

Cloth - Blue

Grass - Large

Metalblech

Oil Paint-3

Static_01

Wood

FIGURE 22
Combining color or pattern and texture

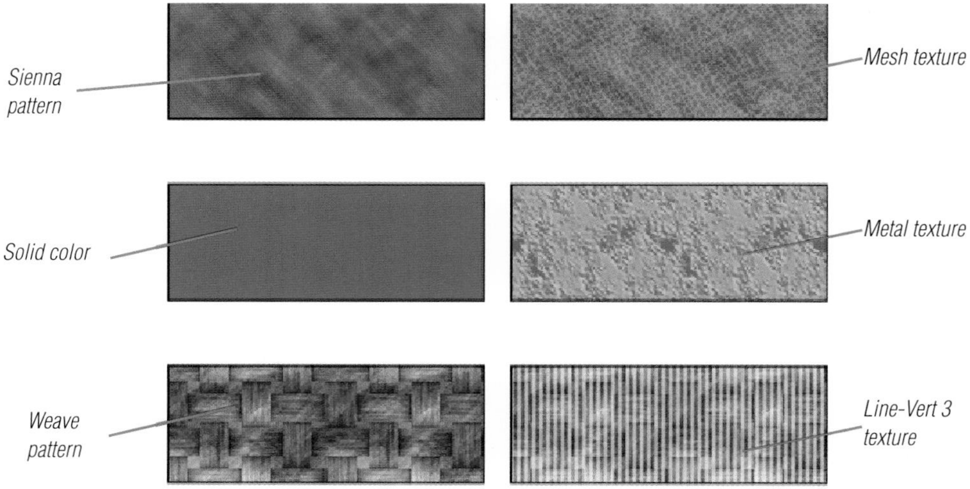

Sienna pattern

Mesh texture

Solid color

Metal texture

Weave pattern

Line-Vert 3 texture

Apply a gradient to an object

1. Click the **Pointer tool** in the Tools panel, then click **cake_donut object** to select it.

2. Click the **Fill category list arrow** in the Property inspector, point to **Gradient**, point to **Ellipse**, as shown in Figure 23, then click **Ellipse**.

   An ellipse gradient is applied to the object, as shown in Figure 24. Gradient fill handles also appear on the gradient.

3. Click the **Fill Color box** in the Property inspector, click the **left color swatch** beneath the color ramp, type **#E5B900** in the Swap colors text box, then press **[Enter]** (Win) or **[return]** (Mac).

4. Repeat Step 3 for the right color swatch, but type **#FF8000** in the Swap colors text box, press **[Enter]** (Win) or **[return]** (Mac) to close the color pop-up window, then compare your color ramp to Figure 25.

5. Click the **Edge of fills list arrow**, click **Feather**, double-click the **Amount of feather text box**, then type **2**.

6. Click the **Texture name list arrow**, click **Parchment**, if necessary, click the **Amount of texture list arrow**, drag the slider to **55**, then verify that the Transparent check box is not selected.

7. Compare your image to Figure 26.

   The new gradient colors and texture are applied to the object.

You selected and modified gradient colors, and applied a texture to an object.

FIGURE 23
Fill and gradient categories

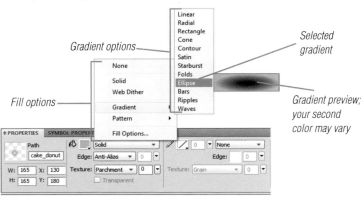

Gradient options

Fill options

FIGURE 24
Gradient applied to object

Selected gradient

Gradient preview; your second color may vary

FIGURE 25
Edit Gradient pop-up window

Opacity swatch affects transparency

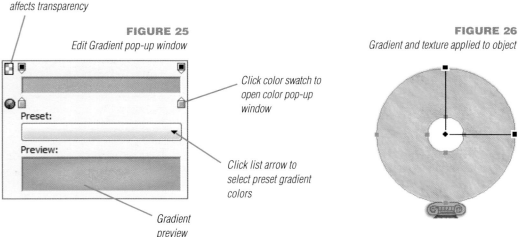

Click color swatch to open color pop-up window

Click list arrow to select preset gradient colors

Gradient preview

FIGURE 26
Gradient and texture applied to object

FIGURE 27

Adjusting fill handles

Drag round handle to top of objects

Drag right square to the object's border

Transform an object and its gradient

1. Verify that the cake_donut object is selected.

2. Click **Modify** on the Application bar, point to **Transform**, then click **Rotate 90°CW** to rotate the object.

   The gradient handles flip position.

3. Drag the **fill handle** up to the top of the objects, then drag the **right handle** to the position shown in Figure 27.

   The placement and shading of the gradient is altered.

4. Click a blank part of the Document window to deselect the cake_donut object, then compare your image to Figure 28.

5. Save your work.

   You rotated the object and adjusted the fill handles to change the gradient.

FIGURE 28

Modified gradient in an object

Existential Pastries

the HOLE *is the* ESSENCE

Understanding basic colors in the Color Mixer

You can open the Color Mixer panel from the Window menu. The Color Mixer displays the color palette of the values of the active solid color, which you can also view in the Fill Color box or Stroke Color box in the Tools panel or in the Property inspector. You can edit color values to create new colors by changing the values for each color component of a color model. You can define colors in five different models: RGB (red, green, blue); Hexadecimal (Fireworks default), which has values similar to RGB; HSB (hue, saturation, and brightness); CMY (cyan, magenta, yellow); and Grayscale. The color model you choose depends on the medium in which the graphic will appear. Generally, the models Fireworks offers are geared toward screen-based and Web-based computer graphics, with the exception of the CMY or Grayscale models. If you want to use a Fireworks-created graphic in print media, you might want to export the graphic into another program that has additional print-specific color models, such as Adobe Illustrator or Adobe Photoshop. All file formats exported by Fireworks are based on the RGB color model.

APPLY FILTERS TO
OBJECTS AND TEXT

What You'll Do

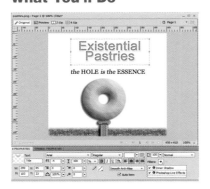

 In this lesson, you will add filters to objects, including text, and change the order of filters in the Filters list.

Understanding Filters

In addition to using the Fill and Stroke sections of the Property inspector, you can use the Filters section to customize the appearance of objects in your document. The Filters section includes the effects found on the Filters menu, as well as bevel, emboss, shadow, and glow effects. For example, you can sharpen, blur, and add the appearance of depth or dimension to an image.

Fireworks calls these **Live Filters** because you can always edit and preview changes to them even after you have saved, closed, and reopened the document. The Filters section lets you experiment with multiple effects. You can add, edit, delete, or hide filters in the Filters list at your convenience. Figure 29 shows the options available in the Filters section and a object with filters applied to it.

> QUICKTIP
>
> To edit a filter, select the object(s) to which the filter is applied, and then click the Info icon or double-click the filter name in the list to open its pop-up window or dialog box.

Using Photoshop Live Effects

In addition to Fireworks Live Filters, you can apply Photoshop Live Effects, known as layer effects in Photoshop. Some effects, such as Bevel and Emboss or Shadow, operate similar to their Fireworks equivalents, although the Photoshop Live Effects dialog box often contains additional adjustment controls. When you open a native Photoshop .psd file in Fireworks, the effects are live and editable, although not every attribute may carry over. Figure 30 shows live effects applied to an object.

Using the Filters Menu

The Filters menu contains commands that correspond to many of the features found in the Filters section. However, be aware that the Filters menu contains fewer effects than the Filters section of the Property inspector and you cannot alter their settings after you apply them. You can remove the effect of these filters only in the current work session—more precisely, you can *undo* these filters, not edit them. After you close the document, the Undo actions are lost, and the filter is permanently applied to your document.

Filters and File Size

Although enabled filters generally contribute to increased file size, disabling a filter instead of deleting it does not significantly add to file size. Some filters, such as the Blur, Blur More, and Gaussian Blur filters, may actually decrease file size because blurring an object decreases the total number of colors in the graphic. The fewer colors used in your document, the less storage space required—hence, smaller file size.

Understanding Transparency

You can adjust the transparency of an image or effect in your document by varying its opacity settings. Fireworks adjusts transparency in terms of percentage, just as it uses percentage settings to adjust the amount of texture in strokes and fills. The **opacity setting** determines if your image is completely opaque (100%) or completely transparent (0%).

FIGURE 29
Viewing filters applied to an object

FIGURE 30
Viewing Photoshop Live Effects applied to objects

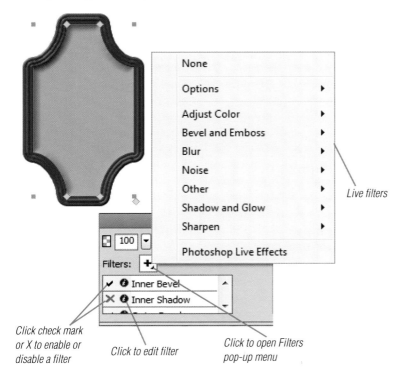

Live filters

Click check mark
or X to enable or
disable a filter

Click to edit filter

Click to open Filters
pop-up menu

Apply filters to objects

1. Select the **cake_donut object**, then click the **Add Filters button** ➕ in the Property inspector.

2. Point to **Bevel and Emboss**, then click **Inner Bevel**.

   The Inner Bevel pop-up window opens.

3. Enter the values shown in Figure 31, then press **[Enter]** (Win) or **[return]** (Mac) to close the Inner Bevel pop-up window.

4. Click the **Add Filters button** ➕ in the Property inspector, then click **Photoshop Live Effects**.

   The Photoshop Live Effects dialog box opens.

5. Click the **Drop Shadow check box**.

6. Enter the values shown in Figure 32, click **Ok**, then click a blank area of the Document window.

   With these filters applied, the cake_donut object now appears to have depth and dimension.

7. Click the **full_column object**, then repeat Steps 4, 5, and 6.

   TIP To delete a filter, select the effect in the Filters list in the Filters section of the Property inspector, then click the Delete Filters button.

8. Deselect the full-column object, then compare your image to Figure 33.

You applied filters to the full_column and cake_donut objects to give them the illusion of three-dimensionality.

FIGURE 31
Inner Bevel pop-up window

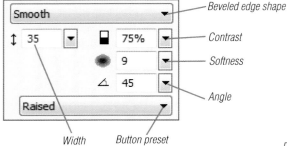

Beveled edge shape

Contrast

Softness

Angle

Width   Button preset

FIGURE 32
Drop Shadow properties in Photoshop Live Effects dialog box

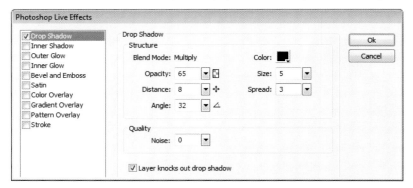

FIGURE 33
Filters added to objects

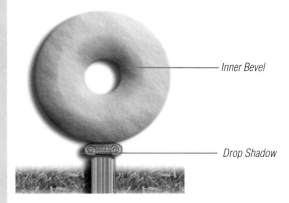

Inner Bevel

Drop Shadow

FIGURE 34

Viewing filters in the Property inspector

*Filters applied
to text*

Reordered filters

1. Click the **Title text object**, click the **Add Filters button** [+] in the Property inspector, click **Photoshop Live Effects**, then click the **Bevel and Emboss check box**.

2. Change the style to **Outer Bevel**, Technique to **Chisel Soft**, the Depth to **50**, then click **OK** to close the Photoshop Live Effects dialog box.

3. Click the **Title text object**, click the **Add Filter button** [+] in the Property inspector, point to **Shadow and Glow**, then click **Inner Shadow**.

4. Double-click the **Distance text box**, type **4**, accept the remaining default settings, then deselect the object.

5. Select the **Title text object**, drag the **Inner Shadow filter** to the top of the Filters list, then notice the difference in the effect.

6. Compare your image to Figure 34, deselect the object, then save your work.

You added filters to a text object, and then rearranged the filters in the Filters list to create a more subtle visual effect.

Using the Measure tool

The Measure tool is a calculating tool located in the vector shapes tool group in the Tools panel. Click the Rectangle tool or currently selected tool, then click Measure Tool. You can use the Measure tool to create precise measurements on the canvas, which can be very helpful when accurate distances are required. The tool does not draw a shape, but it measures distances by height, width, or on the diagonal. Simply click and drag the pointer from one location to another to create a red arrow with start and end points and the pixel dimensions.

APPLY A STYLE
TO TEXT

What You'll Do

**Existential
Pastries**

the HOLE is the ESSENCE

The cake is commentary

In this lesson, you will align objects on the canvas, apply a style to text, and create a new custom style.

Using Live Styles and the Styles Panel

Live Styles contain preset font, color, stroke, or effects attributes that you can apply to objects and text. To access live styles, open the Styles panel from the Window menu, then select a category. Some categories are designed specifically for text, others for objects, including buttons you can use in Web pages. To apply a style, you select an object, and then click a style thumbnail. Figure 35 shows style categories in the Styles panel.

By default the Styles panel opens to the Current Document category, where you can view thumbnails of every style you've added to the current document, even if a style is not currently applied to an object.

You can use the Styles section of the Property inspector to manage styles efficiently. Click the Styles list arrow to view all the styles you've added to the current document. Figure 36 shows styles applied to different objects and text in the current document.

You can customize a style or create a new style and then save it with a unique name. To create a new style, select an object with a style attached to it, adjust the attributes as you wish in the Property inspector, click the New button in the Property inspector, enter a style name, select the attributes you want the style to affect, then click OK.

When you modify a style in the current document, the changes affect objects only in the current document. To modify a current style, select an object with a style applied to it, then change the attributes and effects as desired.

To apply the changes to other objects with that style, click the **Redefine**

Styles button. Be aware that you can permanently adjust the attributes of styles in the Styles panels, so it is best to only modify styles in the current document.

QUICKTIP

To apply the attributes of any object to another object (regardless of style), select the source object, click the Copy command on the Edit menu, select the target object, then click the Paste Attributes command on the Edit menu.

To revert to the original style before it was modified, click the **Clear Overrides button**; to remove the link to a style, click the **Break Link to Style button**; and to delete a style, click the **Delete Style button**.

FIGURE 35
Styles panel; Mac styles may vary

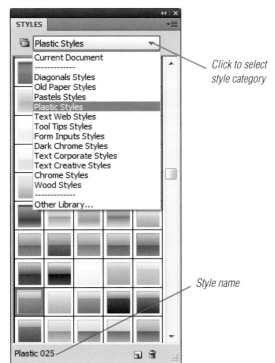

Click to select style category

Style name

FIGURE 36
Viewing objects with applied styles

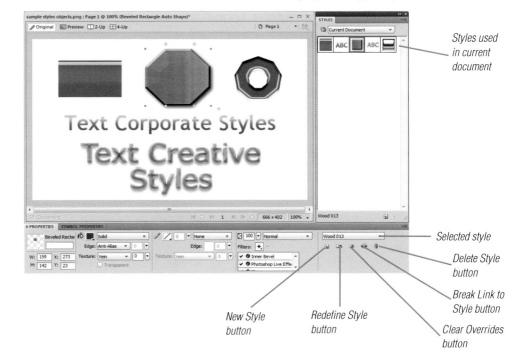

Styles used in current document

Selected style

Delete Style button

Break Link to Style button

Clear Overrides button

New Style button

Redefine Style button

Align objects and apply a style to text

1. Click **Select** on the Application bar, then click **Select All**.

2. Click **Modify** on the Application bar, point to **Align**, then click **Center Vertical**.

   The objects are centered vertically on the canvas.

3. Click the **Text layer** in the Layers panel, create a **new layer**, then name it **Tagline**.

4. Click the **Text tool** T in the Tools panel, then enter the values shown in Figure 37.

5. Click near the **bottom-left corner** of the canvas, then type **The cake is commentary**.

6. Open the **Styles panel**, click the **Category list arrow**, click **Text Corporate Styles**, then click the **Text Corporate Light Bg 010 thumbnail** at the top of the Styles panel, as shown in Figure 38.

   The style is applied to the text, overriding the settings.

   | TIP   To view a style's name, roll the mouse over a thumbnail; the name appears at the bottom of the styles panel.

7. Click the **Category list arrow** in the Styles panel, click **Current Document**, then compare your screen to Figure 39.

You aligned objects, created text, and applied a style to it.

FIGURE 37
Text properties

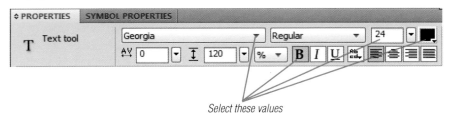

Select these values

FIGURE 38
Selecting a style in the Styles panel

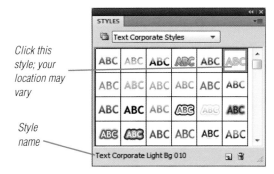

Click this style; your location may vary

Style name

FIGURE 39
Style applied to text

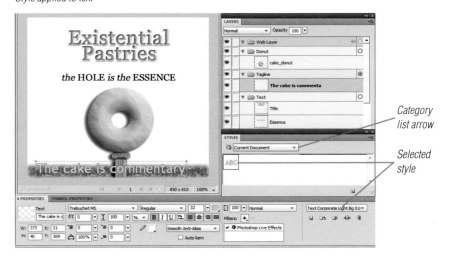

Category list arrow

Selected style

FIGURE 40
New Style dialog box

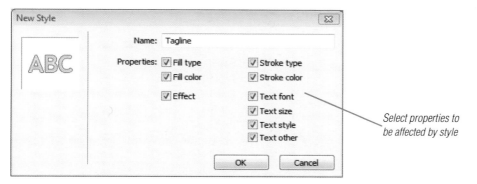

Select properties to be affected by style

FIGURE 41
Viewing new style

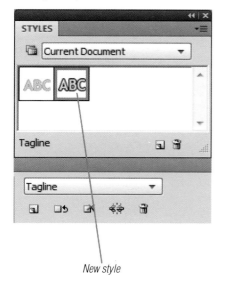

New style

FIGURE 42
New custom style applied to text

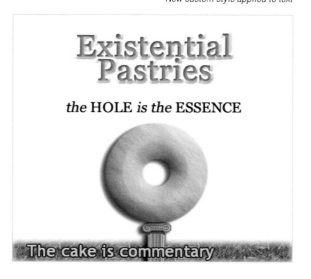

Lesson 5   Apply a Style to Text

Create a custom style

1. Select the text you just created if necessary, double-click the **Font Size text box** in the Property inspector, then type **26**.

2. Double-click the **Photoshop Live Effects filter** in the Filters box, double-click the **Size text box**, type **5**, click the **Fill color box**, double-click the **Swap Colors text box**, type **#333333**, press **[Enter]** (Win) or **[return]** (Mac), then click **OK**.

3. Verify that Current Document is selected in the Styles panel, then click the **New Style button** [icon] at the bottom of the Styles panel.

   The New Style dialog box opens.

4. Type **Tagline** in the Name text box, compare your dialog box to Figure 40, then click **OK**.

   The new style appears in the Styles panel and its name appears in the Styles sections of the Property inspector.

5. Position the mouse over the new style to view the name, then compare your Styles panel and Property inspector to Figure 41.

6. Deselect the text, then compare your screen to Figure 42.

7. Save your work, then close the file and exit Fireworks.

You created a new style and added it to the styles available in the current document.

Create a vector object and modify its path.

1. Open fw2_2.png from where you store your Data Files, then save it as **confection.png**.
2. Select the Pen tool, then set the following properties: Fill color: #66CC99 and Stroke: #3C745C, Pencil 1-Pixel Soft, 1 px.
3. Using the large white gumdrop as a guide, draw a triangle that approximates the gumdrop's height and width.
4. Convert the corner points to curve points, using Figure 43 as a guide.
5. Use the Subselection tool to increase the height of the object, approximately half the distance to the document border.
6. Drag the object to the lower-left corner of the canvas.
7. Rename the object **gumdrop**.
8. Save your work.

Align and group objects.

1. Use the Pointer tool to drag the purple circle in back of the multicolored circle.
2. Align the two objects so that they are centered vertically and horizontally.
3. Group the two circles.
4. Move the grouped circles to the top of the stick, then group them with the stick.

5. Rename the grouped object **lollipop**.
6. Save your work.

Combine objects' paths.

1. Click the red ellipse, then move it on top of the red snowflake.
2. Align the shapes horizontally and vertically.
3. Combine the paths of the two objects, using the Intersect command.
4. Rename the combined object **insignia**.
5. Save your work.

Apply a gradient to an object and modify the gradient.

1. Select the gumdrop object and apply a Ripples gradient to it.
2. Edit the gradient, and change the left color swatch to #006600.
3. Modify the right gradient by dragging the right fill handle to the lower-right corner of the gumdrop. (*Hint*: The fill handle should resemble the hands of a clock set to 4 o'clock.)
4. Add the following fill properties: Edge: Anti-Alias and Texture: Grain, 15%.
5. Save your work.

Apply filters to objects.

1. Select the insignia object.
2. Apply a Photoshop Live Effects, Bevel and Emboss, Pillow Emboss filter with Depth: 75 and the rest the default settings, then close the dialog box.
3. Drag the insignia object to the middle of the gumdrop object. (*Hint*: Move the insignia object on the Layers panel.)
4. Apply a Bevel and Emboss, Inset Emboss filter to the Gumdrop object with default settings.
5. Save your work.

Apply a filter to text.

1. Select the Text tool with the following properties: Font: Times New Roman, Font size: 22, Color: Red, Bold, and Italic. (*Hint*: Change the Fill type to Solid.)
2. Click the upper-left corner of the canvas, then type **Go Sugarfree**.
3. Apply a white Shadow and Glow, Glow filter to the text with a Halo Offset of 1.
4. Save your work.

Apply a style to text.

1. Open the Styles panel, then display the Text Creative Styles category.
2. Select the text.
3. Apply the Text Creative 015 style to the text.
4. Save your work.

Add a new style.

1. Change the Font size to 36.
2. Edit Photoshop Live Effects, change the Inner Shadow color #00FF00, select the Stroke effect, change the Stroke size to 1, close the dialog box, then drag the text to the left edge of the canvas.

3. Display styles for the Current Document, then create a new style named **Candy**.
4. Compare your document to Figure 43.
5. Save your work, close confection.png, then exit Fireworks.

FIGURE 43
Completed Skills Review

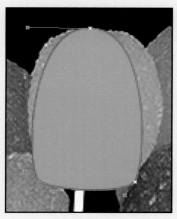

You're in charge of office security at your business. In the last four months, several employees, including the owner, have neglected to engage their screen savers when they've left their desks for lunch, meetings, and so on. So far, friendly reminders and rewards haven't done the trick, so you're going to e-mail the same obnoxious attachment to everyone. You'll develop a simple, but effective, message using Fireworks vector tools and effects.

1. Create a new document that is 504 × 246 pixels with a white background, then save it as **remember_me**.

2. Create a rounded rectangle that fills the background, and apply the following properties to it: Fill Pattern: Paint Blue; Edge: Anti-Alias; Texture: Grain, 25; and Stroke: None.

3. Add an Inner Glow filter with the following properties: Width: 8, Color: White, and Softness: 8, name the object **blue rectangle**, then lock the Background layer.

4. Create and name a new layer **ruler**, then using Figure 44 as a guide, draw a rectangle that has a Linear gradient. Adjust the swatches on the color ramp as follows: Left and Right: #CCCCCC and Middle: #FFFFFF. (*Hint*: Click beneath the color ramp to add a color swatch.)

5. Add a black 1 px Pencil, 1-Pixel-Hard stroke, and Inner Bevel filter with Width 8 and the rest default settings.

6. Use the Line tool to create evenly spaced hash marks that resemble those on a ruler, group the ruler objects, then name the object **ruler base**.

7. Create the following text in the font and filters of your choice: **don't rule out computer security**. (*Hint*: The text in the sample is bold Eras Medium ITC and has a Raised Emboss effect applied to it. It has been converted to a bitmap.)

8. Create a new layer named **Message**, then create **clean up your act** text in the font and color of your choice and apply at least one filter to it using settings of your choice. (*Hint*: The text has Glow and Photoshop Live Effects and Emboss filters applied to it.)

9. Save your work, then compare your document to Figure 44.

10. Close remember_me.png, then exit Fireworks.

FIGURE 44
Sample Completed Project Builder 1

Impact Potions, a new energy drink aimed at the teen market, is sponsoring a design contest. They want you to introduce the drink by using the design in an ad window on other teen websites. They haven't decided on the container yet, so you can create the bottle or can of your choice.

1. If desired, obtain images that will reinforce your message delivery and enhance the vector shapes you will create. You can take your own photographs, or obtain an image from your computer or from the Internet. When downloading from the Internet you should always assume the work is protected by copyright. Be sure to check the website's terms of use to determine if you can use the work for educational, personal, or noncommercial purposes. Always check the copyright information on any media you download.

2. Create a new document and save it as **impact**.

3. Create a beverage container using the vector tools of your choice; apply a fill, style, or stroke; and combine paths as necessary. (*Hint*: The side grips on the can in the sample were created using Punch commands.)

4. Create a label for the container, applying fills, strokes, styles, transparency, and filters as necessary. (*Hint*: The label text has been attached to paths.)

5. Create text for the ad, applying fills, strokes, styles, transparency, and filters as desired.

6. Rename objects or layers on the Layers panel as appropriate.

7. Experiment with changing the order of filters in the Filters list.

FIGURE 45
Sample Completed Project Builder 2

8. Examine the sample shown in Figure 45, then save your work.

One of the many advantages to using Fireworks for your images is the ability to combine vector and bitmap images into one document. For a performance artist, such as the country musician Dwight Yoakam, an official website can reinforce both the artistic message and mood. Photographs and Fireworks-generated images combine to convey the feel of an old-time café and street scene. Many images also link the viewer to other pages within the site. Because dynamic websites are updated frequently to reflect current trends, this page might be different from Figure 46 when you open it online.

1. Connect to the Internet, go to *http://www.dwightyoakam.com/media.html* then enter the site. (*Hint*: Click Music, TV & Films from the Home page, if necessary.)
2. Open a document in a word processor, or open a new Fireworks document, then save the file as **yoakam**. (*Hint*: Use the Text tool in Fireworks to answer the questions below.)
3. Explore the site and answer the following questions:
   - When they were created in Fireworks, which objects could have been grouped?
   - Do objects appear to have been combined?
   - Which gradients, textures, styles, or other effects are applied to objects?

- Are there objects that appear to be a combination of vector shapes, which include photographic images, objects, or that appear to have an effect applied to them?

(*Hint*: Visit the site during the day and during the night and note the differences.)
4. Save your work.

FIGURE 46
Sample Completed Design Project

Dwight Yoakam – www.dwightyoakam.com/media.html

Vintage Wheels, a classic car club, is known for the unusual prizes the club awards to winners of their road rallies. To promote the rallies, the prizes are shown on the group's web page. Your group has been selected to design and promote this year's grand prize: a custom belt buckle. The only requirement is that the buckle honor a classic car and be large enough to be seen from a distance. You can select the classic auto of your choice.

1. If desired, obtain an image for the buckle. You can take your own photos, or obtain an image from your computer or from the Internet. When downloading from the Internet, you should always assume the work is protected by copyright. Be sure to check the website's terms of use to determine if you can use the work for educational, personal, or noncommercial purposes. Always check the copyright information on any media you download.

2. Create a new document and save it as **classic_buckle**.

3. Create two or more vector objects for the buckle, and add fills, styles, strokes, or transparency to them. (*Hint*: The ovals in the sample have a combination of Inner

Shadow, Inner Bevel, and Outer Bevel filters and a style applied to them.)

4. Apply at least one Combine Paths command to the objects.

5. Create text as desired and apply fills, styles, and filters to them.

6. Examine the sample shown in Figure 47, then save your work.

7. Close classic_buckle.png and exit Fireworks.

FIGURE 47
Sample Completed Portfolio Project

chapter

3

IMPORTING, SELECTING, AND MODIFYING GRAPHICS

1. Work with imported files

2. Work with bitmap selection tools

3. Learn about selection areas

4. Select areas based on color

3 IMPORTING, SELECTING,
AND MODIFYING
GRAPHICS

Understanding Importing

Whether you want to create a simple image or a complex Web site, having the right graphic is crucial to the success of your project. Many times, the graphic you need may have been created in another application. Fireworks makes it easy to access such a graphic—regardless of whether it was created within the Adobe CS4 Creative Suite in a program such as Photoshop or Illustrator, or downloaded from a digital camera or scanner.

Fireworks allows you to import several types of files, including vector and bitmap files, as well as HTML tables. Being able to

work with many different file types in the same document has obvious advantages. For example, you can edit Photoshop or Illustrator files directly in Fireworks and export them to Dreamweaver or Flash.

Modifying Images

After you import a bitmap image, you can use an assortment of tools to select and modify the pixels on that image. You can select pixels based on an area or on color. After you select pixels, you can manipulate them independently. For example, you can select and edit a defined set of pixels or blend a selection into surrounding pixels.

Tools You'll Use

Vector File Options

Scale:	100	
Width:	175	Pixels
Height:	270	Pixels
Resolution:	72	Pixels/Inch
Anti-alias:	☑ Paths ☑ Text	Smooth

File conversion

Open a page   Page: 1

Remember layers

☐ Include invisible layers
☑ Include background layers

Render as images

☑ Groups over   30 objects
☐ Blends over   30 steps
☑ Tiled fills over   30 objects

OK   Cancel

Modify

Canvas	▶
Animation	▶
Symbol	▶
Pop-up Menu	▶
Mask	▶
Selective JPEG	▶
Lock Selection	Ctrl+Alt+L
Flatten Selection	Ctrl+Alt+Shift+Z
Merge Down	Ctrl+E
Flatten Layers	Ctrl+Alt+E
Transform	▶
Arrange	▶
Align	▶
Convert Path to Marquee...	
Combine Paths	▶
Alter Path	▶
Group	Ctrl+G
Ungroup	Ctrl+Shift+G

Edit

Undo Select Pixels	Ctrl+Z
Repeat Select Pixels	Ctrl+Y
Insert	▶
Find and Replace...	Ctrl+F
Cut	Ctrl+X
Copy	Ctrl+C
Copy as Vectors	
Copy HTML Code...	Ctrl+Alt+C
Paste	Ctrl+V
Clear	Backspace
Paste as Mask	Ctrl+Alt+V
Paste Inside	Ctrl+Shift+V
Paste Attributes	Ctrl+Alt+Shift+V
Duplicate	Ctrl+Alt+D
Clone	Ctrl+Shift+D
Crop Selected Bitmap	
Crop Document	
Preferences...	Ctrl+U
Keyboard Shortcuts...	

Insert submenu

New Button...	Ctrl+Shift+F8
New Symbol...	Ctrl+F8
Hotspot	Ctrl+Shift+U
Rectangular Slice	Alt+Shift+U
Polygon Slice	Alt+Shift+P
Empty Bitmap	
Bitmap Via Copy	
Bitmap Via Cut	
Layer	Shift+L
State	Shift+F
Page	

Toolbar

Select

Scale tool

Bitmap

Marquee tool   Lasso tool

Magic Wand tool

Vector

Web

Colors

Zoom tool

View

3-3

WORK WITH
IMPORTED FILES

What You'll Do

In this lesson, you will import graphics with different file formats into a Fireworks document, and group and ungroup objects.

Working with Other Adobe Creative Suite 4 Applications

Fireworks has always integrated effortlessly with Flash and Dreamweaver, through a feature known as round-trip editing. The integration features between Fireworks, Dreamweaver, and Flash are discussed at length in the Integrating Adobe CS4 Web Standard chapter. In Fireworks, you can also open and edit native Photoshop and Illustrator files, prepare them for the Web using the excellent optimization features in Fireworks, and then insert them in a Dreamweaver page. You can manage your media using

Adobe Bridge, discussed in Dreamweaver Chapter 3. Adobe Bridge is a media management and organizational tool and includes functions such as Camera Raw support and metadata editing.

Using Files Created in Other Applications

You can open and edit bitmap and vector files created in other applications such as CorelDRAW, or bitmap images created from a scanner or downloaded from a digital camera.

You can bring a Photoshop file into Fireworks in a couple different ways:

Understanding image resolution

For an image displayed on a computer screen—on the Web, attached to an e-mail, or viewed on a cell phone—the unit of measurement is in **PPI** (pixels per inch). The standard resolution setting for Web images is 72 PPI, which is directly related to the display capability of computer monitors. The same picture that looks fabulous in a Web page often appears blurry when you enlarge it in a computer program because the same number of pixels is being spread over a larger number of inches. That picture also looks fuzzy when you print it because the on-screen resolution is too low for printing detailed tone transitions.

---

you can import or open it in Fireworks, where Fireworks retains the file's layer hierarchy, blend modes, and layer effects. Note, however, that Fireworks converts Photoshop vector shapes to bitmap objects.

You can also open or import native Adobe Illustrator .ai files in Fireworks. Fills, layers, masks, vector shapes, and other properties are retained and editable.

QUICKTIP

When you open a Photoshop file in Fireworks and display Guides, the guides will be used to create slices, which are Web objects that contain interactivity such as rollovers.

Importing and Saving Files

Figure 1 shows the import file types available in the Import dialog box (Win). You can determine how Fireworks imports a

FIGURE 1
Import dialog box

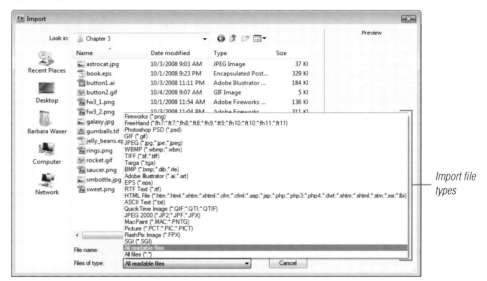

Import file types

Understanding screen resolution

Computer monitors also have resolution settings that refer to the number of pixels contained across the horizontal and vertical axes—that is, how densely packed the pixels are on the screen. For example, a monitor set at a resolution of 1024 × 768 can display 1024 dots on each of 768 lines, totaling around 786,400 pixels. In contrast, a resolution of 800 × 600 displays less than half that amount of pixels, whereas a setting of 1600 × 1200 has nearly 2 million pixels. You can easily notice this when you change the resolution of your computer monitor: the lower the resolution, the larger the image appears, but it displays less detail than it does at a larger resolution.

Photoshop document by selecting different options for layers and text. To do so, open the Preferences dialog box from the Edit menu (Win) or the Fireworks menu (Mac), click the Photoshop Import/Open category, as shown in Figure 2.

When you import a vector-based file, you can select a wide range of importing options in the Vector File Options dialog box, shown in Figure 3 that allow you to ungroup and edit vector objects. In the File Conversion section, you can determine how to treat layers. The Remember layers option maintains the layer configuration of the imported file. Ignore layers places all objects on the currently selected layer. Convert layers to states places layers into individual states. You can change settings in the Render as images section to determine the number of individual objects Fireworks will import.

When you save or close any imported file after you've edited it, Fireworks by default will prompt you to save it as a .png file. To save a file in another format, you can click the Save As command on the File menu to open the Save As dialog box.

FIGURE 2

Photoshop Import/Open options in Preferences dialog box

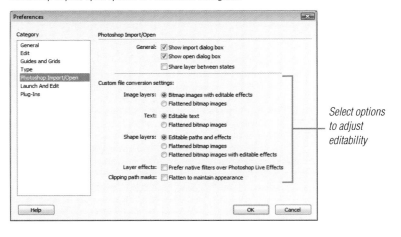

Select options to adjust editability

Click to select layer treatment

FIGURE 3

Vector File Options dialog box

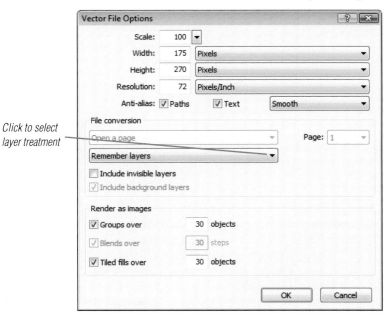

FIGURE 4
Imported GIF

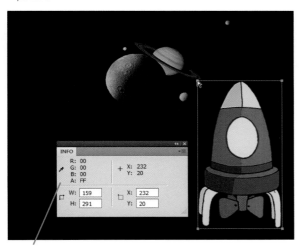

Info panel

FIGURE 5
Imported Fireworks PNG file

Click here

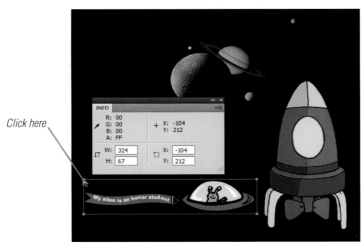

Import a .gif file

1. Open **fw3_1.png**, save it as **horizons.png**, click **Window** on the Application bar, then click **Info**.

2. Change the name of Layer 1 on the Layers panel to **Spaceships**.

3. Click **File** on the Application bar, click **Import**, then navigate to where you store your Data Files.

4. Click the **Files of type list arrow**, then click **All readable files** (if necessary) (Win).
   | TIP   Scroll down the list.

5. Click **rocket.gif**, then click **Open**.

6. Watching coordinates on the Info panel, position the **import pointer** ⌐ on the canvas at approximately **232 X/20 Y**, then click the mouse to import the file.

   | TIP   You can also enter the precise
   | coordinates in the X and Y text boxes
   | in the Property inspector.

7. Compare your image to Figure 4.

You imported a GIF file into a Fireworks document.

Import a Fireworks .png file

1. Click **File** on the Application bar, then click **Import**.

2. Double-click **saucer.png**.

3. Position the **import pointer** ⌐ on the canvas at approximately **–104 X/212 Y**, then click the mouse.

4. Compare your image to Figure 5, then save the file.

You imported a Fireworks .png file.

Import a vector file as editable paths

1. Click the **Background layer** on the Layers panel, click the **New/Duplicate Layer button** at the bottom of the Layers panel, then change the name of the new layer to **Book**.

2. Click **File** on the Application bar, click **Import**, navigate to where you store your Data Files, then double-click **book.eps** to import it.

   The Vector File Options dialog box opens.

   TIP   You can also click the Import button on the Main toolbar (Win) to open the Vector File Options dialog box.

3. Double-click **100** in the Scale text box, (if necessary), type **105**, compare your dialog box to Figure 6, then click **OK**.

   TIP   If the imported file was created in a program that is also designed for print media, such as Illustrator, FreeHand, or Photoshop, Fireworks converts the original color mode from print colors, such as CMYK, to RGB mode, which uses colors designed for the Web.

4. Position the **import pointer** in the top-left corner of the canvas, click the mouse, then compare your image to Figure 7.

   The book appears on the canvas and the object appears in the Layers panel as a grouped object.

   TIP   You might need to undock the Property inspector to match Figure 7.

You imported a vector file into a Fireworks document.

FIGURE 6

Changing an option in the Vector File Options dialog box

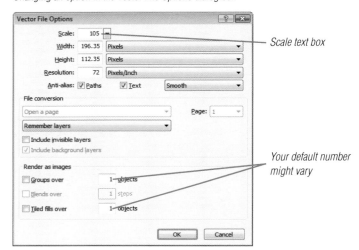

Scale text box

Your default number might vary

FIGURE 7

Vector file imported as a grouped object

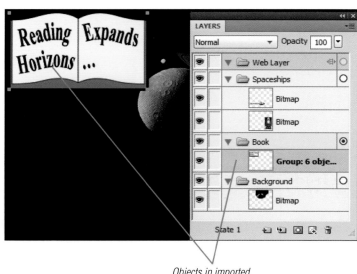

Objects in imported vector file are grouped

FIGURE 8
Ungrouped object made up of paths and grouped objects

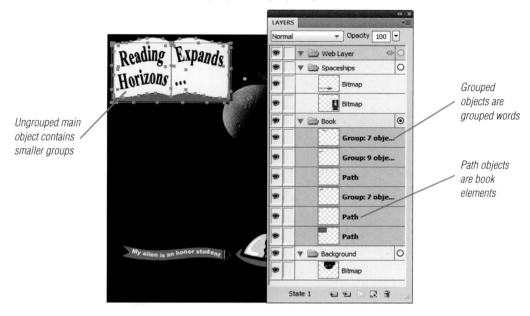

Ungrouped main object contains smaller groups

Grouped objects are grouped words

Path objects are book elements

FIGURE 9
Moved grouped object

Move grouped word here

1. Verify that the grouped object on the book layer is selected, click **Modify** on the Application bar, then click **Ungroup**.

   The book is initially ungrouped into smaller grouped objects and paths.

   TIP   You can also ungroup objects by pressing [Ctrl][Shift][G] (Win) or ⌘ [Shift][G] (Mac).

2. Drag the bottom border of the Layers panel until all the layers are visible (if necessary), then compare your Layers panel to Figure 8.

   Some individual paths are ungrouped, while other objects remain grouped (the individual letters). You could ungroup all the objects if you wanted to edit individually (for a total of 26 objects).

3. Click a blank part of the canvas to deselect the objects, click the **Group: 9 objects object** in the Layers panel to select the word **Horizons**, then drag the selected word to the location shown in Figure 9.

   I TIP   Resize the Layers panel, if necessary.

4. Click the **Book layer** in the Layers panel to select all the objects on the layer, click **Modify** on the Application bar, then click **Group**.

   The numerous book objects are regrouped into one object.

5. Save your work.

You ungrouped and modified an object, and then regrouped the objects.

WORK WITH BITMAP
SELECTION TOOLS

What You'll Do

In this lesson, you will use the marquee tools to select and change pixels in an image.

Using Selection Tools

Being able to select the exact pixels you want is the crucial first step to altering or editing parts of an image. Fireworks offers several ways to select and manipulate pixels in an image. This lesson covers some of those ways. When you select pixels on an image, Fireworks creates a flashing perimeter, known as a **marquee selection**, around the pixels. (This perimeter is also referred to as "marching ants" because of the way it looks.) Marquee selections are temporary areas of selected pixels that exist until you modify the pixels themselves, for example, by cutting, copying, or recoloring them. You can save and recall a bitmap selection, but only one selection at a time. You cannot

save bitmap selections in your document when you close it. You can also use the selection tools in combination to refine a selection.

After you create a marquee selection, you can transfer it to another bitmap by clicking another bitmap object on the same or on a different layer. You can copy or cut a pixel selection as a new object on the active layer in a document by using the Bitmap Via Copy or Bitmap Via Cut Insert command options on the Edit menu. For example, if you select pixels and then click the Bitmap Via Cut command, Fireworks cuts the selected pixels from the original bitmap and then pastes them as a new object above

Moving and copying marquee selections

To move a marquee selection after you have created it, click any of the bitmap selection tools and drag the marquee on the canvas. To copy a selection while a Selection tool is still selected, press [Ctrl][Alt] (Win) or [command][option] (Mac), then drag the selection on the canvas.

the bitmap object on the active layer. Similarly, when you create a bitmap using the Bitmap via Copy command, Fireworks copies the selected pixels and pastes them as a new object on the active layer.

Using the Marquee Tools

Marquee tools select pixels on an image in a specific shape. The properties available for the marquee tools are shown in Figure 10. You can press and hold [Shift] to constrain your rectangle or oval marquee to a square or circle. Use the Fixed Ratio style to constrain the height and width to a precise ratio and the Fixed Size style to set the marquee to an exact dimension.

Using the Transformation Tools

The transformation tool group consists of the Scale tool, Skew tool, Distort tool, and the 9-slice scaling tool. The Scale tool resizes an object, the Skew tool slants an object along the horizontal or vertical axes, and the Distort tool alters the size and proportion of an object and is useful for creating perspective in an object. The 9-slice scaling tool allows you to select part of an object and resize or scale it without distorting it in multiple areas, as often occurs when you use the Scale tool. For vector objects, the tool adds points to the shape. Figure 11 shows skew and distort samples. When you select an object with any of the transformation tools, sizing handles surround the object. You can use these handles to transform or rotate the object. The transformation tool pointer appears when you position the pointer over a sizing handle; the rotation pointer appears when you position the pointer in between the sizing handles or outside the object.

FIGURE 10
Properties for the Marquee and Oval Marquee tools

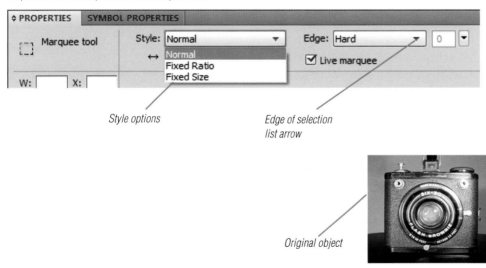

Style options

Edge of selection list arrow

FIGURE 11
Sample skewed and distorted images

Original object

Skewing slants object evenly

Distorting slants points independently

Select pixels using the Marquee tool

1. Verify that horizons.png is open and that Tooltips is selected on the View menu.

2. Click the **Background layer** in the Layers panel, click the **New/Duplicate Layer button** 🔲 , then change the name of the new layer to **Galaxy**.

3. Open **galaxy.jpg** from where you store your Data Files.

4. Click the **Marquee tool** 🔲 in the Tools panel.

   ┃ TIP Mac users may need to click an empty area of the canvas before performing Step 5.

5. Verify that **Normal** is the selected style in the Style list in the Property inspector and that **Anti-alias** is the Edge of selection setting.

6. Place the **pointer** ╋ on the canvas at approximately **65 X/20 Y**, then drag a rectangle to **225 X/330 V** that surrounds the galaxy, as shown in Figure 12.

7. Click **Edit** on the Application bar, click **Copy**, click **Edit** on the Application bar, then click **Paste**.

   The copied pixels are not noticeable because they are pasted on top of the original image on the canvas. The selection appears as the top object in the Layers panel.

8. Deselect the copied selection, click the **Eye icon** 👁 next to the original bitmap in the Layers panel (the bottom one) to hide it, then compare your image to Figure 13.

You set properties for the Marquee tool, created a rectangular marquee, and copied the selection.

FIGURE 12
Making a selection with the Marquee tool

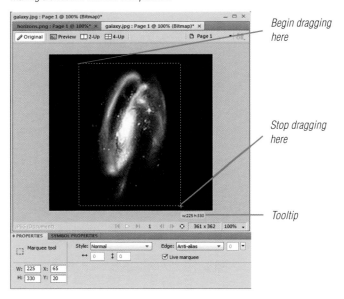

Begin dragging here

Stop dragging here

Tooltip

FIGURE 13
Viewing copied marquee selection

Anti-alias edge is sharp

Importing, Selecting, and Modifying Graphics

FIGURE 14

Using the Oval Marquee tool

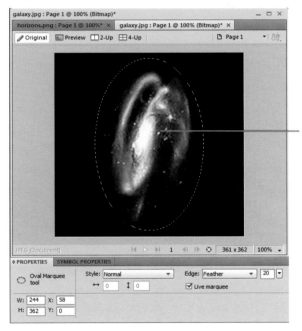

Create marquee by pressing
[Alt] (Win) or [option] (Mac),
then dragging down and to
the right

1. Hide the rectangular selection, then show the original image, respectively, in the Layers panel.

2. Click and hold the **Marquee tool** ⬚ in the Tools panel, then click the **Oval Marquee tool** ⬭.

3. Verify that **Normal** is the selected style in the Style list in the Property inspector, click the **Edge of selection list arrow**, click **Feather**, double-click the **Amount of feather text box**, then type **20**.

   The selection will have a feathered edge. When the Live marquee check box is selected, changes you make in the Property inspector affect the selection marquee.

4. Place the **pointer** ╋ in the middle of the canvas (180 X/180 Y), press and hold **[Alt]** (Win) or **[option]** (Mac), then drag down and to the right to create an oval marquee around the galaxy, as shown in Figure 14.

   Pressing and holding [Alt] (Win) or [option] (Mac) allows you to draw a marquee from the center point outward.

5. Drag the marquee or use the arrow keys to reposition the oval around the galaxy (if necessary).

   TIP You can reselect the marquee as many times as necessary. Notice that the marquee appears to be cropped when you release the mouse button if you extend it beyond the canvas.

(continued)

6. Click **Edit** on the Application bar, point to **Insert**, then click **Bitmap Via Copy** to copy the selection.

7. Click the **Eye icon** 👁 next to the original bottom galaxy bitmap on the Layers panel to hide it, then compare your image to Figure 15.

You set properties for the Oval Marquee tool, created an oval marquee selection, and then created a new bitmap from the original.

Transform a selection

1. Click the oval bitmap to select it, copy the bitmap, click **horizons.png** in the Document window to make it active, then paste the copied oval bitmap.

2. Click the **Pointer tool** ▶ in the Tools panel, then drag the selection to the location shown in Figure 16.

3. Close galaxy.jpg without saving changes.

4. Click the **Scale tool** ▧ in the Tools panel, then open the Align panel (if necessary).

   Rotation handles appear around the selected object.

   | TIP You can press and hold [Alt] (Win) or [option] (Mac) to scale an object from its center.

   (continued)

FIGURE 15
Oval marquee selection

Feathered edge

FIGURE 16
Oval bitmap copied to horizons.png file

Drag oval bitmap here

Importing, Selecting, and Modifying Graphics

FIGURE 17
Rotating an object

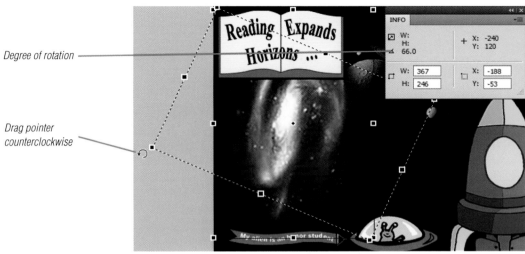

Degree of rotation

Drag pointer
counterclockwise

5. Place the **pointer** outside the object until the rotation pointer appears, drag the selection **counterclockwise 66** degrees, as shown in the Info panel, compare your image to Figure 17, then release the mouse button.

6. Click the **Opacity list arrow** in the Property inspector, drag the slider to **66**, then press **[Enter]** (Win) or **[return]** (Mac).

   | TIP If the Info panel covers the right side of the Property inspector, move or close it.

7. Click the **Pointer tool** in the Tools panel, then drag the **Book object** above the saucer object.

8. Select the book and flying saucer objects, click **Modify** on the Application bar, point to **Align**, then click **Center Vertical** to align the objects.

9. Deselect the objects, compare your screen to Figure 18, then save your work.

You dragged and dropped an object, rotated it, changed its opacity, and aligned it.

FIGURE 18
Moved and aligned objects

Understanding resampling

If the bitmap selection you are copying has a print resolution that differs from the document into which you want to paste, a Resampling dialog box opens, asking if you want to resample the bitmap. Choose Resample if you want to preserve the selection's original dimensions, which will adjust the number of pixels as needed to maintain the bitmap's appearance. Choose Don't Resample to retain the number of original pixels, which may affect the size of the graphic when pasted.

LEARN ABOUT
SELECTION AREAS

What You'll Do

In this lesson, you will select pixels in an image using tools in the Lasso tool group.

Using the Lasso Tools

As you have seen, the marquee tools select an area of pixels in a preset, geometric shape. Using the lasso tools, you can define an exact pixel selection working freeform or following a shape on the canvas. The Lasso tool works well on images that appear to have curves, whereas the Polygon Lasso tool works well on images that have straight lines or asymmetrical outlines. You select pixels by clicking repeatedly around the perimeter of the area you want to select. With the Lasso tool, you create the marquee as you draw it on the canvas—its accuracy is linked to your tracing ability.

QUICKTIP
You can hide the marching ants selection on the screen by pressing [Ctrl][H](Win) or [option][F9](Mac).

Adding and subtracting pixels

To add pixels to an existing lasso selection, press and hold [Shift], and then drag a new marquee. The pixels you select are added to the previously selected marquee. To subtract pixels from a marquee, press and hold [Alt](Win) or [option](Mac). Fireworks deletes the areas where the marquees overlap. To select just the intersection of marquees, create the first marquee, press and hold [Shift][Alt](Win) or [Shift][option](Mac), and then create the second marquee. You can add or subtract pixels using other bitmap selection tools in much the same manner. Note that pressing [Shift] as you use the Polygon Lasso tool constrains the lines that you can draw to 45-degree angle increments.

Using Select Menu Commands

Using commands on the Select menu, you can adjust a pixel selection after you create it, as shown in Figure 19. You can edit the set of selected pixels, or add pixels to or subtract pixels from the selection marquee. The Select Inverse command selects all of the pixels except the ones enclosed by the marquee. Other commands, such as Expand Marquee or Contract Marquee, allow you to enter the number of pixels that add to or subtract from the selection's border. The Smooth Marquee command blends the pixels at the selection edge, eliminating any excess pixels that can create a jagged appearance. You can also transform a marquee to a vector path object using the Convert Marquee to Path command. Creating a marquee can at times be a grueling process. Fortunately, after you are satisfied with a selection, you can use the Save Bitmap Selection and Restore Bitmap Selection commands to save it and recall it at any time during the current editing session or after the file has been saved, closed, and reopened.

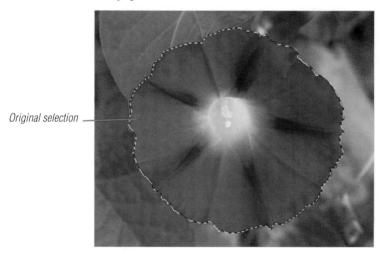

Original selection

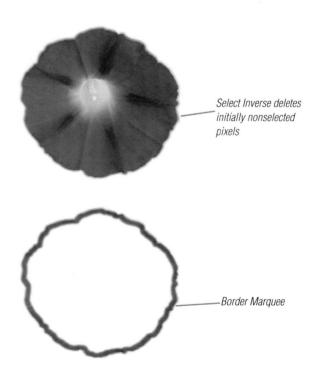

Select Inverse deletes initially nonselected pixels

Border Marquee

Select pixels using the Lasso tool

1. Open **astrocat.jpg**.

2. Click the **Zoom tool** 🔍 in the Tools panel, click the canvas until you can view the image in detail, then drag the borders of the Document window until the entire image is visible.

   You might need to adjust the magnification settings a number of times before you are satisfied.

   > TIP You can also increase magnification by clicking the Set magnification icon on the bottom of the Document window and then clicking a magnification setting from the Set magnification pop-up menu.

3. Click the **Lasso tool** 🔎 in the Tools panel, click the **Edge of selection list arrow** in the Property inspector, click **Feather**, double-click the **Amount of feather text box**, then type **1**.

4. Drag the **pointer** 🔎 along the perimeter of the cat, as shown in Figure 20, then notice the areas where the marquee is off the mark.

   Because the Lasso tool is sensitive to even the slightest deviations from the path you are drawing, the exact shape of your marquee will vary.

   > TIP You can change the pointer of most tools to a crosshair by pressing [Caps Lock], which can make it easier to see the pixels you want to select.

   (continued)

FIGURE 20
Creating a marquee with the Lasso tool

Drag pointer along perimeter of image

Understanding magnification and the Zoom tool

You can increase the magnification of any area on the canvas. To change the magnification in preset increments, click the Zoom tool on the canvas or click a magnification setting in the Set magnification pop-up menu on the bottom of the Document window. To set a magnification between 6% and 6400%, use the Zoom tool to drag a zoom selection box on the canvas. The amount of magnification is based on the size of the zoom selection box. To zoom out of a selection, press and hold [Alt](Win) or [option](Mac), and then click the canvas.

FIGURE 21
Marquee created with the Polygon Lasso tool

Marquee is
less erratic

FIGURE 22
Save Selection dialog box

5. Click **Select** on the Application bar, then click **Deselect**.

> TIP You can also remove a marquee by drawing another one, by clicking an area outside the selection with a tool in the Marquee or Lasso tool groups, or by pressing [Esc].

You selected pixels on an image using the Lasso tool.

Create a selection using the Polygon Lasso tool and save it

1. Press and hold the **Lasso tool** in the Tools panel, then click the **Polygon Lasso tool**.

2. Create a selection by clicking the **pointer** along the perimeter of the image, make sure you connect the start and end points, then compare your image to Figure 21.

> TIP You can readjust your wrist or reposition the mouse on a flat surface in between clicks, which may ensure a more accurate selection.

3. Click **Select** on the Application bar, then click **Save Bitmap Selection**.

4. Type **Kitty** in the Name text box as shown in Figure 22, then click **OK**.

You selected pixels on an image using the Polygon Lasso tool, and then saved the selection.

Transform a selection

1. Click **Select** on the Application bar, click **Expand Marquee**, type **10** in the Expand by text box (if necessary), then click **OK**.

   The marquee expands 10 pixels in each direction.

2. Click **Select** on the Application bar, click **Contract Marquee**, type **20** in the Contract by text box, then click **OK**.

3. Click **Select** on the Application bar, click **Restore Bitmap Selection,** then click **OK** in the Restore Selection dialog box.

   The original marquee selection is restored.

4. Click **Select** on the Application bar, click **Smooth Marquee**, type **10** in the Sample radius text box (if necessary), click **OK**, then compare your image to Figure 23.

   | TIP   Fireworks removes pixels to smooth out the jagged points on the marquee.

5. Click **Select** on the Application bar, click **Restore Bitmap Selection,** then click **OK**.

   | TIP   You can hide the marquee display by clicking the Hide Edges command on the View menu.

6. Click **Select** on the Application bar, click **Select Inverse**, then press **[Delete]**.

7. Click **Select** on the Application bar, click **Restore Bitmap Selection**, then click **OK**.

8. Click **Edit** on the Application bar, then click **Copy**.

9. Close astrocat.jpg without saving changes.

You applied different marquee commands to transform the selection, and then restored the original marquee.

FIGURE 23
Result of Smooth Marquee command

Smoothing removes pixels

FIGURE 24
Result of 50% numeric transform

FIGURE 25
Rotated and repositioned object

Position cat image
in window frame

Transform a copied selection

1. Click the **Pointer tool** ▶ in the Tools panel, (if necessary), then click the **large rocket object** on the canvas.

2. Click **Edit** on the Application bar, then click **Paste**.

3. Click **Modify** on the Application bar, point to **Transform**, then click **Numeric Transform**.

   The Numeric Transform dialog box opens, where you can scale an object by a percentage, resize it by pixels, or rotate an object.

4. Verify that **Scale** is selected in the drop-down list and that the **Scale attributes and Constrain proportions check boxes** are selected.

   The padlock 🔒 indicates that the object will be resized proportionately.

5. Double-click the **width percentage text box**, type **50**, (if necessary), then click **OK**.

6. Drag the **cat image** on top of the rocket window, then compare your image to Figure 24.

7. Verify that the Info panel is open, click the **Scale tool** 📐 in the Tools panel, position the **rotation pointer** ↻ outside the object, then drag the pointer clockwise to **–73** degrees, as indicated on the Info panel.

8. Click the **Pointer tool** ▶ in the Tools panel, drag the image to the location shown in Figure 25, then click a blank part of the Document window.

9. Save your work.

You resized and rotated the copied selection.

SELECT AREAS BASED
ON COLOR

What You'll Do

In this lesson, you will add select areas of color using the Magic Wand tool, merge layers, and then flatten objects and layers in the image.

Using the Magic Wand Tool

The Marquee and Lasso tools select pixels by enclosing them. The Magic Wand tool allows you to select similarly colored areas of a bitmap image. The Magic Wand tool includes edge and tolerance settings. **Tolerance** refers to the range of colors the tool will select. The higher the setting, the larger the selection range. The Magic Wand tool works well on areas of strongly defined or solid color, such as photographic images.

> **QUICK**TIP
>
> Depending on your graphic, you might find it more efficient to add pixels to a Magic Wand selection by pressing and holding [Shift], rather than increasing the tolerance setting and reclicking the bitmap.

The tolerance setting also affects the pixels selected when you click the Select Similar

command on the Select menu. The Magic Wand tool selects pixels of contiguous color tone, not contiguous pixels on the image. When you use the Select Similar command, any matching pixels on the image are selected. Figure 26 shows four selections. The photo on the left shows the pixels selected with a low tolerance setting and those selected at that setting using the Select Similar command. The photo on the right demonstrates the same principle at a higher tolerance setting.

Merging and Flattening Objects and Layers

After you start creating, copying, or importing vector and bitmap objects in a document, your Layers panel can quickly fill up and appear unruly. Although creating and collapsing layers can help manage the large number of objects, you can also flatten or merge the objects you create into a single image, just as grouping objects assembles them into a single arrangement. Flattening and merging objects and layers helps to manage objects, layers, and file size. However, you can no longer edit individual objects after you flatten or merge them.

QUICKTIP

It's a best practice to save an unflattened version of your document as a backup.

The Merge Down command on the Modify menu merges selected objects with the bitmap object that lies beneath the lowest selected object. The Flatten Selection command on the Modify menu flattens two or more objects, even if they are on different layers (the top object moves to the bottom object), converting them to bitmap objects. If you want to move all your objects to a single layer and remove all other layers, you can use the Flatten Layers command.

FIGURE 26
Sample Magic Wand and Select Similar selections

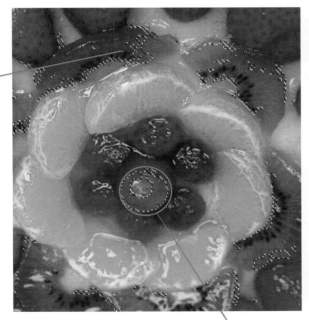
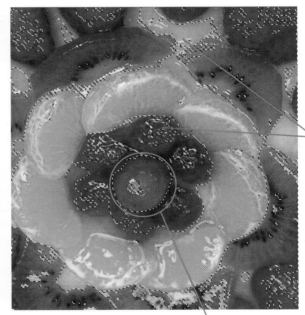

Select Similar command selects more green pixels

Select Similar command selects pixels in more colors

Tolerance 16 selects some green grape pixels

Tolerance 64 selects nearly all of grape